CAMPAIGNING WITH
GRANT

CAMPAIGNING WITH GRANT

BY

GENERAL HORACE PORTER, LL.D.

MALLARD
PRESS

MALLARD PRESS
An imprint of BDD Promotional Book Company, Inc.
666 Fifth Avenue
New York, N.Y. 10103

Mallard Press and its accompanying design and logo
are trademarks of BDD Promotional Book Company, Inc.

This edition first published in the United States of America
in 1991 by The Mallard Press

ISBN 0-7924-5604-1

Printed in the United States of America

TO MY COMRADES OF THE UNION
ARMY AND NAVY, WHOSE VALOR
SAVED THE REPUBLIC, THIS BOOK
IS   RESPECTFULLY   DEDICATED.

PREFACE

THE object aimed at in this narrative is to recount the daily acts of General Grant in the field, to describe minutely his personal traits and habits, and to explain the motives which actuated him in important crises by giving his criticisms upon events in the language employed by him at the time they took place.

The chief effort of the author has been to enable readers to view the Union commander near by, and to bring them into such intimate contact with him that they may know him as familiarly as those who served by his side. It has been no part of the author's purpose to give a detailed history of the campaigns referred to, but to describe the military movements only so far as necessary to show General Grant's intentions and plans and the general results of his operations. Mention of particular commands, subordinate commanders, and topographical features, therefore, had to be in large measure omitted.

While serving as a personal aid to the general-in-chief the author early acquired the habit of making careful and elaborate notes of everything of interest which came under his observation, and these reminiscences are simply a transcript of memoranda jotted down at the time.

THE AUTHOR.

TABLE OF CONTENTS

TABLE OF CONTENTS

TABLE OF CONTENTS

TABLE OF CONTENTS

TABLE OF CONTENTS

LIST OF MAPS AND ILLUSTRATIONS

LIST OF MAPS AND ILLUSTRATIONS

CAMPAIGNING WITH GRANT

CHAPTER I

MY FIRST MEETING WITH GENERAL GRANT—A CONFERENCE
AT THOMAS'S HEADQUARTERS—GRANT'S MANNER OF
WRITING DESPATCHES—OPENING "THE CRACKER LINE"
—GRANT SALUTED BY THE ENEMY—GRANT'S PERSONAL
APPEARANCE

WHILE sitting in my quarters in the little town
of Chattanooga, Tennessee, about an hour
after nightfall, Friday, October 23, 1863, an orderly
brought me a message from General George H.
Thomas, Commander of the Army of the Cumberland, on whose staff I was serving, summoning me to
headquarters. A storm had been raging for two days,
and a chilling rain was still falling. A few minutes'
walk brought me to the plain wooden, one-story dwelling occupied by the commander, which was situated
on Walnut street, near Fourth, and upon my arrival I
found him in the front room on the left side of the
hall, with three members of his staff and several strange
officers. In an arm-chair facing the fireplace was seated
a general officer, slight in figure and of medium stature,
whose face bore an expression of weariness. He was

1

carelessly dressed, and his uniform coat was unbuttoned and thrown back from his chest. He held a lighted cigar in his mouth, and sat in a stooping posture, with his head bent slightly forward. His clothes were wet, and his trousers and top-boots were spattered with mud. General Thomas approached this officer, and, turning to me and mentioning me by name, said, "I want to present you to General Grant." Thereupon the officer seated in the chair, without changing his position, glanced up, extended his arm to its full length, shook hands, and said in a low voice, and speaking slowly, "How do you do?" This was my first meeting with the man with whom I was destined afterward to spend so many of the most interesting years of my life.

The strange officers present were members of General Grant's staff. Charles A. Dana, Assistant Secretary of War, who had been for some time with the Army of the Cumberland, had also entered the room. The next morning he sent a despatch to the War Department, beginning with the words, "Grant arrived last night, wet, dirty, and well."

On the 19th of October General Grant's command had been enlarged so as to cover the newly created military division of the Mississippi, embracing nearly the entire field of operations between the Alleghanies and the Mississippi River, and the Army of the Cumberland had thus been placed under his control. About a month before, that army, after having fought at Chickamauga one of the most gallantly contested and sanguinary battles in the annals of warfare, had fallen back and taken up a defensive position on the south side of the Tennessee River, inclosing within its lines the village of Chattanooga. The opposing forces, under General Bragg, had invested this position, and established such a close siege that the lines of supply had been virtually cut off, rations

and forage were about exhausted, and almost the last
tree-stump had been used for fuel. Most of the men
were without overcoats, and some without shoes; ten
thousand animals had died of starvation, and the gloom
and despondency had been increased by the approach of
cold weather and the appearance of the autumn storms.

General Grant, upon assuming the responsibilities of
his new command, had fully realized the critical condition of the Army of the Cumberland, and had set out
at once for its headquarters to take charge in person of
its future operations. On his way to the front he had
telegraphed General Thomas, from Louisville, to hold
Chattanooga at all hazards, to which that intrepid soldier made the famous reply, " I will hold the town till
we starve."

General Grant had started, the day before the incident I have described, from Bridgeport, a place thirty
miles below Chattanooga, where the Nashville and
Chattanooga Railroad crosses the Tennessee River, and
had ridden by way of Walden's Ridge, the only route
left open by which communication could be had with
the beleaguered town. We had been advised that he
was on his way, but hardly expected that he would
reach Chattanooga that night, considering the state of
the weather, the wretched condition of the roads, or
rather bridle-paths, over the mountain, and the severe
injury to his leg which had been caused by a fall of his
horse several weeks before, and from which he was still
suffering. When he arrived he had to be lifted from his
saddle, and was evidently experiencing much pain, as
his horse had slipped in coming down the mountain,
and had further injured the lame leg; but the general
showed less signs of fatigue than might have been supposed after his hard ride of two days under such trying
circumstances.

As soon as General Grant had partaken of a light supper immediately after his arrival, General Thomas had sent for several general officers and most of the members of his staff to come to headquarters, and the room soon contained an exceedingly interesting group. A member of General Thomas's staff quietly called that officer's attention to the fact that the distinguished guest's clothes were pretty wet and his boots were thoroughly soaked with rain after his long ride through the storm, and intimated that colds were usually no respecters of persons. General Thomas's mind had been so intent upon receiving the commander, and arranging for a conference of officers, that he had entirely overlooked his guest's travel-stained condition; but as soon as his attention was called to it, all of his old-time Virginia hospitality was aroused, and he at once begged his newly arrived chief to step into a bedroom and change his clothes. His urgings, however, were in vain. The general thanked him politely, but positively declined to make any additions to his personal comfort, except to light a fresh cigar. Afterward, however, he consented to draw his chair nearer to the wood fire which was burning in the chimney-place, and to thrust his feet forward to give his top-boots a chance to dry. The extent of his indulgence in personal comfort in the field did not seem to be much greater than that of bluff old Marshal Suvaroff, who, when he wished to give himself over to an excess of luxury, used to go so far as to take off one spur before going to bed.

At General Grant's request, General Thomas, General William F. Smith, his chief engineer, commonly known in the army as "Baldy" Smith, and others, pointed out on a large map the various positions of the troops, and described the general situation. General Grant sat for some time as immovable as a rock and as silent as the sphinx, but listened attentively to all that was said. After a while he straightened himself up in his chair, his features assumed an air of animation, and in a tone of voice which manifested a deep interest in the discussion, he began to fire whole volleys of questions at the officers present. So intelligent were his inquiries, and so pertinent his suggestions, that he made a profound impression upon every one by the quickness of his perception and the knowledge which he had already acquired regarding important details of the army's condition. His questions showed from the outset that his mind was dwelling not only upon the prompt opening of a line of supplies, but upon taking the offensive against the enemy. In this he was only manifesting one of his chief military characteristics — an inborn dislike to be thrown upon the defensive. Even when he had to defend a position, his method of warfare was always that of the "offensive-defensive."

After talking over a plan for communicating with our base of supplies, or, as he called it in his conversation, "opening up the cracker line," an operation which already had been projected and for which preliminary steps had been taken, he turned to me as chief of ordnance of the Army of the Cumberland, and asked, "How much ammunition is there on hand?" I replied, "There is barely enough here to fight one day's battle, but an ample supply has been accumulated at Bridgeport to await the opening of communications."

At about half-past nine o'clock he appeared to have finished his search after information for the time being, and turning to a table, began to write telegrams. Communication by wire had been kept open during all the siege. His first despatch was to General Halleck, the general-in-chief at Washington, and read: "Have just arrived; I will write to-morrow. Please approve

order placing Sherman in command of Department
of the Tennessee, with headquarters in the field."
He had scarcely begun to exercise the authority conferred upon him by his new promotion when his mind
turned to securing advancement for Sherman, who
had been his second in command in the Army of the
Tennessee.

It was more than an hour later when he retired to bed
in an adjoining room to get a much-needed rest. As he
arose and walked across the floor his lameness was very
perceptible. Before the company departed he had
made an appointment with Generals Thomas and Smith
and several staff-officers to accompany him the next
day to make a personal inspection of the lines. Early
on the morning of the 24th the party set out from
headquarters, and most of the day was spent in examining our lines and obtaining a view of the enemy's
position. At Brown's Ferry General Grant dismounted
and went to the river's edge on foot, and made his reconnaissance of that important part of the line in full
view of the enemy's pickets on the opposite bank, but,
singularly enough, he was not fired upon.

Being informed that the general wished to see me that
evening, I went into the room he was occupying at
headquarters, and found two of his staff-officers seated
near him. As I entered he gave a slight nod of the
head by way of recognition, and pointing to a chair, said
rather bluntly, but politely, " Sit down." In reply to a
question which he asked, I gave him some information
he desired in regard to the character and location of
certain heavy guns which I had recently assisted in
putting in position on the advanced portion of our lines,
and the kind and amount of artillery ammunition. He
soon after began to write despatches, and I arose to go,
but resumed my seat as he said, " Sit still." My atten-

tion was soon attracted to the manner in which he went
to work at his correspondence. At this time, as throughout his later career, he wrote nearly all his documents
with his own hand, and seldom dictated to any one even
the most unimportant despatch. His work was performed swiftly and uninterruptedly, but without any
marked display of nervous energy. His thoughts flowed
as freely from his mind as the ink from his pen; he was
never at a loss for an expression, and seldom interlined
a word or made a material correction. He sat with his
head bent low over the table, and when he had occasion
to step to another table or desk to get a paper he wanted,
he would glide rapidly across the room without straightening himself, and return to his seat with his body still
bent over at about the same angle at which he had been
sitting when he left his chair. Upon this occasion he
tossed the sheets of paper across the table as he finished
them, leaving them in the wildest disorder. When he
had completed the despatch, he gathered up the scattered
sheets, read them over rapidly, and arranged them in
their proper order. Turning to me after a time, he
said, "Perhaps you might like to read what I am sending." I thanked him, and in looking over the despatches
I found that he was ordering up Sherman's entire force
from Corinth to within supporting distance, and was
informing Halleck of the dispositions decided upon for
the opening of a line of supplies, and assuring him that
everything possible would be done for the relief of Burnside in east Tennessee. Directions were also given for
the taking of vigorous and comprehensive steps in every
direction throughout his new and extensive command.
At a late hour, after having given further directions in
regard to the contemplated movement for the opening
of the route from Bridgeport to Chattanooga, and in the
mean time sending back to be foraged all the animals

that could be spared, he bid those present a pleasant good night, and limped off to his bedroom.

I cannot dwell too forcibly on the deep impression made upon those who had come in contact for the first time with the new commander, by the exhibition they witnessed of his singular mental powers and his rare military qualities. Coming to us crowned with the laurels he had gained in the brilliant campaign of Vicksburg, we naturally expected to meet a well-equipped soldier, but hardly anybody was prepared to find one who had the grasp, the promptness of decision, and the general administrative capacity which he displayed at the very start as commander of an extensive military division, in which many complicated problems were presented for immediate solution.

After remaining three days as General Thomas's guest, General Grant established his headquarters in a modest-looking two-story frame-house on the bluff near the river, situated on what is now known as First street. In the evening of the 26th I spent some time in the front room on the left side of the hall, which he used as his office, and in which several members of his staff were seated with him. It was a memorable night in the history of the siege, for the troops were being put in motion for the hazardous attempt to open the river route to our base of supplies at Bridgeport. The general sat at a table, smoking, and writing despatches. After finishing several telegrams and giving some directions to his staff, he began to describe the probabilities of the chances of the expedition down the river, expressing a confident belief in its success. General W. F. Smith, who had been so closely identified with the project, was given command of the movement. At midnight he began his march down the north bank of the river with 2800 men. At three o'clock on the morning of the 27th, Hazen started silently down the stream, with his pontoons carrying 1800 men; at five he made a landing at Brown's Ferry, completely surprising the guard at that point, and taking most of them prisoners; at seven o'clock Smith's force had been ferried across, and began to fortify a strong position; and at ten a bridge had been completed. Hooker's advance, coming up from Bridgeport, arrived the next afternoon, the 28th, at Brown's Ferry. The river was now open from Bridgeport to Kelley's Ferry, and the wagon road from that point to Chattanooga by way of Brown's Ferry, about eight miles in length, was in our possession. The success of the movement had been prompt and complete, and there was now established a good line of communication with our base. This changed condition of affairs had been accomplished within five days after General Grant's arrival at the front.

As soon as the enemy recovered from his surprise, he woke up to the importance of the achievement; Longstreet was despatched to retrieve, if possible, the lost ground. His troops reached Wauhatchie in the night of the 28th, and made an attack upon Geary's division of Hooker's forces. The fight raged for about three hours, but Geary succeeded in holding his ground against greatly superior numbers. During the fight Geary's teamsters had become scared, and had deserted their teams, and the mules, stampeded by the sound of battle raging about them, had broken loose from their wagons and run away. Fortunately for their reputation and the safety of the command, they started toward the enemy, and with heads down and tails up, with trace-chains rattling and whiffletrees snapping over the stumps of trees, they rushed pell-mell upon Longstreet's bewildered men. Believing it to be an impetuous charge of cavalry, his line broke and fled. The quartermaster in charge of the animals, not willing to see such distinguished services go unrewarded, sent in the following communication : " I respectfully request that the mules, for their gallantry in this action, may have conferred upon them the brevet rank of horses." Brevets in the army were being bestowed pretty freely at the time, and when this recommendation was reported to General Grant he laughed heartily at the humor of the suggestion. Our loss in the battle, including killed, wounded, and missing, was only 422 men. The enemy never made a further attempt to interrupt our communications.

The much-needed supplies, which had been hurried forward to Bridgeport in anticipation of this movement, soon reached the army, and the rejoicing among the troops manifested itself in lively demonstrations of delight. Every man now felt that he was no longer to remain on the defensive, but was being supplied and equipped for a forward movement against his old foe, whom he had driven from the Ohio to the Cumberland, and from the Cumberland to the Tennessee.

As soon as communication had been opened with our base of supplies, General Grant manifested an eagerness to acquaint himself minutely with the position of the enemy, with a view to taking the offensive. One morning he started toward our right, with several staff-officers, to make a personal examination of that portion of the line. When he came in sight of Chattanooga Creek, which separated our pickets from those of the enemy, he directed those who had accompanied him to halt and remain out of sight while he advanced alone, which he supposed he could do without attracting much attention. The pickets were within hailing distance of one another on opposite banks of the creek. They had established a temporary truce on their own responsibility, and the men of each army were allowed to get water from the same stream without being fired upon by those on the

other side. A sentinel of our picket-guard recognized
General Grant as he approached, and gave the customary cry, "Turn out the guard — commanding general!"
The enemy on the opposite side of the creek evidently
heard the words, and one of his sentinels cried out,
"Turn out the guard — General Grant!" The confederate guard took up the joke, and promptly formed, facing our line, and presented arms. The general returned
the salute by lifting his hat, the guard was then dismissed, and he continued his ride toward our left. We
knew that we were engaged in a civil war, but such
civility largely exceeded our expectations.

In company with General Thomas and other members
of his staff, I was brought into almost daily contact with
General Grant, and became intensely interested in the
progress of the plans he was maturing for dealing with
the enemy at all points of the theater of war lying
within his command. Early in November instructions
came from the Secretary of War calling me to Washington, and in accordance therewith General Thomas
issued an order relieving me from duty with his army.[1]

I had heard through personal letters that the Secretary wished to reorganize the Ordnance Bureau at
Washington, and wished my services in that connection on account of my long experience in that depart-

[1] HEADQUARTERS, DEPARTMENT OF THE CUMBERLAND, CHATTANOOGA, TENN., November 5, 1863.

General Orders, No. 261.

1. Captain Thomas G. Baylor, ordnance corps, having, pursuant to orders from the Secretary of War, relieved Captain Horace Porter from duty at these headquarters, is announced as chief of ordnance for this army, and will at once enter upon the discharge of his duties.

The general commanding takes this occasion to express his appreciation of the valuable service rendered by Captain Porter during his connection with this army. His thorough knowledge of the duties of his position, his good judgment and untiring industry, have increased the efficiency of the army, and entitle him to the thanks of the general commanding. . . . By command of Major-general George H. Thomas.

C. GODDARD, Assistant Adjutant-general.—EDITOR.

ment in the field. The order was interpreted as a compliment, but was distasteful to me for many reasons, although I understood that the assignment was to be only temporary, and it was at a season when active operations in the field were usually suspended. It was a subject of much regret to leave General Thomas, for I had become greatly attached to him, and had acquired that respect and admiration for the character of this distinguished soldier which was felt by all who had ever come in contact with him. "Old Pap Thomas," as we all loved to call him, was more of a father than a commander to the younger officers who served under his immediate command, and he possessed their warmest affections. He and his corps commanders now made a written appeal to General Grant, requesting him to intercede and endeavor to retain me in the command. In the evening of the 5th of November I was sent for by General Grant to come to his headquarters. On my arrival, he requested me to be seated at the opposite side of the table at which he sat smoking, offered me a cigar, and said: "I was sorry to see the order of the Secretary of War calling you to Washington. I have had some other views in mind regarding your services, and I still hope that I may be able to secure the recall of the order, and to have you assigned to duty with me, if that would be agreeable to you." I replied eagerly, "Nothing could possibly be more agreeable, and I should feel most highly honored by such an assignment." He went on to say, "With this step in view, I have just written a letter to the general-in-chief," which he then handed me to read.[1]

[1] CHATTANOOGA, TENN.,
    Nov. 5, 1863.
MAJ.-GEN. H. W. HALLECK,
    General-in-Chief of the Army.
Capt. Horace Porter, who is now being relieved as chief ordnance officer in the Department of the Cumberland, is represented by all officers who know him as one of the most meritorious and valuable young

Hardly allowing me to finish my expressions of surprise and gratification, he continued: "Of course, you will have to obey your present orders and proceed to Washington. I want you to take this letter with you, and see that it is put into the hands of General Halleck; perhaps you will soon be able to rejoin me here. My requests are not always complied with at headquarters, but I have written pretty strongly in this case, and I hope favorable action may be taken." I replied that I would make my preparations at once to start East, and then withdrew. The next day I called to bid the general good-by, and, after taking leave of General Thomas and my comrades on the staff, set out for the capital by way of the new line of communication which had just been opened.

A description of General Grant's personal appearance at this important period of his career may not be out of place here, particularly as up to that time the public had received such erroneous impressions of him. There were then few correct portraits of him in circulation. Some of the earliest pictures purporting to be photographs of him had been manufactured when he was at the distant front, never stopping in one place long enough to be "focused." Nothing daunted, the practisers of that art which is the chief solace of the vain had photographed a burly beef-contractor, and spread the pictures broadcast as representing the determined, but rather robust, features of the coming hero, and it was some time before the real photographs which followed

officers in the service. So far as I have heard from general officers there is a universal desire to see him promoted to the rank of brigadier-general and retained here. I feel no hesitation in joining in the recommendation, and ask that he may be assigned for duty with me. I feel the necessity for just such an officer as Captain Porter is described to be, at headquarters, and, if permitted, will retain him with me if assigned here for duty. I am, &c.,

U. S. GRANT, Major-general.

were believed to be genuine. False impressions of him were derived, too, from the fact that he had come forth from a country leather store, and was famous chiefly for striking sledge-hammer blows in the field, and conducting relentless pursuits of his foes through the swamps of the Southwest. He was pictured in the popular mind as striding about in the most approved swash-buckler style of melodrama. Many of us were not a little surprised to find in him a man of slim figure, slightly stooped, five feet eight inches in height, weighing only a hundred and thirty-five pounds, and of a modesty of mien and gentleness of manner which seemed to fit him more for the court than for the camp. His eyes were dark-gray, and were the most expressive of his features. Like nearly all men who speak little, he was a good listener; but his face gave little indication of his thoughts, and it was the expression of his eyes which furnished about the only response to the speaker who conversed with him. When he was about to say anything amusing, there was always a perceptible twinkle in his eyes before he began to speak, and he often laughed heartily at a witty remark or a humorous incident. His mouth, like Washington's, was of the letter-box shape, the contact of the lips forming a nearly horizontal line. This feature was of a pattern in striking contrast with that of Napoleon, who had a bow mouth, which looked as if it had been modeled after a front view of his cocked hat. The firmness with which the general's square-shaped jaws were set when his features were in repose was highly expressive of his force of character and the strength of his will-power. His hair and beard were of a chestnut-brown color. The beard was worn full, no part of the face being shaved, but, like the hair, was always kept closely and neatly trimmed. Like Crom-

well, Lincoln, and several other great men in history, he
had a wart on his cheek.   In his case it was small, and
located on the right side just above the line of the
beard.   His face was not perfectly symmetrical, the left
eye being a very little lower than the right.   His brow
was high, broad, and rather square, and was creased
with several horizontal wrinkles, which helped to emphasize the serious and somewhat careworn look which
was never absent from his countenance.   This expression, however, was in no wise an indication of his nature, which was always buoyant, cheerful, and hopeful.
His voice was exceedingly musical, and one of the clear-
est in sound and most distinct in utterance that I have
ever heard.   It had a singular power of penetration, and
sentences spoken by him in an ordinary tone in camp
could be heard at a distance which was surprising.   His
gait in walking might have been called decidedly unmilitary.   He never carried his body erect, and having
no ear for music or rhythm, he never kept step to the
airs played by the bands, no matter how vigorously the
bass drums emphasized the accent.   When walking in
company there was no attempt to keep step with others.
In conversing he usually employed only two gestures;
one was the stroking of his chin beard with his left
hand; the other was the raising and lowering of his
right hand, and resting it at intervals upon his knee or
a table, the hand being held with the fingers close together and the knuckles bent, so that the back of the
hand and fingers formed a right angle.   When not
pressed by any matter of importance he was often slow
in his movements, but when roused to activity he was
quick in every motion, and worked with marvelous
rapidity.   He was civil to all who came in contact with
him, and never attempted to snub any one, or treat

anybody with less consideration on account of his inferiority in rank. With him there was none of the puppyism so often bred by power, and none of the dogmatism which Samuel Johnson characterized as puppyism grown to maturity.

CHAPTER II

WHEN I reached Washington I went at once to
headquarters, and endeavored to see the com-
mander-in-chief for the purpose of presenting General
Grant's letter, but found, after two or three attempts,
that it would be impossible to secure an interview. I
therefore gave the letter to Colonel Kelton, his adjutant-
general, who placed it in General Halleck's hands. Not
only was there no action taken in regard to the request
which the letter contained, but its receipt was not even
acknowledged. This circumstance, with others of its
kind, made it plain that General Grant would never be
free to make his selection of officers, and organize his
forces as he desired, until he should be made general-in-
chief. Elihu B. Washburne, the member of Congress
from the Galena district in Illinois, General Grant's old
home, soon introduced a bill creating the grade of lieutenant-general, and it was passed by both houses of
Congress, with the implied understanding that General
Grant was to fill the position. The highest grade in the

17

army theretofore created during the war had been that
of major-general.   The act became a law on February
26, 1864, and the nomination of General Grant was sent
to the Senate by Mr. Lincoln on the 1st of March, and
confirmed on the 2d.   On the 3d the general was ordered
to Washington.   I had set to work upon my duties in
the Ordnance Bureau, and in the mean time had received
several very kind messages from the general regarding
the chances of my returning to the field.

On the evening of March 8 the President and Mrs.
Lincoln gave a public reception at the White House,
which I attended.   The President stood in the usual
reception-room, known as the "Blue Room," with several cabinet officers near him, and shook hands cordially
with everybody, as the vast procession of men and
women passed in front of him.   He was in evening
dress, and wore a turned-down collar a size too large.
The necktie was rather broad and awkwardly tied.   He
was more of a Hercules than an Adonis.   His height of
six feet four inches enabled him to look over the heads
of most of his visitors.   His form was ungainly, and
the movements of his long, angular arms and legs bordered at times upon the grotesque.   His eyes were gray
and disproportionately small.   His face wore a general
expression of sadness, the deep lines indicating the sense
of responsibility which weighed upon him; but at times
his features lighted up with a broad smile, and there
was a merry twinkle in his eyes as he greeted an old
acquaintance and exchanged a few words with him in
a tone of familiarity.   He had sprung from the common people to become one of the most uncommon of
men.   Mrs. Lincoln occupied a position on his right.
For a time she stood on a line with him and took part
in the reception, but afterward stepped back and conversed with some of the wives of the cabinet officers

and other personal acquaintances who were in the room.
At about half-past nine o'clock a sudden commotion
near the entrance to the room attracted general attention, and, upon looking in that direction, I was surprised to see General Grant walking along modestly
with the rest of the crowd toward Mr. Lincoln. He
had arrived from the West that evening, and had come
to the White House to pay his respects to the President.
He had been in Washington but once before, when he
visited it for a day soon after he had left West Point.
Although these two historical characters had never
met before, Mr. Lincoln recognized the general at
once from the pictures he had seen of him. With a
face radiant with delight, he advanced rapidly two or
three steps toward his distinguished visitor, and cried
out: "Why, here is General Grant! Well, this is a
great pleasure, I assure you," at the same time seizing
him by the hand, and shaking it for several minutes
with a vigor which showed the extreme cordiality of
the welcome.

The scene now presented was deeply impressive.
Standing face to face for the first time were the two
illustrious men whose names will always be inseparably
associated in connection with the war of the rebellion.
Grant's right hand grasped the lapel of his coat; his
head was bent slightly forward, and his eyes upturned
toward Lincoln's face. The President, who was eight
inches taller, looked down with beaming countenance
upon his guest. Although their appearance, their training, and their characteristics were in striking contrast,
yet the two men had many traits in common, and there
were numerous points of resemblance in their remarkable careers. Each was of humble origin, and had been
compelled to learn the first lessons of life in the severe
school of adversity. Each had risen from the people,

possessed an abiding confidence in them, and always
retained a deep hold upon their affections.   Each might
have said to those who were inclined to sneer at his
plain origin what a marshal of France, who had risen
from the ranks to a dukedom, said to the hereditary
nobles who attempted to snub him in Vienna: " I am an
ancestor; you are only descendants."   In a great crisis
of their country's history both had entered the public
service from the same State.   Both were conspicuous
for the possession of that most uncommon of all vir-
tues, common sense.   Both despised the arts of the
demagogue, and shrank from posing for effect, or indulging in mock heroics.   Even when their characteristics differed, they only served to supplement each
other, and to add a still greater strength to the cause
for which they strove.   With hearts too great for rivalry, with souls untouched by jealousy, they lived to
teach the world that it is time to abandon the path of
ambition when it becomes so narrow that two cannot
walk it abreast.

The statesman and the soldier conversed for a few
minutes, and then the President presented his distinguished guest to Mr. Seward.   The Secretary of State
was very demonstrative in his welcome, and after exchanging a few words, led the general to where Mrs.
Lincoln was standing, and presented him to her.   Mrs.
Lincoln expressed much surprise and pleasure at the
meeting, and she and the general chatted together very
pleasantly for some minutes.   The visitors had by this
time become so curious to catch a sight of the general
that their eagerness knew no bounds, and they became
altogether unmanageable.   Mr. Seward's consummate
knowledge of the wiles of diplomacy now came to the
rescue and saved the situation.   He succeeded in struggling through the crowd with the general until they

reached the large East Room, where the people could circulate more freely. This, however, was only a temporary relief. The people by this time had worked themselves up to a state of uncontrollable excitement. The vast throng surged and swayed and crowded until alarm was felt for the safety of the ladies. Cries now arose of "Grant! Grant! Grant!" Then came cheer after cheer. Seward, after some persuasion, induced the general to stand upon a sofa, thinking the visitors would be satisfied with a view of him, and retire; but as soon as they caught sight of him their shouts were renewed, and a rush was made to shake his hand. The President sent word that he and the Secretary of War would await the general's return in one of the small drawing-rooms, but it was fully an hour before he was able to make his way there, and then only with the aid of several officers and ushers.

The story has been circulated that at the conference which then took place, or at the interview the next day, the President and the Secretary of War urged General Grant to make his campaign toward Richmond by the overland route, and finally persuaded him to do so, although he had set forth the superior advantages of the water route. There is not the slightest foundation for this rumor. General Grant some time after repeated to members of his staff just what had taken place, and no reference whatever was made to the choice of these two routes.

The next day, March 9, the general went to the White House, by invitation of Mr. Lincoln, for the purpose of receiving his commission from the hands of the President. Upon his return to Willard's Hotel, I called to pay my respects. Curiosity led me to look at the hotel register, and the modesty of the entry upon the book, in the general's handwriting, made an impression upon me.

It read simply, " U. S. Grant and son, Galena, Ill." His eldest boy, Fred, accompanied him.

The act which created the grade of lieutenant-general authorized a personal staff, to consist of a chief of staff with the rank of brigadier-general, four aides-de-camp, and two military secretaries, each with the rank of lieutenant-colonel. In our conversation the general referred to this circumstance, and offered me one of the positions of aide-de-camp, which I said I would accept very gladly.

The next day, the 10th, he paid a visit by rail to the headquarters of the Army of the Potomac, near Brandy Station, in Virginia, about seventy miles from Washington. He returned the day after, and started the same night for Nashville, to meet Sherman and turn over to him the command of the Military Division of the Mississippi. While in Washington General Grant had been so much an object of curiosity, and had been so continually surrounded by admiring crowds when he appeared in the streets, and even in his hotel, that it had become very irksome to him. With his simplicity and total lack of personal vanity, he did not seem able to understand why he should attract so much attention. The President had given him a cordial invitation to dine that evening at the White House, but he begged to be excused for the reason that he would lose a whole day, which he could not afford at that critical period. " Besides," he added, " I have become very tired of this show business."

On the 12th the official order was issued placing General Grant in command of all the armies of the United States.

I soon learned that the Secretary of War, in spite of General Grant's request to have me assigned to his staff, wanted to insist upon my continuing my duties in the department at Washington, and I resolved to have an interview with him, and to protest against such action. The Secretary had a wide reputation for extreme brusqueness in his intercourse even with his friends, and seemed determined, as an officer once expressed it, to administer discipline totally regardless of previous acquaintance.   A Frenchman once said that during the Revolution, while the guillotine was at work, he never heard the name of Robespierre that he did not take off his hat to see whether his head was still on his shoulders; some of our officers were similarly inclined when they heard the name of Stanton.   However, I found the Secretary quite civil, and even patient, and, to all appearances, disposed to allow my head to continue to occupy the place where I was in the habit of wearing it. Nevertheless, the interview ended without his having yielded.   I certainly received a very cold bath at his hands, and to this day I never see the impress of his unrelenting features upon a one-dollar treasury note without feeling a chill run down my back.

General Grant returned to the capital on March 23. I went to Willard's to call upon him that evening, and encountered him on the stairs leading up to the first floor.   He stopped, shook hands, and greeted me with the words, "How do you do, colonel?"   I replied: "I had hoped to be colonel by this time, owing to your interposition, but what I feared has been realized. Much against my wishes, the Secretary of War seems to have made up his mind to keep me here."   "I will see him to-morrow, and urge the matter in person," answered the general.   He then invited me to accompany him to his room, and in the course of a conversation which followed said that he had had Sheridan ordered East to take command of the cavalry of the Army of the Potomac.

Sheridan arrived in Washington on April 4.   He had

been worn down almost to a shadow by hard work and
exposure in the field; he weighed only a hundred and
fifteen pounds, and as his height was but five feet six
inches, he looked anything but formidable as a candidate for a cavalry leader. He had met the President and
the officials at the War Department that day for the
first time, and it was his appearance on this occasion
which gave rise to a remark made to General Grant the
next time he visited the department: "The officer you
brought on from the West is rather a little fellow to
handle your cavalry." To which Grant replied, "You
will find him big enough for the purpose before we get
through with him."

General Grant had started for the field on the 26th of
March, and established his headquarters in the little
town of Culpeper Court-house in Virginia, twelve miles
north of the Rapidan. He visited Washington about
once a week to confer with the President and the Secretary of War.

I continued my duties in the department at Washington till my fate should be decided, and on the 27th of
April I found that the request of the general-in-chief
had prevailed, and my appointment was officially announced as an aide-de-camp on his personal staff.

The afternoon of April 29 I arrived at Culpeper,
and reported to him for duty. A plain brick house near
the railway-station had been taken for headquarters,
and a number of tents had been pitched in the yard to
furnish additional accommodations.

The next morning the general called for his horse, to
ride over to General Meade's headquarters, near Brandy
Station, about six miles distant. He selected me as the
officer who was to accompany him, and we set out together on the trip, followed by two orderlies. He was
mounted upon his large bay horse, "Cincinnati," which

afterward became so well known throughout the army. The animal was not called after the family of the ancient warrior who beat his sword into a plowshare, but after our modern city of that name. He was a half-brother to "Asteroid" and "Kentucky," the famous racers, and was consequently of excellent blood. Noticing the agility with which the general flung himself into the saddle, I remarked, "I am very glad to see that your injured leg no longer disables you." "No," he replied; "it gives me scarcely any trouble now, although sometimes it feels a little numb." As we rode along he began to speak of his new command, and said: "I have watched the progress of the Army of the Potomac ever since it was organized, and have been greatly interested in reading the accounts of the splendid fighting it has done. I always thought the territory covered by its operations would be the principal battle-ground of the war. When I was at Cairo, in 1861, the height of my ambition was to command a brigade of cavalry in this army. I suppose it was my fondness for horses that made me feel that I should be more at home in command of cavalry, and I thought that the Army of the Potomac would present the best field of operations for a brigade commander in that arm of the service."

He then changed the subject to Chattanooga, and in speaking of that battle interjected into his descriptions brief criticisms upon the services and characteristics of several of the officers who had taken part in the engagement. He continued by saying: "The difficulty is in finding commanding officers possessed of sufficient breadth of view and administrative ability to confine their attention to perfecting their organizations, and giving a general supervision to their commands, instead of wasting their time upon details. For instance, there is General G——. He is a very gallant officer, but at a

critical period of the battle of Chattanooga he neglected
to give the necessary directions to his troops, and concentrated all his efforts upon aiming and firing some
heavy guns, a service which could have been better performed by any lieutenant of artillery. I had to order
him peremptorily to leave the battery and give his attention to his troops."

He then spoke of his experiences with Mr. Lincoln,
and the very favorable impression the President had
made upon him. He said: " In the first interview I had
with the President, when no others were present, and
he could talk freely, he told me that he did not pretend
to know anything about the handling of troops, and it
was with the greatest reluctance that he ever interfered
with the movements of army commanders: but he had
common sense enough to know that celerity was absolutely necessary; that while armies were sitting down
waiting for opportunities to turn up which might, perhaps, be more favorable from a strictly military point
of view, the government was spending millions of dollars every day; that there was a limit to the sinews of
war, and a time might be reached when the spirits and
resources of the people would become exhausted. He
had always contended that these considerations should
be taken into account, as well as purely military questions, and that he adopted the plan of issuing his ' executive orders' principally for the purpose of hurrying
the movements of commanding generals; but that he
believed I knew the value of minutes, and that he was
not going to interfere with my operations. He said,
further, that he did not want to know my plans; that
it was, perhaps, better that he should not know them,
for everybody he met was trying to find out from him
something about the contemplated movements, and
there was always a temptation 'to leak.' I have not

communicated my plans to him or to the Secretary of War. The only suggestion the President made — and it was merely a suggestion, not a definite plan — was entirely impracticable, and it was not again referred to in our conversations. He told me in our first private interview a most amusing anecdote regarding a delegation of 'cross-roads wiseacres,' as he called them, who came to see him one day to criticize my conduct in paroling Pemberton's army after the surrender at Vicksburg, who insisted that the men would violate their paroles, and in less than a month confront me anew in the field, and have to be whipped all over again. Said Mr. Lincoln: 'I thought the best way to get rid of them was to tell them the story of Sykes's dog. "Have you ever heard about Sykes's yellow dog?" said I to the spokesman of the delegation. He said he had n't. "Well, I must tell you about him," said I. "Sykes had a yellow dog he set great store by, but there were a lot of small boys around the village, and that 's always a bad thing for dogs, you know. These boys did n't share Sykes's views, and they were not disposed to let the dog have a fair show. Even Sykes had to admit that the dog was getting unpopular; in fact, it was soon seen that a prejudice was growing up against that dog that threatened to wreck all his future prospects in life. The boys, after meditating how they could get the best of him, finally fixed up a cartridge with a long fuse, put the cartridge in a piece of meat, dropped the meat in the road in front of Sykes's door, and then perched themselves on a fence a good distance off, holding the end of the fuse in their hands. Then they whistled for the dog. When he came out he scented the bait, and bolted the meat, cartridge and all. The boys touched off the fuse with a cigar, and in about a second a report came from that dog that sounded like a clap of thunder. Sykes came

bouncing out of the house, and yelled, 'What 's up?
Anything busted?' There was no reply, except a snicker
from the small boys roosting on the fence; but as Sykes
looked up he saw the whole air filled with pieces of yellow dog. He picked up the biggest piece he could find,
a portion of the back with a part of the tail still hanging to it, and after turning it round and looking it all
over, he said, ' Well, I guess he 'll never be much account
again — as a dog.' And I guess Pemberton's forces will
never be much account again — as an army." The delegation began looking around for their hats before I had
quite got to the end of the story, and I was never both-
ered any more after that about superseding the commander of the Army of the Tennessee.'"

The general related this anecdote with more animation than he usually displayed, and with the manifestation of a keen sense of the humorous, and remarked
afterward, "But no one who does not possess the President's unequaled powers of mimicry can pretend to
convey an idea of the amusing manner in which he told
the story."

This characteristic illustration employed by the President was used afterward in a garbled form by writers,
in an attempt to apply it to other events. I give the
original version.

When we reached General Meade's camp, that officer,
who was sitting in his quarters, came out and greeted
the general-in-chief warmly, shaking hands with him
before he dismounted. General Meade was then forty-
nine years of age, of rather a spare figure, and graceful
in his movements. He had a full beard, which, like his
hair, was brown, slightly tinged with gray. He wore a
slouched felt hat with a conical crown and a turned-
down rim, which gave him a sort of Tyrolese appearance. The two commanders entered Meade's quarters,

sat down, lighted their cigars, and held a long interview regarding the approaching campaign. I now learned that, two days before, the time had been definitely named at which the opening campaign was to begin, and that on the next Wednesday, May 4, the armies were to move. Meade, in speaking of his troops, always referred to them as "my people." During this visit I had an opportunity to meet a number of old acquaintances whom I had not seen since I served with the Army of the Potomac on General McClellan's staff two years before. After the interview had ended I returned with the general to headquarters, riding at a brisk trot. His conversation now turned upon the commander of the Army of the Potomac, in the course of which he remarked: "I had never met General Meade since the Mexican war until I visited his headquarters when I came East last month. In my first interview with him he talked in a manner which led me to form a very high opinion of him. He referred to the changes which were taking place, and said it had occurred to him that I might want to make a change in the commander of the Army of the Potomac, and to put in his place Sherman or some other officer who had served with me in the West, and urged me not to hesitate on his account if I desired to make such an assignment. He added that the success of the cause was much more important than any consideration for the feelings of an individual. He spoke so patriotically and unselfishly that even if I had had any intention of relieving him, I should have been inclined to change my mind after the manly attitude he assumed in this frank interview."

This was the first long personal talk I had with the general-in-chief, as our intercourse heretofore had been only of an official character, and the exhibition of the remarkable power he possessed as a conversationalist was a revelation. I began to learn that his reputed reticence did not extend to his private intercourse, and that he had the ability to impart a peculiar charm to almost any topic.

That evening a large correspondence was conducted in relation to the final preparations for the coming movements.

A few days before, an occurrence had happened which came very near depriving the armies of the services of General Grant in the Virginia campaign. On his return to headquarters after his last visit to the President in Washington, when his special train reached Warrenton Junction he saw a large cloud of dust to the east of the road. Upon making inquiries of the station master as to its cause, he learned that Colonel Mosby, who commanded a partizan Confederate force, called by his own people Mosby's "conglomerates," and who had become famous for his cavalry raids, had just passed, driving a detachment of our cavalry before him. If the train had been a few minutes earlier, Mosby, like Christopher Columbus upon his voyage to this country, would have discovered something which he was not looking for. As the train carried no guard, it would not have been possible to make any defense. In such case the Union commander would have reached Richmond a year sooner than he finally arrived there, but not at the head of an army.

General Grant now held a command the magnitude of which has seldom been equaled in history. His troops consisted of twenty-one army-corps, and the territory covered by the field of operations embraced eighteen military departments, besides the region held by the Army of the Potomac, which had never been organized into a department. The total number of troops under his command, "present for duty, equipped," was

533,000. In all purely military questions his will was at this time almost supreme, and his authority was usually unquestioned. He occupied the most conspicuous position in the nation, not excepting that of the President himself, and the eyes of all the loyal people in the land were turned to him appealingly as the one man upon whom their hopes were centered and in whom their chief faith reposed. The responsibilities imposed were commensurate with the magnitude of the undertaking which had been confided to him. While commanding all the armies of the nation, he had wisely decided to establish his headquarters with the Army of the Potomac, and give his immediate supervision to the operations of that force and the troops which were intended to coöperate with it in the State of Virginia. Telegraphic communication was then open with nearly all the armies.

The staff consisted of fourteen officers only, and was not larger than that of some division commanders. The chief of staff was Brigadier-general John A. Rawlins. When the war broke out he was a practising lawyer in Galena, Illinois, and had gained some prominence in politics as a Democrat. After the firing upon Fort Sumter a public meeting was held in Galena, and Captain Grant, being an ex-army officer, was called upon to preside. Rawlins attended the meeting, and made a stirring and effective speech, declaring it to be the duty of all good citizens to sink their political predilections, and urging them to pledge themselves to the support of the Union and the enforcement of the laws. General Grant was much impressed with the vigor and logic of the address, and when he was afterward assigned to the command of a brigade, he appointed Rawlins on his staff. He was at first aide-de-camp, afterward assistant adjutant-general, and finally chief of staff. The general

had a high regard for him officially, and was warmly
attached to him personally.   Rawlins in his youth had
worked on a farm, and assisted his father in burning
charcoal, obtaining what education he could acquire at
odd times in the district school and at a neighboring
seminary.   He was frank, honest, and resolute, and
loyally devoted to his chief.   He always had the courage of his convictions, and was capable of stating them
with great force.   He was plain and simple in manner,
of a genial disposition, and popular with all the other
members of the staff.   He had never served in a military organization, nor made a study of the art of war;
but he possessed natural executive ability of a high
order, and developed qualities which made him exceedingly useful to his chief and to the service.

The rest of the staff consisted of the following
officers:

Lieutenant-colonel C. B. Comstock, aide-de-camp, an
officer of the United States corps of engineers, with a
well-deserved reputation for scientific attainments, who
had shown great efficiency while serving with General
Grant in the Vicksburg campaign.

Lieutenant-colonel Horace Porter, aide-de-camp.

Lieutenant-colonel O. E. Babcock, aide-de-camp, an
accomplished officer of engineers, who had gained an
excellent reputation in several campaigns, in which he
had been conspicuous for his good judgment and great
personal courage.

Lieutenant-colonel F. T. Dent, aide-de-camp, a classmate of General Grant, and brother of Mrs. Grant.   He
had served with credit in the Mexican war, and in
Scott's advance upon the city of Mexico had been
severely wounded, and was twice promoted for gallant
and meritorious conduct in battle.

The four officers just named were of the regular

army, and were graduates of the West Point Military Academy.

Lieutenant-colonel Adam Badeau, military secretary, who had first gone to the field as a newspaper correspondent, and was afterward made an aide-de-camp to General T. W. Sherman. He was badly wounded in the foot at Port Hudson, and when convalescent was assigned to the staff of General Grant. He had had a good training in literature, and was an accomplished writer and scholar.

Lieutenant-colonel William R. Rowley, military secretary, was also from Galena. He entered an Illinois regiment as a lieutenant, and after the battle of Donelson was made a captain and aide-de-camp to General Grant. His gallant conduct at Shiloh, where he greatly distinguished himself, commended him still more highly to his commander. He resigned August 30, 1864, and was succeeded by Captain Parker.

Lieutenant-colonel T. S. Bowers, assistant adjutant-general, was a young editor of a country newspaper in Illinois when hostilities began. He raised a company of volunteers for the Forty-eighth Illinois Infantry, but declined the captaincy, and fought in the ranks. He was detailed as a clerical assistant at General Grant's headquarters in the Donelson campaign, and was soon made a lieutenant, and afterward a captain and aide-de-camp. His services in all the subsequent campaigns were highly appreciated by his chief.

Lieutenant-colonel W. L. Duff had been for a time acting chief of artillery under General Grant in the West, and was now assigned to duty as assistant inspector-general.

Captain Ely S. Parker, assistant adjutant-general, who was a full-blooded Indian, a grand nephew of the famous Red Jacket, and reigning chief of the tribes

known as the Six Nations.   His Indian name was Done-
hogawa.   Colonel Parker had received a good education,
and was a civil engineer employed upon the United
States government building in Galena at the breaking
out of the war.   He commended himself to General
Grant by his conduct in the Vicksburg campaign, and
was there placed on his staff, and served in the adjutant-
general's department.

Captain George K. Leet, assistant adjutant-general,
who had come East with General Grant from the Army
of the Tennessee, and who was assigned to duty at the
headquarters of the army in Washington, and remained
there during the campaign.

Captain H. W. Janes, assistant quartermaster.

Captain Peter T. Hudson, a volunteer officer from the
State of Iowa, had served with the general in the West,
and was retained as an aide-de-camp.

Lieutenant William McKee Dunn, Jr., a beardless boy
of nineteen, was assigned as an acting aide-de-camp to
General Rawlins, but performed general staff duty at
headquarters, and under many trying circumstances
proved himself as cool and gallant as the most experienced veteran.

All the members of the staff had had abundant experience in the field, and were young, active, and ready
for any kind of hard work.

CHAPTER III

THE night of May 3 will always be memorable in the recollection of those who assembled in the little front room of the house occupied as headquarters at Culpeper. The eight senior members of the staff seated themselves that evening about their chief to receive their final instructions, and participated in an intensely interesting discussion of the grand campaign, which was to begin the next morning with all its hopes, its uncertainties, and its horrors. Sherman had been instructed to strike Joseph E. Johnston's army in northwest Georgia, and make his way to Atlanta. Banks was to advance up the Red River and capture Shreveport. Sigel was ordered to make an expedition down the valley of Virginia, and endeavor to destroy a portion of the East Tennessee, Virginia, and Georgia Railroad. His movement was expected to keep Lee from withdrawing troops from the valley, and reinforcing his principal army, known as the Army of Northern Virginia. Butler was directed to move up the James River, and endeavor to secure Petersburg and the railways leading into it, and, if opportunity offered, to seize Richmond itself. Burnside, with the Ninth Corps, which had been moved from Annapolis into Virginia, was to support the Army of the Potomac. The subsequent movements of all the forces operating in Virginia were to depend largely upon the result of the first battles between the Army of the Potomac and the Army of Northern Virginia. General Grant felt, as he afterward expressed it in his official report, that our armies had acted heretofore too independently of one another — "without concert, like a balky team, no two ever pulling together." To obviate this, he had made up his mind to launch all his armies against the Confederacy at the same time, to give the enemy no rest, and to allow him no opportunity to reinforce any of his armies by troops which were not themselves confronted by Union forces.

The general sat for some time preparing a few final instructions in writing. After he had finished he turned his back to the table, crossed one leg over the other, lighted a fresh cigar, and began to talk of the momentous movement which in a few hours was to begin. He said: "I weighed very carefully the advantages and disadvantages of moving against Lee's left and moving against his right. The former promised more decisive results if immediately successful, and would best prevent Lee from moving north to make raids, but it would deprive our army of the advantages of easy communication with a water base of supplies, and compel us to carry such a large amount of ammunition and rations in wagon-trains, and detach so many troops as train guards, that I found it presented too many serious difficulties; and when I considered especially the sufferings of the wounded in being transported long distances overland, instead of being carried by short routes to water, where they could be comfortably moved by boats, I had no longer any hesitation in deciding to cross the Rapidan below the position occupied by Lee's army, and move by our left.   This plan will also enable us to cooperate better with Butler's forces, and not become separated too far from them.   I shall not give my attention so much to Richmond as to Lee's army, and I want all commanders to feel that hostile armies, and not cities, are to be their objective points."   It was the understanding that Lee's army was to be the objective point of the Army of the Potomac, and it was to move against Richmond only in case Lee went there.   To use Grant's own language to Meade, "Wherever Lee goes, there you will go also."   He of course thought it likely that Lee would fall back upon Richmond in case of defeat, and place himself behind its fortifications; for he had said to Meade, in his instructions to him, "Should a siege of Richmond become necessary, ammunition and equipments can be got from the arsenals at Washington and Fort Monroe"; and during the discussion that evening he rose from his seat, stepped up to a map hanging upon the wall, and with a sweep of his forefinger indicated a line around Richmond and Petersburg, and remarked: "When my troops are there, Richmond is mine.   Lee must retreat or surrender."

He then communicated verbal instructions to his staff, which gave the key to his method of handling troops in actual battle, and showed the value he placed upon celerity and the overcoming of delays in communicating orders.   He said to us: "I want you to discuss with me freely from time to time the details of the orders given for the conduct of a battle, and learn my views as fully as possible as to what course should be pursued in all the contingencies which may arise. I expect to send you to the critical points of the lines to keep me promptly advised of what is taking place, and in cases of great emergency, when new dispositions have to be made on the instant, or it becomes suddenly necessary to reinforce one command by sending to its aid troops from another, and there is not time to communicate with headquarters, I want you to explain my views to commanders, and urge immediate action, looking to coöperation, without waiting for specific orders from me." He said he would locate his headquarters near those of Meade, and communicate his instructions through that officer, and through Burnside, whose command at this time was independent of the Army of the Potomac; but that emergencies might arise in which he himself would have to give immediate direction to troops when actually engaged in battle.

He never made known his plans far in advance to any one. It was his invariable custom to keep his contemplated movements locked up in his own mind to avoid all possibility of their being mentioned. What impressed every one most was the self-reliance displayed in perfecting his plans, and his absolute faith in their success. His calm confidence communicated itself to all who listened to him, and inspired them with a feeling akin to that of their chief.

The discussion did not end till long past midnight. As usual on the eve of a battle, before the general retired he wrote a letter to Mrs. Grant. I did not know the nature of the contents of the letters to his wife until after the war, when Mrs. Grant, in speaking of them, said that they always contained words of cheer and comfort, expressed an abiding faith in victory, and never failed to dwell upon the sad thought which always oppressed him when he realized that many human lives would have to be sacrificed, and great sufferings would have to be endured by the wounded. The general's letters to his wife were very frequent during a campaign, and no pressure of official duties was ever permitted to interrupt this correspondence.

The Rapidan separated the two hostile forces in northern Virginia. Lee's headquarters were at Orange Court-house, a distance of seventeen miles from Culpeper. The Army of the Potomac consisted of the Second Corps, commanded by Hancock; the Fifth, commanded by Warren; the Sixth, commanded by Sedgwick; and the cavalry corps under Sheridan. Besides these, there was Burnside's separate command, consisting of the Ninth Army Corps. These troops numbered in all about 116,000 present for duty, equipped. The Army of Northern Virginia consisted of three infantry corps, commanded respectively by Longstreet, Ewell, and A. P. Hill, and a cavalry corps commanded by J. E. B. Stuart. Its exact strength has never been accurately ascertained, but from the best data available it has been estimated at about 70,000 present for duty, equipped. General Grant, in his "Memoirs," puts the number as high as 80,000.

Those familiar with military operations, and unprejudiced in their opinion, will concede that, notwithstanding Lee's inferiority in numbers, the advantages were, nevertheless, in his favor in the approaching campaign. Having interior lines, he was able to move by shorter marches, and to act constantly on the defensive at a period of the war when troops had learned to intrench themselves with marvelous rapidity, and force the invading army continually to assault fortified positions. The task to be performed by the Union forces was that of conducting a moving siege.   The field of operations, with its numerous rivers and creeks difficult of approach, its lack of practicable roads, its dense forests, its impassable swamps, and its trying summer climate, debilitating to Northern troops, seemed specially designed by nature for purposes of defense.   Lee and his officers were familiar with every foot of the ground, and every inhabitant was eager to give them information.   His army was in a friendly country, from which provisions could be drawn from all directions, and few troops had to be detached to guard lines of supply.   The Union army, on the contrary, was unfamiliar with the country, was without accurate maps, could seldom secure trustworthy guides, and had to detach large bodies of troops from the main command to guard its long lines of communication, protect its supply-trains, and conduct the wounded to points of safety.   The Southern Confederacy was virtually a military despotism, with a soldier at the head of its government, and officers were appointed in the army entirely with reference to their military qualifications.   Since Lee had taken command he had not lost a single battle fought in the State of Virginia, and the prestige of success had an effect upon his troops the importance of which cannot easily be over-estimated.   His men were made to feel that they were fighting for their homes and firesides; the pulpit, the press, and the women were making superhuman efforts to "fire the Southern heart"; disasters were concealed, temporary advantages were magnified into triumphant victories, and crushing defeats were hailed as blessings in disguise.   In the North there was a divided press, with much carping criticism on the part of journals opposed to the war, which was fitted to discourage the troops and destroy their confidence in their leaders.   There were hosts of Southern sympathizers, constituting a foe in the rear, whose threats and overt acts often necessitated the withdrawal of troops from the front to hold them in check. In all the circumstances, no just military critic will claim that the advantage was on the side of the Union army merely because it was numerically larger.

The campaign in Virginia was to begin by throwing the Army of the Potomac with all celerity to the south side of the Rapidan, below Lee's position. The infantry moved a little after twelve o'clock in the morning of May 4. The cavalry dashed forward in advance under cover of the night, drove in the enemy's pickets, secured Germanna Ford, and also Ely's Ford, six miles below, and before six o'clock in the morning had laid two pontoon-bridges at each place, and passed to the south side of the river. Warren's corps crossed at Germanna Ford, followed by Sedgwick's, while Hancock's corps made the passage at Ely's Ford. At 8 A. M. the general-in-chief, with his staff, started from headquarters, and set out for Germanna Ford, following Warren's troops. He was mounted upon his bay horse "Cincinnati," equipped with a saddle of the Grimsley pattern, which was somewhat the worse for wear, as the general had used it in all his campaigns from Donelson to the present time. Rawlins was on his left, and rode a "clay-bank" horse he had brought from the West named "General Blair," in honor of Frank P. Blair, who commanded a corps in the Army of the Tennessee. General Grant was dressed in a uniform coat and waistcoat, the coat being unbuttoned. On his hands were a pair of yellowish-brown thread gloves. He wore a pair of plain top-boots, reaching to his knees, and was equipped with a regulation sword, spurs, and sash. On his head was a slouch hat of black felt with a plain gold cord around it. His orderly carried strapped behind his saddle the general's overcoat, which was that of a private soldier of cavalry. A sun as bright as the "sun of Austerlitz" shone down upon the scene. Its light brought out in vivid colors the beauties of the landscape which lay before us, and its rays were reflected with dazzling brilliancy from the brass field-pieces and the white covers of the wagons as they rolled lazily along in the distance. The crisp, bracing air seemed to impart to all a sense of exhilaration. As far as the eye could reach the troops were wending their way to the front. Their war banners, bullet-riddled and battle-stained, floated proudly in the morning breeze. The roads resounded to the measured tread of the advancing columns, and the deep forests were lighted by the glitter of their steel. The quick, elastic step and easy, swinging gait of the men, the cheery look upon their faces, and the lusty shouts with which they greeted their new commander as he passed, gave proof of the temper of their metal, and the superb spirit which animated their hearts. If the general's nature had been as emotional as that of Napoleon, he might have been moved to utter the words of the French emperor as his troops filed past him in moving to the field of Waterloo: "Magnificent, magnificent!" But as General Grant was neither demonstrative nor communicative, he gave no expression whatever to his feelings.

With the party on the way to the front rode a citizen whose identity and purposes soon became an object of anxious inquiry among the troops. His plain black, funereal-looking citizen's clothes presented a sight not often witnessed on a general's staff, and attracted no little attention on the part of the soldiers, who began to make audible side remarks, evincing a searching curiosity to know whether the general had brought his private undertaker with him, or whether it was a parson who had joined headquarters so as to be on hand to read the funeral service over the Southern Confederacy when the boys succeeded in getting it into the "last ditch." The person was Mr. E. B. Washburne, member of Congress from General Grant's district, who had arrived at headquarters a few days before, and had expressed a desire to accompany the army upon the opening campaign, to which the general had readily assented.

A short time before noon the general-in-chief crossed one of the pontoon-bridges at Germanna Ford to the south side of the Rapidan, rode to the top of the bluff overlooking the river, and there dismounted, and established temporary headquarters at an old farm-house with Dutch gables and porch in front. It was rather dilapidated in appearance, and looked as if it had been deserted for some time. The only furniture it contained was a table and two chairs. Meade's headquarters were located close by. General Grant sat down on the steps of the house, lighted a cigar, and remained silent for some time, quietly watching Sedgwick's men passing over the bridge. After a while he said: "Well, the movement so far has been as satisfactory as could be desired. We have succeeded in seizing the fords and crossing the river without loss or delay. Lee must by this time know upon what roads we are advancing, but he may not yet realize the full extent of the movement. We shall probably soon get some indications as to what he intends to do."

A representative of a newspaper, with whom the general was acquainted, now stepped up to him and said, "General Grant, about how long will it take you to get to Richmond?" The general replied at once: "I will agree to be there in about four days—that is, if General Lee becomes a party to the agreement; but if

he objects, the trip will undoubtedly be prolonged."
The correspondent looked as if he did not see just how
he could base any definite predictions upon this oracu-
lar response.

I happened to be looking over a field map at the time,
and, at the general's request, handed it to him. He examined it attentively for a few minutes, and then
returned it without making any remarks. The main
roads were pretty well represented on our maps. The
Germanna road runs a little east of south; five miles
from the Rapidan it is crossed by a road running east
and west, called the Orange turnpike; a mile beyond it
intersects the Brock road, which runs north and south;
and a mile farther on the Brock road is crossed by the
Orange plank-road running east and west. There were
also some narrow cross-roads cut through the woods in
various places.

About one o'clock word came from Meade that our
signal-officers had succeeded in deciphering a message
sent to General Ewell, which read as follows: "We are
moving. Had I not better move D. and D. toward New
Verdierville? (Signed) R." The general manifested
considerable satisfaction at receiving this news, and remarked: "That gives just the information I wanted.
It shows that Lee is drawing out from his position, and
is pushing across to meet us." He now called for writing material, and placing a book upon his knee, laid the
paper upon it, and wrote a despatch to Burnside at
Rappahannock Station, saying: "Make forced marches
until you reach this place. Start your troops now in
the rear the moment they can be got off, and require
them to make a night march."

A cold lunch was then eaten off a pine table in the
dining-room of the deserted house. Later in the afternoon our tents arrived, and were pitched near the house,

and a little before dark the "mess" sat down to dinner. The table had been laid under the fly of a large tent of the pattern known as the "hospital tent." Perhaps no headquarters of a general in supreme command of great armies ever presented so democratic an appearance. All the officers of the staff dined at the table with their chief, and the style of conversation was as familiar as that which occurs in the household of any private family. Nothing could have been more informal or unconventional than the manner in which the mess was conducted. The staff-officers came to the table and left it at such times as their duties permitted, sometimes lingering over a meal to indulge in conversation, at other times remaining to take only a few mouthfuls in all haste before starting out upon the lines. The chief ate less and talked less than any other member of the staff, and partook only of the plainest food.

A camp-fire of dry fence-rails had been built in front of the general's tent, not because the evening was particularly cold, but for the reason that the fire lighted up the scene and made the camp look more cheerful. General Meade came over to headquarters after dinner, and took a seat upon a folding camp-chair by our fire, and he and General Grant entered into a most interesting discussion of the situation and the plans for the next day. The general-in-chief offered Meade a cigar. The wind was blowing, and he had some difficulty in lighting it, when General Grant offered him his flint and steel, which overcame the difficulty. The general always carried in the field a small silver tinder-box, in which there was a flint and steel with which to strike a spark, and a coil of fuse which was easily ignited by the spark and not affected by the wind. The French would call it a *briquet*. While the two generals were talking, and a number of staff-officers sitting by listening, tele-

grams were received from Washington saying that
Sherman had advanced in Georgia, Butler had ascended
the James River, and Sigel's forces were moving down
the valley of Virginia.   These advances were in obedience to General Grant's previous orders.   He said: "I
don't expect much from Sigel's movement; it is made
principally for the purpose of preventing the enemy in
his front from withdrawing troops to reinforce Lee's
army.   To use an expression of Mr. Lincoln's, employed
in my last conversation with him, when I was speaking
of this general policy, 'If Sigel can't skin himself, he
can hold a leg while somebody else skins.'   It is very
gratifying to know that Hancock and Warren have
made a march to-day of over twenty miles, with scarcely
any stragglers from their commands."   Telegrams were
now sent to Washington announcing the entire success
of the crossing of the Rapidan, and saying that it would
be demonstrated before long whether the enemy intended to give battle on that side of Richmond.   Meade
soon after retired to his headquarters, and a little while
before midnight General Grant entered his tent and
turned in for the night.   Its only furniture consisted of
a portable cot made of a coarse canvas stretcher over a
light wooden frame, a tin wash-basin which stood on an
iron tripod, two folding camp-chairs, and a plain pine
table.   The general's baggage was limited to one small
camp trunk, which contained his underclothing, toilet
articles, a suit of clothes, and an extra pair of boots.

General Longstreet, then commanding a corps in Lee's
army, told me, several years after the war, that the
evening on which news was received that Grant intended
to give personal direction to the army which was to
operate against Lee, he had a conversation on the subject at Lee's headquarters.   An officer present talked
very confidently of being able to whip with all ease the

western general who was to confront them, at which Longstreet said: "Do you know Grant?" "No," the officer replied. "Well, I do," continued Longstreet. "I was in the corps of cadets with him at West Point for three years, I was present at his wedding, I served in the same army with him in Mexico, I have observed his methods of warfare in the West, and I believe I know him through and through; and I tell you that we cannot afford to underrate him and the army he now commands. We must make up our minds to get into line of battle and to stay there; for that man will fight us every day and every hour till the end of this war. In order to whip him we must outmanœuver him, and husband our strength as best we can."

After the officers at headquarters had obtained what sleep they could get, they arose about daylight, feeling that in all probability they would witness before night either a fight or a foot-race—a fight if the armies encountered each other, a foot-race to secure good positions if the armies remained apart.

General Meade had started south at dawn, moving along the Germanna road. General Grant intended to remain in his present camp till Burnside arrived, in order to give him some directions in person regarding his movements. The general sat down to the breakfast-table after nearly all the staff-officers had finished their morning meal. While he was slowly sipping his coffee, a young newspaper reporter, whose appetite, combined with his spirit of enterprise, had gained a substantial victory over his modesty, slipped up to the table, took a seat at the farther end, and remarked, "Well, I would n't mind taking a cup of something warm myself, if there 's no objection." Thereupon seizing a coffee-pot, he poured out a full ration of that soothing army beverage, and, after helping himself to some of the other dishes, proceeded to eat breakfast with an appetite which had evidently been stimulated by long hours of fasting. The general paid no more attention to this occurrence than he would have paid to the flight of a bird across his path. He scarcely looked at the intruder, did not utter a word at the time, and made no mention of it afterward. It was a fair sample of the imperturbability of his nature as to trivial matters taking place about him. General Grant sent a message to Meade at 8:24 A. M., saying, among other things, "If an opportunity presents itself for pitching into a part of Lee's army, do so without giving time for dispositions." It will be observed from this despatch, and many others which follow, that nearly all of our commanding officers in the field indulged in a certain amount of colloquialism in their communications. Perhaps it seemed to them to make the style less stilted, to give more snap to their language, and express their meaning more briefly. It certainly savored less of the "pomp" and more of the "circumstance" of war than the correspondence of European commanders.

Sheridan's cavalry had been assigned to the duty of guarding the train of four thousand wagons, and feeling out to the left for the enemy. The head of Burnside's leading division was now seen crossing the river; but as General Grant was anxious to go to the front, he decided not to wait to see Burnside in person, but to send him a note instead, urging him to close up as rapidly as possible upon Sedgwick's corps. This communication was despatched at 8:41 A. M., and the general immediately after directed the staff to mount and move forward with him along the Germanna road. After riding a mile, an officer was seen coming toward us at a gallop, and was soon recognized as Colonel Hyde of Sedgwick's staff. He halted in front of General Grant and said: "General Meade directed me to ride back and meet you, and say that the enemy is still advancing along the turnpike, and that Warren's and Sedgwick's troops are being put in position to meet him." The general now started forward at an accelerated pace, and, after riding four miles farther along the Germanna road, came to the crossing of the Orange turnpike. Here General Meade was seen standing near the roadside. He came forward on foot to give General Grant the latest information. The general now dismounted, and the two officers began to discuss the situation.

It had become evident that the enemy intended to give battle in the heart of the Wilderness, and it was decided to establish the headquarters of both generals near the place where they were holding their present conference, at the junction of these two important roads. As this spot became the central point from which nearly all the orders of the commander were issued during one of the most desperate battles in the annals of history, a description of the location is important, in order to give the reader a clear understanding of the memorable events which took place in its vicinity.

A little to the east of the cross-roads stood the old Wilderness tavern, a deserted building surrounded by a rank growth of weeds, and partly shut in by trees. A few hundred yards to the west, and in the northwest angle formed by the two intersecting roads, was a knoll from which the old trees had been cut, and upon which was a second growth of scraggy pine, scrub-oak, and other timber. The knoll was high enough to afford a view for some little distance, but the outlook was limited in all directions by the almost impenetrable forest with its interlacing trees and tangled undergrowth. The ground upon which the battle was fought was in-

tersected in every direction by winding rivulets, rugged
ravines, and ridges of mineral rock. Many excavations
had been made in opening iron-ore beds, leaving pits
bordered by ridges of earth. Trees had been felled in a
number of places to furnish fuel and supply sawmills.
The locality is well described by its name. It was a
wilderness in the most forbidding sense of the word.

The headquarters wagons had followed the staff, the
tents were soon pitched, and a camp was established on
low ground at the foot of the knoll just described, between it and the Germanna road. Grant and Meade
had, in the mean time, taken up their positions on top
of the knoll and stood there talking over the situation;
Warren had joined them, and had communicated the
latest news from his front. As soon as General Grant
learned the situation, he followed his habitual custom in
warfare, and, instead of waiting to be attacked, took the
initiative and pushed out against the enemy. Warren
had been directed to move out in force on the Orange
turnpike, Getty's division of Sedgwick's corps was put
into position on Warren's left, and as soon as it was
found that the enemy was advancing on the Orange
plank-road, orders were sent to Hancock to hurry up
his troops, and take up a position on the left of Getty.
While these preparations were progressing, General
Grant lighted a cigar, sat down on the stump of a tree,
took out his penknife, and began to whittle a stick. He
kept on his brown thread gloves, and did not remove
them once during the entire day. Everything was
comparatively quiet until the hour of noon, when the
stillness was suddenly broken by the sharp rattle of
musketry and the roar of artillery. These sounds were
the quick messengers which told that Warren had met
the enemy and begun the conflict. He encountered
Ewell's corps, and drove it nearly a mile, but was soon

compelled to fall back and restore the connection which
had been lost between his divisions.

Warren then had a conference with General Grant,
who proposed that they should ride out to the front.
He called for his horse, which had remained saddled,
and directed me and another of the aides to accompany
him.   As General Warren was more familiar with the
ground, he rode ahead.   He was mounted on a fine-look-
ing white horse, was neatly uniformed, and wore the
yellow sash of a general officer.   He was one of the few
officers who wore their sashes in a campaign, or paid
much attention to their dress.   The party moved to the
front along a narrow country road bordered by a heavy
undergrowth of timber and bristling thickets.   The infantry were struggling with difficulty through the dense
woods, the wounded were lying along the roadside, firing still continued in front, and dense clouds of smoke
hung above the tops of the trees.   It was the opening
scene of the horrors of the Wilderness.

After having learned from personal inspection the
exact character of the locality in which the battle was to
be fought, General Grant returned to headquarters, in
order to be able to communicate more promptly with
the different commands.   News had been received that
Hill's corps of Lee's army was moving up rapidly on
the Orange plank-road.   Grant was now becoming impatient to take the initiative against the enemy, and
staff-officers were sent with important orders to all parts
of the line.   It was soon seen that the infantry would
have to fight it out without much aid from the artillery,
as it was impossible to move many batteries to the front,
owing to the difficult nature of the ground.   Hancock,
with great energy, had thrown forward two of his divisions to support Getty, who had already attacked Hill.
I was sent to communicate with Hancock during this

part of the engagement. The fighting had become exceedingly severe on that part of the field. General Alexander Hays, one of the most gallant officers in the service, commanding one of Hancock's brigades, finding that his line had broken, rushed forward to encourage his troops, and was instantly killed. Getty and Carroll were severely wounded. After remaining for some time with Hancock's men, I returned to headquarters to report the situation to the general-in-chief, and carried to him the sad intelligence of Hays's death. General Grant was by no means a demonstrative man, but upon learning the intelligence I brought, he was visibly affected. He was seated upon the ground with his back against a tree, still whittling pine sticks. He sat for a time without uttering a word, and then, speaking in a low voice, and pausing between the sentences, said: "Hays and I were cadets together for three years. We served for a time in the same regiment in the Mexican war. He was a noble man and a gallant officer. I am not surprised that he met his death at the head of his troops; it was just like him. He was a man who would never follow, but would always lead in battle."

Wadsworth's division of Warren's corps was sent to support Hancock; but it encountered great difficulty in working its way through the woods, and darkness set in before it could get within striking distance of the enemy. Sedgwick had some fighting on the right of Warren, but no important results had been accomplished on his front. About eight o'clock in the evening the firing died away, and the troops in the immediate presence of the enemy lay on their arms to await the events of the morning.

Sheridan had left a force in the rear sufficient to protect the trains, and had formed the rest of his command so as to confront the enemy's cavalry, which had been moved around by the right of the enemy's line. He had severe fighting on our extreme left. When we sat down at the mess-table at headquarters that evening, the events of the day were fully discussed, and each staff-officer related to the general in detail the scenes which had occurred upon the particular portion of the front which he had visited. Soon after we had risen from the table and left the mess-tent, Meade walked over from his headquarters, and he and the general-in-chief seated themselves by the camp-fire, and talked over the events of the day and the plans for the morrow. Mr. Washburne and our staff-officers made part of the group. The general manifested intense anxiety in regard to relieving the wounded, and the medical officers and the commanders of troops were urged to make every possible effort to find the sufferers and convey them to the rear. Even in daylight it would have been a difficult undertaking to penetrate the thickets and carry the wounded to a place of safety, but at night it was almost impossible, for every time a lantern was shown, or a noise made, it was certain to attract the fire of the enemy. However, those who had been slightly wounded made their own way to the field-hospitals, and by dint of extraordinary exertions, great numbers of the seriously injured were brought to positions where they could be cared for.

During the conversation General Grant remarked: "As Burnside's corps, on our side, and Longstreet's, on the other side, have not been engaged, and the troops of both armies have been occupied principally in struggling through thickets and fighting for position, to-day's work has not been much of a test of strength. I feel pretty well satisfied with the result of the engagement; for it is evident that Lee attempted by a bold movement to strike this army in flank before it could be put into line of battle and be prepared to fight to advantage; but in this he has failed."

The plan agreed upon that night for the coming struggle was as follows: Hancock and Wadsworth were to make an attack on Hill at 4:30 A.M., so as to strike him if possible before Longstreet could arrive to reinforce him. Burnside, who would arrive early in the morning with three divisions, was to send one division (Stevenson's) to Hancock, and to put the other two divisions between Wadsworth and Warren's other divisions, and attack Hill in flank, or at least obliquely, while Warren and Sedgwick were to attack along their fronts, inflict all the damage they could, and keep the troops opposed to them from reinforcing Hill and Longstreet. Burnside's fourth division was to guard the wagon-trains. This division was composed of colored troops, and was commanded by General Ferrero. General Meade, through whom all orders were issued to the Army of the Potomac, was of the opinion that the troops could not be got into position for the attack as early as half-past four o'clock, and recommended six; but General Grant objected, as he was apprehensive that this might give the enemy an opportunity to take the initiative. However, he agreed to postpone the time till five o'clock, and the final orders were given for that hour. Meade now arose, said good night, and walked over to his headquarters. Before eleven o'clock the general-in-chief remarked to the staff: "We shall have a busy day to-morrow, and I think we had better get all the sleep we can to-night. I am a confirmed believer in the restorative qualities of sleep, and always like to get at least seven hours of it, though I have often been compelled to put up with much less." "It is said," remarked Washburne, "that Napoleon often indulged in only four hours of sleep, and still preserved all the vigor of his mental faculties." "Well, I, for one, never believed those stories," the general replied. "If the truth were known, I have no doubt it would be found that he made up for his short sleep at night by taking naps during the day." The chief then retired to his tent, and his example was followed by all the officers who could be spared from duty. The marked stillness which now reigned in camp formed a striking contrast to the shock and din of battle which had just ceased, and which was so soon to be renewed.

CHAPTER IV

GRANT'S PREPARATIONS FOR THE SECOND DAY IN THE WILDER-
NESS — HANCOCK FLUSHED WITH VICTORY — GRANT AT A
CRITICAL MOMENT — THE CRISIS OF THE WILDERNESS —
GRANT'S DEMEANOR ON THE FIELD — GRANT'S PECULIAR-
ITIES IN BATTLE — GRANT'S CONFIDENCE IN SUCCESS —
THE GENERAL-IN-CHIEF AS AID TO A DROVER — CONFU-
SION CAUSED BY A NIGHT ATTACK — GRANT ADMINISTERS
A REPRIMAND — GRANT AFTER THE BATTLE — THE WIL-
DERNESS A UNIQUE COMBAT

AT four o'clock the next morning, May 6, we were
awakened in our camp by the sound of Burnside's
men moving along the Germanna road. They had been
marching since 1 A. M., hurrying on to reach the left of
Warren. The members of the headquarters mess soon
after assembled to partake of a hasty breakfast. The
general made rather a singular meal preparatory to so
exhausting a day as that which was to follow. He took
a cucumber, sliced it, poured some vinegar over it, and
partook of nothing else except a cup of strong coffee.
The first thing he did after rising from the table was to
call for a fresh supply of cigars. His colored servant
"Bill" brought him two dozen. After lighting one of
them, he filled his pockets with the rest. He then went
over to the knoll, and began to walk back and forth
slowly upon the cleared portion of the ridge. While
listening for Hancock's attack on the left, we heard the

sound of heavy firing on the right, and found that the enemy had attacked Sedgwick and Warren. Warren afterward had one brigade pretty roughly handled, and driven back some distance; but no ground was permanently lost or gained by either side on that part of the line. Promptly at five o'clock the roar of battle was heard in Hancock's front, and before seven he had broken the enemy's line, and driven him back in confusion more than a mile. The general now instructed me to ride out to Hancock's front, inform him of the progress of Burnside's movement, explain the assistance that officer was expected to render, and tell him more fully the object of sending to his aid Stevenson's division of Burnside's corps.

I met Hancock on the Orange plank-road, not far from its junction with the Brock road, actively engaged in directing his troops, and restoring the confusion in their alinement caused by the desperate fighting and the difficult character of the ground. All thought of the battle which raged about us was to me for a moment lost in a contemplation of the dramatic scene presented in the person of the knightly corps commander. He had just driven the enemy a mile and a half. His face was flushed with the excitement of victory, his eyes were lighted by the fire of battle, his flaxen hair was thrust back from his temples, his right arm was extended to its full length in pointing out certain positions as he gave his orders, and his commanding form towered still higher as he rose in his stirrups to peer through the openings in the woods. He was considered the handsomest general officer in the army, and at this moment he looked like a spirited portrait from the hands of a master artist, with the deep brown of the dense forest forming a fitting background. It was itself enough to inspire the troops he led to deeds of unmatched heroism.   He had been well dubbed "Hancock the Superb."   This expression dated back to the field of Williamsburg.   At the close of that battle, General McClellan sent a telegram to his wife in New York announcing his victory, and as she and Hancock were old friends, he added the words, "Hancock was superb." The newspapers got hold of the despatch, and the designation was heralded in prominent head-lines throughout the entire press.   The description was so appropriate that the designation clung to him through life.

Along the line of Hancock's advance the enemy's dead were everywhere visible; his wounded strewed the roads; prisoners had been captured, and battle-flags had been taken: but Hancock was now compelled to halt and restore the contact between his commands.   Before nine o'clock, however, he was pushing out again on the Orange plank-road, and another fierce fight soon began.

Sheridan had become engaged in a spirited contest with Stuart's cavalry on the left at Todd's tavern, in which our troops were completely victorious.   The sound of this conflict was mistaken for a time for an attack by Longstreet from that direction, and made Hancock anxious to strengthen his exposed left flank. His embarrassments were increased by one of those singular accidents which, though trivial in themselves, often turn the tide of battle.   A body of infantry was reported to be advancing up the Brock road, and moving upon Hancock's left and rear.   A brigade which could ill be spared was at once thrown out in that direction to resist the threatened attack.   It soon appeared that the body of infantry consisted of about seven hundred of our convalescents, who were returning to join their commands.   The incident, however, had caused the loss of valuable time.   These occurrences prevented Hancock from further taking the offensive.

After waiting for some time, and hearing nothing of Burnside's contemplated assault, I told Hancock I would ride over to Burnside, explain to him fully the situation on the left, and urge upon him the importance of making all possible haste. Upon reaching his position, I found that he was meeting with many difficulties in moving his men into position, and was making very little progress. I explained the absolute necessity of going to the relief of Hancock, and Colonel Comstock and I labored vigorously to help to find some means of getting the troops through the woods. Seeing the difficulties in the way, I returned to General Grant to let him know the true situation, and that an early attack from that quarter could not be depended upon.

Warren's troops were driven back on a portion of his line in front of general headquarters, stragglers were making their way to the rear, the enemy's shells were beginning to fall on the knoll where General Grant was seated on the stump of a tree, and it looked for a while as if the tide of battle would sweep over that point of the field. He rose slowly to his feet, and stood for a time watching the scene, and mingling the smoke of his cigar with the smoke of battle, without making any comments. His horse was in charge of an orderly just behind the hill, but he evidently had no thought of mounting. An officer ventured to remark to him, "General, would n't it be prudent to move headquarters to the other side of the Germanna road till the result of the present attack is known?" The general replied very quietly, between the puffs of his cigar, "It strikes me it would be better to order up some artillery and defend the present location." Thereupon a battery was brought up, and every preparation made for defense. The enemy, however, was checked before he reached the knoll. In this instance, as in many others, the general was true to the motto of his Scottish ancestors of the Grant clan: " Stand fast, Craig Ellachie."

About eleven o'clock the battle raged again with renewed fury on Hancock's front. He had been attacked in front and on the flank by a sudden advance of the enemy, who, concealed by the dense wood, had approached near at several points before opening fire. This caused some confusion among Hancock's troops, who had become in great measure exhausted by their fighting since five o'clock in the morning, and they were now compelled to fall back to their breastworks along the Brock road. The enemy pressed on to within a few hundred yards of the intrenchments, but did not venture to assault. In this attack Longstreet was badly wounded, and the Confederate general Jenkins was killed, both having been accidently shot by their own men. We suffered a severe loss in the death of the gallant General Wadsworth. After Longstreet's removal from the field, Lee took command of his right in person, as we learned afterward, and ordered that any further assault should be postponed till a later hour.

Colonel Leasure's brigade of Burnside's corps now executed a movement of striking brilliancy. It had been sent to Hancock, and posted on the left of his line, and was ordered by him to sweep along his front from left to right. Leasure moved out promptly, facing to the right, with his right flank about a hundred yards from our line of breastworks, and dashed along the entire front with such boldness and audacity that the portions of the enemy he encountered fell back without attempting to make any serious resistance.

General Grant was becoming more anxious still about Burnside's attack, and I soon after galloped over to the latter with instructions to move on without a moment's delay, and connect with Hancock's right at all hazards.

I found his troops endeavoring to obey orders as best they could, but, in struggling through underbrush and swamps, all efforts to keep up their alinement were futile. General Burnside, when I met him this time, was dismounted and seated by the roadside. A champagne basket filled with lunch had been brought up, and at his invitation I joined him and some of his staff in sampling the attractive contents of the hamper. In doing so we acted upon the recognized principle of experienced campaigners, who always eat a meal wherever they can get it, not knowing where the next one is to come from. It was called "eating for the future."

A little after noon Burnside's advance became engaged for about a quarter of an hour, but did not accomplish any important result. I worked my way out on foot to his extreme front line at this time, to obtain a more accurate knowledge of the difficulties which impeded the advance of his troops, and then returned again to headquarters to report the situation.

About half the army was now under Hancock's command, and it was probable that he would need still more reinforcements, and the general-in-chief was devoting a good deal of thought to our right, which had been weakened. At 10:30 A. M. Sedgwick and Warren had been ordered to intrench their fronts and do everything possible to strengthen their positions. A portion of the wagon-train guards had been ordered to report to Sedgwick for duty on his front. Every one on the right was on the alert, and eager to hear particulars about the fighting on the left. The various commands had been advised from time to time of the events which occurred, for it was General Grant's invariable custom to have commanding officers on different points of the line promptly informed of what occurred at other points.

Generals Grant and Meade, after discussing the situa-

tion, now decided to have Hancock and Burnside make
a simultaneous attack at 6 P. M. It was then supposed
that Burnside would certainly be in position by that hour
to unite in such an assault. I started for Hancock's
front to confer with him regarding this movement, and
just as I joined his troops, the enemy, directed by Lee
in person, as we afterward discovered, made a desperate
assault upon our line. It began at 4:15 P. M. The
woods in front of Hancock had now taken fire, and the
flames were communicated to his log breastworks and
abatis of slashed timber. The wind was, unfortunately,
blowing in our direction, and the blinding smoke was
driven in the faces of our men, while the fire itself swept
down upon them. For a time they battled heroically
to maintain their position, fighting both the conflagration and the enemy's advancing columns. At last, however, the breastworks became untenable, and some of
the troops who had displayed such brilliant qualities
during the entire day now fell back in confusion. The
enemy took advantage of the disorder, and, rushing forward with cheers, succeeded in planting some of his
battle-flags upon our front line of breastworks; but
Hancock and all the staff-officers present made strenuous exertions to rally the men, and many of them were
soon brought back to the front. General Carroll's brigade was now ordered to form and retake the line of
intrenchments which had been lost. These gallant
troops, led by the intrepid Carroll in person, dashing
forward at a run, and cheering as they went, swept
everything before them, and in a few minutes were in
possession of the works. Both the attack and counter-
attack were so handsomely made that they elicited
praise from friend and foe alike. Some of Hancock's
artillery was served with great efficiency in this engagement, and added much to the result. At five o'clock

the enemy had been completely repulsed, and fell back, leaving a large number of his dead and wounded on the field.

Burnside made an attack at half-past five, but with no important results. The nature of the ground was a more formidable obstruction than the enemy. Warren and Sedgwick had been engaged during part of the day, and had prevented the enemy in front of them from withdrawing any troops, but notwithstanding their gallant fighting they had substantially gained no ground.

While the most critical movements were taking place, General Grant manifested no perceptible anxiety, but gave his orders, and sent and received communications, with a coolness and deliberation which made a marked impression upon those who had been brought into contact with him for the first time on the field of battle. His speech was never hurried, and his manner betrayed no trace of excitability or even impatience. He never exhibited to better advantage his peculiar ability in moving troops with unparalleled speed to the critical points on the line of battle where they were most needed, or, as it was sometimes called, "feeding a fight." There was a spur on the heel of every order he sent, and his subordinates were made to realize that in battle it is the minutes which control events. He said, while waiting for Burnside to get into position and attack: "The only time I ever feel impatient is when I give an order for an important movement of troops in the presence of the enemy, and am waiting for them to reach their destination. Then the minutes seem like hours." He rode out to important points of the line twice during the day, in company with General Meade and two officers of the staff. It was noticed that he was visibly affected by his proximity to the wounded, and especially by the sight of blood. He would turn his face away from such scenes, and show by the expression of his countenance, and sometimes by a pause in his conversation, that he felt most keenly the painful spectacle presented by the field of battle. Some reference was made to the subject in camp that evening, and the general said: "I cannot bear the sight of suffering. The night after the first day's fight at Shiloh I was sitting on the ground, leaning against a tree, trying to get some sleep. It soon began to rain so hard that I went into a log-house near by to seek shelter; but I found the surgeons had taken possession of it, and were amputating the arms and legs of the wounded, and blood was flowing in streams. I could not endure such a scene, and was glad to return to the tree outside, and sit there till morning in the storm." I thought of this remark while sitting by his bedside twenty-one years afterward, when he, in the last days of his fatal illness, was himself undergoing supreme physical torture.

As the general felt that he could be found more readily, and could issue his orders more promptly, from the central point which he had chosen for his headquarters, he remained there almost the entire day. He would at times walk slowly up and down, but most of the day he sat upon the stump of a tree, or on the ground, with his back leaning against a tree. The thread gloves remained on his hands, a lighted cigar was in his mouth almost constantly, and his penknife was kept in active use whittling sticks. He would pick up one small twig after another, and sometimes holding the small end away from him would rapidly shave it down to a point; at other times he would turn the point toward him and work on it as if sharpening a lead-pencil; then he would girdle it, cut it in two, throw it away, and begin on another. We had long been accused of being a nation of whittlers, and this practice on the part of such a conspicuous representative American seemed to give color to the charge. He seldom indulged in this habit in subsequent battles. The occupation played sad havoc with the thread gloves, and before nightfall several holes had been worn in them, from which his finger-nails protruded. After that day the gloves disappeared, and the general thereafter went without them in camp, and wore the usual buckskin gauntlets when on horseback. It was not till the Appomattox campaign that another pair of thread gloves was donned. There was a mystery about the use of those gloves which was never entirely solved. The impression was that Mrs. Grant had purchased them, and handed them to the general before he started from Washington, and that, either in deference to her, or because he had a notion that the officers in the Eastern armies were greater sticklers for dress than those in the armies of the West, he wore the gloves continuously for the first three days of his opening campaign in Virginia; that is to say, as long as they lasted under the wear and tear to which he subjected them.

His confidence was never for a moment shaken in the outcome of the general engagement in the Wilderness, and he never once doubted his ability to make a forward movement as the result of that battle. At a critical period of the day he sent instructions to have all the pontoon-bridges over the Rapidan in his rear taken up, except the one at Germanna Ford. A short time after giving this order he called General Rawlins, Colonel Babcock, and me to him, and asked for a map. As we sat together on the ground, his legs tucked under him, tailor fashion, he looked over the map, and said: "I do not hope to gain any very decided advantage from the fighting in this forest. I did expect excellent results from

Hancock's movement early this morning, when he started the enemy on the run; but it was impossible for him to see his own troops, or the true position of the enemy, and the success gained could not be followed up in such a country. I can certainly drive Lee back into his works, but I shall not assault him there; he would have all the advantage in such a fight. If he falls back and intrenches, my notion is to move promptly toward the left. This will, in all probability, compel him to try and throw himself between us and Richmond, and in such a movement I hope to be able to attack him in a more open country, and outside of his breastworks." This was the second time only that he had looked at the maps since crossing the Rapidan, and it was always noticeable in a campaign how seldom he consulted them, compared with the constant examination of them by most other prominent commanders. The explanation of it is that he had an extraordinary memory as to anything that was presented to him graphically. After looking critically at a map of a locality, it seemed to become photographed indelibly upon his brain, and he could follow its features without referring to it again. Besides, he possessed an almost intuitive knowledge of topography, and never became confused as to the points of the compass. He was a natural "bushwhacker," and was never so much at home as when finding his way by the course of streams, the contour of the hills, and the general features of the country. I asked him, one day, whether he had ever been deceived as to the points of the compass. He said: "Only once—when I arrived at Cairo, Illinois. The effect of that curious bend in the river turned me completely around, and when the sun came up the first morning after I got there, it seemed to me that it rose directly in the west."

During a lull in the battle late in the afternoon, General Grant, in company with two staff-officers, strolled over toward the Germanna road. While we stood on the bank of a small rivulet, a drove of beef-cattle was driven past. One of the animals strayed into the stream, and had evidently made up its mind to part company with its fellows and come over to our side. One of the drovers yelled out to the general, who was a little in advance of his officers: "I say, stranger, head off that beef-critter for me, will you?" The general, having always prided himself upon being a practical farmer, felt as much at home in handling cattle as in directing armies, and without changing countenance at once stepped forward, threw up his hands, and shouted to the animal. It stopped, took a look at him, and then, as if sufficiently impressed with this show of authority, turned back into the road. The general made no comment whatever upon this incident, and seemed to think no more about the salutation he had received than if some one had presented arms to him. He knew, of course, that the man did not recognize him. If he had supposed the man was lacking in proper military respect, he would perhaps have administered to him the same lesson which he once taught a soldier in the Twenty-first Illinois, when he commanded that regiment. An officer who had served under him at the time told me that Colonel Grant, as he came out of his tent one morning, found a strapping big fellow posted as sentinel, who nodded his head good-naturedly, smiled blandly, and said, "Howdy, colonel?" His commander cried, "Hand me your piece," and upon taking it, faced the soldier and came to a "present arms"; then handing back the musket, he remarked, "That is the way to say 'How do you do' to your colonel."

It was now about sundown; the storm of battle which had raged with unabated fury from early dawn had been succeeded by a calm. The contemplated general attack at six o'clock had been abandoned on account of the assault of the enemy on Hancock's front, and the difficulty of perfecting the alinements and supplying the men with ammunition. It was felt that the day's strife had ended, unless Lee should risk another attack. Just then the stillness was broken by heavy volleys of musketry on our extreme right, which told that Sedgwick had been assaulted, and was actually engaged with the enemy. The attack against which the general-in-chief during the day had ordered every precaution to be taken had now been made. Meade was at Grant's headquarters at the time. They had just left the top of the knoll, and were standing in front of General Grant's tent talking to Mr. Washburne. Staff-officers and couriers were soon seen galloping up to Meade's headquarters, and his chief of staff, General Humphreys, sent word that the attack was directed against our extreme right, and that a part of Sedgwick's line had been driven back in some confusion. Generals Grant and Meade, accompanied by me and one or two other staff-officers, walked rapidly over to Meade's tent, and found that the reports still coming in were bringing news of increasing disaster. It was soon reported that General Shaler and part of his brigade had been captured; then that General Seymour and several hundred of his men had fallen into the hands of the enemy; afterward that our right had been turned, and Ferrero's division cut off and forced back upon the Rapidan. General Humphreys, on receiving the first reports, had given prompt instructions with a view to strengthening the point of the line attacked. General Grant now took the matter in hand with his accustomed vigor. Darkness had set in, but the firing still continued. Aides came galloping in from the right, laboring under intense excitement, talking wildly, and giving the most exaggerated reports of the engagement. Some declared that a large force had broken and scattered Sedgwick's entire corps. Others insisted that the enemy had turned our right completely, and captured the wagon-train. It was asserted at one time that both Sedgwick and Wright had been captured. Such tales of disaster would have been enough to inspire serious apprehension in daylight and under ordinary circumstances. In the darkness of the night, in the gloom of a tangled forest, and after men's nerves had been racked by the strain of a two days' desperate battle, the most immovable commander might have been shaken. But it was in just such sudden emergencies that General Grant was always at his best. Without the change of a muscle of his face, or the slightest alteration in the tones of his voice, he quietly interrogated the officers who brought the reports; then, sifting out the truth from the mass of exaggerations, he gave directions for relieving the situation with the marvelous rapidity which was always characteristic of him when directing movements in the face of an enemy. Reinforcements were hurried to the point attacked, and preparations made for Sedgwick's corps to take up a new line, with the front and right thrown back. General Grant soon walked over to his own camp, seated himself on a stool in front of his tent, lighted a fresh cigar, and there continued to receive further advices from the right.

A general officer came in from his command at this juncture, and said to the general-in-chief, speaking rapidly and laboring under considerable excitement: "General Grant, this is a crisis that cannot be looked upon too seriously. I know Lee's methods well by past experience; he will throw his whole army between us and the Rapidan, and cut us off completely from our communications." The general rose to his feet, took his cigar out of his mouth, turned to the officer, and replied, with a degree of animation which he seldom manifested: "Oh, I am heartily tired of hearing about what Lee is going to do. Some of you always seem to think he is suddenly going to turn a double somersault, and land in our rear and on both of our flanks at the same time. Go back to your command, and try to think what we are going to do ourselves, instead of what Lee is going to do." The officer retired rather crestfallen, and without saying a word in reply. This recalls a very pertinent criticism regarding his chief once made in my presence by General Sherman. He said: "Grant always seemed pretty certain to win when he went into a fight with anything like equal numbers. I believe the chief reason why he was more successful than others was that while they were thinking so much about what the enemy was going to do, Grant was thinking all the time about what he was going to do himself."

Hancock came to headquarters about 8 P. M., and had a conference with the general-in-chief and General Meade. He had had a very busy day on his front, and while he was cheery, and showed that there was still plenty of fight left in him, he manifested signs of fatigue after his exhausting labors. General Grant, in offering him a cigar, found that only one was left in his pocket. Deducting the number he had given away from the supply he had started out with in the morning showed that he had smoked that day about twenty, all very strong and of formidable size. But it must be remembered that it was a particularly long day. He never afterward equaled that record in the use of tobacco.

The general, after having given his final orders providing for any emergency which might arise, entered his tent, and threw himself down upon his camp-bed. Ten minutes thereafter an alarming report was received from the right. I looked in his tent, and found him sleeping as soundly and as peacefully as an infant. I waked him, and communicated the report. His military instincts convinced him that it was a gross exaggeration, and as he had already made every provision for meeting any renewed attempts against the right, he turned over in his bed, and immediately went to sleep again. Twenty-one years thereafter, as I sat by his death-bed, when his sufferings had become agonizing, and he was racked by the tortures of insomnia, I recalled to him that night in the Wilderness. He said: " Ah, yes; it seems strange that I, who always slept so well in the field, should now pass whole nights in the quiet of this peaceful house without being able to close my eyes."

It was soon ascertained that although Sedgwick's line had been forced back with some loss, and Shaler and Seymour had been made prisoners, only a few hundred men had been captured, and the enemy had been compelled to withdraw. General Grant had great confidence in Sedgwick in such an emergency, and the event showed that it was not misplaced.

The attack on our right, and its repulse, ended the memorable battle of the Wilderness. The losses were found to be: killed, 2246; wounded, 12,037; missing, 3383; total, 17,666. The damage inflicted upon the enemy is not known, but as he was the assaulting party as often as the Union army, there is reason to believe that the losses on the two sides were about equal. Taking twenty-four hours as the time actually occupied in fighting, and counting the casualties in both armies, it will be found that on that bloody field every minute recorded the loss of twenty-five men.

As the staff-officers threw themselves upon the

ground that night, sleep came to them without coaxing. They had been on the move since dawn, galloping over bad roads, struggling about through forest openings, jumping rivulets, wading swamps, helping to rally troops, dodging bullets, and searching for commanding officers in all sorts of unknown places. Their horses had been crippled, and they themselves were well-nigh exhausted. For the small part I had been able to perform in the engagement, the general recommended me for the brevet rank of major in the regular army, "for gallant and meritorious services." His recommendation was afterward approved by the President. This promotion was especially gratifying for the reason that it was conferred for conduct in the first battle in which I had served under the command of the general-in-chief.

There were features of the battle which have never been matched in the annals of warfare. For two days nearly 200,000 veteran troops had struggled in a death-grapple, confronted at each step with almost every obstacle by which nature could bar their path, and groping their way through a tangled forest the impenetrable gloom of which could be likened only to the shadow of death. The undergrowth stayed their progress, the upper growth shut out the light of heaven. Officers could rarely see their troops for any considerable distance, for smoke clouded the vision, and a heavy sky obscured the sun. Directions were ascertained and lines established by means of the pocket-compass, and a change of position often presented an operation more like a problem of ocean navigation than a question of military manœuvers. It was the sense of sound and of touch rather than the sense of sight which guided the movements. It was a battle fought with the ear, and not with the eye. All circumstances seemed to combine to make the scene one of unutterable horror. At times the wind howled through the tree-tops, mingling its moans with the groans of the dying, and heavy branches were cut off by the fire of the artillery, and fell crashing upon the heads of the men, adding a new terror to battle. Forest fires raged; ammunition-trains exploded; the dead were roasted in the conflagration; the wounded, roused by its hot breath, dragged themselves along, with their torn and mangled limbs, in the mad energy of despair, to escape the ravages of the flames; and every bush seemed hung with shreds of blood-stained clothing. It was as though Christian men had turned to fiends, and hell itself had usurped the place of earth.

CHAPTER V

THE next morning, May 7, General Grant was almost
the first one up. He seated himself at the camp-
fire at dawn, and looked thoroughly refreshed after the
sound sleep he had enjoyed. In fact, a night's rest had
greatly reinvigorated every one. A fog, combined with
the smoke from the smoldering forest fires, rendered it
difficult for those of us who were sent to make reconnaissances to see any great distance, even where there
were openings in the forest. A little after 6 A. M. there
was some artillery-firing from Warren's batteries, which
created an impression for a little while that the enemy
might be moving against him; but he soon sent word
that he had been firing at some skirmishers who had
pushed down to a point near his intrenchments and discharged a few shots. At 6:30 A. M. the general issued
his orders to prepare for a night march of the entire
army toward Spottsylvania Court-house, on the direct
road to Richmond. At 8:30 Burnside pushed out a

74

skirmishing party to feel the enemy, and found that he had withdrawn from a portion of his line.   Skirmishing continued along parts of Warren's front till 11 A. M.   In fact, each army was anxious to learn promptly the position and apparent intentions of the other, so as to be able to act intelligently in making the next move in the all-absorbing game.   The enemy was found to be occupying a strongly intrenched line defended by artillery, and at an average distance from our front of nearly a mile.

While sitting at the mess-table taking breakfast, I asked the general-in-chief: "In all your battles up to this time, where do you think your presence upon the field was most useful in the accomplishing of results?" He replied: "Well, I don't know"; then, after a pause, "perhaps at Shiloh."   I said: "I think it was last night, when the attack was made on our right."   He did not follow up the subject, for he always spoke with great reluctance about anything which was distinctly personal to himself.   The only way in which we could ever draw him out, and induce him to talk about events in his military career, was to make some misstatement intentionally about an occurrence.   His regard for truth was so great that his mind always rebelled against inaccuracies, and in his desire to correct the error he would go into an explanation of the facts, and in doing so would often be led to talk with freedom upon the subject.

An officer related to the general an incident of the attack the night before, which showed that even the gravest events have a comical side.   In the efforts to strengthen our right, a number of teamsters had been ordered into the ranks and sent hurriedly to the front. As they were marching past their teams, one of the men was recognized by his favorite "lead" mule, who proceeded to pay his respects to him in a friendly heehaw, which reverberated through the forest until the sound bid fair to rival the report of the opening gun at Lexington, which fired the " shot heard round the world." The teamster turned to him and cried: " Oh, you better not laugh, old Simon Bolivar. Before this fight's through I bet they 'll pick you up and put you into the ranks, too ! "

After leaving the breakfast-table, the general lighted a cigar and took his seat on a camp-stool in front of his tent. In a conversation with the staff he then began to discuss the operations of the day before. He expressed himself as satisfied with the result in the main, saying: " While it is in one sense a drawn battle, as neither side has gained or lost ground substantially since the fighting began, yet we remain in possession of the field, and the forces opposed to us have withdrawn to a distance from our front and taken up a defensive position. We cannot call the engagement a positive victory, but the enemy have only twice actually reached our lines in their many attacks, and have not gained a single advantage. This will enable me to carry out my intention of moving to the left, and compelling the enemy to fight in a more open country and outside of their breastworks."

An old officer who was passing by, an acquaintance of the general's, now stepped up to the group. He had recently been ordered in from the plains, and his wild tales of red-handed slaughter in the land of the savages had already made him known in the army as the " Injun-slayer." An aide remarked to him, " Well, as you 've been spoiling for a fight ever since you joined this army, how did yesterday's set-to strike you by way of a skirmish ? " " Oh," was the reply, " you had large numbers engaged, and heavy losses; but it was n't the

picturesque, desperate hand-to-hand fighting that you
see when you 're among the Injuns." "No; but we got
in some pretty neat work on the white man," said the
aide. "Yes; but it did n't compare with the time the
Nez Percés and the Shoshonee tribes had their big battle," continued the veteran. "Why, how was that?"
cried all present in a chorus. "Well, you see," explained
the narrator, "first the Nez Percés set up a yell louder
than a blast of Gabriel's trumpet, and charged straight
across the valley; but the Shoshonees stood their ground
without budging an inch, and pretty soon they went for
the Nez Percés and drove 'em back again. As soon as
the Nez Percés could catch their breath they took another turn at the Shoshonees, and shoved them back
just about where they started from. By this time the
ground between 'em was so covered by the killed and
wounded that you could n't see as much as a blade of
grass. But still they kept on charging back and forth
across that valley, and they moved so fast that when
their lines of battle passed me, the wind they made was
so strong that I had to hold my hat on with both hands,
and once I came mighty near being blown clear off my
feet." "Why, where were *you* all this time?" asked
several voices. "Oh," said he, "I was standing on a
little knoll in the middle of the valley, looking on."
"Why," remarked an officer, "I should think they
would have killed you in the scrimmage." Then the
face of the veteran of the plains assumed an air of
offended innocence, and in a tone of voice which made
it painfully evident that he felt the hurt, he said,
"What?—the Injuns! Lord, they all knew *me!*" The
general joined in the smiles which followed this bit of
sadly mutilated truth. Similar Munchausenisms, indulged in from time to time by this officer, demonstrated
the fact that he had become so skilled in warping ve-

racity that one of his lies could make truth look mean alongside of it, and he finally grew so untrustworthy that it was unsafe even to believe the contrary of what he said.

At 3 P. M. despatches were received by way of Washington, saying that General Butler had reached the junction of the James and Appomattox rivers the night of the 5th, had surprised the enemy, and successfully disembarked his troops, and that Sherman was moving out against Johnston in Georgia, and expected that a battle would be fought on the 7th.

All preparations for the night march had now been completed. The wagon-trains were to move at 4 P.M., so as to get a start of the infantry, and then go into park and let the troops pass them. The cavalry had been thrown out in advance; the infantry began the march at 8:30 P. M. Warren was to proceed along the Brock road toward Spottsylvania Court-house, moving by the rear of Hancock, whose corps was to remain in its position during the night to guard against a possible attack by the enemy, and afterward to follow Warren. Sedgwick was to move by way of Chancellorsville and Piney Branch Church. Burnside was to follow Sedgwick, and to cover the trains which moved on the roads that were farthest from the enemy.

Soon after dark, Generals Grant and Meade, accompanied by their staffs, after having given personal supervision to the starting of the march, rode along the Brock road toward Hancock's headquarters, with the intention of waiting there till Warren's troops should reach that point. While moving close to Hancock's line, there occurred an unexpected demonstration on the part of the troops, which created one of the most memorable scenes of the campaign. Notwithstanding the darkness of the night, the form of the commander was recognized, and word was passed rapidly along that the chief who had led them through the mazes of the Wilderness was again moving forward with his horse's head turned toward Richmond. Troops know but little about what is going on in a large army, except the occurrences which take place in their immediate vicinity; but this night ride of the general-in-chief told plainly the story of success, and gave each man to understand that the cry was to be "On to Richmond!" Soldiers weary and sleepy after their long battle, with stiffened limbs and smarting wounds, now sprang to their feet, forgetful of their pains, and rushed forward to the roadside. Wild cheers echoed through the forest, and glad shouts of triumph rent the air. Men swung their hats, tossed up their arms, and pressed forward to within touch of their chief, clapping their hands, and speaking to him with the familiarity of comrades. Pine-knots and leaves were set on fire, and lighted the scene with their weird, flickering glare. The night march had become a triumphal procession for the new commander. The demonstration was the emphatic verdict pronounced by the troops upon his first battle in the East. The excitement had been imparted to the horses, which soon became restive, and even the general's large bay, over which he possessed ordinarily such perfect control, became difficult to manage. Instead of being elated by this significant ovation, the general, thoughtful only of the practical question of the success of the movement, said: "This is most unfortunate. The sound will reach the ears of the enemy, and I fear it may reveal our movement." By his direction, staff-officers rode forward and urged the men to keep quiet so as not to attract the enemy's attention; but the demonstration did not really cease until the general was out of sight.

When Hancock's headquarters were reached, the party remained with him for some time, awaiting the arrival of the head of Warren's troops. Hancock's wound received at Gettysburg had not thoroughly healed, and he suffered such inconvenience from it when in the saddle that he had applied for permission to ride in a spring ambulance while on the march and when his troops were not in action. He was reclining upon one of the seats of the ambulance, conversing with General Grant, who had dismounted and was sitting on the ground with his back against a tree, whittling a stick, when the sound of firing broke forth directly in front. Hancock sprang up, seized his sword, which was lying near him, buckled it around his waist, and cried: "My horse! my horse!" The scene was intensely dramatic, and recalled vividly to the bystanders the cry of Richard III on the field of Bosworth. Grant listened a moment without changing his position or ceasing his whittling, and then remarked: "They are not fighting; the firing is all on one side. It takes two sides to start a fight." In a few minutes the firing died away, and it was found that the enemy was not advancing. The incident fairly illustrates the contrast in the temperaments of these two distinguished soldiers.

At eleven o'clock word came to Grant and Meade that their headquarters escorts and wagons were delaying the advance of Warren's corps, and they decided to move on to Todd's tavern in order to clear the way. The woods were still on fire along parts of the main road, which made it almost impassable, so that the party turned out to the right into a side road. The intention was to take the same route by which the cavalry had advanced, but it was difficult to tell one road from another. The night was dark, the dust was thick, the guide who was directing the party became confused, and it was uncertain whether we were going in the right direction or riding into the lines of the enemy. The guide was for a time suspected of treachery, but he was innocent of such a charge, and had only lost his bearings. Colonel Comstock rode on in advance, and hearing the sound of marching columns not far off on our right, came back with this news, and it was decided to return to the Brock road. General Grant at first demurred when it was proposed to turn back, and urged the guide to try and find some cross-road leading to the Brock road, to avoid retracing our steps. This was an instance of his marked aversion to turning back, which amounted almost to a superstition. He often put himself to the greatest personal inconvenience to avoid it. When he found he was not traveling in the direction he intended to take, he would try all sorts of cross-cuts, ford streams, and jump any number of fences to reach another road rather than go back and take a fresh start. If he had been in the place of the famous apprentice boy who wandered away from London, he would never have been thrice mayor of that city, for with him Bow Bells would have appealed to deaf ears when they chimed out, "Turn again, Whittington." The enemy who encountered him never failed to feel the effect of this inborn prejudice against turning back. However, a slight retrograde movement became absolutely necessary in the present instance, and the general yielded to the force of circumstances. An orderly was stationed at the fork of the roads to indicate the right direction to Warren's troops when they should reach that point, and our party proceeded to Todd's tavern, reaching there soon after midnight. It was learned afterward that Anderson's (Longstreet's) corps had been marching parallel with us, and at a distance of less than a mile, so that the apprehension felt was well founded.

The general and staff bivouacked upon the ground.
The night was quite chilly, and a couple of fires were
lighted to add to our comfort.   General Grant lay down
with his officers beside one of the fires, without any
covering; when asleep, an aide quietly spread an overcoat over him.   For about four hours we all kept turning over every few minutes so as to get warmed on
both sides, imitating with our bodies the diurnal motion
of the earth as it exposes its sides alternately to the
heat of the sun.   When daylight broke it was seen that
a low board structure close to which the general-in-
chief had lain down was a pig-pen; but its former occupants had disappeared, and were probably at that
time nourishing the stomachs of the cavalry troopers of
the invading army.   Unfortunately, the odors of the
place had not taken their departure with the pigs, but
remained to add to the discomfort of the bivouackers.
Sheridan's cavalry had had a fight at this place the
afternoon before, in which he had defeated the opposing
force, and the ground in the vicinity, strewn with the
dead, offered ample evidence of the severity of the
struggle.

At daylight on the morning of the 8th active operations were in progress throughout the columns.   General Sheridan had ordered his cavalry to move by
different roads to seize the bridges crossing the Po
River.   General Meade modified these orders, and
directed a portion of the cavalry to move in front of
Warren's infantry on the Spottsylvania Court-house
road.   The enemy were felling trees and placing other
obstacles in the way, in order to impede the movement,
and the cavalry was afterward withdrawn and the infantry directed to open the way.

About sunrise General Grant, after taking off his coat
and shaking it to rid it of some of the dust in which he

had lain down, shared with the staff-officers some soldiers' rations, and then seated himself on the ground by the roadside to take his morning smoke.

Soon afterward he and General Meade rode on, and established their respective headquarters near Piney Branch Church, about two miles to the east of Todd's tavern. It was Sunday, but the overrunning of the country by contending armies had scattered the little church's congregation. The temple of prayer was voiceless, the tolling of its peaceful bell had given place to the echo of hostile guns, and in the excitement which prevailed it must be confessed that few recalled the fact that it was the Sabbath day.

A drum corps in passing caught sight of the general, and at once struck up a then popular negro camp-meeting air. Every one began to laugh, and Rawlins cried, "Good for the drummers!" "What's the fun?" inquired the general. "Why," was the reply, "they are playing, 'Ain't I glad to get out ob de wilderness!'" The general smiled at the ready wit of the musicians, and said, "Well, with me a musical joke always requires explanation. I know only two tunes: one is 'Yankee Doodle,' and the other is n't."

Charles A. Dana, Assistant Secretary of War, joined us during the forenoon, coming from Washington by way of Rappahannock Station, and remained at headquarters most of the time through the entire campaign. His daily, and sometimes hourly, despatches to the War Department, giving the events occurring in the field, constituted a correspondence which is a rare example of perspicuity, accuracy, and vividness of description.

Sheridan had been sent for by Meade to come to his headquarters, and when he arrived, between eleven and twelve o'clock that morning, a very acrimonious dispute took place between the two generals. Meade was pos-

sessed of an excitable temper which under irritating
circumstances became almost ungovernable. He had
worked himself into a towering passion regarding the
delays encountered in the forward movement, and when
Sheridan appeared went at him hammer and tongs, ac-
cusing him of blunders, and charging him with not
making a proper disposition of his troops, and letting
the cavalry block the advance of the infantry. Sheridan was equally fiery, and, smarting under the belief
that he was unjustly treated, all the hotspur in his
nature was aroused. He insisted that Meade had created the trouble by countermanding his (Sheridan's)
orders, and that it was this act which had resulted in
mixing up his troops with the infantry, exposing to
great danger Wilson's division, which had advanced as
far as Spottsylvania Court-house, and rendering in-
effectual all his combinations regarding the movements
of the cavalry corps. Sheridan declared with great
warmth that he would not command the cavalry any
longer under such conditions, and said if he could have
matters his own way he would concentrate all the cavalry, move out in force against Stuart's command, and
whip it. His language throughout was highly spiced
and conspicuously italicized with expletives. General
Meade came over to General Grant's tent immediately
after, and related the interview to him. The excitement
of the one was in singular contrast with the calmness
of the other. When Meade repeated the remarks made
by Sheridan, that he could move out with his cavalry
and whip Stuart, General Grant quietly observed, " Did
Sheridan say that? Well, he generally knows what he
is talking about. Let him start right out and do it."
By one o'clock Sheridan had received his orders in
writing from Meade for the movement. Early the next
morning he started upon his famous raid to the vicinity

of Richmond in rear of the enemy's army, and made good his word.

After the interview just mentioned, the general-in-chief talked for some time with officers of the staff about the results of the battle of the previous days. He said in this connection: "All things in this world are relative. While we were engaged in the Wilderness I could not keep from thinking of the first fight I ever saw—the battle of Palo Alto. As I looked at the long line of battle, consisting of three thousand men, I felt that General Taylor had such a fearful responsibility resting upon him that I wondered how he ever had the nerve to assume it; and when, after the fight, the casualties were reported, and the losses ascertained to be nearly sixty in killed, wounded, and missing, the engagement assumed a magnitude in my eyes which was positively startling. When the news of the victory reached the States, the windows in every household were illuminated, and it was largely instrumental in making General Taylor President of the United States. Now, such an affair would scarcely be deemed important enough to report to headquarters." He little thought at that moment that the battles then in progress would be chiefly instrumental in making the commander himself President of the United States.

The movements of the opposing armies now became one of the most instructive lessons in the art of modern warfare. They showed the closeness of the game played by the two great masters who commanded the contending forces, and illustrated how thoroughly those skilled fencers had carte and tierce at their fingers' ends. They demonstrated, also, how far the features of a campaign may be affected by accidents and errors. In the Wilderness the manœuvers had been largely a game of blindman's-buff; they now became more like the play of

pussy-wants-a-corner.   Anderson had been ordered by
Lee, on the evening of May 7, to start for Spottsylvania
Court-house the next morning; but Anderson, finding
the woods on fire, and no good place to go into camp,
kept his troops in motion, continued his march all
night, and reached Spottsylvania in the morning.   The
cavalry which Sheridan had placed at the bridges over
the Po River might have greatly impeded Anderson's
march; but owing to conflicting orders the movements
of the cavalry had been changed, and Anderson occupied a position at Spottsylvania that morning as the
result of a series of accidents.   When Lee found our
wagon-trains were moving in an easterly direction, he
made up his mind that our army was retreating, and
telegraphed on the 8th to his government at Richmond:
" The enemy has abandoned his position, and is moving
toward Fredericksburg."   He sent an order the same
day to Early, then commanding Hill's corps, saying:
" Move by Todd's tavern along the Brock road as soon
as your front is clear of the enemy."   It will be seen
that in this order he directed a corps to move by a
road which was then in full possession of our forces, and
Early did not discover this fact till he actually encountered Hancock's troops at Todd's tavern.   Early was
then compelled to take another road.   It was after these
movements that General Grant uttered the aphorism,
" Accident often decides the fate of battle."

At 11:30 A. M. General Grant sent a telegram to Halleck, saying: " The best of feeling prevails. . . . Route
to the James River . . . not yet definitely marked out."
In talking over the situation at headquarters, he said:
" It looks somewhat as if Lee intends to throw his army
between us and Fredericksburg, in order to cut us off
from our base of supplies.   I would not be at all sorry

to have such a move made, as in that case I would be in rear of Lee, and between him and Richmond."

That morning, May 8, the troops under Warren encountered those of Anderson's corps, who were intrenched near Spottsylvania. Warren attacked, but was not able to make much progress, and decided to strengthen his own position and wait until other troops came to his assistance before giving battle. His men had suffered great hardships. They had been under fire for four days, and had just made a long night march to reach their present position. Late in the afternoon Warren and Sedgwick were ordered to attack with all their forces, but it was nearly dark before the assault could be made, and then only half of Sedgwick's command and but one of Warren's divisions participated. There was no decided result from this day's fighting.

Late in the afternoon of the 8th headquarters were moved south about two miles, and camp was pitched in the angle formed by the intersection of the Brock road with the road running south from Piney Branch Church. Lee had by this time comprehended Grant's intentions, and was making all haste to throw his troops between the Union army and Richmond, and take up a strong defensive position. Most of the officers of the staff had been in the saddle since daylight, communicating with the corps commanders, designating the lines of march, and urging forward the troops; and as soon as the tents were pitched that night all who could be spared for a while from duty "turned in" to catch as many winks of sleep as possible.

Every one at headquarters was up at daylight the next morning, prepared for another active day's work. Hancock was now on the right, Warren next, then Sedgwick; Burnside was moving down to go into position on the extreme left.   The general expressed his intention to devote the day principally to placing all the troops in position, reconnoitering the enemy's line, and getting in readiness for a combined attack as soon as proper preparations for it could be made.   The country was more open than the Wilderness, but it still presented obstacles of a most formidable nature.   Four rivers run in a southeasterly direction.   Some early pioneer, ingenious in systematic nomenclature, and who was evidently possessed of a due regard for "helps to human memory," had named the streams respectively, beginning with the most southerly, the Mat, the Ta, the Po, and the Ny, and then deployed these terms in single line, closed them in until they were given a touch of the elbow, and called the formation the Mattapony, the name by which the large river is known into which the four smaller ones flow.

Spottsylvania Court-house lies between the Po and the Ny.   While these streams are not wide, their banks are steep in some places and lined by marshes in other. The country is undulating, and was at that time broken by alternations of cleared spaces and dense forests.   In the woods there was a thick tangled undergrowth of hazel, dwarf pine, and scrub-oak.

A little before eight o'clock on the morning of May 9, the general mounted his horse, and directed me and two other staff-officers to accompany him to make an examination of the lines in our immediate front.   This day he rode a black pony called "Jeff Davis" (given that name because it had been captured in Mississippi on the plantation of Joe Davis, a brother of the Confederate president).   It was turned into the quartermaster's department, from which it was purchased by the general on his Vicksburg campaign.   He was not well at that time, being afflicted with boils, and he took a fancy to the pony because it had a remarkably easy pace, which enabled the general to make his long daily rides with much more comfort than when he used the horses he usually rode. "Little Jeff" soon became a conspicuous figure in the Virginia campaign.

We proceeded to Sedgwick's command, and the general had a conference with him in regard to the part his corps was to take in the contemplated attack. Both officers remained mounted during the interview. The gallant commander of the famous Sixth Corps seemed particularly cheerful and hopeful that morning, and looked the picture of buoyant life and vigorous health. When his chief uttered some words of compliment upon his recent services, and spoke of the hardships he had encountered, Sedgwick spoke lightly of the difficulties experienced, and expressed every confidence in the ability of his troops to respond heroically to every demand made upon them. When the general-in-chief left him, Sedgwick started with his staff to move farther to the front. Our party had ridden but a short distance to the left when General Grant sent me back to Sedgwick to discuss with him further a matter which it was thought had not been sufficiently emphasized in their conversation. While I was following the road I had seen him take, I heard musketry-firing ahead, and soon saw the body of an officer being borne from the field. Such a sight was so common that ordinarily it would have attracted no attention, but my apprehensions were aroused by seeing several of General Sedgwick's staff beside the body. As they came nearer I gave an inquiring look. Colonel Beaumont, of the staff, cast his eyes in the direction of the body, then looked at me with an expression of profound sorrow, and slowly shook his head. His actions told the whole sad story. His heroic chief was dead. I was informed that as he was approaching an exposed point of the line to examine the enemy's position more closely, General McMahon, of his staff, reminded him that one or two officers had just been struck at that spot by sharp-shooters, and begged him not to advance farther. At this suggestion the general only smiled, and soon after had entirely forgotten the warning. Indifferent to every form of danger, such an appeal made but little impression upon him. His movements led him to the position against which he had been cautioned, and he had scarcely dismounted and reached the spot on foot when a bullet entered his left cheek just below the eye, and he fell dead. As his lifeless form was carried by, a smile still remained upon his lips. Sedgwick was essentially a soldier. He had never married; the camp was his home, and the members of his staff were his family. He was always spoken of familiarly as "Uncle John," and the news of his death fell upon his comrades with a sense of grief akin to the sorrow of a personal bereavement.

I rode off at once to bear the sad intelligence to the general-in-chief. For a few moments he could scarcely realize it, and twice asked, "Is he really dead?" The shock was severe, and he could ill conceal the depth of his grief. He said: "His loss to this army is greater than the loss of a whole division of troops." General Wright was at once placed in command of the Sixth Corps.

At daylight on May 9 Burnside had moved down the road from Fredericksburg, crossed the Ny, driven back a force of the enemy, and finally reached a position within less than two miles of Spottsylvania. By noon it was found that the Confederate army occupied an almost continuous line in front of Spottsylvania, in the form of a semicircle, with the convex side facing north.

The demonstrations made by Lee, and the strengthening of his right, revived in General Grant's mind the impression that the enemy might attempt to work around our left, and interpose between us and Fredericksburg; and preparations were made in such case to attack Lee's left, turn it, and throw the Union army between him and Richmond. At noon a package of despatches from Washington reached headquarters, and were eagerly read. They announced that Sherman's columns were moving successfully in northwestern Georgia, that Resaca was threatened, and that Joe Johnston was steadily retreating. A report from Butler, dated the 5th, stated that he had landed at City Point, and reports of the 6th and 7th announced that he had sent out reconnoitering parties on the Petersburg Railroad, and had despatched troops to take possession of it; that he had had some hard fighting, and was then intrenching, and wanted reinforcements. General Grant directed the reinforcements to be sent. Sigel reported that he had not yet met the enemy, and expected to move up the Shenandoah Valley and try to connect with Crook. General Grant did not express any particular gratification regarding these reports, except the one from Sherman, and in fact made very few comments upon them.

Hancock had crossed the Po, and was now threatening Lee's left. On the morning of the 10th Hancock found the enemy's line strongly intrenched, and no general attack was made upon it. Lee had realized the danger threatened, and had hurried troops to his left to protect that flank. Grant, perceiving this, decided that Lee must have weakened other portions of his line, and at once determined to assault his center.

At 9:30 A. M. the general-in-chief sat down in his tent at his little camp-table, and wrote with his own hand, as usual, a despatch to Halleck which began as follows: " The enemy hold our front in very strong force, and evince a strong determination to interpose between us and Richmond to the last. *I shall take no backward steps. . . .*" The last sentence, which I have italicized, attracted no notice at the time on the part of those who read it, but it afterward became historic and took a prominent place among the general's famous sayings.

It was now suggested to him that it would be more convenient to move our camp farther to the left, so as to be near the center, where the assault was to take place, and orders were given to establish it a little more than a mile to the southeast, near the Alsop house. The tents were pitched in a comfortable-looking little dell, on the edge of a deep wood, and near the principal roads of communication.

CHAPTER VI

COMMUNICATING WITH BURNSIDE — GRANT ATTACKS THE
ENEMY'S CENTER — HOW A FAMOUS MESSAGE WAS DE-
SPATCHED — NEWS FROM THE OTHER ARMIES — PRE-
PARING TO ATTACK THE "ANGLE" — AN EVENTFUL
MORNING AT HEADQUARTERS — TWO DISTINGUISHED
PRISONERS — HOW THE "ANGLE" WAS CAPTURED —
SCENES AT THE "BLOODY ANGLE"

AT half-past ten on the morning of May 10 the general-in-chief called me to where he was standing
in front of his tent, spoke in much detail of what he
wanted Burnside to accomplish, and directed me to go
to that officer, explain to him fully the situation and
the wishes of the commander, and remain with him on
the left during the rest of the day. As I was mounting
the general added: "I had started to write a note to
Burnside; just wait a moment, and I 'll finish it, and
you can deliver it to him." He stepped into his tent,
and returned in a few minutes and handed me the note.
I set out at once at a gallop toward our left. There
were two roads by which Burnside could be reached.
One was a circuitous route some distance in rear of our
lines; the other was much shorter, but under the enemy's
fire for quite a distance. The latter was chosen on account of the time which would thereby be saved. When
the exposed part of the road was reached, I adopted the
method to which aides so often resorted when they had

93

to take the chances of getting through with a message, and when those chances were not particularly promising—putting the horse on a run, and throwing the body down along his neck on the opposite side from the enemy. Although the bullets did considerable execution in clipping the limbs of the trees and stirring up the earth, they were considerate enough to skip me. The horse was struck, but only slightly, and I succeeded in reaching Burnside rather ahead of schedule time. His headquarters had been established on the north side of the river Ny. I explained to him that a general attack was to be made in the afternoon on the enemy's center by Warren's and Hancock's troops, and that he was to move forward for the purpose of reconnoitering Lee's extreme right, and keeping him from detaching troops from his flanks to reinforce his center. If Burnside could see a chance to attack, he was to do so with all vigor, and in a general way make the best coöperative effort that was possible.

A little while before, the heroic Stevenson, commander of his first division, had been struck by a sharpshooter and killed. He had served with Burnside in the North Carolina expedition, and the general was much attached to him. He felt his loss keenly, and was profuse in his expressions of grief.

The forward movement was ordered at once. Burnside was in great doubt as to whether he should concentrate his three divisions and attack the enemy's right vigorously, or demonstrate with two divisions, and place the third in rear of Mott, who was on his right. I felt sure that General Grant would prefer the former, and urged it strenuously; but Burnside was so anxious to have General Grant make a decision in the matter himself that he sent him a note at 2:15 P. M. He did not get an answer for nearly two hours. The general said in his reply that it was then too late to bring up the third division, and he thought that Burnside would be secure in attacking as he was.

I had ridden with General Burnside to the front to watch the movement. The advance soon reached a point within a quarter of a mile of Spottsylvania, and completely turned the right of the enemy's line; but the country was so bewildering, and the enemy so completely concealed from view, that it was impossible at the time to know the exact relative positions of the contending forces. Toward dark Willcox's division had constructed a line of fence-rail breastworks, and held pretty securely his advanced position.

I had sent two bulletins to General Grant describing the situation on the left, but the orderly who carried one of the despatches never arrived, having probably been killed, and the other did not reach the general till quite late, as he was riding among the troops in front of the center of the line, and it was difficult to find him. I started for headquarters that evening, but owing to the intense darkness, the condition of the roads, and the difficulty of finding the way, did not arrive till long after midnight.

The same day, May 10, had witnessed important fighting on the right and center of our line. Hancock moved his troops back to the north side of the Po. Barlow's division, while withdrawing, became isolated, and was twice assaulted, but each time repulsed the enemy. The losses on both sides were heavy. Wright had formed an assaulting force of twelve regiments, and placed Colonel Emory Upton in command. At 4 P. M. Wright, Warren, and Mott moved their commands forward, and a fierce struggle ensued. Warren was repulsed with severe loss, and Mott's attack failed; but Upton's column swept through the enemy's line, carry-

ing everything before it, and capturing several guns
and a number of prisoners. Unfortunately the troops
ordered to his support were so slow in reaching him that
he had to be withdrawn. The men had behaved so
handsomely, however, and manifested such a desire to
retake the position, that General Grant had additional
troops brought up, and ordered another assault. Again
a rush was made upon the enemy's line, and again the
same gallantry was shown. Many of our men succeeded
in getting over the earthworks, but could not secure a
lodgment which could be held; and as the assaults at
other points were not made with the dash and spirit
exhibited by Upton, his troops were withdrawn after
nightfall to a position of greater security, in which they
would not be isolated from the rest of the forces. He
was compelled to abandon his captured guns, but he
brought away all his prisoners. Upton had been
severely wounded. General Grant had obtained permission of the government before starting from Washington to promote officers on the field for conspicuous
acts of gallantry, and he now conferred upon Upton the
well-merited grade of brigadier-general. Colonel Samuel
S. Carroll was also promoted to the rank of brigadier-
general for gallantry displayed by him in this action.

Lee had learned by this time that he must be on the
lookout for an attack from Grant at any hour, day or
night. He sent Ewell a message on the evening of the
10th, saying: "It will be necessary for you to reëstab-
lish your whole line to-night. . . . Perhaps Grant will
make a night attack, as it was a favorite amusement of
his at Vicksburg."

While the general-in-chief was out on the lines supervising the afternoon attack, he dismounted and sat
down on a fallen tree to write a despatch. While thus
engaged a shell exploded directly in front of him. He

looked up from his paper an instant, and then, without the slightest change of countenance, went on writing the message. Some of the Fifth Wisconsin wounded were being carried past him at the time, and Major E. R. Jones of that regiment said, and he mentions it in his interesting book of reminiscences published since, that one of his men made the remark: "Ulysses don't scare worth a d—n."

The 11th of May gave promise of a little rest for everybody, as the commander expressed his intention to spend the day simply in reconnoitering for the purpose of learning more about the character and strength of the enemy's intrenchments, and discovering the weakest points in his line, with a view to breaking through. He sat down at the mess-table that morning, and made his entire breakfast off a cup of coffee and a small piece of beef cooked almost to a crisp; for the cook had by this time learned that the nearer he came to burning up the beef the better the general liked it. During the short time he was at the table he conversed with Mr. Elihu B. Washburne, who had accompanied headquarters up to this time, and who was now about to return to Washington. After breakfast the general lighted a cigar, seated himself on a camp-chair in front of his tent, and was joined there by Mr. Washburne and several members of the staff. At half-past eight o'clock the cavalry escort which was to accompany the congressman was drawn up in the road near by, and all present rose to bid him good-by. Turning to the chief, he said: "General, I shall go to see the President and the Secretary of War as soon as I reach Washington. I can imagine their anxiety to know what you think of the prospects of the campaign, and I know they would be greatly gratified if I could carry a message from you giving what encouragement you can as to the situation."

The general hesitated a moment, and then replied:
"We are certainly making fair progress, and all the
fighting has been in our favor; but the campaign prom-
ises to be a long one, and I am particularly anxious not
to say anything just now that might hold out false
hopes to the people"; and then, after a pause, added,
"However, I will write a letter to Halleck, as I generally communicate through him, giving the general
situation, and you can take it with you." He stepped
into his tent, sat down at his field-table, and, keeping
his cigar in his mouth, wrote a despatch of about
two hundred words. In the middle of the communication occurred the famous words, *"I propose to fight
it out on this line if it takes all summer."* When the
letter had been copied, he folded it and handed it to Mr.
Washburne, who thanked him warmly, wished him a
continuation of success, shook hands with him and with
each of the members of the staff, and at once mounted
his horse and rode off. The staff-officers read the retained copy of the despatch, but neither the general
himself nor any one at headquarters realized the epigrammatic character of the striking sentence it contained until the New York papers reached camp a few
days afterward with the words displayed in large head-
lines, and with conspicuous comments upon the force
of the expression. It was learned afterward that the
President was delighted to read this despatch giving
such full information as to the situation, and that he
had said a few days before, when asked by a member
of Congress what Grant was doing: "Well, I can't tell
much about it. You see, Grant has gone to the Wilderness, crawled in, drawn up the ladder, and pulled in the
hole after him, and I guess we'll have to wait till he
comes out before we know just what he's up to."

The general was now awaiting news from Butler and

Sheridan with some anxiety. While maturing his plans for striking Lee, he was at the same time keeping a close lookout to see that Lee was not detaching any troops with the purpose of crushing Butler's or Sheridan's forces. This day, May 11, the looked-for despatches arrived, and their contents caused no little excitement at headquarters. The general, after glancing over the reports hurriedly, stepped to the front of his tent, and read them aloud to the staff-officers, who had gathered about him, eager to learn the news from the coöperating armies. Butler reported that he had a strongly intrenched position at Bermuda Hundred, in the angle formed by the James and Appomattox rivers; that he had cut the railroad, leaving Beauregard's troops south of the break, and had completely whipped Hill's force. Sheridan sent word that he had torn up ten miles of the Virginia Central Railroad between Lee's army and Richmond, and had destroyed a large quantity of medical supplies and a million and a half of rations. The general-in-chief expressed himself as particularly pleased with the destruction of the railroad in rear of Lee, as it would increase the difficulty of moving troops suddenly between Richmond and Spottsylvania for the purpose of reinforcing either of those points. As usual, the contents of these despatches were promptly communicated to Generals Meade and Burnside.

The result of the day's work on our front was to discover more definitely the character of the salient in Lee's defenses on the right of his center. It was in the shape of a V with a flattened apex. The ground in front sloped down toward our position, and was in most places thickly wooded. There was a clearing, however, about four hundred yards in width immediately in front of the apex. Several of the staff-officers were on that part of the field a great portion of the day. At three o'clock in the afternoon the general had thoroughly matured his plans, and sent instructions to Meade directing him to move Hancock with all possible secrecy under cover of night to the left of Wright, and to make a vigorous assault on the "angle" at dawn the next morning. Warren and Wright were ordered to hold their corps as close to the enemy as possible, and to take advantage of any diversion caused by this attack to push in if an opportunity should present itself. A personal conference was held with the three corps commanders, and every effort made to have a perfect understanding on their part as to exactly what was required in this important movement. Colonels Comstock and Babcock were directed to go to Burnside that afternoon, and to remain with him during the movements of the next day, in which he was to attack simultaneously with Hancock. The other members of the staff were sent to keep in communication with the different portions of Hancock's line. The threatening sky was not propitious for the movement, but in this entertainment there was to be "no postponement on account of the weather," and the preparations went on regardless of the lowering clouds and falling rain. All those who were in the secret anticipated a memorable field-day on the morrow.

Hancock's troops made a difficult night march, groping their way through the gloom of the forests, their clothing drenched with rain, and their feet ankle-deep in Virginia mud. A little after midnight they reached their position, and formed for the attack at a distance of about twelve hundred yards from the enemy's intrenchments.

I had been out all night looking after the movements of the troops which were to form the assaulting columns. After they had all been placed in position I started for headquarters, in obedience to instructions, to report the situation to the general-in-chief. He counted upon important results from the movement, although he appreciated fully the difficulties to be encountered, and was naturally anxious about the dispositions which were being made for the attack. The condition of the country was such that a horseman could make but slow progress in moving from one point of the field to another. The rain was falling in torrents, the ground was marshy, the roads were narrow, and the movements of the infantry and artillery had churned up the mud until the country was almost impassable. In the pitchy darkness one's horse constantly ran against trees, was shoved off the road by guns or wagons, and had to squeeze through lines of infantry, who swore like "our army in Flanders" when a staff-officer's horse manifested a disposition to crawl over them. By feeling the way for some hours I reached headquarters about daylight the next morning, May 12.

When I arrived the general was up and sitting wrapped in his overcoat close to a camp-fire which was struggling heroically to sustain its life against the assaults of wind and rain. It had been decided to move headquarters a little nearer to the center of the lines, and most of the camp equipage had been packed up ready to start. The general seemed in excellent spirits, and was even inclined to be jocose. He said to me: "We have just had our coffee, and you will find some left for you"; and then, taking a critical look at my drenched and bespattered clothes and famished appearance, added, "But perhaps you are not hungry." To disabuse the chief's mind on this score, I sent for a cup of coffee, and drank it with the relish of a shipwrecked mariner, while I related the incidents of the embarrassments encountered in Hancock's movement, and the position he had

taken up.   Before I had quite finished making my report the stillness was suddenly broken by artillery-
firing, which came from the direction of Burnside's position.   A few minutes after came the sound of cheers
and the rattle of musketry from Hancock's front, telling
that the main assault upon the "angle" had begun.
No one could see a hundred yards from our position on
account of the dense woods, and reports from the front
were eagerly awaited.   It was nearly an hour before
anything definite was received, but at 5:30 an officer
came galloping through the woods with a report from
Hancock saying he had captured the first line of the
enemy's works.   This officer was closely followed by
another, who reported that many prisoners had been
taken.   Fifteen minutes later came the announcement
that Hancock had captured two general officers.   General Grant sent Burnside this news with a message saying, "Push on with all vigor."   Wright's corps was
now ordered to attack on the right of Hancock.   Before
six o'clock a message from Hancock's headquarters reported the capture of two thousand prisoners, and a
quarter of an hour later Burnside sent word that he had
driven the enemy back two miles and a half in his front.
Hancock called for reinforcements, but Grant had anticipated him and had already ordered troops to his
support.   The scene at headquarters was now exciting
in the extreme.   As aides galloped up one after the
other in quick succession with stirring bulletins, all bearing the glad tidings of overwhelming success, the group
of staff-officers standing about the camp-fire interrupted
their active work of receiving, receipting for, and an-
swering despatches by shouts and cheers which made
the forest ring.   General Grant sat unmoved upon his
camp-chair, giving his constant thoughts to devising
methods for making the victory complete.   At times

the smoke from the struggling camp-fire would for a moment blind him, and occasionally a gust of wind would blow the cape of his greatcoat over his face, and cut off his voice in the middle of a sentence.   Only once during the scene he rose from his seat and paced up and down for about ten minutes.   He made very few comments upon the stirring events which were crowding so closely upon one another until the reports came in regarding the prisoners.   When the large numbers captured were announced, he said, with the first trace of animation he had shown: "That's the kind of news I like to hear.   I had hoped that a bold dash at daylight would secure a large number of prisoners.   Hancock is doing well."   This remark was eminently characteristic of the Union commander.   His extreme fondness for taking prisoners was manifested in every battle he fought.   When word was brought to him of a success on any part of the line, his first and most eager question was always, "Have any prisoners been taken?"   The love for capturing prisoners amounted to a passion with him.   It did not seem to arise from the fact that they added so largely to the trophies of battle, and was no doubt chiefly due to his tenderness of heart, which prompted him to feel that it was always more humane to reduce the enemy's strength by captures than by slaughter.   His desire in this respect was amply gratified, for during the war it fell to his lot to capture a larger number of prisoners than any general of modern times.

Meade had come over to Grant's headquarters early, and while they were engaged in discussing the situation, about 6:30 A. M., a horseman rode up wearing the uniform of a Confederate general.   Halting near the camp-fire, he dismounted and walked forward, saluting the group of Union officers as he approached.   His clothing was covered with mud, and a hole had been torn in the crown of his felt hat, through which a tuft of hair protruded, looking like a Sioux chief's warlock. Meade looked at him attentively for a moment, and then stepped up to him, grasped him cordially by the hand, and cried, "Why, how do you do, general?" and then turned to the general-in-chief and said, "General Grant, this is General Johnson—Edward Johnson." General Grant shook hands warmly with the distinguished prisoner, and exclaimed, "How do you do? It is a long time since we last met." "Yes," replied Johnson; "it is a great many years, and I had not expected to meet you under such circumstances." "It is one of the many sad fortunes of war," answered General Grant, who offered the captured officer a cigar, and then picked up a camp-chair, placed it with his own hands near the fire, and added, "Be seated, and we will do all in our power to make you as comfortable as possible." Johnson sat down, and said in a voice and with a manner which showed that he was deeply touched by these manifestations of courtesy, "Thank you, general, thank you; you are very kind." He had been in the corps of cadets with General Meade, and had served in the Mexican war with General Grant, but they probably would not have recognized him if they had not already heard that he had been made a prisoner. I had known Johnson very well, and it was only four years since I had seen him. We recognized each other at once, and I extended a cordial greeting to him, and presented the members of our staff. He was soon quite at his ease, and bore himself under the trying circumstances in a manner which commanded the respect of every one present. General Hancock had already provided him with a horse to make his trip to the rear with the rest of the prisoners as comfortably as possible. After some pleasant conversation with Grant and Meade about old times and the strange chances of war, he bade us good-by, and started under escort for our base of supplies. General George H. Steuart was also captured, but was not sent in to general headquarters on account of a scene which had been brought about by an unseemly exhibition of temper on his part. Hancock had known him in the old army, and in his usual frank way went up to him, greeted him kindly, and offered his hand. Steuart drew back, rejected the offer, and said rather haughtily, "Under the present circumstances, I must decline to take your hand." Hancock, who was somewhat nettled by this remark, replied, "Under any other circumstances, general, I should not have offered it." No further attempt was made to extend any courtesies to his prisoner, who was left to make his way to the rear on foot with the others who had been captured.

While Generals Grant and Meade were talking with General Johnson by the camp-fire, a despatch came in from Hancock, saying, "I have finished up Johnson, and am now going into Early." General Grant passed this despatch around, but did not read it aloud, as usual, out of consideration for Johnson's feelings. Soon after came another report that Hancock had taken three thousand prisoners; then another that he had turned his captured guns upon the enemy and made a whole division prisoners, including the famous Stonewall Brigade. Burnside now reported that his right had lost its connection with Hancock's corps. General Grant sent him a brief, characteristic note in reply, saying, "Push the enemy with all your might; that 's the way to connect."

The general-in-chief showed again upon that eventful morning the value he placed upon minutes. Aides were kept riding at a full run carrying messages, and the terseness, vigor, and intensity manifested in every line of his field orders were enough to spur the most sluggish to prompt action.

After giving such instructions as would provide for the present emergencies, the general ordered the pony "Jeff Davis" to be saddled, and started for the front. He left an adjutant-general behind, with orders to forward to him promptly all communications. The staff rode with the general, and after a while reached a clearing on a piece of elevated ground from which a view of portions of the line could be obtained. It was found, upon learning the details of the assault upon the "angle," that, notwithstanding the fatigues and hardships to which the troops had been subjected, they had moved forward with the step of veterans, and had marched half-way across the open ground which separated them from the well-defended earthworks in their front with a steady pace and unbroken alinement. At that point they sent up cheers which rent the air, and the columns dashed forward at a run, scattering the enemy's pickets before them in their swift advance. A brisk fire was opened by the Confederate line from a position to the left, but, unheeding it, and without firing a shot, the assaulting column tore away the slashed timber and other obstacles in its path, and rushed like a mighty torrent over the intrenchments. A desperate hand-to-hand encounter now followed, in which men fought like demons, using their bayonets and clubbed muskets when in too close contact to load and fire. The main assault fell on Johnson's division of Lee's army. Lee was led to believe that there was an intention to attack his left, and he had sent most of Johnson's artillery to strengthen that flank. Johnson had his suspicions aroused during the night that there were preparations under way for attacking his front, and had induced Lee to order the artillery back.   By a strange coincidence, it arrived just as Johnson's line was carried, and before the guns could fire a shot they fell into Hancock's hands.   Besides capturing Generals Steuart and Johnson, he took nearly four thousand prisoners, thirty pieces of artillery, several thousand stands of small arms, and about thirty colors.   His troops swept on half a mile, driving the enemy before them in confusion, and did not pause till they encountered a second line of intrenchments.   The enemy was now driven to desperation, and every effort was bent toward retaking his lost works.   Reinforcements were rushed forward by Lee as soon as he saw the threatening condition of matters at the "angle"; and a formidable counter-movement was rapidly organized against Hancock.   As our troops were upon unknown territory, and as their formations had been thrown into considerable confusion by the rapidity of their movements, they withdrew slowly before the attack to the main line of works they had captured, and turning them against the enemy, held them successfully during all the terrific struggle that followed.

By six o'clock A. M. Wright was on that portion of the field, and his men were placed on the right of the "angle." Scarcely had he taken up this position when the Confederates made a determined and savage attack upon him; but despite their well-directed efforts they failed to recapture the line.   Wright was wounded early in the fight, but refused to leave the field.   Hancock had placed some artillery upon high ground, and his guns fired over the heads of our troops and did much execution in the ranks of the enemy.   Warren had been directed to make an attack before eight o'clock, in order to prevent the enemy from massing troops upon the center in an effort to retake the "angle," but he was slow in carrying out the order.   Although the instructions were of the most positive and urgent character, he did not accomplish the work expected of him. A little before eleven o'clock General Grant became so anxious that he directed General Meade to relieve Warren if he did not attack promptly, and to put General Humphreys in command of his corps. General Meade concurred in this course, and said that he would have relieved Warren without an order to that effect if there had been any further delay. General Grant said to one or two of us who were near him: "I feel sorry to be obliged to send such an order in regard to Warren. He is an officer for whom I had conceived a very high regard. His quickness of perception, personal gallantry, and soldierly bearing pleased me, and a few days ago I should have been inclined to place him in command of the Army of the Potomac in case Meade had been killed; but I began to feel, after his want of vigor in assaulting on the 8th, that he was not as efficient as I had believed, and his delay in attacking and the feeble character of his assaults to-day confirm me in my apprehensions." This was said in a kindly spirit, but with an air of serious disappointment. Longstreet's troops had continued to confront Warren, knowing that to lose that part of the enemy's line would expose the troops at the "angle" to a flank attack, and the obstacles to a successful assault were really very formidable. Warren was blamed not so much for not carrying the line in his front as for delays in making the attack.

The general now started for another part of the field, and kept moving from point to point to get a close view of the fighting on different parts of the line. Once or twice he called for a powerful field-glass belonging to Badeau. This was rather unusual, for the general never carried a glass himself, and seldom used one. He was exceptionally far-sighted, and generally trusted to his natural vision in examining the field. Badeau's near-sightedness made him very dependent on his glass. A few days before, while he was using it, a battery commander who was passing attempted a professional joke by remarking, " I say, Badeau ; can you see Richmond ? " " Not quite," answered the colonel; " though I hope to some day." " Better have the barrels of your glass rifled so that it will carry farther," suggested the artillerist.

Before riding far the general came to a humble-looking farm-house, which was within range of the enemy's guns, and surrounded by wounded men, sullen-looking prisoners, and terror-stricken stragglers. The fences were broken, the ground was furrowed by shells; and the place presented a scene which depicted war in its most repulsive aspect. An old lady and her daughter were standing on the porch. When the mother was told that the officer passing was the general-in-chief, she ran toward him, and with the tears running down her cheeks, threw up her arms and cried, " Thank God! thank God! I again behold the glorious flag of the Union, that I have not laid eyes on for three long, terrible years. Thank the Lord that I have at last seen the commander of the Union armies! I am proud to say that my husband and my son went from here to serve in those armies, but I have been cut off from all communication, and can get no tidings of them. Oh, you don't know, sir, what a loyal woman suffers in this land; but the coming of the Union troops makes me feel that deliverance is at last at hand, and that the gates have been opened for my escape from this hell." The general was so touched by this impassioned speech, and felt so firmly convinced that the woman was telling the truth, that he dismounted and went into the yard, and sat for a little time on the porch, to learn the details of her story, and to see what he could do to comfort and succor her. She gave an account of her persecutions and sufferings which would have moved the sternest heart. The general, finding that she was without food, ordered a supply of rations to be issued to her and her daughter, and promised to have inquiries set on foot to ascertain the whereabouts of her husband and son. She was profuse in her expressions of gratitude for these acts of kindness. Her story was afterward found to be true in every particular.

I had been anxious to participate in the scenes occurring at the "angle," and now got permission to go there and look after some new movements which had been ordered. Lee made five assaults, in all, that day, in a series of desperate and even reckless attempts to retake his main line of earthworks; but each time his men were hurled back defeated, and he had to content himself in the end with throwing up a new line farther in his rear.

The battle near the "angle" was probably the most desperate engagement in the history of modern warfare, and presented features which were absolutely appalling. It was chiefly a savage hand-to-hand fight across the breastworks. Rank after rank was riddled by shot and shell and bayonet-thrusts, and finally sank, a mass of torn and mutilated corpses; then fresh troops rushed madly forward to replace the dead, and so the murderous work went on. Guns were run up close to the parapet, and double charges of canister played their part in the bloody work. The fence-rails and logs in the breastworks were shattered into splinters, and trees over a foot and a half in diameter were cut completely in two by the incessant musketry fire. A section of the trunk of a stout oak-tree thus severed was afterward sent to Washington, where it is still on exhibition at the National Museum. We had not only shot down an army, but also a forest. The opposing flags were in places thrust against each other, and muskets were fired with muzzle against muzzle. Skulls were crushed with clubbed muskets, and men stabbed to death with swords and bayonets thrust between the logs in the parapet which separated the combatants. Wild cheers, savage yells, and frantic shrieks rose above the sighing of the wind and the pattering of the rain, and formed a demoniacal accompaniment to the booming of the guns as they hurled their missiles of death into the contending ranks. Even the darkness of night and the pitiless storm failed to stop the fierce contest, and the deadly strife did not cease till after midnight. Our troops had been under fire for twenty hours, but they still held the position which they had so dearly purchased.

My duties carried me again to the spot the next day, and the appalling sight presented was harrowing in the extreme. Our own killed were scattered over a large space near the "angle," while in front of the captured breastworks the enemy's dead, vastly more numerous than our own, were piled upon each other in some places four layers deep, exhibiting every ghastly phase of mutilation. Below the mass of fast-decaying corpses, the convulsive twitching of limbs and the writhing of bodies showed that there were wounded men still alive and struggling to extricate themselves from their horrid entombment. Every relief possible was afforded, but in too many cases it came too late. The place was well named the "Bloody Angle."

The results of the battle are best summed up in the report which the general-in-chief sent to Washington. At 6:30 p. m., May 12, he wrote to Halleck as follows: "The eighth day of battle closes, leaving between three and four thousand prisoners in our hands for the day's work, including two general officers, and over thirty pieces of artillery. The enemy are obstinate, and seem to have found the last ditch.   We have lost no organization, not even that of a company, whilst we have destroyed and captured one division (Johnson's), one brigade (Doles's), and one regiment entire of the enemy." The Confederates had suffered greatly in general officers. Two had been killed, four severely wounded, and two captured.   Our loss in killed, wounded, and missing was less than seven thousand; that of the enemy, between nine and ten thousand, as nearly as could be ascertained.

CHAPTER VII

GRANT AND MEADE—FIELD DIVERSIONS—SEIZING VANTAGE-
GROUND — GRANT AND THE WOUNDED CONFEDERATE
— GRANT'S TOILET IN CAMP—IMPORTANT DESPATCHES
— THROUGH RAIN AND MUD — GRANT AND THE DYING
SOLDIER — BAD NEWS

O N the morning of May 13 General Grant expressed
some anxiety as to the possibility of Lee's falling
back toward Richmond without our knowing it in time to
follow him up closely enough to attack him, although it
was thought that the almost impassable condition of the
roads would probably prevent such an attempt. Skirmishers were pushed forward near enough to discover the
meaning of a movement of some of the organizations in
Lee's center, and it was found that the enemy was merely
taking up a new position in rear of the works which had
been captured from him. There was no other fighting
that day. The general busied himself principally with
inquiries about the care of the wounded and the burial
of the killed. He thought not only of the respect due
the gallant dead, but of proper rewards for the living
whose services had contributed conspicuously to the
victory. He wrote a communication to the Secretary
of War, in which he urged the following promotions:
Meade and Sherman to be major-generals, and Hancock
a brigadier-general, in the regular army; Wright and
Gibbon to be major-generals of volunteers; and Carroll,

Upton, and McCandless to be brigadier-generals in that service. He had already promoted Upton on the field, but this promotion had to be confirmed at Washington. He said in his letter: "General Meade has more than met my most sanguine expectations. He and Sherman are the fittest officers for large commands I have come in contact with." An animated discussion took place at headquarters that day regarding General Meade's somewhat anomalous position, and the embarrassments which were at times caused on the field by the necessity of issuing orders through him instead of direct to the corps commanders. The general-in-chief always invited the most frank and cordial interchange of views, and never failed to listen patiently to the more prominent members of his staff. He seldom joined in the discussions, and usually reserved what he had to say till the end of the argument, when he gave his views and rendered his decision. It was now urged upon him, with much force, that time was often lost in having field orders pass through an intermediary; that there was danger that, in transmitting orders to corps commanders, the instructions might be either so curtailed or elaborated as to change their spirit; that no matter how able General Meade might be, his position was in some measure a false one; that few responsibilities were given him, and yet he was charged with the duties of an army commander; that if he failed the responsibility could not be fixed upon him, and if he succeeded he could not reap the full reward of his merits; that, besides, he had an irascible temper, and often irritated officers who came in contact with him, while General Grant was even-tempered, and succeeded in securing a more hearty coöperation of his generals when he dealt with them direct. The discussion became heated at times.

At the close of the arguments the general said: "I am

fully aware that some embarrassments arise from the present organization, but there is more weight on the other side of the question. I am commanding all the armies, and I cannot neglect others by giving my time exclusively to the Army of the Potomac, which would involve performing all the detailed duties of an army commander, directing its administration, enforcing discipline, reviewing its court-martial proceedings, etc. I have Burnside's, Butler's, and Sigel's armies to look after in Virginia, to say nothing of our Western armies, and I may make Sheridan's cavalry a separate command. Besides, Meade has served a long time with the Army of the Potomac, knows its subordinate officers thoroughly, and led it to a memorable victory at Gettysburg. I have just come from the West, and if I removed a deserving Eastern man from the position of army commander, my motives might be misunderstood, and the effect be bad upon the spirits of the troops. General Meade and I are in close contact on the field; he is capable and perfectly subordinate, and by attending to the details he relieves me of much unnecessary work, and gives me more time to think and to mature my general plans. I will always see that he gets full credit for what he does."

This was a broad view of the situation, and one to which the general mainly adhered throughout the war; but after that day he gave a closer personal direction in battle to the movements of subdivisions of the armies.

General Meade manifested an excellent spirit through all the embarrassments which his position at times entailed. He usually showed his orders to General Grant before issuing them, and as their camps in this campaign were seldom more than a pistol-shot distant from each other, despatches from the corps commanders directed to Meade generally reached the general-in-chief about the same time. In fact, when they were together, Meade frequently handed despatches to his chief to read before he read them himself. As Grant's combativeness displayed itself only against the enemy, and he was a man with whom an associate could not quarrel without furnishing all the provocation himself, he and Meade continued on the best of terms officially and personally throughout this long and eventful campaign.

During the ten days of battle through which we had just passed very little relief, physical or mental, had been obtained; but there was one staff-officer, a Colonel B——, who often came as bearer of messages to our headquarters, who always managed to console himself with novel-reading, and his peculiarity in this respect became a standing joke among those who knew him. He went about with his saddle-bags stuffed full of thrilling romances, and was seen several times sitting on his horse under a brisk fire, poring over the last pages of an absorbing volume to reach the dénouement of the plot, and evincing a greater curiosity to find how the hero and the heroine were going to be extricated from the entangled dilemma into which they had been plunged by the unsympathetic author than to learn the result of the surrounding battle. One of his peculiarities was that he took it for granted that all the people he met were perfectly familiar with his line of literature, and he talked about nothing but the merits of the latest novel. For the last week he had been devouring Victor Hugo's "Les Misérables." It was an English translation, for the officer had no knowledge of French. As he was passing a house in rear of the "angle" he saw a young lady seated on the porch, and, stopping his horse, bowed to her with all the grace of a Chesterfield, and endeavored to engage her in conversation. Before he had gone far he took occasion to remark: "By the way, have you seen 'Lees Miserables'?" anglicizing the pronunciation. Her black eyes snapped with indignation as she tartly replied: "Don't you talk to me that way; they 're a good deal better than Grant's miserables anyhow!" This was retold so often by those who heard it that, for some time after, its repetition seriously endangered the colonel's peace of mind.

On the morning of the 14th it was decided to move the headquarters of Generals Grant and Meade farther east to a position on some high ground three quarters of a mile north of the Ny River, and near the Fredericksburg and Spottsylvania Court-house road. The two generals and their staff-officers rode forward on the Massaponax Church road, and came to a halt and dismounted at a house not far from the Ny River. About half a mile south of that stream, at a place near the Gayle house, there was a hill held by the enemy, which overlooked both the Massaponax and the Fredericksburg roads, and as it commanded an important position, it was decided to try to get possession of it.

Just then General Upton rode up, joined the group, and addressing himself to both Generals Grant and Meade, said, with his usual enthusiasm and confidence, and speaking with great rapidity: "I can take that hill with my brigade. I hope you will let me try it; I 'm certain I can take it." He was asked how many men he had left, as his brigade had seen very hard fighting in the last few days. He replied, "About eight or nine hundred men."

It was soon decided to let him make the attempt, and General Wright, who was supervising the movement, gave Upton orders to start forward at once and seize the position. Upton put his brigade in motion with his usual promptness, but the regular brigade had preceded him and captured the hill. Upton relieved the regular brigade and occupied the place, but his possession of it was not of long duration. The enemy sent forward a portion of Mahone's infantry and Chambliss's cavalry, and Upton was compelled to fall back before superior numbers. However, there was no intention to allow the enemy to hold such an important position, and Meade directed Warren to send one of his brigades to recapture it. Ayres's brigade moved forward with spirit, and the position was soon retaken and held. General Grant expressed to General Meade his pleasure at seeing Warren's troops making so prompt and successful a movement, and as both officers had censured Warren on the 13th, they were anxious now to give him full credit for his present conduct. General Meade sent him the following despatch: "I thank you and Ayres for taking the hill. It was handsomely done." General Wright then moved forward two brigades to relieve Ayres. This was the only fighting on that day.

While riding about the field General Grant stopped at a house and expressed a desire to prepare some despatches. A number of wounded were lying upon the porch and in the rooms; they had made their way there in accordance with the usual custom of wounded men to seek a house. It seems to be a natural instinct, as a house conveys the idea of shelter and of home. I walked with the general into a back room to see whether there was a dry spot which he might take possession of for a short time, to write messages and look over the maps.

As we entered, there was seen sitting in the only chair a Confederate corporal of infantry who had been shot in the right cheek just under the eye, the ball coming out near the left ear. A mass of coagulated blood covered his face and neck, and he presented a shocking appearance. He arose the moment we entered, pushed his chair forward toward the general, and said, with a bow and a smile, " Here, take my chair, sir." General Grant looked at him, and replied: " Ah, you need that chair much more than I; keep your seat. I see you are badly hurt." The officer answered good-naturedly : " If you folks let me go back to our lines, I think I ought to be able to get a leave to go home and see my girl; but I reckon she would n't know me now." The general said, " I will see that one of our surgeons does all in his power for you"; and soon after he told one of the surgeons who was dressing the wounds of our own men to do what he could for the Confederate. The despatches were afterward written in another room. Thirty-three years afterward I discovered that this corporal's name was W. R. Thraxton, and that he was in excellent health and living in Macon, Georgia.

The enemy had now set to work to discover the real meaning of our present movements. In the afternoon skirmishers pushed forward on our right, and found that Warren's corps was no longer there.

In the night of the 14th Lee began to move troops to his right. Grant now directed Hancock's corps to be withdrawn and massed behind the center of our line, so that it could be moved promptly in either direction. When the general got back to camp that evening his clothes were a mass of mud from head to foot, his uniform being scarcely recognizable. He sat until bedtime without making any change in his dress; he never seemed particularly incommoded by the travel-stained condition of his outer garments, but was scrupulously careful, even in the most active campaigns, about the cleanliness of his linen and his person. The only chance for a bath was in having a barrel sawed in two and using the half of it as a sort of sitz-bath. During most of this campaign the general, like the staff-officers, used this method of bathing, or, as our English friends would say, "tubbing." Afterward he supplied himself with a portable rubber bath-tub. While campaign life is not a good school for the cultivation of squeamishness, and while the general was always ready to rough it in camp, yet he was particularly modest in performing his toilet, and his tent fronts were always tied close, and the most perfect privacy was secured, when he was washing, or changing his clothes. While thus engaged even his servant was not allowed to enter his quarters.

The next day, May 15, the rain continued, and the difficulties of moving became still greater. Important despatches were received from the other armies. They informed the general-in-chief that General Averell's cavalry had cut a portion of the East Tennessee Railroad, and had also captured and destroyed a depot of supplies in West Virginia. Butler reported that he had captured some works near Drewry's Bluff, on the James River. The next day, the 16th, came a despatch from Sherman saying that he had compelled Johnston to evacuate Dalton and was pursuing him closely. Sheridan reported that he had destroyed a portion of the Virginia Central and the Fredericksburg railroads in Lee's rear, had killed General J. E. B. Stuart, completely routed his cavalry, and captured a portion of the outer lines of Richmond. He said he might possibly have taken Richmond by assault, but, being ignorant of the operations of General Grant and General Butler, and knowing the rapidity with which the enemy could throw troops against him, he decided that it would not be wise to make such an attempt.

The loss of General Stuart was a severe blow to the enemy. He was their foremost cavalry leader, and one in whom Lee reposed great confidence. We afterward heard that he had been taken to Richmond, and had reached there before he died; that Jefferson Davis visited his death-bed, and was greatly affected when he found that there was no hope of saving the life of this accomplished officer.

The continual rain was most disheartening. On May 16 Grant wrote to Halleck: "We have had five days' almost constant rain, without any prospect yet of its clearing up. The roads have now become so impassable that ambulances with wounded men can no longer run between here and Fredericksburg. All offensive operations must necessarily cease until we can have twenty-four hours of dry weather. The army is in the best of spirits, and feels the greatest confidence in ultimate success. . . . The elements alone have suspended hostilities."

In the Wilderness the army had to struggle against fire and dust; now it had to contend with rain and mud. An ordinary rain, lasting for a day or two, does not embarrass troops; but when the storm continues for a week it becomes one of the most serious obstacles in a campaign. The men can secure no proper shelter and no comfortable rest; their clothing has no chance to dry; and a tramp of a few miles through tenacious mud requires as much exertion as an ordinary day's march. Tents become saturated and weighted with water, and draft-animals have increased loads, and heavier roads over which to haul them. Dry wood cannot be found; cooking becomes difficult; the men's spirits are affected by the gloom, and even the most buoyant natures become disheartened. It is much worse for an army acting on the offensive, for it has more marching to do, being compelled to move principally on exterior lines.

Staff-officers had to labor day and night during the present campaign in making reconnaissances and in cross-questioning natives, deserters, prisoners, and fugi-

tive negroes, in an attempt to secure data for the purpose of constructing local maps from day to day. As
soon as these were finished they were distributed to the
subordinate commanders. Great confusion arose from
the duplication of the names of houses and farms.
Either family names were particularly scarce in that
section of the State, or else the people were united by
close ties of relationship, and country cousins abounded
to a confusing extent. So many farm-houses in some
of the localities were occupied by people of the same
name that, when certain farms were designated in orders,
serious errors arose at times from mistaking one place
for another.

The weather looked a little brighter on May 17, but
the roads were still so heavy that no movement was
attempted. A few reinforcements were received at this
time, mainly some heavy-artillery regiments from the
defenses about Washington, who had been drilled to
serve as infantry. On the 17th Brigadier-general R. O.
Tyler arrived with a division of these troops, number-
ing, with the Corcoran Legion, which had also joined,
nearly 8000 men. They were assigned to Hancock's
corps.

Headquarters were this day moved about a mile and
a quarter to the southeast, to a point not far from Massaponax Church. We knew that the enemy had depleted
the troops on his left in order to strengthen his right
wing, and on the night of the 17th Hancock and Wright
were ordered to assault Lee's left the next morning,
directing their attack against the second line he had
taken up in rear of the "angle," or, as some of the troops
now called it, "Hell's Half-acre." The enemy's position,
however, had been strengthened at this point more than
it was supposed, and his new line of intrenchments had
been given a very formidable character. Our attacking

party found the ground completely swept by a heavy and destructive fire of musketry and artillery, but in spite of this the men moved gallantly forward and made desperate attempts to carry the works. It was soon demonstrated, however, that the movement could not result in success, and the troops were withdrawn.

General Grant had ridden over to the right to watch the progress of this attack. While he was passing a spot near the roadside where there were a number of wounded, one of them, who was lying close to the roadside, seemed to attract his special notice. The man's face was beardless; he was evidently young; his countenance was strikingly handsome, and there was something in his appealing look which could not fail to engage attention, even in the full tide of battle. The blood was flowing from a wound in his breast, the froth about his mouth was tinged with red, and his wandering, staring eyes gave unmistakable evidence of approaching death. Just then a young staff-officer dashed by at a full gallop, and as his horse's hoofs struck a puddle in the road, a mass of black mud was splashed in the wounded man's face. He gave a piteous look, as much as to say, "Could n't you let me die in peace and not add to my sufferings?" The general, whose eyes were at that moment turned upon the youth, was visibly affected. He reined in his horse, and seeing from a motion he made that he was intending to dismount to bestow some care upon the young man, I sprang from my horse, ran to the side of the soldier, wiped his face with my handkerchief, spoke to him, and examined his wound; but in a few minutes the unmistakable death-rattle was heard, and I found that he had breathed his last. I said to the general, who was watching the scene intently, "The poor fellow is dead," remounted my horse, and the party rode on. The chief had turned round twice to look after the officer who had splashed the mud and who had passed rapidly on, as if he wished to take him to task for his carelessness. There was a painfully sad look upon the general's face, and he did not speak for some time. While always keenly sensitive to the sufferings of the wounded, this pitiful sight seemed to affect him more than usual.

When General Grant returned to his headquarters, greatly disappointed that the attack had not succeeded, he found despatches from the other armies which were by no means likely to furnish consolation to him or to the officers about him. Sigel had been badly defeated at New Market, and was in retreat; Butler had been driven from Drewry's Bluff, though he still held possession of the road to Petersburg; and Banks had suffered defeat in Louisiana. The general was in no sense depressed by the information, and received it in a philosophic spirit; but he was particularly annoyed by the despatches from Sigel, for two hours before he had sent a message urging that officer to make his way to Staunton to stop supplies from being sent from there to Lee's army. He immediately requested Halleck to have Sigel relieved and General Hunter put in command of his troops. General Canby was sent to supersede Banks; this was done by the authorities at Washington, and not upon General Grant's suggestion, though the general thought well of Canby and made no objection.

In commenting briefly upon the bad news, General Grant said: "Lee will undoubtedly reinforce his army largely by bringing Beauregard's troops from Richmond, now that Butler has been driven back, and will call in troops from the Valley since Sigel's defeated forces have retreated to Cedar Creek. Hoke's troops will be needed no longer in North Carolina, and I am prepared to see Lee's forces in our front materially strengthened. I thought the other day that they must feel pretty blue in Richmond over the reports of our victories; but as they are in direct telegraphic communication with the points at which the fighting took place, they were no doubt at the same time aware of our defeats, of which we have not learned till to-day; so probably they did not feel as badly as we imagined."

The general was not a man to waste any time over occurrences of the past; his first thoughts were always to redouble his efforts to take the initiative and overcome disaster by success. Now that his coöperating armies had failed him, he determined upon still bolder movements on the part of the troops under his immediate direction. As the weather was at this time more promising, his first act was to sit down at his field-desk and write an order providing for a general movement by the left flank toward Richmond, to begin the next night, May 19. He then sent to Washington asking the coöperation of the navy in changing our base of supplies to Port Royal on the Rappahannock.

CHAPTER VIII

ATTEMPT TO TURN THE UNION RIGHT — "BILL" — GRANT'S
UNPROTECTED HEADQUARTERS — GRANT AND THE VIR-
GINIA LADY — A RACE FOR THE NORTH ANNA — A NOON-
DAY HALT AT MRS. TYLER'S

THE fact that a change had been made in the position of our troops, and that Hancock's corps had
been withdrawn from our front and placed in rear of our
center, evidently made Lee suspect that some movement
was afoot, and he determined to send General Ewell's
corps to try to turn our right, and to put Early in
readiness to coöperate in the movement if it should
promise success.

In the afternoon of May 19, a little after five o'clock,
I was taking a nap in my tent, to try to make up for
the sleep lost the night before. Aides-de-camp in this
campaign were usually engaged in riding back and forth
during the night between headquarters and the different
commands, communicating instructions for the next
day, and had to catch their sleep in instalments. I was
suddenly awakened by my colored servant crying out
to me: "Wake up, sah, fo' God's sake! De whole ob
Lee's army am in our reah!" He was in a state of
feverish excitement, and his face seemed two shades
lighter than its ordinary hue. The black boys were not
to be blamed for manifesting fright, for they all had a
notion that their lives would not be worth praying for
if they fell into the hands of the enemy and were recog-

nized as persons who had made their escape from slavery to serve in the Yankee army. Hearing heavy firing in the direction of our rear, I put my head out of the tent, and seeing the general and staff standing near their horses, which had been saddled, I called for my horse and hastened to join them. Upon my inquiring what the matter was, the general said: "The enemy is detaching a large force to turn our right. I wish you would ride to the point of attack, and keep me posted as to the movement, and urge upon the commanders of the troops in that vicinity not only to check the advance of the enemy, but to take the offensive and destroy them if possible. You can say that Warren's corps will be ordered to coöperate promptly." General Meade had already sent urgent orders to his troops nearest the point threatened. I started up the Fredericksburg road, and saw a large force of infantry advancing, which proved to be the troops of Ewell's corps who had crossed the Ny River. In the vicinity of the Harris house, about a mile east of the Ny, I found General Tyler's division posted on the Fredericksburg road, with Kitching's brigade on his left. By Meade's direction Hancock had been ordered to send a division to move at double-quick to Tyler's support, and Warren's Maryland brigade arrived on the ground later. The enemy had made a vigorous attack on Tyler and Kitching, and the contest was raging fiercely along their lines. I rode up to Tyler, who was an old army friend, found him making every possible disposition to check the enemy's advance, and called out to him: "Tyler, you are in luck to-day. It is n't every one who has a chance to make such a début on joining an army. You are certain to knock a brevet out of this day's fight." He said: "As you see, my men are raw hands at this sort of work, but they are behaving like veterans."

Hancock had arrived on the ground in person, and when Birney's troops of his corps came up they were put into action on Tyler's right. Crawford, of Warren's corps, arrived about dark, and was put in position on the left. The brunt of the attack, however, had been broken by the troops upon which it first fell. Each regiment of Tyler's heavy artillery was as large as some of our brigades. These regiments had been thoroughly drilled and disciplined in the defenses about Washington, but this was their first engagement, and their new uniforms and bright muskets formed a striking contrast to the travel-stained clothing and dull-looking arms of the other regiments. When the veterans arrived they cracked no end of jokes at the expense of the new troops. They would cry out to them: "How are you, heavies? Is this work heavy enough for you? You're doing well, my sons. If you keep on like this a couple of years, you'll learn all the tricks of the trade." They were particularly anxious to get hold of the new arms of the fresh troops, and when a man was shot down a veteran would promptly seize his gun in exchange for his own, which had become much the worse for wear in the last week's rain-storms.

The fighting was exceedingly obstinate, and continued until after nine o'clock; but by that hour the enemy had been driven back at all points, and forced to beat a rapid retreat across the Ny. His loss in killed and wounded was severe, and we captured over four hundred prisoners from him. We did not escape a considerable loss on our side, six hundred of our men having been killed and wounded. A staff-officer, passing over the ground after dark, saw in the vicinity of the Fredericksburg road a row of men stretched upon the ground, looking as if they had lain down in line of battle to sleep. He started to shake several of them, and cried out: "Get up!

What do you mean by going to sleep at such a time as this?" He was shocked to find that this row consisted entirely of dead bodies lying as they fell, shot down in ranks with their alinement perfectly preserved. The scene told with mute eloquence the story of their valor and the perfection of their discipline. The brevet rank predicted for Tyler was conferred upon him for his services in this engagement, and it had been fairly won.

Lee had evidently intended to make Ewell's movement a formidable one, for Early had received orders to coöperate in the attack if it should promise success, and during the afternoon he sent forward a brigade which made an assault in his front. The attempt, however, was a complete failure.

This attack by Ewell on the 19th prevented the orders previously issued for the general movement by the left flank from being carried out until the night of the 20th.

The Army of the Potomac had been embarrassed by having too much artillery. Finding that the country through which it had to move was more difficult than had been supposed, General Grant gave an order on the 19th to send ninety-two guns back to Washington.

The next morning, May 20, the general was later than usual in making his appearance, in consequence of having overslept. Finally his voice was heard calling from his tent to his colored servant: "Bill! Ho, Bill! What time is it?" The servant ran to him, found he was still in bed, and told him the hour. In scarcely more than ten minutes the general appeared at the mess-table. We were not surprised at the rapidity with which he had dressed himself, for we had learned by this time that in putting on his clothes he was as quick as a lightning-change actor in a variety theater. When the officers at headquarters were called up particularly early to start on the march, every one did his utmost to be on time and not keep the general waiting; but, however vigorous the effort, no one could match him in getting on his clothes.   There was seldom any occasion for such hurried dressing, but with him it was a habit which continued through life.

Bill, the servant who waited on the general, was a notable character.   He was entirely a creature of accident.   When the general was at Cairo in 1861, Bill suddenly appeared one day at headquarters with two other slave boys, who had just escaped from their former masters in Missouri.   They belonged to that class of fugitive blacks who were characterized by those given to artistic comparisons as "charcoal sketches from the hands of the old masters."   Bill was of a genuine burnt-cork hue, and no white blood contaminated the purity of his lineage.   He at once set himself to work without orders, taking care of one of the aides, and by dint of his force of character resisted all efforts of that officer to discharge him.   When any waiter was absent, or even when all were present, he would turn up in the headquarters mess-tent and insist on helping the general at table.   Then he attached himself to Colonel Boomer, and forced that officer in spite of himself to submit to his services.   After the colonel had been killed in the assault on Vicksburg, Bill suddenly put in an appearance again at headquarters, and was found making himself useful to the general, notwithstanding the protests of the other servants, and before long he had himself regularly entered upon the general's private pay-roll. When his chief came East, Bill followed, and gradually took entire charge of the general's personal comfort as valet, waiter, and man of all work.   He was devoted, never known to be beyond call, had studied the general's habits so carefully that he could always anticipate his few wants, and became really very useful.   I had a

striking illustration one morning in front of Spottsylvania of how devoted Bill was to the general's comfort.
While we were camping in the region of wood-ticks,
garter-snakes, and beetles, I saw Bill in front of the
general's tent thrusting his hand first into one of the
chief's boots and then into the other. "What are you
doing that for, Bill?" I asked. "Oh," he explained, "I
allers feels around in de gin'ral's boots afore I lets him
put dem on, to see dat no insec's done got into dem de
prev'us night." He followed in the general's shadow all
through his Presidential terms, then he insisted upon
attempting business in Washington, and afterward tried
his hand at preaching; but he had fed so long at the
public crib that his appetite had been spoiled for any
other means of sustaining life, and he finally made his
way into a government department as messenger, where
he still is and where it is hoped that his eventful life
may be rounded out in the quiet and comfort to which
his public services entitle him. He will not be as
dramatic an historical character as Napoleon's Mame-
luke, but in his humble way he was as faithful and
devoted to his chief as the famous Roustan.

In discussing the contemplated movement to the left,
General Grant said on the morning of May 20: "My
chief anxiety now is to draw Lee out of his works and
fight him in the open field, instead of assaulting him
behind his intrenchments. The movement of Early
yesterday gives me some hope that Lee may at times
take the offensive, and thus give our troops the desired
opportunity." In this, however, the general was disappointed; for the attack of the 19th was the last offensive
movement in force that Lee ventured to make during
the entire campaign.

The series of desperate battles around Spottsylvania
had ended, but other soil was now to be stained by the

blood of fratricidal war.   Torbert's cavalry division
began the march to the South on May 20, and as soon
as it was dark Hancock's corps set out for Milford Station, a distance of about twenty miles, to take up a
position on the south bank of the Mattapony.   Guiney's
Station was reached the next morning, after a night
march of eight miles.   Hancock's advance crossed the
Mattapony at noon and intrenched its position.   At ten
o'clock that morning Warren had moved south, and that
night he reached the vicinity of Guiney's Station.
Burnside put his corps in motion as soon as the road
was clear of Hancock's troops, and was followed by
Wright.

Generals Grant and Meade, with their staffs, took up
their march on May 21, following the road taken by
Hancock's corps, and late in the afternoon reached
Guiney's Station.   Our vigilant signal-officers, who had
made every effort to read the enemy's signals, now succeeded in deciphering an important despatch, from which
it was learned that Lee had discovered the movement
that our forces were making.   Hancock was now many
miles in advance, and the head of Warren's corps was a
considerable distance in the rear.   Our party, besides a
small cavalry and infantry escort, consisted entirely of
officers, many of them of high rank.   One might have
said of it what Curran said of the books in his library,
"Not numerous, but select."   It was suggested by some
that, before pitching camp for the night, the headquarters had better move back upon the road on which we
had advanced until Warren's troops should be met; but
General Grant made light of the proposition and ordered
the camp to be established where we were, saying, "I
think, instead of our going back, we had better hurry
Warren forward."   Suggestions to the general to turn
back fell as usual upon deaf ears.

While our people were putting up the tents and making preparations for supper, General Grant strolled over to a house near by, owned by a Mr. Chandler, and sat down on the porch. I accompanied him, and took a seat beside him. In a few minutes a lady came to the door, and was surprised to find that the visitor was the general-in-chief. He was always particularly civil to ladies, and he rose to his feet at once, took off his hat, and made a courteous bow. She was ladylike and polite in her behavior, and she and the general soon became engaged in a pleasant talk. Her conversation was exceedingly entertaining. She said, among other things: "This house has witnessed some sad scenes. One of our greatest generals died here just a year ago—General Jackson—Stonewell Jackson of blessed memory." "Indeed!" remarked General Grant. "He and I were at West Point together for a year, and we served in the same army in Mexico." "Then you must have known how good and great he was," said the lady. "Oh, yes," replied the general; "he was a sterling, manly cadet, and enjoyed the respect of every one who knew him. He was always of a religious turn of mind, and a plodding, hard-working student. His standing was at first very low in his class, but by his indomitable energy he managed to graduate quite high. He was a gallant soldier and a Christian gentleman, and I can understand fully the admiration your people have for him."

"They brought him here the Monday after the battle of Chancellorsville," she continued. "You probably know, sir, that he had been wounded in the left arm and right hand by his own men, who fired upon him accidentally in the night, and his arm had been amputated on the field. The operation was very successful, and he was getting along nicely; but the wet applications made to the wound brought on pneumonia, and it was that which caused his death. He lingered till the next Sunday afternoon, May 10, and then he was taken from us." Here the lady of the house became very much affected, and almost broke down in recalling the sad event.

Our tents had by this time been pitched, and the general, after taking a polite leave of his hostess, and saying he would place a guard over her house to see that no damage was done to her property, walked over to camp, and soon after sat down with the mess to a light supper.

The question has been asked why General Grant in this movement left so great a distance between Hancock's corps and the rest of his army. He did it intentionally, and under the circumstances it was unquestionably wise generalship. He was determined to try by every means in his power to tempt Lee to fight outside of his intrenched lines. He had in the battles of the last two weeks thoroughly measured Lee's capacity as an opponent, and he believed it would be difficult to force him to take the offensive unless some good opportunity were offered. He knew that Lee, from the distance over which he would have to move his troops, could not attack the isolated Hancock with more than an army-corps. Such a force he was certain Hancock could whip; and Grant, being in close communication with the several corps, felt that he could bring up reinforcements as rapidly as the enemy, and that the chances would be greatly in his favor if he could thus bring on an engagement in the open field. There was no question in his mind as to whipping his opponent; the only problem was how to get at him.

The next morning, May 22, headquarters moved south, following the line which had been taken by Hancock's troops, which ran parallel with the Fredericksburg Railroad. The officers and men had never experienced a more sudden change of feelings and prospects. The weather was pleasant, the air was invigorating, the sun was shining brightly, and the roads were rapidly drying up. The men had been withdrawn from the scenes of their terrific struggles at Spottsylvania, and were no longer confronting formidable earthworks. The features of the country had also entirely changed. Though there were many swamps, thickets, and streams with difficult approaches, the deep gloom of the Wilderness had been left behind. The country was now more open, and presented many clearings, and the range of vision was largely increased. The roads were broad, the land was well cultivated, and the crops were abundant. The men seemed to breathe a new atmosphere, and were inspired with new hope. It was again " on to Richmond," and the many miles they were now gaining toward the enemy's capital, and out of reach of fire, made them experience that buoyancy of feeling which always accompanies the prestige of success. But while the country was covered with farms and houses, there was scarcely an inhabitant to be seen. Most of the able-bodied men were serving in the armies, and the slaves had been driven farther south. Many of the non-combatants had gone away to escape the invading army, and the only people encountered were women and children and old and decrepit men.

The corps were now rapidly moving toward Hanover Junction, which is about twenty-five miles north of Richmond. Lee, notwithstanding his superior means of obtaining information, had not begun to move until Hancock's corps had crossed the Mattapony at Milford. He then started rapidly down the Telegraph road, and as he had a shorter route than the Union forces, it appears that he reached Hanover Court-house at the head of Ewell's corps at 9:30 o'clock on May 22. His tele-

grams and manœuvers all go to show that he was entirely deceived in regard to Grant's movements. He
reported at that time: " I have learned, as yet, nothing
of the movements of the enemy east of the Mattapony."
The day before, in speaking of the position of Grant's
army, he said: " I fear [this] will secure him from attack
until he crosses the Pamunkey."   Even after Grant had
crossed the Mattapony, Lee spoke of the Union forces
as being east of that river, and was hurrying forward
troops in order to prevent Grant from crossing the
Pamunkey, a stream formed by the junction of the
North Anna and the South Anna rivers, while Grant
was in reality moving toward the North Anna.   In
these movements Lee was entirely outgeneraled.

On the morning of May 22 Hancock was instructed to
remain at Milford during the day, while the other corps
were directed to move south by roads which would not
separate them by distances of more than four miles.   It
appears to have been about midday of the 22d when
Lee obtained information, through his cavalry, of our
advance toward the North Anna.   Hancock could not
well have reached Hanover Junction before Lee, for
Lee's route from the right of his intrenchments on the
Po to Hanover Junction by the Telegraph road was
about twenty-eight miles, while the route of Hancock's
corps from Anderson's Mill to Hanover Junction via
Bowling Green was about thirty-four miles; besides, as
Hancock was advancing with a detached corps through
an enemy's country and over unknown roads, he had to
move with caution.

Early in the afternoon General Grant decided to halt
for a couple of hours, to be in easy communication with
the troops that were following.   He selected for the halt
a plantation which was beautifully situated on high
ground, commanding a charming view of the valley of

the Mattapony. A very comfortable house stood not
far from the road along which Burnside's corps was
marching. In making halts of this kind a house was
usually selected, for the reason that good water was
easily obtainable, and facilities were afforded for looking
at maps and conducting correspondence. General Grant
never entered any of the houses, as they were usually
occupied by ladies, and he did not wish to appear to
invade their dwellings; he generally sat on the porch.
When we reached this plantation, the escort and the
junior staff-officers lounged about the grounds in the
shade of the trees, while General Grant, accompanied by
two or three of us who were riding with him, dismounted,
and ascended the steps of the porch. A very gentle and
prepossessing-looking lady standing in the doorway was
soon joined by an older woman. General Grant bowed
courteously and said, " With your permission, I will
spend a few hours here." The younger lady replied
very civilly, " Certainly, sir." The older one exclaimed
abruptly, " I do hope you will not let your soldiers ruin
our place and carry away our property." The general
answered politely, " I will order a guard to keep the
men out of your place, and see that you are amply protected "; and at once gave the necessary instructions.
The ladies, seeing that the officer with whom they were
conversing was evidently one of superior rank, became
anxious to know who he was, and the older one stepped
up to me, and in a whisper asked his name. Upon being
told that he was General Grant, she seemed greatly surprised, and in a rather excited manner informed the
other lady of the fact. The younger lady, whose name
was Mrs. Tyler, said that she was the wife of a colonel
in the Confederate army, who was serving with General
Joe Johnston in the West; but she had not heard from
him for some time, and she was very anxious to learn

through General Grant what news he had from that quarter. The general said, "Sherman is advancing upon Rome, and ought to have reached that place by this time." Thereupon the older lady, who proved to be the mother-in-law of the younger one, said very sharply: "General Sherman will never capture that place. I know all about that country, and you have n't an army that will ever take it. We all know very well that Sherman is making no headway against General Johnston's army."

We could see that she was entertaining views which everywhere prevailed in the South. The authorities naturally put the best face upon matters, and the newspapers tried to buoy up the people with false hopes. It was not surprising that the inhabitants of the remote parts of the country were in ignorance of the true progress of the war. General Grant replied in a quiet way: " General Sherman is certainly advancing rapidly in that direction; and while I do not wish to be the communicator of news which may be unpleasant to you, I have every reason to believe that Rome is by this time in his possession." The older lady then assumed a bantering tone, and became somewhat excited and defiant in her manner; and the younger one joined with her in scouting the idea that Rome could ever be taken. Just then a courier rode up with despatches from Washington containing a telegram from Sherman. General Grant glanced over it, and then read it to the staff. It announced that Sherman had just captured Rome. The ladies had caught the purport of the communication, although it was not intended that they should hear it. The wife burst into tears, and the mother-in-law was much affected by the news, which was of course sad tidings to both of them.

The mother then began to talk with great rapidity

and with no little asperity, saying: "I came from Richmond not long ago, where I lived in a house on the James River which overlooks Belle Isle; and I had the satisfaction of looking down every day on the Yankee prisoners. I saw thousands and thousands of them, and before this campaign is over I want to see the whole of the Yankee army in Southern prisons."

Just then Burnside rode into the yard, dismounted, and joined our party on the porch. He was a man of great gallantry and elegance of manner, and was always excessively polite to the gentler sex. He raised his hat, made a profound bow to the ladies, and, as he looked at his corps filing by on the road, said to the older one, who was standing near him, "I don't suppose, madam, that you ever saw so many Yankee soldiers before." She replied instantly: "Not at liberty, sir." This was such a good shot that every one was greatly amused, and General Grant joined heartily in the laugh that followed at Burnside's expense.

CHAPTER IX

HANCOCK'S corps had been fighting and marching
almost continuously for over a week, both day and
night, and the halt on May 22 was made to give a much-
needed rest. It was a curious study to watch the effect
which the constant exposure to fire had produced upon
the nervous system of the troops. Their nerves had
become so sensitive that the men would start at the
slightest sound, and dodge at the flight of a bird or the
sight of a pebble tossed past them. One of their
amusements in camp at that time was to throw stones
and chips past one another's heads, and raise a laugh at
the active dodging and bending the body low, or "jack-
knifing," as the men called it. This did not indicate
any loss of courage; it was merely an effect produced
by a temporary physical condition which the men could
not control, and gave ample evidence of the nervous
strain to which they had so long been subjected. Dodging the head under fire is often as purely involuntary as
winking. I have known, in my experience, only two
men who could remain absolutely immovable under a
heavy fire, without even the twitching of a muscle. One

140

was a bugler in the cavalry, and the other was General Grant.

In the evening of the 22d the general-in-chief issued written orders directing the movement of the troops for the next day. The march was to begin at five o'clock in the morning, and the several corps were to send out cavalry and infantry in advance on all the roads to ascertain the position of the enemy. The purpose was to cross the North Anna River west of the Fredericksburg Railroad, and to strike Lee wherever he could be found. To understand the topography of the country, it is necessary to explain that the North Anna and the South Anna run in an easterly direction, at a distance from each other of eight or ten miles in the vicinity of the region in which Grant's operations took place, and unite and form the Pamunkey River about five miles east of the line of the Fredericksburg Railroad. This road crossed the North Anna about two miles north of Hanover Junction, the intersection of the Fredericksburg and the Virginia Central railroads. The Telegraph road crossed the river by a wooden bridge half a mile west of the railroad bridge. Farther up the river there were three fords about a mile and a half apart. Hancock marched to the Telegraph-road bridge, Burnside to Ox Ford, and Warren to Jericho Ford. Wright followed Warren; Burnside's corps used plantation roads which ran between the main roads which had been taken by the corps of Hancock and Warren.

Hancock approached the river at the Telegraph-road bridge about noon. He found the enemy holding an earthwork on the north side, and saw a force posted on the opposite bank. Seeing the importance of gaining possession of the defensive work, he determined to take it by assault, and did so handsomely, some of the enemy being captured, and the rest driven over the bridge, followed closely by our men. The retreating force was thrown into great confusion, and in the rush a number were crowded off the bridge and drowned.

Burnside, on reaching Ox Ford, found it held by the enemy strongly intrenched on the south bank of the river, and no attack was made. Warren reached Jericho Ford soon after noon, seized it, laid a pontoon-bridge, and by 4:30 P. M. had moved his whole corps to the south bank. At six o'clock Hill's corps attacked Warren's line before his troops were all in position, and forced it back some distance; but the enemy was soon repulsed. Wright's corps was moved up to support Warren, but it was not deemed necessary to send it across the river until the next morning.

General Grant rode during this day, May 23, with Hancock's corps. While halting in the afternoon at a house not far from the river, he was told by the people living there that Lee had rested for a few hours at the same house the day before, and that his entire army had crossed the river. On the morning of the 24th Hancock crossed to the south side. Crittenden's division crossed the river and joined Warren's corps. They advanced against the enemy with a view of dislodging him from his position at Ox Ford, but his lines were found so strong that after a brief encounter our forces withdrew. They had not been able to take with them any artillery. That night our whole army, except one division of Burnside's corps, was on the south side of the river and close up to the enemy's lines.

General headquarters were established near Chesterfield Station on May 24. That day Sheridan returned from his memorable cavalry raid, and was warmly greeted by General Grant at headquarters, and heartily congratulated upon his signal success. He related some of the principal incidents in the raid very graphically,

but with becoming modesty.   In describing a particularly hot fight, he would become highly animated in
manner and dramatic in gesture; then he would turn to
some ludicrous incident, laugh heartily, and seem to
enjoy greatly the recollection of it.   It will be remembered that he started out suddenly on May 8, passed
round the right of Lee's army, keeping out of reach of
his infantry, crossed the North Anna in the night, destroyed ten miles of the Virginia Central Railroad,
together with cars, locomotives, and a large amount of
army supplies, recaptured three hundred and seventy-
five of our prisoners on their way from Spottsylvania to
Richmond, crossed the South Anna, struck the Fredericksburg road at Ashland, and destroyed the depot,
many miles of road, a train of cars, and a large supply
of army stores.   Finding that the enemy's cavalry were
concentrating, he united his divisions, which had been
operating at different points in the work of destruction,
and fought a pitched battle at Yellow Tavern, about
seven miles north of Richmond, capturing two pieces of
artillery, mortally wounding the commander, J. E. B.
Stuart, and killing Brigadier-general James B. Gordon.
He then entered the advanced lines of intrenchments
north of Richmond, crossed the Chickahominy, and
reached Haxall's Landing, on the James, where he re-
plenished his supplies from stores sent to him by Butler.
After remaining there from the 14th to the 17th of May,
he started on his return to the Army of the Potomac.
He had lost only four hundred and twenty-five men in
killed, wounded, and missing.   One important effect of
Sheridan's operations was that he compelled all of the
enemy's cavalry to be moved against him, which left our
large train of four thousand wagons free from their
attacks.

General Grant at times had a peculiar manner of

teasing officers with whom he was on terms of intimacy, and in this interview he began to joke with his cavalry leader by saying to those who were gathered about him: "Now, Sheridan evidently thinks he has been clear down to the James River, and has been breaking up railroads, and even getting a peep at Richmond; but probably this is all imagination, or else he has been reading something of the kind in the newspapers. I don't suppose he seriously thinks that he made such a march as that in two weeks."

Sheridan joined in the fun, and replied: "Well, after what General Grant says, I do begin to feel doubtful as to whether I have been absent at all from the Army of the Potomac." Sheridan had become well bronzed by his exposure to the sun, and looked the picture of health. It was seen at once that the general-in-chief did not intend to give him or his command any rest. He told him of the movements he had in contemplation, and Sheridan saw that all his troopers would be wanted immediately at the front.

That evening, the 24th, General Grant issued an order, which he had been considering for some time, assigning Burnside's corps to the Army of the Potomac, and putting him under the command of Meade. It was found that such a consolidation would be much better for purposes of administration, and give more unity to the movements. It had been heretofore necessary to inform Meade of the instructions given to Burnside, and to let Burnside know of the movements that were to be undertaken by Meade, in order that the commanders might understand fully what was intended to be accomplished, and be in a position to coöperate intelligently. This involved much correspondence and consumed time. The new order was intended to avoid this, and simplify the methods which had been employed. While General

Grant was riding past the headquarters of Burnside the next morning, Burnside came out of his tent, and in company with several of his officers came up to General Grant, who had now halted by the roadside, shook hands with him, and said: "I have received the instructions assigning my command to the Army of the Potomac. That order is excellent; it is a military necessity, and I am glad it has been issued." This conduct of Burnside gave the greatest satisfaction to the general-in-chief, and he commented very favorably upon it afterward. It must be recollected in this connection that Burnside was senior in rank to Meade, and had commanded the Army of the Potomac when Meade was a division commander under him; and the manner in which Burnside acquiesced in his new assignment, and the spirit he manifested in his readiness to set aside all personal aims and ambitions for the public good, were among the many instances of his patriotism and his absolute loyalty to the cause he served.

The general headquarters were moved farther west on May 25, and established on the north side of the North Anna, near Quarles's Ford, at a place known as Quarles's Mills. That day it became evident that Lee was going to make a permanent stand between the North and the South Anna. His position was found to be exceedingly strong, and was somewhat similar to the one taken up at Spottsylvania. The lines were shaped something like the letter U, with the base resting on the river at Ox Ford. It had one face turned toward Hancock, and the other toward Warren. The lines were made exceedingly formidable by means of strong earthworks with heavy obstructions planted in front, and were flanked on the right by an impenetrable swamp, and on the left by Little River. General Grant said, in discussing the situation at this time: " It now looks as if Lee's position were such that it would not be prudent to fight a battle in the narrow space between these two rivers, and I shall withdraw our army from its present position, and make another flank march to the left; but I want, while we are here, to destroy a portion of the Virginia Central Railroad, as that is the road by which Lee is receiving a large part of his supplies and reinforcements." He ended the conversation by directing me to cross the river and superintend this operation.

I went with a portion of Russell's division of Wright's corps, which began the work of destruction at a point on the railroad about eight hundred yards from the enemy's extreme left. A brigade was extended along one side of the road in single rank, and at a given signal the men took hold of the rails, lifted up the road, and turned it upside down. Then, breaking the rails loose, they used them as levers in prying off the cross-ties, which they piled up at different points, laid the rails across them, and set fire to the ties. As soon as the rails became sufficiently hot they bent in the middle by their own weight; efforts were then made to twist them so as to render them still more unserviceable. Several miles of railway were thus destroyed.

The reinforcements which General Grant had predicted would be sent to Lee's army had reached him. Between 12,000 and 15,000 men arrived from the 22d to the 25th of May. Breckinridge had come from the valley of Virginia with nearly all of his forces; Pickett brought a division from the vicinity of Richmond; and Hoke's brigade of Early's division had also been sent to Lee from the Confederate capital. On the 22d, as soon as Grant had learned the extent of the disaster to Butler's army on the James, he said that Butler was not detaining 10,000 men in Richmond, and not even keeping the roads south of that city broken, and he considered it advisable to have the greater part of Butler's troops join in the campaign of the Army of the Potomac. On May 25 he telegraphed orders to Halleck, saying: "Send Butler's forces to White House, to land on the north side, and march up to join this army. The James River should be held to City Point, but leave nothing more than is absolutely necessary to hold it, acting purely on the defensive. The enemy will not undertake any offensive operations there, but will concentrate everything here." At the same time he said: "If Hunter can possibly get to Charlottesville and Lynchburg, he should do so, living on the country. The railroads and canals should be destroyed beyond the possibility of repair for weeks." These instructions were given in consequence of the withdrawal of Breckinridge's command, which left the valley of Virginia undefended.

When I recrossed the river and returned to headquarters in the evening, I found General Grant sitting in front of his tent smoking a cigar and anxious to hear the report as to the extent of the damage to the railroad. About the time I finished relating to him what had been accomplished, an old woman who occupied a small house near by strolled over to headquarters, apparently bent upon having a friendly chat with the commander of the Yankee armies. The number of questions she asked showed that she was not lacking in the quality of curiosity which is supposed to be common to her sex. She wore an old-fashioned calico dress about six inches too short, with the sleeves rolled up to the elbows. She had a nose so sharp that it looked as if it had been caught in the crack of a door, and small gray eyes that twinkled and snapped as she spoke. She began by nodding a familiar "How do you do?" to the general, and saying in a voice which squeaked like the high notes of an E-flat clarinet with a soft reed: "I believe you command all these h'yah Yankees that are comin' down h'yah and cavortin' round over this whole section of country." The general bowed an assent, and she continued: "I'm powerful glad General Lee has been lickin' you-all from the Rapidan cl'ah down h'yah, and that now he's got you jes wh'ah he wants you."

Then she drew up a camp-chair alongside the general, seated herself on it, and finding that her remarks seemed to be received good-naturedly, grew still more familiar, and went òn to say: "Yes, and afo' long Lee'll be a-chasin' you-all up through Pennsylvany ag'in. Was you up thah in Pennsylvany when he got aftah you-all last summer?" The general had great difficulty in keeping his face straight as he replied: "Well, no; I was n't there myself. I had some business in another direction." He did not explain to her that Vicksburg was at that time commanding something of his attention. Said she: "I notice our boys got away with lots of 'em Conestoga hosses up thah, and they brought lots of 'em back with 'em. We've got a pretty good show of 'em round this section of country, and they're jes the best draft-hosses you ever see. Hope the boys'll get up thah ag'in soon, and bring back some more of 'em."

The general kept on smoking his cigar, and was greatly amused by the conversation. After a little while the woman went back to her house, but returned later, and said: "See h'yah; I'm all alone in my house, and I'm kinder skeerd. I expect them Yankee soldiers of yourn'll steal everything I have, and murder me afo' morning, if you don't give me some protection." "Oh," replied the general, "we will see that you are not hurt"; and turning to Lieutenant Dunn of the staff, he said: "Dunn, you had better go and stay in the old lady's house to-night. You can probably make yourself more comfortable there than in camp, anyhow; and I don't want her to be frightened."

Dunn followed the old woman rather reluctantly to her house, and played guardian angel to her till the next morning.

General Grant had now presented to him for solution a very formidable military problem. Lee's position, from the strength and location of his intrenchments and the defensive character of the country, was impregnable, or at least it could not be carried by assault without involving great loss of life. The general had therefore decided to withdraw, and make another movement by the left flank, in the hope of so manœuvering as to afford another opportunity of getting a chance to strike Lee outside his earthworks. However, a withdrawal in the face of a vigilant foe, and the crossing of a difficult river within sight of the enemy, constitute one of the most hazardous movements in warfare. There was the possibility, also, that Lee might mass his artillery on his left flank, and try to hold it by this means and with a minimum of his infantry, and with the bulk of his army move out on his right in an attempt to crush Hancock's corps. This is exactly what Grant himself would have done under similar circumstances; but he had by this time become familiar with Lee's methods, and had very little apprehension that he would take the offensive. Nevertheless, Hancock was ordered to take every precaution against a possible assault. The withdrawal of the army was conducted with consummate skill, and furnishes an instructive lesson in warfare. In the first place, the enemy had to be deceived and thrown off his guard to make the movement at all safe. For this purpose Wilson's division of cavalry was transferred to the right of the army on May 25, and ordered to cross the North Anna and proceed to Little River on Lee's extreme left, and make a vigorous demonstration, to convey the impression that there was a movement of the army in that direction with a view to turning Lee's left. This was done so effectually that Lee telegraphed to Richmond the next morning: "From present indications the enemy seems to contemplate a movement on our left flank." During the night of the 25th the trains and all of the artillery, which was in position on our right wing, were quietly moved to the north bank of the river. Russell's division of the Sixth Corps was also withdrawn and moved in the rear of Burnside, and at daylight the next morning halted in a place where its movements could not be seen by the enemy during the day. Its position in front of the enemy had been skilfully filled with men from the other parts of the command, and its absence was not discovered. Early in the morning of May 26 instructions were issued for the withdrawal of the entire army that night. After these orders had been despatched, the general seated himself in front of his tent for a quiet smoke. In a few minutes the old woman who had had the familiar chat with him the evening before rushed over to his tent in a high state of excitement. Swinging her arms like the fans of a windmill, and screaming at the top of her shrill voice, she cried out: "See h'yah; these Yankees o' yourn got into my bahn last night, and stole the only hoss I had, and I want you to send some of your folks out to find him and bring him back." The general listened to her story, and when she had finished remarked quietly: "Madam, perhaps it is one of those Conestoga horses you spoke, of that belong up in Pennsylvania, and some of our men have made up their minds to take him back home." The old lady at this remark was rather crestfallen, and said with a grin: "Well, I reckon you 've got me on that; but you Yankees have no business down h'yah

anyhow, and I think you might get me back that hoss."
The general replied: "I'm very sorry indeed that this
has occurred, and if the army were in camp I would send
you around with a guard to see whether the horse could
be recognized by you and recovered; but the troops are
moving constantly, and it would be utterly impossible to
find the animal." She finally went off, shaking her fist
and muttering: "I'm sart'in of one thing, anyhow:
General Lee 'll just dust you-all out of this place afo'
you kin say scat."

The operations of the last two days had made the
duties of staff-officers particularly arduous, and a great
many of us were feeling the effects of the last week's
hard work and exposure, the loss of sleep, and the
breathing of a malarious atmosphere. In connection
with the renewal of the work of destroying the railroad,
I was sent across the river again on the 26th, and on
returning that afternoon to headquarters found myself
suffering severely from fever and sick-headache. About
dark General Grant wished me to make another trip to
the extreme right, to assist in the work of withdrawing
the troops, as I was particularly familiar with that part
of the lines. Sickness is no excuse in the field, so I
started across the river again without making my condition known to the general. To make matters worse, a
thunder-storm came up, accompanied by vivid lightning,
and between the flashes the darkness was so impenetrable
that it was slow work finding the roads. Babcock, seeing my condition, volunteered to accompany me, so that
if I gave out, the orders I was carrying might still reach
their destination. We remained in the saddle the greater
part of the night. On my return to headquarters a surgeon supplied me liberally with round-shot in the form
of quinine pills, which were used so effectively that my
fever was soon forced to beat a retreat.

As soon as it was dark the other divisions of Wright's corps had begun the recrossing of the river. This corps followed the route which had been taken by Russell's division, while Warren took a road a little farther to the north. Burnside and Hancock next withdrew, and so cautiously that their movements entirely escaped detection by the enemy. All the corps left strong guards in their fronts, which were withdrawn at the last moment. The pontoon-bridges were taken up after crossing the river, and cavalry was sent to the several fords to hold them after they had been abandoned by the infantry, and to destroy any facilities for crossing which had been neglected. The withdrawal from the North Anna had now been successfully accomplished.

CHAPTER X

AS soon as all the commands had safely recrossed the
North Anna, General Grant set out on the morning of May 27, and marched with the troops in the new
movement to the left. Sheridan, with two divisions of
his cavalry, had started east the afternoon of the day
before, and had moved rapidly to Hanovertown on the
Pamunkey, a distance of nearly thirty miles.

On the march the general-in-chief, as he rode by, was
vociferously cheered, as usual, by the troops. Every
movement directed by him inspired the men with new
confidence in his ability and his watchfulness over their
interests; and not only the officers, but the rank and
file, understood fully that he had saved them on the
North Anna from the slaughter which would probably
have occurred if they had been thrown against Lee's
formidable intrenchments, and had had to fight a battle
with their backs to a river; that he had skilfully withdrawn them without the loss of a man or a wagon, and
that they were again making an advance movement.

153

The soldiers by this time were getting on intimate terms with their commander—in fact, becoming quite chummy. One man in the ranks touched his hat as the chief rode by, and asked, "Is it all right, general?" He received a nod of the head in reply, and the words, "Yes, I think so." Another man looked up at him, and said in an earnest tone, "General, we 'll lick 'em sure pop next time." These remarks were not attempts at undue familiarity, but expressions of a genuine sentiment of soldierly fellowship which the men had learned to entertain toward their chief. That night general headquarters were established at Mangohick Church, about twenty miles in a southeasterly direction from Quarles's Ford.

The cavalry had been handled with great skill. It made a feint as if to cross at Littlepage's and Taylor's fords on the Pamunkey, and after dark moved rapidly to Hanover Ferry, about twelve miles farther down the stream, where the actual crossing took place on the morning of the 27th. It was followed by Russell's division of infantry. The rest of the troops had made a good march, and soon after midday on May 28, Wright, Hancock, and Warren had crossed the river and gone into position about a mile and a half beyond. Burnside had reached the ferry, but remained on the north side to guard the trains. General Grant had pushed on to Hanover Ferry, and expressed himself as greatly pleased at the success of the movement. He had abundant reason to congratulate himself upon the thorough carrying out of his instructions. In each of his three attempts to move close to Lee's troops and cross difficult rivers in his very face, Grant had been completely successful, and had manœuvered so as to accomplish a most formidable task in warfare with insignificant loss.

In the operations of the last few days General Grant

had employed with wonderful skill his chief military characteristics of quickness of thought, celerity of action, and fertility of resource. While his plans were always well matured, and much thought and investigation were expended upon perfecting them in advance, yet they were sufficiently general in their nature to admit readily of those changes which often have to be made upon the instant in consequence of some unanticipated movement of the enemy, or some unexpected discovery in the topography of the field of operations. It seemed a little singular to him that Lee, after falling back behind the North Anna River, had allowed the Union army to advance across that difficult stream without any substantial resistance, and that, when across, he had made a stand with his back to another river, the South Anna, and remained there entirely passive, and that three days afterward he had permitted the Union army to withdraw across the North Anna under his very nose without even attacking its rear-guards. It was these circumstances which made Grant say at this time, and also write to the government: "Lee's army is really whipped. . . . A battle with them outside of intrenchments cannot be had. . . ."

Our base of supplies was now transferred from Port Royal to White House on the York River.

Before describing the personal incidents connected with what is known as the Cold Harbor campaign, it is important to give the reader a general idea of the character of the country in which the manœuvering and fighting occurred. Hanovertown, near which place our army had now been concentrated, is about seventeen miles in a straight line northeast from Richmond. The country is crossed by two streams, Totopotomoy Creek and the Chickahominy River, both running in a southeasterly direction, the latter being about four miles from

Richmond at the nearest point. Between these are a number of smaller creeks and rivulets. Their banks are low, and their approaches swampy and covered with woods and thickets. Three main roads lead from Hanovertown to Richmond. The most northerly is called the Hanovertown or Shady Grove road; the second route, the Mechanicsville road; the third and most southerly, which runs through Old Cold Harbor, New Cold Harbor, and Gaines's Mill, is known as the Cold Harbor road. Old Cold Harbor, half-way between Hanovertown and Richmond, consisted merely of a few scattered houses; but its strategic position was important for reasons which will hereafter appear. New Cold Harbor was little more than the intersection of cross-roads about a mile and a half west of Old Cold Harbor. It was at first supposed that Cold Harbor was a corruption of the phrase Cool Arbor, and the shade-trees in the vicinity seemed to suggest such a name; but it was ascertained afterward that the name Cold Harbor was correct, that it had been taken from the places frequently found along the highways of England, and means "shelter without fire."

On May 28 Sheridan was pushed out toward Mechanicsville to discover the enemy's position, and after a sharp fight at Haw's Shop, drove a body of the enemy out of some earthworks in which it was posted. That night the Ninth Corps crossed the river. Wilson's cavalry division remained on the north side until the morning of the 30th to cover the crossing of the trains. General headquarters had crossed the Pamunkey on the pontoon-bridge in the afternoon of May 28, after a hard, dusty ride, and had gone into camp on the south side. In the mean time Lee had moved his entire army rapidly from the North Anna, and thrown it between our army and Richmond.

On the morning of the 29th, Wright, Hancock, and Warren were directed to move forward and make a reconnaissance in force, which brought about some spirited fighting. The movement disclosed the fact that all of Lee's troops were in position on the north side of the Chickahominy, and were well intrenched.

General Grant was particularly anxious, that evening, to obtain information of the enemy from some inside source. Several prisoners had been taken, and one of them who was disposed to be particularly talkative was brought in to headquarters, it being thought that the general might like to examine him in person. He was a tall, slim, shock-headed, comical-looking creature, and proved to be so full of native humor that I give the portion of his conversation which afforded us the most amusement. He, of course, did not know in whose presence he was as he rattled off his quick-witted remarks. "What command do you belong to?" asked the general. "I'm in Early's corps, and I belong to a No'th Ca'lina reegiment, suh," was the reply. "Oh, you're from North Carolina," remarked the general. "Yes," said the prisoner, "and a good deal fa'thah from it jes' now than I'd like to be, God knows." "Well, where were you taken, and how did you get here?" was next asked. "How did I get h'yah! Well, when a man has half a dozen o' them thah reckless and desp'rit dragoons o' yourn lammin' him along the road on a tight run, and wallopin' him with the flats o' thah sabahs, he don't have no trouble gittin' h'yah." "Is your whole corps in our front, and when did it arrive?" inquired the general. "Well, now, jes' let me tell you about that," said the prisoner; "and let me begin right from the sta't. I'm not goin' to fool you, 'cause I'm fast losin' interest in this fight. I was a peaceful man, and I did n't want to hurt nobody, when a conscript officah down thah in the ole Tar State come around, and told me I 'd have to git into the ranks, and go to fightin' fo' my rights. I tried to have him p'int 'em out fo' me. I told him I 'd as lief have 'em all, but I was n't strenuous about it. Then he begun to put on more airs than a buckin' hoss at a county fair, and told me to come right along—that the country wanted me. Well, I had noticed that our folks was losin' a good many battles; that you-all was too much for 'em; and I got to flatterin' myself that perhaps it was only right fo' me to go and jine our army, jes' to kind o' even things up. But matters has been goin' pretty rough with us ever since, and I 'm gettin' to feel peacefuller and peacefuller every day. They 're feedin' us half the time on crumbs, and thah 's one boy in my company that 's got so thin you have to throw a tent-fly over him to get up a respectable shadow. Then they have a way of campin' us alongside o' creeks not much biggah than a slate-pencil; and you have to be powerful quick about gittin' what watah you want, or some thirsty cow 'll come along and drink up the whole stream. I thought, from all the fuss she had made at the sta't, that South Ca'lina was goin' to fight the whole wah through herself, and make it a picnic for the rest of us; but when thah 's real trouble she has to get the ole Tar State to do the solid work."

"Are there any men from South Carolina in your brigade?" was the next question. The answer came with a serio-comic expression of countenance: "Yas; a few—in the band." The general suppressed the laugh with which he was now struggling, and feeling that an effort to get any useful information from the North Carolinian would be a slow process, disappeared into his tent to attend to some correspondence, and left the prisoner to be further interviewed by the staff. "I tell

you, gentlemen," went on the Confederate, "thah 's lots
o' cobwebs in my throat, and I could talk to you-all a
good deal bettah if I only had a dish o' liquor.   Thah 's
nothin' braces a man up like takin' a little o' the tangle-
foot."

Thereupon a canteen and cup were brought, and after
the man had poured out about four fingers of commissary whisky and tossed it off as if it were water, he
looked considerably invigorated.   "Nothin' as soothin'
as co'n-juice, aftah all," he continued.   "I 'd like to live
in Kaintucky; them Kaintucky fellers say they can
walk right into a co'n-field, strip off an eah, and jes'
squeeze a drink of whisky right out'n it."   "How did
you happen to be picked up?" was now asked.   "Well,
you see, suh," he replied, " our cap'n, Jimmy Skipwo'th,
marched me out on the picket-line.   Cap'n Jimmy 's
one o' them thah slack-twisted, loose-belted, toggle-
j'inted kind o' fellers that sends you straight out to the
front; and if you don't get killed right off, why, he gets
all out o' patience, an' thinks you want to live fo'evah.
You can't get away, because he 's always keepin' tab on
you.   When he marched us out to-day I says to him:
'Cap'n Jimmy, thah don't 'pear to be enough of the
boys a-comin' along with us.   Now I tell you, when we
go to monkeyin' with them Yankees we ought to have
plenty o' company; we don't want to feel lonesome.'
Well, we got thah, and went to diggin' a ditch so we
could flop down in it and protect our heads, and could
use it afterward fo' buryin' you-all in it, ef we could get
hold o' you.   Well, jes' then you opened lively, and
come at us a-whoopin' and a-careerin' like sin; and ez
fo' me, I took a header fo' the ditch.   The boys saw
somethin' drop, and I did n't make any effo't to pick it
up ag'in till the misunderstandin' was ovah.   The fust
thing I knowed aftah that, you lighted onto me, yanked

me out o' the hole, and then turned me ovah to some of you' dragoons; and Lo'd! how they did run me into you' lines! And so h'yah I am."

After the provost-marshal's people had been told to take the prisoner to the rear and treat him well, the man, before moving on, said: "Gentlemen, I would like mighty well to see that thah new-fangled weepon o' yourn that shoots like it was a whole platoon. They tell me, you can load it up on Sunday and fiah it off all the rest o' the week." He had derived this notion from the Spencer carbine, the new magazine-gun which fired seven shots in rapid succession. After this exhibition of his talent for dialogue, he was marched off to join the other prisoners.

On May 30, Wright, Hancock, and Warren engaged the enemy in their respective fronts, which led to some active skirmishing, the enemy's skirmishers being in most places strongly intrenched. Burnside this day crossed the Totopotomoy. Early's (formerly Ewell's) corps moved out with the evident intention of turning our left, and made a heavy attack, but was repulsed, and forced to fall back, after suffering a severe loss, particularly in field-officers.

About noon Grant received word that transports bringing W. F. Smith's troops from Butler's army were beginning to arrive at White House; and they were ordered to move forward at once, and join the Army of the Potomac. General Grant thought that it was not improbable that the enemy would endeavor to throw troops around our left flank, in the hope of striking Smith a crushing blow before we could detach a force from the Army of the Potomac to prevent it. Sheridan was directed to watch for such a movement, and an infantry brigade was sent out early that morning to join Smith, and march back with him so as to strengthen his forces. General Grant said at this time: "Nothing would please me better than to have the enemy make a movement around our left flank. I would in that case move the whole army to the right, and throw it between Lee and Richmond." But this opportunity did not arise.

On May 30 the general headquarters had been established in a clearing on the north side of the Shady Grove road, about a mile and three quarters west of Haw's Shop. General Grant this day sent a despatch to Halleck at Washington saying: "I wish you would send all the pontoon-bridging you can to City Point to have it ready in case it is wanted." As early as May 26 staff-officers had been sent from the Army of the Potomac to collect all the bridging material at command, and hold it in readiness. This was done in order to be prepared to cross the James River, if deemed best, and attack Richmond and Petersburg from the south side, and carry out the views expressed by Grant in the beginning of the Wilderness campaign as to his movements in certain contingencies.

It was seen by him from the operations of the 30th that the enemy was working his way southward by extending his right flank, with a view to securing Old Cold Harbor, and holding the roads running from that point toward the James River and White House. This would cut off Grant's short route to the James in case he should decide to cross that river, and would also command the principal line of communication with his base at White House. Old Cold Harbor was therefore a point much desired by both the contending generals, and the operations of the 31st were watched with much interest to see which army would secure the prize.

That morning my orders took me to the extreme left in connection with the movements of the cavalry.

Sheridan advanced rapidly upon Old Cold Harbor, attacked a body of the enemy intrenched there, and after a severe fight carried the position. The place, however, was too important to be abandoned by the enemy without a further struggle, and he soon returned, bringing up a force so large that it appeared for a time impossible for Sheridan to hold his position. Finding no troops advancing to his support, the only course which seemed open to him was to fall back; but just as he had withdrawn he received an order to hold the place at all hazards until reinforcements could reach him. With his usual zeal and boldness, he now reoccupied the enemy's breastworks, dismounted his men, and determined to make a desperate struggle to hold the position against whatever force might be sent against him. Darkness set in, however, before the enemy made another assault. In anticipation of a hard fight for the possession of Cold Harbor, General Grant had ordered Wright's corps to make a night march and move to Sheridan's relief. Lee, discovering this, ordered Anderson's corps to Cold Harbor. On Sheridan's front during the night we could distinctly hear the enemy's troops making preparations for the next morning's attack, and could even hear some of the commands given by their officers. Soon after daylight on June 1 the assault began. Sheridan kept quiet till the attacking party came within a short distance of his breastworks, and then opened with a destructive fire, under which the enemy fell back in considerable confusion. He soon rallied, however, and rushed again to the assault, but once more recoiled before Sheridan's well-delivered volleys. Wright had been instructed to arrive at daylight, but the night march had been exceptionally difficult, and the head of his column did not appear until nine o'clock. The troops were footsore and jaded, but they moved promptly into line, and relieved Sheridan's little force, which had been fighting desperately against great odds for about four hours. Grant had secured Old Cold Harbor, and won the game.

Smith's corps consisted of 13,000 men. He left about 2500 to guard White House, and with the rest started for the front, reaching there at three o'clock in the afternoon of June 1. At five o'clock Wright's and Smith's commands advanced and captured the earthworks in their front, taking about 750 prisoners.

The enemy had made three attacks upon Warren, but had been handsomely repulsed. Hancock and Burnside had also been attacked, no doubt to prevent them from sending troops to reinforce our left.

The enemy seemed roused to desperation in his struggle to gain the much-coveted strategic point at Old Cold Harbor, and made several savage attacks in that direction during the night; but they were all successfully repelled. In gaining and holding the important position sought, the Union army that day lost nearly 2000 men in killed and in wounded; the enemy probably suffered to about the same extent.

Headquarters were moved about two miles this day, June 1, to the Via House, which was half a mile south of Totopotomoy Creek on the road leading from Haw's Shop to Bethesda Church. Before starting, the general's servant asked whether he should saddle "Jeff Davis," the horse Grant had been riding for two days. "No," was the reply; "we are getting into a rather swampy country, and I fear little 'Jeff's' legs are not quite long enough for wading through the mud. You had better saddle 'Egypt.'" This horse was large in size and a medium-colored bay. He was called "Egypt," not because he had come from the region of the Nile, but from the junction of the Mississippi and Ohio rivers in southern Illinois, a section of country named after the land of the Ptolemies.

When the horse was brought up the general mounted as usual in a manner peculiar to himself. He made no perceptible effort, and used his hands but little to aid him; he put his left foot in the stirrup, grasped the horse's mane near the withers with his left hand, and rose without making a spring, by simply straightening the left leg till his body was high enough to enable him to throw the right leg over the saddle. There was no "climbing" up the animal's side, and no jerky movements. The mounting was always done in an instant and with the greatest possible ease.

Rawlins rode with the general at the head of the staff. As the party turned a bend in the road near the crossing of the Totopotomoy, the general came in sight of a teamster whose wagon was stalled in a place where it was somewhat swampy, and who was standing beside his team beating his horses brutally in the face with the butt-end of his whip, and swearing with a volubility calculated to give a sulphurous odor to all the surrounding atmosphere. Grant's aversion to profanity and his love of horses caused all the ire in his nature to be aroused by the sight presented. Putting both spurs into "Egypt's" flanks, he dashed toward the teamster, and raising his clenched fist, called out to him: "What does this conduct mean, you scoundrel? Stop beating those horses!" The teamster looked at him, and said coolly, as he delivered another blow aimed at the face of the wheel-horse: "Well, who's drivin' this team anyhow—you or me?" The general was now thoroughly angered, and his manner was by no means as angelic as that of the celestial being who called a halt when Balaam was disciplining the ass. "I'll show you, you infernal villain!" he cried, shaking his fist in the man's face.

Then calling to an officer of the escort, he said: "Take this man in charge, and have him tied up to a tree for six hours as a punishment for his brutality." The man slunk off sullenly in charge of the escort to receive his punishment, without showing any penitence for his conduct. He was evidently a hardened case. Of course he was not aware that the officer addressing him was the general-in-chief, but he evidently knew that he was an officer of high rank, as he was accompanied by a staff and an escort, so that there was no excuse for the insubordinate and insolent remark. During the stirring scenes of that day's battle the general twice referred to the incident in vehement language, showing that the recollection of it was still rankling in his mind. This was the one exhibition of temper manifested by him during the entire campaign, and the only one I ever witnessed during my many years of service with him. I remarked that night to Colonel Bowers, who had served with his chief ever since the Fort Donelson campaign: "The general to-day gave us his first exhibition of anger. Did you ever see him fire up in that way in his earlier campaigns?" "Never but once," said Bowers: "and that was in the Iuka campaign. One day on the march he came across a straggler who had stopped at a house and assaulted a woman. The general sprang from his horse, seized a musket from the hands of a soldier, and struck the culprit over the head with it, sending him sprawling to the ground." He always had a peculiar horror of such crimes. They were very rare in our war, but when brought to his attention the general showed no mercy to the culprit.

Grant and Meade rode along the lines that day, and learned from personal observation the general features of the topography. About noon they stopped at Wright's headquarters, and the commander of the Sixth

Corps gave the party some delicious ice-water. He had found an ice-house near his headquarters, and after a hot and dusty ride since daylight the cool draught was gratefully relished by those whose thirst it slaked. The previous winter had been unusually cold, and an abundance of ice had formed upon the streams in Virginia. The well-filled ice-houses found on the line of march were a great boon to the wounded. General Wright had assumed command of the Sixth Corps at a critical period of the campaign, and under very trying circumstances; but he had conducted it with such heroic gallantry and marked ability that he had commended himself highly to both Grant and Meade.

That night the variety of food at the headquarters mess was increased by the arrival of a supply of oysters received by way of White House. Shell-fish were among the few dishes which tempted the general's appetite, and as he had been living principally on roast beef and hard bread during the whole campaign, and had not eaten enough of these to sustain life in an ordinary person, every one was delighted that evening, when sitting down at the mess-table, to see the general attack the oysters with evident relish, and make a hearty meal of them. Thereafter every effort was made to get a supply of that species of sea food as often as possible. At the dinner-table he referred again to the brutality of the teamster, saying: " If people knew how much more they could get out of a horse by gentleness than by harshness, they would save a great deal of trouble both to the horse and the man. A horse is a particularly intelligent animal; he can be made to do almost anything if his master has intelligence enough to let him know what is required. Some men, for instance, when they want to lead a horse forward, turn toward him and stare him in the face. He, of course, thinks they are barring his way, and he stands still. If they would turn their back to him and move on he would naturally follow. I am looking forward longingly to the time when we can end this war, and I can settle down on my St. Louis farm and raise horses. I love to train young colts, and I will invite you all to visit me and take a hand in the amusement. When old age comes on, and I get too feeble to move about, I expect to derive my chief pleasure from sitting in a big arm-chair in the center of a ring,—a sort of training-course,—holding a colt's leading-line in my hand, and watching him run around the ring." He little foresaw that a torturing disease was to cut short his life before he could realize his cherished hopes of enjoying the happiness of the peaceful old age which he anticipated.

No warrior was ever more anxious for peace, and all of the general's references to the pending strife evinced his constant longing for the termination of the struggle upon terms which would secure forever the integrity of the Union. When he prepared his letter of acceptance of his first nomination for the Presidency, he wrote no random phrase, but expressed the genuine sentiments of his heart, when he said, " Let us have peace."

The night of the 1st of June was a busy one for both officers and men. Grant, eager as usual to push the advantage gained, set about making such disposition of the troops as would best accomplish this purpose. Hancock was ordered to move after nightfall from the extreme right to the extreme left of the army. The night was extremely dark, especially when passing through the woods, no one was familiar with the roads, the heat was intense, and the dust stifling; but notwithstanding all the difficulties encountered, Hancock arrived at Old Cold Harbor on the morning of June 2, after a march of over twelve miles. As the men were greatly exhausted, however, from hunger and fatigue, they had to be given an opportunity to rest and eat their rations, and it was found impossible to make a formidable assault until five o'clock in the afternoon. Warren and Burnside were both attacked while. they were moving their troops, but they repelled all assaults, and caused the enemy considerable loss.

At daylight on June 2 the headquarters were moved about two miles south to a camp near Bethesda Church, so as to be nearer the center of the line, which had been extended toward the left. Upon reaching the church, and while waiting for the arrival of the wagons and the pitching of the tents, a number of important orders were issued. The pews had been carried out of the church and placed in the shade of the trees surrounding it. The general-in-chief and his officers seated themselves in the pews, while the horses were taken to a little distance in the rear. The ubiquitous photographers were promptly on the ground, and they succeeded in taking several fairly good views of the group. A supply of New York papers had just been received, and the party, with the exception of the general, were soon absorbed in reading the news. He was too much occupied at the time in thinking over his plans for the day to give attention to the papers, and was content to hear from the staff a summary of anything of importance mentioned in the press. He was usually a diligent reader of the newspapers and of all current literature. There was one New York morning journal which claimed a special previous knowledge of his movements, and made some very clever guesses concerning his plans. He used to call this paper his "organ," and upon the arrival of the mail he would generally pick it up first, and remark: "Now let me see what my organ has to say, and then I can tell better what I am going to do."

A large delegation of the Christian Commission had arrived at White House, and was now moving up toward the lines with a supply-train which carried many comforts for the wounded. I saw among the number a person whom I recognized as the pastor of a church which I had attended some years before. He was trudging along like the others in his shirt-sleeves, wearing a broad-brimmed slouch-hat, and was covered with Virginia dust. I presented him to General Grant and the rest of the officers, and then brought up a number of the other members of the Commission, and presented them in turn. General Grant rose to his feet, shook hands with them, and greeted them all with great cordiality; then, resuming his seat, he said: "Sit down, gentlemen, and rest; you look tired after your march." They thanked him, and several of them took seats in the church pews near him, though, considering their professional training, most of them would have doubtless felt more at home in the pulpit than in the pews. The general continued by saying: "I am very glad to see you coming to the army on your present mission; unfortunately, you will find an extensive field for your work. My greatest concern in this campaign is the care of the large number of wounded. Our surgeons have been unremitting in their labors, and I know you can be of great assistance."

The gentlemen replied: "We have brought with us everything that we thought could minister to the comfort of the wounded, and we will devote ourselves religiously to the work." After the general had assured them that they should have all necessary transportation put at their disposal, they bid him good-by, and continued their march. His parting words were: "Remember, gentlemen, whatever instructions you may receive, let your first care be for the wounded." Before leaving they expressed to the staff their great delight in having had this unexpected chat with the commander of the armies, and having been treated by him with so much consideration.

The Christian Commission, as well as the Sanitary Commission, was often of inestimable service to the wounded, and many a gallant fellow owed his life to its kindly and devoted ministerings.

CHAPTER XI

LEE had manœuvered and fought over this ground
two years before, and was perfectly acquainted
with every detail of topography, while to Grant it was
entirely new. There were, however, in the Army of
the Potomac a great many prominent officers who had
served with McClellan on the Peninsula, and were
familiar with the locality.

General Grant, as usual, had not only to give direction to the active movements taking place under his
own eye, but was compelled to bestow much thought
upon the coöperating armies at a distance; and the
double responsibility was a severe tax upon his energies. He expected that much would be accomplished
in the valley of Virginia by Hunter, now that the
forces opposed to him had withdrawn, and was urging
him to increased exertion; but he had to communicate
with him by way of Washington, which created much
delay, and added greatly to the anxieties of the general-
in-chief. In the afternoon of the 2d, Lee became aware
that we were sending troops against his right, and was
active in moving his forces to meet an attack on that

171

flank. His left now rested on Totopotomoy Creek, and his right was near New Cold Harbor, and was protected by an impassable swamp. A strong parapet was thrown up on his right in the rear of a sunken road which answered the purpose of a ditch. On the left center the ground was lower and more level, but difficult of approach on account of swamps, ravines, and thickets. Added to this were the usual obstacles of heavy slashings of timber. General Grant had manœuvered skilfully with a view to compelling Lee to stretch out his line and make it as thin and weak as possible, and it was at present over six miles long.

A serious problem now presented itself to General Grant's mind—whether to attempt to crush Lee's army on the north side of the James, with the prospect in case of success of driving him into Richmond, capturing the city perhaps without a siege, and putting the Confederate government to flight; or to move the Union army south of the James without giving battle, and transfer the field of operations to the vicinity of Petersburg. It was a nice question of judgment. After discussing the matter thoroughly with his principal officers, and weighing all the chances, he decided to attack Lee's army in its present position. He had succeeded in breaking the enemy's line at Chattanooga, Spottsylvania, and other places under circumstances which were not more favorable, and the results to be obtained now would be so great in case of success that it seemed wise to make the attempt.

The general considered the question not only from a military standpoint, but he took a still broader view of the situation. The expenses of the war had reached nearly four million dollars a day. Many of the people in the North were becoming discouraged at the prolongation of the contest. If the army were transferred

south of the James without fighting a battle on the
north side, people would be impatient at the prospect
of an apparently indefinite continuation of operations;
and as the sickly season of summer was approaching,
the deaths from disease among the troops meanwhile
would be greater than any possible loss encountered in
the contemplated attack. The loss from sickness on the
part of the enemy would naturally be less, as his troops
were acclimated and ours were not. Besides, there
were constant rumors that if the war continued much
longer European powers would recognize the Confederacy, and perhaps give it material assistance; but this
consideration influenced Grant much less than the
others. Delays are usually dangerous, and there was at
present too much at stake to admit of further loss of
time in ending the war, if it could be avoided.

The attack was ordered to be made at daylight on
the morning of June 3. The eve of battle was, as usual,
an anxious and tiresome night at headquarters, and
some changes in the detailed orders specifying the part
the troops were to perform in the coming action were
made nearly as late as midnight. Lee's position was
such that no turning movement was practicable, and it
was necessary that one of his flanks should be crushed
by a direct assault. An attack on the enemy's right
promised the better results, and Grant had decided to
strike the blow there. Of course the exact strength of
the enemy's position could not be ascertained until developed by a close attack, as changes were constantly
being made in it, and new batteries were likely to be
put in position at any time. The general's intention,
therefore, was to attack early in the morning, and
make a vigorous effort to break Lee's right, and if it
were demonstrated that the assault could not succeed
without too great a sacrifice of life, to desist, and have

the men throw up cover for their protection with a view
of holding all the ground they had gained.   Our troops
were disposed as follows: Hancock on the extreme left,
Wright next, then Smith and Warren, with Burnside on
the extreme right.

Everything was now in readiness for the memorable
battle of Cold Harbor.   Headquarters had been moved
two miles farther to our left, and established near Old
Cold Harbor, so as to be within easy reach of the main
point of attack.   It has been stated by inimical critics
that the men had become demoralized by the many
assaults in which they had been engaged; that they had
lost much of their spirit, and were even insubordinate,
refusing to move against the earthworks in obedience
to the orders of their immediate commanders.   This is
a gross slander upon the troops, who were as gallant and
subordinate as any forces in the history of modern warfare, although it is true that many of the veterans had
fallen, and that the recruits who replaced them were
inferior in fighting qualities.

In passing along on foot among the troops at the
extreme front that evening while transmitting some of
the final orders, I observed an incident which afforded
a practical illustration of the deliberate and desperate
courage of the men.   As I came near one of the regiments which was making preparations for the next
morning's assault, I noticed that many of the soldiers
had taken off their coats, and seemed to be engaged in
sewing up rents in them.   This exhibition of tailoring
seemed rather peculiar at such a moment, but upon
closer examination it was found that the men were
calmly writing their names and home addresses on slips
of paper, and pinning them on the backs of their coats,
so that their dead bodies might be recognized upon the
field, and their fate made known to their families at

home. They were veterans who knew well from terrible experience the danger which awaited them, but their minds were occupied not with thoughts of shirking their duty, but with preparation for the desperate work of the coming morning. Such courage is more than heroic—it is sublime.

At 4:30 A. M., June 3, Hancock, Wright, and Smith moved forward promptly to the attack. Hancock's troops struck a salient of the enemy's works, and after a desperate struggle captured it, taking a couple of hundred prisoners, three guns, and a stand of colors. Then, turning the captured guns upon the enemy, they soon drove him from that part of the line into his main works, a short distance in the rear. The second line, however, did not move up in time to support the first, which was finally driven back and forced out of the works it had captured. The men resisted stubbornly, and taking advantage of the crest of a low hill at a distance of fifty or sixty yards from the captured works, they rapidly threw up enough cover to enable them to hold that position. Another division had rushed forward in column to effect a lodgment, if possible, in the enemy's works; but an impassable swamp divided the troops, who were now subjected to a galling fire of artillery and musketry; and although a portion of them gained the enemy's intrenchments, their ranks had become too much weakened and scattered to hold their position, and they were compelled to fall back.

Wright's corps had moved forward, and carried the rifle-pits in its front, and then assaulted the main line. This was too strong, however, to be captured, and our troops were compelled to retire. Nevertheless, they held a line, and protected it as best they could, at a distance of only thirty or forty yards from the enemy.

Smith made his assault by taking advantage of a

ravine which sheltered his troops somewhat from the cross-fire of the enemy. His men drove the enemy's skirmishers before them, and carried the rifle-pits with great gallantry; but the line had to be readjusted at close quarters, and the same cross-fire from which Wright had suffered made further advances extremely hazardous. Smith now reported that his troops were so cut up that there was no prospect of carrying the works in his front unless the enfilading fire on his flank could be silenced. Additional artillery was then sent forward to try to keep down the enemy's fire.

Burnside had captured the advance rifle-pits in front of Early's left, and had taken up a position close to the enemy's main line. Warren's line was long and thin, and his troops, from the position they occupied, could not do much in the way of assaulting. These demonstrations against the enemy's left were principally to keep him engaged, and prevent him from withdrawing troops to reinforce his right. Warren had coöperated with Burnside in driving Early from the Shady Grove road, upon which he had advanced and made an attack. Gordon had attacked Warren's center, but was handsomely repulsed. Wilson's division of cavalry, which had returned from destroying the Virginia Central Railroad, moved across the Totopotomoy to Haw's Shop, drove the enemy from that place, made a further advance, carried some rifle-pits and held them for an hour, but was unable to connect with Burnside's infantry, and withdrew to Haw's Shop.

The reports received by General Grant were at first favorable and encouraging, and he urged a continuance of the successes gained; but finding the strength of the position greater than any one could have supposed, he sent word at 7 A. M. to General Meade, saying: "The moment it becomes certain that an assault cannot suc-

ceed, suspend the offensive; but when one does succeed, push it vigorously, and if necessary pile in troops
at the successful point from wherever they can be
taken." Troops had again pushed forward at different
points of the line. General Grant had established himself at a central position, which had been made known
to all the commanders and staff-officers, so that he
could at that point receive promptly all reports. Some
of these messages were rather contradictory, and became still more conflicting as the attack proceeded.
His staff-officers were active in bringing information
from every important point, but the phases of battle were
changing more rapidly than they could be reported.

At eleven o'clock the general rode out along the lines
to consult with commanding officers on the spot.
Hancock now reported that the position in his front
could not be taken. Wright stated that a lodgment
might be made in his front, but that nothing would be
gained by it unless Hancock and Smith were to advance at the same time. Smith thought that he might
be able to carry the works before him, but was not
sanguine. Burnside believed that he could break the
enemy's line in his front, but Warren on his left did not
agree in this opinion.

The general-in-chief now felt so entirely convinced
that any more attacks upon the enemy's works would
not result in success that at half-past twelve o'clock he
wrote the following order to General Meade: "The
opinion of the corps commanders not being sanguine of
success in case an assault is ordered, you may direct a
suspension of farther advance for the present. Hold
our most advanced positions, and strengthen them. . . .
To aid the expedition under General Hunter, it is necessary that we should detain all the army now with Lee
until the former gets well on his way to Lynchburg.

To do this effectually, it will be better to keep the
enemy out of the intrenchments of Richmond than to
have them go back there. Wright and Hancock should
be ready to assault in case the enemy should break
through General Smith's lines, and all should be ready
to resist an assault."

After finishing this despatch the general discussed
at some length the situation, saying: "I am still of the
opinion I have held since leaving the North Anna, that
Lee will not come out and take the offensive against us;
but I want to prepare for every contingency, and I am
particularly anxious to be able to turn the tables upon
the enemy in case they should, after their success this
morning in acting on the defensive, be tempted to make
a counter-attack upon our lines."

At two o'clock Grant announced the result of the
engagement to Halleck. At three o'clock, while waiting
for news in regard to the casualties of the morning and
reports in detail from the corps commanders, he busied
himself in sending instructions in regard to Banks's
command in Louisiana, and advised a movement against
Mobile.

There was a good deal of irregular firing along the
lines, and in the afternoon it became heavy on Burnside's right. The enemy had made an attack there, and
while it lasted he attempted to haul off some of his
batteries; but Burnside's return fire was so vigorous
that this attempt was prevented. In the night the
enemy's troops withdrew from Burnside's front, leaving
some of their wounded in his hands and their dead un-
buried.

General Grant's time was now given up almost entirely
to thinking of the care of the wounded. Our entire
loss in killed, wounded, and missing was nearly 7000.
Our surgeons were able to give prompt relief to the

ULYSSES S. GRANT AS LIEUTENANT-GENERAL.

From a photograph.

General Rawlins.   General W. F. Smith.   General Thomas.   Captain Porter.
   Charles A. Dana.   General Wilson.   General Grant.

GENERAL GRANT AT THE HEADQUARTERS OF GENERAL THOMAS.

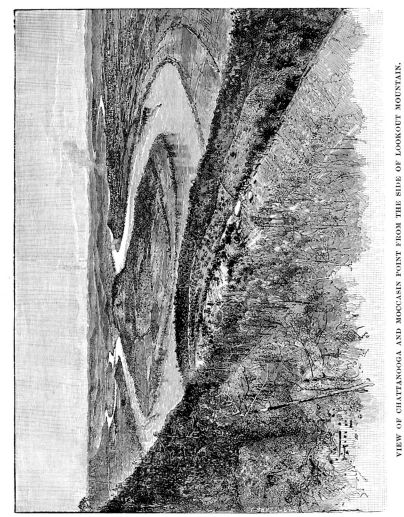

VIEW OF CHATTANOOGA AND MOCCASIN POINT FROM THE SIDE OF LOOKOUT MOUNTAIN.

From a photograph.

MAJOR-GENERAL GEORGE G. MEADE.

From a photograph by Brady.

GRANT'S HEADQUARTERS IN THE WILDERNESS.

GENERAL HORACE PORTER.

From a war-time photograph.

GENERAL GRANT RECONNOITERING THE CONFEDERATE POSITION AT SPOTTSYL-
VANIA COURT-HOUSE.

From a sketch made at the time by C. W. Reed.

MAJOR-GENERAL JOHN SEDGWICK, KILLED AT SPOTTSYLVANIA IN THE
WILDERNESS CAMPAIGN, MAY 9, 1864.

From a photograph.

GENERAL GRANT AND THE WOUNDED CONFEDERATE.

MAJOR-GENERAL HENRY W. HALLECK.

From a photograph.

GRANT AND HIS STAFF AT BETHESDA CHURCH.

From a war-time photograph.

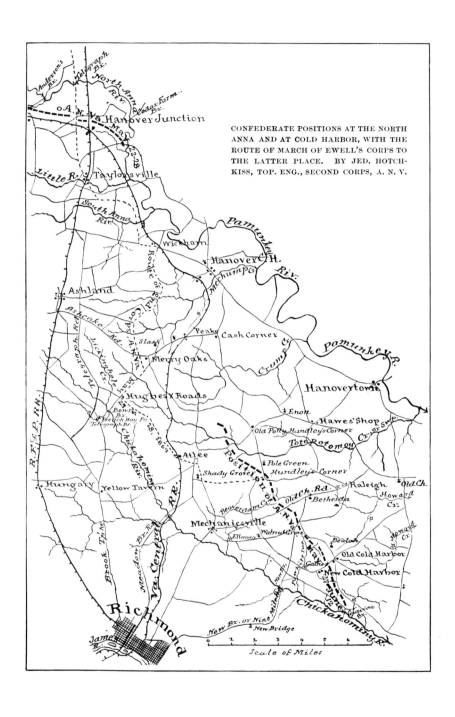

CONFEDERATE POSITIONS AT THE NORTH
ANNA AND AT COLD HARBOR, WITH THE
ROUTE OF MARCH OF EWELL'S CORPS TO
THE LATTER PLACE. BY JED. HOTCH-
KISS, TOP. ENG., SECOND CORPS, A. N. V.

GRANT'S ARMY CROSSING THE JAMES RIVER.

MAP OF THE PETERSBURG AND APPOMATTOX CAMPAIGNS.

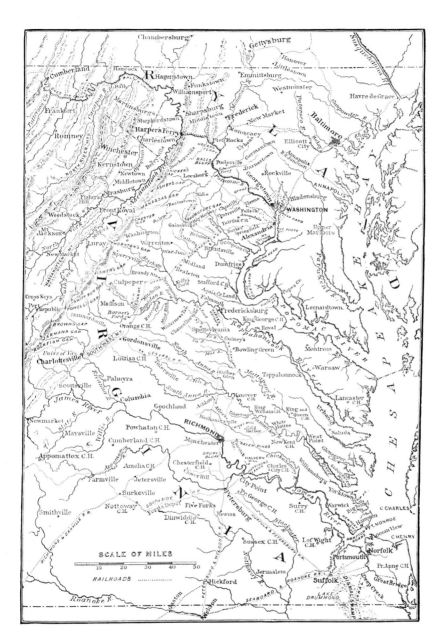

MAP OF THE VIRGINIA CAMPAIGNS OF 1864-65

GENERAL GRANT HASTENING TO ORDER THE RECALL OF THE ASSAULTING COLUMN.

wounded who were recovered, as every preparation had
been made for this emergency, and our army was fortunately only twelve miles from a water base.   Many,
however, were left between the lines; and as the works
were close together, and the intervening ground under
a constant fire, it was not possible to remove a great
number of the wounded or to bury the dead.   The
enemy's wounded in our hands were taken in charge by
our surgeons, and the same care was given to them as
to our own men.

That evening, when the staff-officers had assembled
at headquarters after much hard riding and hot work
during the day, the events which had occurred were
discussed with the commander, and plans talked over
for the next morning.   The general said: "I regret this
assault more than any one I have ever ordered.   I regarded it as a stern necessity, and believed that it
would bring compensating results; but, as it has proved,
no advantages have been gained sufficient to justify the
heavy losses suffered.   The early assault at Vicksburg,
while it was not successful, yet brought compensating
advantages; for it taught the men that they could not
seize the much-coveted prize of that stronghold without
a siege, and it was the means of making them work
cheerfully and patiently afterward in the trenches, and
of securing the capture of the place with but little more
loss of life; whereas if the assault had not been made
the men could not have been convinced that they could
not have captured the city by making a dash upon it
which might have saved them many months of arduous
labor, sickness, and fatigue."   The matter was seldom
referred to again in conversation, for General Grant,
with his usual habit of mind, bent all his energies toward consummating his plans for the future.

There has been brought out recently a remarkable

vindication of Grant's judgment in ordering the assault at Cold Harbor. In a lecture delivered at San Antonio, Texas, April 20, 1896, by ex-United States Senator John H. Reagan, who was postmaster-general in Jefferson Davis's cabinet, he states that he and several of the judges of the courts in Richmond rode out to General Lee's headquarters, and were with him during this attack. In describing the interview he says:

" He [Lee] then said to me that General Grant was at that time assaulting his lines at three different places, with columns of from six to eight deep. Upon this, I asked him if his line should be broken what reserve he had. He replied, 'Not a regiment,' and added that if he should shorten his lines to make a reserve the enemy would turn him, and if he should weaken his lines to make a reserve they would be broken." This is a confirmation of the fact that Grant had succeeded in compelling Lee to stretch out his line almost to the breaking-point, and a proof that if our attacking columns had penetrated it, Lee would have been found without reserves, and the damage inflicted upon him would have been irreparable.

There were critics who were severe in their condemnation of what Grant called "hammering" and Sherman called "pounding"; but they were found principally among the stay-at-homes, and especially the men who sympathized with the enemy. A soldier said one night, when reading by a camp-fire an account of a call issued by a disloyal newspaper at home for a public meeting to protest against the continued bloodshed in this campaign: "Who's shedding this blood, anyhow? They better wait till we fellows down here at the front hollo, 'Enough!'" The soldiers were as anxious as their commander to fight the war to a finish, and be allowed to return to their families and their business.

Grant could have effectually stopped the carnage at any time by withholding from battle. He could have avoided all bloodshed by remaining north of the Rapidan, intrenching, and not moving against his enemy: but he was not placed in command of the armies for that purpose. It had been demonstrated by more than three years of campaigning that peace could be secured only by whipping and destroying the enemy. No one was more desirous of peace; no one was possessed of a heart more sensitive to every form of human suffering than the commander: but he realized that paper bullets are not effective in warfare; he knew better than to attempt to hew rocks with a razor; and he felt that in campaigning the hardest blows bring the quickest relief. He was aware that in Wellington's armies the annual loss from disease was 113 out of 1000; in our Mexican war, 152; and in the Crimea, 600; and that in the campaigns thus far in our own war more men had died from sickness while lying in camp than from shot and shell in battle. He could not select his ground for fighting in this continuous siege of fortified lines; for, though he and his chief officers applied all their experience and skill in endeavors to manœuver the enemy out of strong positions before attacking him, his foe was often too able and wily to fall into the trap set for him, and had to be struck in positions which were far from Grant's choosing. When Lee stopped fighting the cause of secession was lost. If Grant had stopped fighting the cause of the Union would have been lost. He was assigned one of the most appalling tasks ever intrusted to a commander. He did his duty fearlessly to the bitter end, and triumphed. In thirteen months after Lincoln handed him his commission of lieutenant-general, and intrusted to him the command of the armies, the war was virtually ended.

CHAPTER XII

GRANT DECIDES TO CROSS THE JAMES—SUFFERINGS AT THE
FRONT—GRANT'S VISITOR FROM THE PACIFIC SLOPE—
AN IMPORTANT MISSION — DEALING WITH A LIBELER
OF THE PRESS—LOSSES—GRANT RELATES SOME AN-
ECDOTES

THE time had now come when Grant was to carry
out his alternative movement of throwing the
entire army south of the James River. Halleck, who
was rather fertile in suggestions, although few of them
were ever practicable, had written Grant about the advisability of throwing his army round by the right flank,
taking up a line northeast of Richmond, controlling the
railroads leading north of Richmond, and using them to
supply the Union army. This view may have been
favored in Washington for the reason that it was
thought it would better protect the capital. Grant said,
in discussing this matter at headquarters: "We can
defend Washington best by keeping Lee so occupied
that he cannot detach enough troops to capture it. If
the safety of the city should really become imperiled, we
have water communication, and can transport a sufficient number of troops to Washington at any time to hold
it against attack. This movement proposed by Halleck
would separate the Army of the Potomac by a still
greater distance from Butler's army, while it would
leave us a long vulnerable line of communication, and

182

require a large part of our effective force to properly guard it. I shall prepare at once to move across the James River, and in the mean time destroy to a still greater extent the railroads north of Richmond."

On June 5, General J. G. Barnard, of the United States engineer corps, was assigned to duty as chief engineer at Grant's headquarters.

The general-in-chief realized that he was in a swampy and sickly portion of the country. The malaria was highly productive of disease, and the Chickahominy fever was dreaded by all the troops who had a recollection of its ravages when they campaigned in that section of the country two years before. The operations had been so active that precautions against sickness had necessarily been much neglected, and the general was anxious, while giving the men some rest, to improve the sanitary conditions. By dint of extraordinary exertions the camps were well policed, and large quantities of fresh vegetables were brought forward and distributed. Cattle were received in much better condition than those which had made long marches and had furnished beef which was far from being wholesome. Greater attention was demanded in the cooking of the food and the procuring of better water. Dead animals and offal were buried, and more stringent sanitary regulations were enforced throughout the entire command.

What was most distressing at this time was the condition of affairs at the extreme front. No one who did not witness the sights on those portions of the line where the opposing troops were in exceptionally close contact can form an idea of the sufferings experienced. Staff-officers used to work their way on foot daily to the advanced points, so as to be able to report with accuracy these harrowing scenes. Some of the sights

were not unlike those of the "bloody angle" at Spottsylvania. Between the lines where the heavy assaults
had been made there was in some places a distance of
thirty or forty yards completely covered by the dead and
wounded of both sides. The bodies of the dead were
festering in the sun, while the wounded were dying a
torturing death from starvation, thirst, and loss of blood.
In some places the stench became sickening. Every
attempt to make a change in the picket-line brought on
heavy firing, as both sides had become nervous from
long watchfulness, and the slightest movement on either
front led to the belief that it was the beginning of an
assault. In the night there was often heavy artillery-
firing, sometimes accompanied by musketry, with a view
to deterring the other side from attacking, or occasioned
by false rumors of an attempt to assault. The men on
the advanced lines had to lie close to the ground in narrow trenches, with little water for drinking purposes,
except that obtained from surface drainage. They were
subjected to the broiling heat by day and the chilling
winds and fogs at night, and had to eat the rations that
could be got to them under the greatest imaginable discomfort.

The staff-officers, in their frequent visits to the front
of our lines, had learned the most exposed points, and
in passing them usually quickened their speed so as to
be a shorter time under the enemy's fire. There was
one particularly dangerous place where a dirt road ran
along the foot of a knoll on the side toward the enemy.
A prominent citizen from the Pacific coast, whom General Grant knew, had arrived from Washington, and
was spending a few days at headquarters to see what an
army in the field looked like. One morning, as the
general was mounting with a portion of his staff to
make one of his frequent reconnoitering trips along the

lines, the visitor proposed to ride with him, but said before starting: "Is there going to be much shooting where you 're going, general? For I 've got a wife and children waiting for me on the Pacific slope, and I don't want to get pinked by the Johnny Rebs." "Well, they 're not very particular over there where their shots strike when they begin firing. I always advise persons who have no business to transact with them to keep away," replied the general. "Yes; but I want to see as much of this show as possible, now that I 've come here," said the guest; and mounting a horse which had been ordered up for him, he rode along with the party. Pretty soon some stray artillery shots flew in our direction, but the visitor rode on without showing any signs of disturbance, except a very active ducking of the head, accompanied by a running comment upon the utter carelessness and waste of ammunition on the part of the enemy, and the evident disposition to mow down a mild-mannered and harmless civilian with as little hesitation as they would the general-in-chief who was crowding them with all his armies.

After a while we came to the dangerous portion of the dirt road, and the staff-officers reminded the general that it was usually pretty hot there; but he passed over it at a walk without paying attention to the warning, and stopped at the most exposed point to examine the position in front, which seemed to him to present some features of importance. A battery instantly opened, and shot and shell shrieked through the air, and plowed the ground in a most enlivening manner. The visitor, whose head was now bobbing from one side to the other like a signal-flag waving a message, cried out to the commander: "See here, general; it don't appear to me that this place could have been selected by you with special reference to personal safety." The general was absorbed in his examination of the ground, and made no reply for a minute or two. Then, looking at his guest, who was growing red and pale by turns, and rolling nearly out of his saddle in dodging to the right and left, remarked with a smile: "You are giving yourself a great deal of useless exercise. When you hear the sound of a shot it has already passed you." Just then a shell exploded close by, scattering the dirt in every direction. This was too great a trial for the overstrained nerves of the visitor. He turned his horse's head to the rear, drove both spurs into the animal's flanks, and as he dashed away with the speed of a John Gilpin, he cried back to us: "I have a wife and family waiting for me, and I'm pressed for time. Besides, I'm not much of a curiosity-seeker anyway." Just then his black silk hat blew off, but he did not stop to recover it, and was soon out of sight. He had evidently reached a state of mind when the best of hats appears to be of no special value.

That evening in camp the general perpetrated a number of jokes at the visitor's expense, saying to him: "Well, you appear to have won that race you entered your horse for this afternoon." "Yes," said the visitor; "I seem to have got in first." "Perhaps," continued the general, "you felt like that soldier in one of our retreats who, when asked by an officer where he was going, said: 'I'm trying to find the rear of this army, but it don't appear to have any.'" "I don't know why it was, but Lee seemed to have some personal grudge against me," remarked the guest. "I think," said the general, "it must have been that high hat which attracted his attention." "Great Scott!" screamed the visitor, springing from his camp-stool as if the enemy had again opened fire on him; "do you know that that hat had a card in it with my name on? Holy smoke!

If the boys get hold of it, and give me away, and the news gets out to the Pacific slope, I 'll be a dead duck in the next political campaign!"

General Grant was now stimulating every one to increased activity in making preparations for the formidable movement he was about to undertake in throwing the army with all its impedimenta across the James. He was fully impressed with its hazardous nature, but was perfectly confident that he could carry it out without encountering extraordinary risks. The army had to be withdrawn so quietly from its position that it would be able to gain a night's march before its absence should be discovered. The fact that the lines were within thirty or forty yards of each other at some points made this an exceedingly delicate task. Roads had to be constructed over the marshes leading to the lower Chickahominy, and bridges thrown over that stream preparatory to crossing. The army was then to move to the James, and cross upon pontoon-bridges and improvised ferries. This would involve a march of about fifty miles in order to reach Butler's position, while Lee, holding interior lines, could arrive there by a march of less than half that distance.

In the afternoon of June 6 the general called Colonel Comstock and me into his tent, asked us to be seated, and said with more impressiveness of manner than he usually manifested: "I want you to undertake an important mission preliminary to moving the army from its present position. I have made up my mind to send Smith's corps by a forced night march to Cole's Landing on the Chickahominy, there to take boats and be transferred to Butler's position at Bermuda Hundred. These troops are to move without their wagons or artillery. Their batteries will accompany the Army of the Potomac. That army will be held in readiness to pull out on short notice, and by rapid marches reach the James River and prepare to cross. I want you to go to Bermuda Hundred, and explain the contemplated movement fully to General Butler, and see that the necessary preparations are made by him to render his position secure against any attack from Lee's forces while the Army of the Potomac is making its movement. You will then select the best point on the river for the crossing, taking into consideration the necessity of choosing a place which will give the Army of the Potomac as short a line of march as practicable, and which will at the same time be far enough down-stream to allow for a sufficient distance between it and the present position of Lee's army to prevent the chances of our being attacked successfully while in the act of crossing. You should be guided also by considerations of the width of the river at the point of crossing, and of the character of the country by which it will have to be approached."

Early the next morning Comstock and I rode rapidly to White House, and then took a steamboat down the Pamunkey and York rivers, and up the James, reaching Butler's headquarters at Bermuda Hundred the next day. After having obtained a knowledge of the topography along the James, and secured the best maps that could be had, we despatched a message to the general and started down the James on the 10th, making further careful reconnaissances of the banks and the approaches on each side. Comstock and I had served on General McClellan's staff when his army occupied the north bank of the James two years before, and the country for many miles along the river was quite familiar to us. This knowledge was of much assistance on the present mission. We returned by the same route by which we had come, and reached headquarters on the 12th. We had noted one or two places on the river which might have served the purpose of crossing; but, all things considered, we reported unhesitatingly in favor of a point familiarly known as Fort Powhatan, about ten miles below City Point, the latter place being at the junction of the James and Appomattox rivers. Several roads led to the point selected for crossing both on the north and the south side of the James, and it was found that they could be made suitable for the passage of wagon-trains by repairing and in some places corduroying them. The principal advantage of the place selected was that it was the narrowest point that could be found on the river below City Point, being twenty-one hundred feet in width from Wilcox's Landing on the north side to Windmill Point on the south side.

General Grant had been anxiously awaiting our return, and had in the mean time made every preparation for withdrawing the army from its present position. On our arrival we went at once to his tent, and were closeted with him for nearly an hour discussing the contemplated operation. While listening to our verbal report and preparing the orders for the movement which was to take place, the general showed the only anxiety and nervousness of manner he had ever manifested on any occasion. After smoking his cigar vigorously for some minutes, he removed it from his mouth, put it on the table, and allowed it to go out; then relighted it, gave a few puffs, and laid it aside again. In giving him the information he desired, we could hardly get the words out of our mouths fast enough to suit him. He kept repeating, "Yes, yes," in a manner which was equivalent to saying, "Go on, go on"; and the numerous questions he asked were uttered with much greater rapidity than usual. This would not have been noticed by persons unfamiliar with his habit; but to us it was evident that he was wrought up to an intensity of thought and action which he seldom displayed. At the close of the interview he informed us that he would begin the movement that night.

The same day on which Comstock and I started from Cold Harbor (June 7), Sheridan had been sent north with two divisions of cavalry to break up the Virginia Central Railroad, and, if practicable, to push west and join General Hunter's force, which was moving down the valley. It was expected that the enemy's cavalry would be compelled to follow Sheridan, and that our large trains would be safe from its attacks during the contemplated movement across the James River. Nothing was left unthought of by the trained mind of the commander who was conducting these formidable operations.

On June 9 a portion of the Army of the Potomac had been set to work fortifying a line to our left and rear on ground overlooking the Chickahominy, under cover of which the army could move down that stream. Boats for making the ferriage of the James had been ordered from all available places. Preparations had been made for bridging necessary points on the Chickahominy, and a large force had been put to work under engineer officers to repair the roads. This day (June 12) was Sunday, but it was by no means a day of rest. All was now ready for the important movement.

General Meade had been untiring in his efforts during this eventful week. He was General Grant's senior by seven years, was older than any of the corps commanders, and was naturally of an excitable temperament, and with the continual annoyances to which he was subjected he not infrequently became quite irritable. He was greatly disturbed at this time by some newspaper reports stating that on the second night of the battle of the Wilderness he had advised a retreat across the

Rapidan; and in talking this matter over with General Grant, his indignation became so great that his wrath knew no bounds. He said that the rumor had been circulated throughout the press, and would be believed by many of the people, and perhaps by the authorities in Washington. Mr. Dana, the Assistant Secretary of War, who was still with the army, was present at the interview, and he and General Grant tried to console Meade by assurances that the story would not be credited, and that they would give a broad contradiction to it. Mr. Dana at once sent a despatch to the Secretary of War, alluding to the rumor, and saying: "This is entirely untrue. He has not shown any weakness of the sort since moving from Culpeper, nor once intimated a doubt as to the successful issue of the campaign." The Secretary replied the next day (June 10), saying: "Please say to General Meade that the lying report alluded to in your telegram was not even for a moment believed by the President or myself. We have the most perfect confidence in him. He could not wish a more exalted estimation of his ability, his firmness, and every quality of a commanding general than is entertained for him." The newspaper correspondent who had been the author of this slander was seized and placed on a horse, with large placards hung upon his breast and back bearing the inscription, "Libeler of the Press," and drummed out of camp. There had never been a moment when Meade had not been in favor of bold and vigorous advances, and he would have been the last man to counsel a retreat.

While at the mess-table taking our last meal before starting upon the march to the James on the evening of the 12th, the conversation turned upon the losses which had occurred and the reinforcements which had been received up to that time. The figures then known did not differ much from those contained in the accurate official reports afterward compiled. From the opening of the campaign, May 4, to the movement across the James, June 12, the total casualties in the Army of the Potomac, including Sheridan's cavalry and Burnside's command, had been: killed, 7621; wounded, 38,339; captured or missing, 8966; total, 54,926. The services of all the men included in these figures were not, however, permanently lost to the army. A number of them were prisoners who were afterward exchanged, and many had been only slightly wounded, and were soon ready for duty again. Some were doubtless counted more than once, as a soldier who was wounded in a battle twice, and afterward killed, may have been counted three times in making up the list of casualties, whereas the army had really lost but one man. The losses of the enemy have never been ascertained. No precise information on the subject has been discovered, and not even a general statement can be made of his casualties. In a few of the battles of this campaign his losses were greater than the losses suffered by the Union troops; in the greater part of the battles they were less. Our reinforcements had amounted to just about the same number as the losses. It was estimated from the best sources of information that Lee had also received reinforcements equal to his losses, so that the armies were now of about the same size as when the campaign began.

All the reinforcements organized in the North and reported as on their way to the front did not reach us. There was a good deal of truth in the remark reported to have been made by Mr. Lincoln: "We get a large body of reinforcements together, and start them to the front; but after deducting the sick, the deserters, the stragglers, and the discharged, the numbers seriously diminish by the time they reach their destination. It 's like trying to shovel fleas across a barnyard; you don't get 'em all there."

General Grant said during the discussion: "I was with General Taylor's command in Mexico when he not only failed to receive reinforcements, but found that nearly all his regulars were to be sent away from him to join General Scott. Taylor was apt to be a little absent-minded when absorbed in any perplexing problem, and the morning he received the discouraging news he sat down to breakfast in a brown study, poured out a cup of coffee, and instead of putting in the sugar, he reached out and got hold of the mustard-pot, and stirred half a dozen spoonfuls of its contents into the coffee. He did n't realize what he had done till he took a mouthful, and then he broke out in a towering rage.

"We learned something at Shiloh about the way in which the reports of losses are sometimes exaggerated in battle. At the close of the first day's fight Sherman met a colonel of one of his regiments with only about a hundred of his soldiers in ranks, and said to him, 'Why, where are your men?' The colonel cast his eyes sadly along the line, wiped a tear from his cheek, and replied in a whimpering voice: 'We went in eight hundred strong, and that's all that's left of us.' 'You don't tell me!' exclaimed Sherman, beginning to be deeply affected by the fearful result of the carnage. 'Yes,' said the colonel; 'the rebs appeared to have a special spite against us.' Sherman passed along some hours afterward, when the commissary was issuing rations, and found that the colonel's men were returning on the run from under the bank of the river, where they had taken shelter from the firing; and in a few minutes nearly all of the lost seven hundred had rejoined, and were boiling coffee and eating a hearty meal with an appetite that showed they were still very much alive."

CHAPTER XIII

THE START FOR THE JAMES — GRANT'S SECRETIVENESS — STEALING A MARCH ON THE ENEMY — THE PASSAGE OF THE JAMES — A BRILLIANT SPECTACLE — GENERAL W. F. SMITH'S ATTACK ON PETERSBURG — DONNING SUMMER UNIFORM

AT dark on the evening of June 12 the famous march to the James began. General Grant had acted with his usual secrecy in regard to important movements, and had spoken of his detailed plans to only a few officers upon whose reticence he could rely implicitly, and whom he was compelled to take into his secret in order to make the necessary preparations. The orders for the movement were delivered to commanders in the strictest confidence. Smith's corps began its march that night to White House, its destination having been changed from Coles's Landing on the Chickahominy; and on its arrival it embarked for Bermuda Hundred, the position occupied by Butler in the angle between the James River and the Appomattox. A portion of Wilson's division of cavalry which had not accompanied Sheridan pushed forward to Long Bridge on the Chickahominy, fifteen miles below Cold Harbor. All the bridges on that river had been destroyed, and the cavalry had to dismount and wade across the muddy stream under great difficulty; but they soon succeeded in reaching the opposite bank in sufficient numbers to drive

áway the enemy's cavalry pickets. A pontoon-bridge
was then rapidly constructed. Warren had kept close
to the cavalry, and on the morning of the 13th his whole
corps had crossed the bridge. Hancock's corps followed.
Burnside set out on the road to Jones's Bridge, twenty
miles below Cold Harbor, and was followed by Wright.
Cavalry covered the rear. Warren moved out some distance on the Long Bridge road, so as to watch the routes
leading toward Richmond and hold the bridge across
the White Oak Swamp. He was to make demonstrations which were intended to deceive Lee and give him
the impression that our army was turning his right with
the intention of either moving upon Richmond or crossing the James above City Point. How completely successful this movement was in confusing the enemy will
be seen later.

General Grant started from his camp near Old Cold
Harbor on the night of June 12. Although there was
moonlight, the dust rose in such dense clouds that it
was difficult to see more than a short distance, and the
march was exceedingly tedious and uncomfortable. The
artillerymen would at times have to walk ahead of the
battery horses, and locate the small bridges along the
road by feeling for them.

After the general had got some miles out on the march
from Cold Harbor, an officer of rank joined him, and as
they rode along began to explain a plan which he had
sketched, providing for the construction of another line
of intrenchments, some distance in rear of the lines then
held by us, to be used in case the army should at any
time want to fall back and move toward the James, and
should be attacked while withdrawing. The general
kept on smoking his cigar, listened to the proposition
for a time, and then quietly remarked to the astonished
officer: "The army has already pulled out from the

enemy's front, and is now on its march to the James." This is mentioned as an instance of how well his secrets could be kept. He had never been a secretive man until the positions of responsibility in which he was placed compelled him to be chary in giving expression to his opinions and purposes. He then learned the force of the philosopher's maxim that "the unspoken word is a sword in the scabbard, while the spoken word is a sword in the hand of one's enemy." In the field there were constant visitors to the camp, ready to circulate carelessly any intimations of the commander's movements, at the risk of having such valuable information reach the enemy. Any encouraging expression given to an applicant for favors was apt to be tortured into a promise, and the general naturally became guarded in his intercourse. When questioned beyond the bounds of propriety, his lips closed like a vise, and the obtruding party was left to supply all the subsequent conversation. These circumstances proclaimed him a man who studied to be uncommunicative, and gave him a reputation for reserve which could not fairly be attributed to him. He was called the "American Sphinx," "Ulysses the Silent," and the "Great Unspeakable," and was popularly supposed to move about with sealed lips. It is true that he had no "small talk" introduced merely for the sake of talking, and many a one will recollect the embarrassment of a first encounter with him resulting from this fact; but while, like Shakspere's soldier, he never wore his dagger in his mouth, yet in talking to a small circle of friends upon matters to which he had given special consideration, his conversation was so thoughtful, philosophical, and original that he fascinated all who listened to him.

The next morning (June 13) the general made a halt at Long Bridge, where the head of Hancock's corps had arrived, and where he could be near Warren's movement and communicate promptly with him. That evening he reached Wilcox's Landing, and went into camp on the north bank of the James, at the point where the crossing was to take place.

Hancock's corps made a forced march, and reached the river at Wilcox's Landing on the afternoon of June 13. Wright's and Burnside's corps arrived there the next day. Warren's corps withdrew on the night of the 13th from the position to which it had advanced, and reached the James on the afternoon of the 14th. The several corps had moved by forced marches over distances of from twenty-five to fifty-five miles, and the effect of the heat and dust, and the necessity of every man's carrying an ample supply of ammunition and rations, rendered the marches fatiguing in the extreme.

Although the army started on the night of the 12th, it was not until the next morning that Lee had any knowledge of the fact, and even then he wholly misunderstood the movement. He telegraphed to Richmond at 10 P. M. on the 13th: "At daybreak this morning it was discovered that the army of General Grant had left our front. Our skirmishers were advanced between one and two miles, but failing to discover the enemy, were withdrawn, and the army was moved to conform to the route taken by him. . . ." It will be seen from this that Lee was occupied with Warren's advance directly toward Richmond, and made his army conform to this route, while Grant, with the bulk of his forces, was marching in an entirely different direction. On the 14th General Grant took a small steamer and ran up the river to Bermuda Hundred, to have a personal interview with General Butler and arrange plans for his forces to move out at once and make an attack

upon Petersburg. Grant knew now that he had stolen
a march on Lee, and that Petersburg was almost undefended; and with his usual fondness for taking the
offensive, he was anxious to hasten the movement
which he had had in contemplation against that place,
to be begun before the Army of the Potomac should
arrive. His instructions were that as soon as Smith's
troops reached their destination they should be reinforced by as many men as could be spared from Butler's
troops,—about 6000,—and move at once against Petersburg. General Grant returned to Wilcox's Landing at
1 P. M. He had sent a despatch from Bermuda Hundred to Washington, giving briefly the situation of the
army and the progress of the movement. That afternoon reports were received showing pretty definitely
Lee's present position; for Grant, with the energy and
system which he never failed to employ in securing
prompt information regarding his opponent's movements, had had Lee's operations closely watched.

The work of laying the great pontoon-bridge across
the James began after 4 P. M. on June 14, and was finished by eleven o'clock that night. It was twenty-one
hundred feet in length, and required one hundred and
one pontoons. The pontoons, which were in the channel of the river, where the water was swift and deep,
were attached to vessels that were anchored above and
below for this purpose. Admiral Lee's fleet took position in the river, and assisted in covering the passage
of the troops. Hancock began to move his corps on
ferry-boats on the 14th, and before daylight on the
morning of the 15th his entire infantry had been transferred to the south side of the James, with four batteries of artillery. By 6:30 A. M. three ferry-boats had
been added to the number in use, which greatly facil-
itated the passage of his wagons and artillery. Butler

had been ordered to send sixty thousand rations to Hancock that morning. Hancock waited for them till eleven o'clock, and then started for Petersburg without them. General Grant now received the following answer to his despatch of the day before to the President: "I begin to see it. You will succeed. God bless you all. A. LINCOLN."

By midnight of the 16th the army, with all its artillery and trains, had been safely transferred to the south side of the James without a serious accident or the loss of a wagon or an animal, and with no casualties except those which occurred in the minor encounters of Warren's corps and the cavalry with the enemy. This memorable operation, when examined in all its details, will furnish one of the most valuable and instructive studies in logistics.

As the general-in-chief stood upon the bluff on the north bank of the river on the morning of June 15, watching with unusual interest the busy scene spread out before him, it presented a sight which had never been equaled even in his extended experience in all the varied phases of warfare. His cigar had been thrown aside, his hands were clasped behind him, and he seemed lost in the contemplation of the spectacle. The great bridge was the scene of a continuous movement of infantry columns, batteries of artillery, and wagon-trains. The approaches to the river on both banks were covered with masses of troops moving briskly to their positions or waiting patiently their turn to cross. At the two improvised ferries steamboats were gliding back and forth with the regularity of weavers' shuttles. A fleet of transports covered the surface of the water below the bridge, and gunboats floated lazily upon the stream, guarding the river above. Drums were beating the march, bands were playing stirring quicksteps, the

distant booming of cannon on Warren's front showed
that he and the enemy were still exchanging compli-
ments; and mingled with these sounds were the cheers
of the sailors, the shouting of the troops, the rumbling
of wheels, and the shrieks of steam-whistles. The
bright sun, shining through a clear sky upon the scene,
cast its sheen upon the water, was reflected from the
burnished gun-barrels and glittering cannon, and
brought out with increased brilliancy the gay colors of
the waving banners. The calmly flowing river reflected
the blue of the heavens, and mirrored on its surface the
beauties of nature that bordered it. The rich grain
was standing high in the surrounding fields. The har-
vest was almost ripe, but the harvesters had fled. The
arts of civilization had recoiled before the science of
destruction; and in looking from the growing crops to
the marching columns, the gentle smile of peace con-
trasted strangely with the savage frown of war. It was
a matchless pageant that could not fail to inspire all
beholders with the grandeur of achievement and the
majesty of military power. The man whose genius had
conceived and whose skill had executed this masterly
movement stood watching the spectacle in profound
silence. Whether his mind was occupied with the contemplation of its magnitude and success, or was busied
with maturing plans for the future, no one can tell.
After a time he woke from his reverie, mounted his
horse, and gave orders to have headquarters ferried
across to the south bank of the river. On arriving
there, he set out for City Point; but he had ridden only
a short distance when a small steamer came along, and
as he wished to reach City Point as quickly as possible
to direct operations from there, he decided to go aboard
the boat. It was hailed, and took him on, with Parker
and a couple of other staff-officers. The rest of us

went by land, so as to take some instructions to Hancock's corps and to familiarize ourselves with that part of the country.

Upon reaching City Point, headquarters were established on a high bluff at the junction of the James and the Appomattox rivers. I have said that the passage of the James had been effected without the loss of an animal. A proper regard for strict veracity requires a modification of the statement. The headquarters mess had procured a Virginia cow, the rich milk of which went far toward compensating for the shortcomings in other supplies. While preparing to ferry across the river, the cow was tied to a tree to prevent her from turning deserter, and in the hurry of embarking was entirely forgotten. The mess felt the loss keenly until another animal was procured. That evening at the dinner-table, when reference was made to the incident, the general said: " Well, it seems that the loss of animals in this movement falls most heavily upon headquarters."

General William F. Smith had disembarked his troops at Bermuda Hundred during the preceding night (the 14th), had started immediately upon his movement against Petersburg, and had struck the Confederate pickets the next morning, June 15. The enemy was protected by a line of rifle-pits and heavy thickets. After some hard fighting he was driven from his position; our troops then moved forward, and by half-past one o'clock arrived at a point from which it was thought that an assault could be made upon the intrenchments. Reconnaissances were made during the afternoon, and finally Smith decided that a direct assault would be too hazardous, and at half-past seven o'clock threw forward his troops in strong skirmish-lines. After a short struggle the enemy was forced back from his intrenchments in front of our center and left, and Smith's second line then made an attack upon the rest of the works. The Confederates were now driven back at all points, four guns were taken and turned upon the retreating troops, the line of intrenchments was carried, and three hundred prisoners and sixteen pieces of artillery captured. Instead of following up this advantage with his whole force in an attempt to seize the city, Smith made no further advance. Staff-officers from Grant had reached Smith at four o'clock, saying that Hancock was marching toward him. The head of Hancock's troops reached a point a mile in the rear of Hinks's division of Smith's command about half-past six, and two divisions of Hancock's corps were ordered to push on and coöperate in the pending movement. Night soon after set in, and Smith contented himself with having two divisions of Hancock's corps occupy the works which had been captured. Reinforcements from Lee's army were now arriving in Smith's front. General Grant's belief regarding the inferior force in Petersburg proved to be entirely correct. While the works were well supplied with artillery, about the only available troops to defend them were Wise's brigade of 2500 men, and Deering's cavalry of 2000. Besides this force there was only the local militia, composed of old men and young boys, who had never seen active service.

The general-in-chief had used all the arts of which he was master in preparing and conducting this memorable movement across the James, which was beset at all points by innumerable difficulties. He had thrown nearly 16,000 troops against Petersburg before Lee had sent a single reinforcement there, and had moved them by transports so that they might not arrive exhausted by a long march. With a perfect knowledge of Lee's movements, Grant had brought the advance of his army in front of Petersburg on the 15th, while Lee was still groping about to discover his opponent's movements. In reaching this point, Grant had marched more than twice the distance of Lee's route, and had crossed two rivers, one a most formidable obstacle. In commenting in his "Memoirs" (Vol. II., page 186) on this movement, he says: "I believed then, and still believe, that Petersburg could have been easily captured at that time."

The weather had become so warm that the general and most of the staff had ordered thin, dark-blue flannel blouses to be sent to them to take the place of the heavy uniform coats which they had been wearing. The summer clothing had arrived, and was now tried on. The general's blouse, like the others, was of plain material, single-breasted, and had four regulation brass buttons in front. It was substantially the coat of a private soldier, with nothing to indicate the rank of an officer except the three gold stars of a lieutenant-general on the shoulder-straps. He wore at this time a turn-down white linen collar and a small, black "butterfly" cravat, which was hooked on to his front collar-button. The general, when he put on the blouse, did not take the pains to see whether it fitted him or to notice how it looked, but thought only of the comfort it afforded, and said, "Well, this is a relief," and then added: "I have never taken as much satisfaction as some people in making frequent changes in my outer clothing. I like to put on a suit of clothes when I get up in the morning, and wear it until I go to bed, unless I have to make a change in my dress to meet company. I have been in the habit of getting one coat at a time, putting it on and wearing it every day as long as it looked respectable, instead of using a best and a second best. I know that is not the right way to manage, but a comfortable coat seems like an old friend, and I don't like

to change it." The general had also received a pair of
light, neatly fitting calfskin boots, to which he seemed
to take a fancy; thereafter he wore them most of the
time in place of his heavy top-boots, putting on the
latter only when he rode out in wet weather.

CHAPTER XIV

PETERSBURG — LEE MYSTIFIED AS TO GRANT'S MOVEMENTS
— A CHANGE OF COMPLEXION — MEADE IN ACTION —
CONDITION OF THE ARMY — GRANT'S CAMP AT CITY
POINT — GRANT AT THE MESS-TABLE

ON the morning of June 16 General Grant went to the Petersburg front. He was accompanied by most of his staff, and by Mr. Dana, Assistant Secretary of War. The enemy was then constantly arriving and occupying his intrenchments in strong force. Burnside's corps had just come up, and was put in position on Hancock's left. At 10:15 A. M. Grant sent an order to Meade to hurry Warren forward, and start up the river himself by steamer and take command in person at Petersburg.

The enemy's intrenchments which protected Petersburg were well located, and were in some places strong. They started at a point on the south bank of the Appomattox, about a mile from the eastern outskirts of the city, and extended in the form of a semicircle to a point on the river at about the same distance from the western limits of the city. Petersburg had at that time a population of 18,000, and was called the "Cockade City" from the fact that at the breaking out of the war of 1812 it furnished a company which was peculiarly uniformed and in which each man wore in his hat a conspicuous cockade.

The probability of Lee's attacking Bermuda Hundred

in force induced General Grant to return to City Point
to direct the movements on Butler's lines. While riding
in that direction he met Meade hurrying forward from
the steamer-landing. In a short interview, and without dismounting from his horse, he instructed that officer to move at once to the front and make a vigorous
attack upon the works at Petersburg at six o'clock in
the evening, and drive the enemy, if possible, across the
Appomattox. It was discovered before that hour that
the enemy was advancing upon Butler's front, and
General Grant directed me to ride at full speed to
Meade and tell him that this made it still more important that his attack should be a vigorous one, and that
the enemy might be found weaker there on account of
troops having been collected at Bermuda Hundred. I
found Meade standing near the edge of a piece of woods,
surrounded by some of his staff, and actively engaged
in superintending the attack, which was then in progress. His usual nervous energy was displayed in the
intensity of his manner and the rapid and animated
style of his conversation. He assured me that no additional orders could be given which could add to the
vigor of the attack. He was acting with great earnestness, and doing his utmost to carry out the instructions
which he had received. He had arrived at the front
about two o'clock, and his plans had been as well matured as possible for the movement. Three redans, as
well as a line of earthworks connecting them, were captured. The enemy felt the loss keenly, and made several desperate attempts during the night to recover the
ground, but in this he did not succeed.

When I got back to City Point that evening General
Grant felt considerably encouraged by the news brought
him, and spent most of the night in planning movements for the next day.

After further consultation with the general-in-chief I started again for the front at Petersburg before dawn on the 17th, carrying instructions looking to the contemplated attacks that day. Burnside's troops surprised the enemy at daybreak by making a sudden rush upon his works, captured his intrenchments, swept his line for a mile, and took 600 prisoners, a stand of colors, 4 guns, and 1500 stands of small arms. Attacks were also made by Hancock and Warren, and more of the enemy's line was captured, but not permanently held.

Telegrams sent by General Lee on June 17 show how completely mystified he was, even at that late day, in regard to Grant's movements. At 12 M. he sent a despatch to Beauregard, saying: "Until I can get more definite information of Grant's movements, I do not think it prudent to draw more troops to this side of the river." At 1:45 P. M. he telegraphed: "Warren's corps crossed the Chickahominy at Long Bridge on the 13th; . . . that night it marched to Westover. Some prisoners were taken from it on the 14th; have not heard of it since." At 4:30 he sent Beauregard another despatch, saying: "Have no information of Grant's crossing the James River, but upon your report have ordered troops up to Chaffin's Bluff." Grant, on the contrary, had ascertained from watchers on Butler's tall signal-tower, which had been erected at Bermuda Hundred, just how many railway-trains with troops had passed toward Petersburg, and learned from the columns of dust that large forces were marching south. From scouts, prisoners, and refugees he had secured each day a close knowledge of Lee's movements.

Colonel Parker, the Indian, had been diligently employed in these busy days helping to take care of General Grant's correspondence. He wrote an excellent hand, and as one of the military secretaries often overhauled the general's correspondence and prepared answers to his private letters. This evening he was seated at the writing-table in the general's tent, while his chief was standing at a little distance outside talking with some of the staff. A citizen who had come to City Point in the employ of the Sanitary Commission, and who had been at Cairo when the general took command there in 1861, approached the group and inquired: "Where is the old man's tent? I'd like to get a look at him; have n't seen him for three years." Rawlins, to avoid being interrupted, said, "That's his tent," at the same time pointing to it. The man stepped over to the tent, looked in, and saw the swarthy features of Parker as he sat in the general's chair. The visitor seemed a little puzzled, and as he walked away was heard to remark: "Yes, that's him; but he's got all-fired sunburnt since I last had a look at him." The general was greatly amused by the incident, and repeated the remark afterward to Parker, who enjoyed it as much as the others.

At daylight on the 18th Meade's troops advanced to the assault which had been ordered, but made the discovery that the enemy's line of the day before had been abandoned. By the time new formations could be made Lee's army had arrived in large force, great activity had been displayed in strengthening the fortifications, and the difficulties of the attacking party had been greatly increased. The Second Corps was temporarily commanded by D. B. Birney, as Hancock's Gettysburg wound had broken out afresh the day before, entirely disabling him. Gallant assaults were repeatedly made by Burnside, Warren, and Birney; and while they did not succeed in the object of carrying the enemy's main line of fortifications, positions were gained closer to his works, and these were held and strongly intrenched.

Both of the opposing lines on this part of the ground were now strengthened, and remained substantially the same in position from that time until the capture of Petersburg.

General Grant realized the nature of the ground and the circumstances that prevented the troops from accomplishing more than had been done, and he complimented Meade upon the promptness and vigor with which he had handled his army on this day of active operations. Indeed, Meade had shown brilliant qualities as commander of a large army, and under the general directions given him had made all the dispositions and issued all the detailed orders. Grant felt it necessary to remain at City Point in order to be in communication with both Meade and Butler, as Lee's troops were that day moving rapidly south past Butler's front.

My duties kept me on Meade's front a large part of the day. He showed himself the personification of earnest, vigorous action in rousing his subordinate commanders to superior exertions. Even his fits of anger and his resort to intemperate language stood him at times in good stead in spurring on every one upon that active field. He sent ringing despatches to all points of the line, and paced up and down upon the field in his nervous, restless manner, as he watched the progress of the operations and made running comments on the actions of his subordinates. His aquiline nose and piercing eyes gave him something of the eagle's look, and added to the interest of his personality. He had much to try him upon this occasion, and if he was severe in his reprimands and showed faults of temper, he certainly displayed no faults as a commander. When the battle was over no one was more ready to make amends for the instances in which he felt that he might have done injustice to his subordinates. He said to them: " Sorry

to hear you cannot carry the works. Get the best line
you can and be prepared to hold it. I suppose you
cannot make any more attacks, and I feel satisfied all
has been done that can be done." Lee himself did not
arrive at Petersburg until noon that day.

After I had returned to headquarters that evening,
and had given the general-in-chief reports of the battle
in more detail than he had received them by despatches
during the day, he sat in his tent and discussed the situation philosophically, saying: "Lee's whole army has
now arrived, and the topography of the country about
Petersburg has been well taken advantage of by the
enemy in the location of strong works. I will make no
more assaults on that portion of the line, but will give
the men a rest, and then look to extensions toward our
left, with a view to destroying Lee's communications on
the south and confining him to a close siege." At ten
o'clock he turned to his table and wrote the following
message to Meade: "I am perfectly satisfied that all has
been done that could be done, and that the assaults of
to-day were called for by all the appearances and information that could be obtained. Now we will rest the
men, and use the spade for their protection until a new
vein can be struck. . . ."

It was apparent in the recent engagements that the men
had not attacked with the same vigor that they had displayed in the Wilderness campaign; but this was owing
more to the change in their physical than in their moral
condition. They had moved incessantly both day and
night, and had been engaged in skirmishing or in giving
battle from the 4th of May to the 18th of June. They had
seen their veteran comrades fall on every side, and their
places filled by inexperienced recruits, and many of the
officers in whom they had unshaken confidence had been
killed or wounded. Officers had been in the saddle day

and night, securing snatches of sleep for a few hours at a time as best they could. Sleeping on horseback had become an art, and experienced riders had learned to brace themselves in their saddles, rest their hands on the pommel, and catch many a cat-nap while riding. These snatches of sleep were of short duration and accomplished under many difficulties, but often proved more refreshing than might be supposed.

There was considerable suffering from sickness in many of the camps. It may be said that the enemy had suffered equally from the same causes that impaired the efficiency of our men, but there was a vast difference between the conditions of the two armies. The enemy had been engaged principally in defending strong intrenchments and in making short marches; he was accustomed to the Southern climate, and was buoyed up with the feeling that he was defending his home and fireside.

A controversy had arisen as to the cause of Hancock's not reaching Petersburg earlier on the 15th. Hancock conceived the idea that the circumstances might be construed as a reproach upon him, and he asked for an official investigation; but General Grant had no intention of reflecting either upon him or Meade. He assured them that, in his judgment, no investigation was necessary. He recommended them both for promotion to the grade of major-general in the regular army, and each was appointed to that rank.

The headquarters camp at City Point was destined to become historic and to be the scene of some of the most memorable events of the war. It was located at the junction of the James and the Appomattox rivers, and was within easy water communication with Fort Monroe and Washington, as well as with Butler's army, which was to occupy positions on both sides of the upper James. The City Point Railroad was repaired, and a branch was constructed to points south of Petersburg, immediately in rear of the line held by the Army of the Potomac, so that there might be convenient communication with that army. The new portion of the road was built, like most of our military railroads, upon the natural surface of the ground, with but little attempt at grading. It ran up hill and down dale, and its undulations were so marked that a train moving along it looked in the distance like a fly crawling over a corrugated washboard. At City Point there was a level piece of ground on a high bluff, on which stood a comfortable house. This building was assigned to the chief quartermaster, and General Grant's headquarters camp was established on the lawn. The tents occupied a line a little over a hundred feet back from the edge of the bluff. In the middle of the line were General Grant's quarters. A hospital tent was used as his office, while a smaller tent connecting in the rear was occupied as his sleeping-apartment. A hospital tent-fly was stretched in front of the office tent so as to make a shaded space in which persons could sit. A rustic bench and a number of folding camp-chairs with backs were placed there, and it was beneath this tent-fly that most of the important official interviews were held. When great secrecy was to be observed the parties would retire to the office tent. On both sides of the general's quarters were pitched close together enough officers' tents to accommodate the staff. Each tent was occupied by two officers. The mess-tent was pitched in the rear, and at a short distance still farther back a temporary shelter was prepared for the horses. A wooden staircase was built reaching from headquarters to the steamboat-landing at the foot of the bluff; ample wharves, storehouses, and hospitals were rapidly constructed, and a commodious base of supplies was established in the vicinity. The day the wharf was completed and planked over the general took a stroll along it, his hands thrust in his trousers pockets, and a lighted cigar in his mouth. He had recently issued instructions to take every precaution against fire, and had not gone far when a sentinel called out: " It 's against orders to come on the wharf with a lighted cigar." The general at once took his Havana out of his mouth and threw it into the river, saying: " I don't like to lose my smoke, but the sentinel 's right. He evidently is n't going to let me disobey my own orders."

Each staff-officer took his turn in acting as " caterer " of the mess, usually for a month at a time. His duties consisted in giving general directions to the steward as to ordering the meals, keeping an account of the bills, and at the end of his tour dividing up the expenses and collecting the amount charged to each officer. General Grant insisted upon paying two shares of the expenses instead of one, upon the ground that he invited more guests to meals than any one else in the mess, although this was not always the case, for each officer was allowed to entertain guests, and there were at times as many visitors at table as members of the mess. The officer acting as caterer sat at the head of the mess-table, with the general on his right.

It now came my turn to take a hand in managing the affairs of the mess. The general, while he never complained, was still the most difficult person to cater for in the whole army. About the only meat he enjoyed was beef, and this he could not eat unless it was so thoroughly well done that no appearance of blood could be seen. If blood appeared in any meat which came on the table, the sight of it seemed entirely to destroy his appetite. (This was the man

whose enemies delighted in calling him a butcher.)
He enjoyed oysters and fruit, but these could not be
procured on an active campaign. He never ate mutton
when he could obtain anything else, and fowl and game
he abhorred. As he used to express it: " I never could
eat anything that goes on two legs." Evidently he
could never have been converted to cannabalism. He
did not miss much by declining to eat the chickens
which were picked up on a campaign, for they were
usually tough enough to create the suspicion that they
had been hatched from hard-boiled eggs, and were so
impenetrable that an officer said of one of them that he
could not even stick his fork through the gravy. The
general was fonder of cucumbers than of anything else,
and often made his entire meal upon a sliced cucumber
and a cup of coffee. He always enjoyed corn, pork and
beans, and buckwheat cakes. In fact, he seemed to be
particularly fond of only the most indigestible dishes.
He had been eating so little for several days just before
I took my turn as caterer that I looked about to try to
find some delicacy that would tempt his appetite, and
after a good deal of pains succeeded in getting some
sweetbreads sent down from Washington. They had
been nicely cooked, and I announced them, when they
came on the table, with an air of ill-disguised triumph;
but he said: " I hope these were not obtained especially
for me, for I have a singular aversion to them. In my
young days I used to eat them, not knowing exactly
what part of the animal they came from; but as soon
as I learned what they were my stomach rebelled
against them, and I have never tasted them since."

When any fruit could be procured, it was placed on
the table by way of helping to ornament it, and afterward used as dessert. Between the courses of the dinner
the general would often reach over to the dish of fruit and

pick out a berry or a cherry and eat it slowly. He used to do this in a sly way, like a child helping itself to some forbidden dish at the table, and afraid of being caught in the act. He said one day: "I suppose I ought not to eat a course out of its turn, but I take the greatest delight in picking out bits of fruit and eating them during a meal. One of the reasons I do not enjoy dining out as much as I do at home is because I am compelled to sit through a long list of courses, few of which I eat, and to resist the constant temptation to taste a little fruit in the meanwhile to help pass away the time." Napoleon was famous for eating out of the various dishes before him with his fingers. General Grant's use of the fingers never went beyond picking out small fruits. He was always refined in his manners at table, and no matter how great was the hurry, or what were the circumstances of the occasion, he never violated the requirements of true politeness.

He ate less than any man in the army; sometimes the amount of food taken did not seem enough to keep a bird alive, and his meals were frugal enough to satisfy the tastes of the most avowed anchorite. It so happened that no one in the mess had any inclination to drink wine or spirits at meals, and none was carried among the mess's supplies. The only beverage ever used at table besides tea and coffee was water, although on the march it was often taken from places which rendered it not the most palatable or healthful of drinks. If a staff-officer wanted anything stronger he would carry some commissary whisky in a canteen. Upon a few occasions, after a hard day's ride in stormy weather, the general joined the officers of the staff in taking a whisky toddy in the evening. He never offered liquor of any kind to visitors at headquarters. His hospitality consisted in inviting them to meals and to smoke cigars.

CHAPTER XV

ON June 21 Butler had thrown a pontoon-bridge
across the James, and seized a position on the
north side known as Deep Bottom, ten miles below
Richmond. General Grant had directed this with a
view to divide the attention of the enemy's troops, and
to confuse them as to whether to expect an attack upon
Richmond or Petersburg, and because he had in contemplation some operations on the north side of the
James, which he intended to carry out under certain
contingencies, in which case the occupation of Deep
Bottom might become important.

On Tuesday, June 21, a white river-steamer arrived
at the wharf, bringing President Lincoln, who had embraced this opportunity to visit for the first time the
armies under General Grant's immediate command.
As the boat neared the shore, the general and several
of us who were with him at the time walked down to
the wharf, in order that the general-in-chief might meet
his distinguished visitor and extend a greeting to him
as soon as the boat made the landing. As our party

stepped aboard, the President came down from the upper deck, where he had been standing, to the after-gangway, and reaching out his long, angular arm, he wrung General Grant's hand vigorously, and held it in his for some time, while he uttered in rapid words his congratulations and expressions of appreciation of the great task which had been accomplished since he and the general had parted in Washington. The group then went into the after-cabin. General Grant said: "I hope you are very well, Mr. President." "Yes, I am in very good health," Mr. Lincoln replied; "but I don't feel very comfortable after my trip last night on the bay. It was rough, and I was considerably shaken up. My stomach has not yet entirely recovered from the effects." An officer of the party now saw that an opportunity had arisen to make this scene the supreme moment of his life, in giving him a chance to soothe the digestive organs of the Chief Magistrate of the nation. He said: "Try a glass of champagne, Mr. President. That is always a certain cure for seasickness." Mr. Lincoln looked at him for a moment, his face lighting up with a smile, and then remarked: " No, my friend; I have seen too many fellows seasick ashore from drinking that very stuff." This was a knockdown for the officer, and in the laugh at his expense Mr. Lincoln and the general both joined heartily.

General Grant now said: " I know it would be a great satisfaction for the troops to have an opportunity of seeing you, Mr. President; and I am sure your presence among them would have a very gratifying effect. I can furnish you a good horse, and will be most happy to escort you to points of interest along the line." Mr. Lincoln replied: "Why, yes; I had fully intended to go out and take a look at the brave fellows who have fought their way down to Petersburg in this wonderful campaign, and I am ready to start at any time."

General Grant presented to Mr. Lincoln the officers
of the staff who were present, and he had for each one
a cordial greeting and a pleasant word. There was a
kindliness in his tone and a hearty manner of expression which went far to captivate all who met him. The
President soon stepped ashore, and after sitting awhile
at headquarters mounted the large bay horse "Cincinnati," while the general rode with him on "Jeff Davis."
Three of us of the staff accompanied them, and the
scenes encountered in visiting both Butler's and Meade's
commands were most interesting. Mr. Lincoln wore a
very high black silk hat and black trousers and frock-
coat. Like most men who had been brought up in the
West, he had good command of a horse, but it must be
acknowledged that in appearance he was not a very
dashing rider. On this occasion, by the time he had
reached the troops he was completely covered with dust,
and the black color of his clothes had changed to Confederate gray. As he had no straps, his trousers gradually worked up above his ankles, and gave him the appearance of a country farmer riding into town wearing
his Sunday clothes. A citizen on horseback is always
an odd sight in the midst of a uniformed army, and the
picture presented by the President bordered upon the
grotesque. However, the troops were so lost in admiration of the man that the humorous aspect did not
seem to strike them. The soldiers rapidly passed the
word along the line that "Uncle Abe" had joined them,
and cheers broke forth from all the commands, and enthusiastic shouts and even words of familiar greeting
met him on all sides. After a while General Grant said:
"Mr. President, let us ride on and see the colored
troops, who behaved so handsomely in Smith's attack
on the works in front of Petersburg last week." "Oh,
yes," replied Mr. Lincoln; "I want to take a look at

those boys. I read with the greatest delight the account given in Mr. Dana's despatch to the Secretary of War of how gallantly they behaved. He said they took six out of the sixteen guns captured that day. I was opposed on nearly every side when I first favored the raising of colored regiments; but they have proved their efficiency, and I am glad they have kept pace with the white troops in the recent assaults. When we wanted every able-bodied man who could be spared to go to the front, and my opposers kept objecting to the negroes, I used to tell them that at such times it was just as well to be a little color-blind. I think, general, we can say of the black boys what a country fellow who was an old-time abolitionist in Illinois said when he went to a theater in Chicago and saw Forrest playing *Othello*. He was not very well up in Shakspere, and did n't know that the tragedian was a white man who had blacked up for the purpose. After the play was over the folks who had invited him to go to the show wanted to know what he thought of the actors, and he said: 'Waal, layin' aside all sectional prejudices and any partiality I may have for the race, derned ef I don't think the nigger held his own with any on 'em.'" The Western dialect employed in this story was perfect.

The camp of the colored troops of the Eighteenth Corps was soon reached, and a scene now occurred which defies description. They beheld for the first time the liberator of their race — the man who by a stroke of his pen had struck the shackles from the limbs of their fellow-bondmen and proclaimed liberty to the enslaved. Always impressionable, the enthusiasm of the blacks now knew no limits. They cheered, laughed, cried, sang hymns of praise, and shouted in their negro dialect, "God bress Massa Linkum!" "De Lord save Fader Abraham!" "De day ob jubilee am come, shuah."

They crowded about him and fondled his horse; some of them kissed his hands, while others ran off crying in triumph to their comrades that they had touched his clothes. The President rode with bared head; the tears had started to his eyes, and his voice was so broken by emotion that he could scarcely articulate the words of thanks and congratulation which he tried to speak to the humble and devoted men through whose ranks he rode. The scene was affecting in the extreme, and no one could have witnessed it unmoved.

In the evening Mr. Lincoln gathered with General Grant and the staff in front of the general's tent, and then we had an opportunity of appreciating his charm as a talker, and hearing some of the stories for which he had become celebrated. He did not tell a story merely for the sake of the anecdote, but to point a moral or to clench a fact. So far as our experience went, his anecdotes possessed the true geometric requisite of excellence: they were neither too broad nor too long. He seemed to recollect every incident in his experience and to weave it into material for his stories. One evening a sentinel whose post was near enough to enable him to catch most of the President's remarks was heard to say, " Well, that man 's got a powerful memory and a mighty poor forgettery."

He seldom indulged even in a smile until he reached the climax of a humorous narration; then he joined heartily with the listeners in the laugh which followed. He usually sat on a low camp-chair, and wound his legs around each other as if in an effort to get them out of the way, and with his long arms he accompanied what he said with all sorts of odd gestures. An officer once made the remark that he would rather have a single photograph of one of Mr. Lincoln's jokes than own the negative of any other man's. In the course of the conversation that evening he spoke of the improvement in arms and ammunition, and of the new powder prepared for the fifteen-inch guns. He said he had never seen the latter article, but he understood it differed very much from any other powder that had ever been used. I told him that I happened to have in my tent a specimen which had been sent to headquarters as a curiosity, and that I would bring it to him. When I returned with a grain of the powder about the size of a walnut, he took it, turned it over in his hand, and after examining it carefully, said: "Well, it 's rather larger than the powder we used to buy in my shooting days. It reminds me of what occurred once in a country meeting-house in Sangamon County. You see, there were very few newspapers then, and the country storekeepers had to resort to some other means of advertising their wares. If, for instance, the preacher happened to be late in coming to a prayer-meeting of an evening, the shopkeepers would often put in the time while the people were waiting by notifying them of any new arrival of an attractive line of goods. One evening a man rose up and said: 'Brethren, let me take occasion to say, while we 're a-waitin', that I have jest received a new inv'ice of sportin' powder. The grains are so small you kin sca'cely see 'em with the naked eye, and polished up so fine you kin stand up and comb yer ha'r in front of one o' them grains jest like it was a lookin'-glass. Hope you 'll come down to my store at the cross-roads and examine that powder for yourselves.' When he had got about this far a rival powder-merchant in the meeting, who had been boiling over with indignation at the amount of advertising the opposition powder was getting, jumped up and cried out: 'Brethren, I hope you 'll not believe a single word Brother Jones has been sayin' about that powder. I 've been down thar and seen it for myself, and I pledge you my word that the grains is bigger than the lumps in a coal-pile; and any one of you, brethren, ef you was in your future state, could put a bar'l o' that powder on your shoulder and march squar' through the sulphurious flames surroundin' you without the least danger of an explosion.'" We thought that grain of powder had served even a better purpose in drawing out this story than it could ever serve in being fired from a fifteen-inch gun.

As the party broke up for the night I walked into my quarters to put back the grain of powder, and upon turning round to come out, I found that the President had followed me and was looking into my tent, from curiosity, doubtless, to see how the officers were quartered. Of course I made haste to invite him in. He stepped inside for a moment, and his eye fell upon a specimen artillery trace, a patented article which some inventor had left the day before in order to have it examined at headquarters. The President exclaimed, "Why, what 's that?" I replied, "That is a trace." "Oh," remarked Mr. Lincoln, "that recalls what the poet wrote: 'Sorrow had fled, but left her traces there.' What became of the rest of the harness he did n't mention."

That night Mr. Lincoln slept aboard the boat which had brought him to City Point. He had expressed to General Grant a desire to go up the James the next day, to see that portion of our lines and visit the flagship of Admiral Lee, who commanded the gunboats. All arrangements were made for the trip, and the President's boat started up the river about eight o'clock the next morning, stopping at Bermuda Hundred to take on General Butler. Admiral Lee came aboard from his flag-ship, and the party proceeded up the river as far as it was safe to ascend. Mr. Lincoln was in excellent spirits, and listened with great eagerness to the descriptions of the works, which could be seen from the river, and the objects for which they had been constructed. When his attention was called to some particularly strong positions which had been seized and fortified, he remarked to Butler: "When Grant once gets possession of a place, he holds on to it as if he had inherited it." Orders had been sent to have the pontoon-bridge at Deep Bottom opened for the passage of the President's boat, so that he could proceed some distance beyond that point. His whole conversation during his visit showed the deep anxiety he felt and the weight of responsibility which was resting upon him. His face would light up for a time while telling an anecdote illustrating a subject under discussion, and afterward his features would relax and show the deep lines which had been graven upon them by the mental strain to which he had been subjected for nearly four years. The National Republican Convention had renominated him for the Presidency just two weeks before, and some reference was made to it and to the number of men who composed the Electoral College. He remarked: "Among all our colleges, the Electoral College is the only one where they choose their own masters." He did not show any disposition to dwell upon the subject, or upon the approaching political campaign. His mind seemed completely absorbed in the operations of the armies. Several times, when contemplated battles were spoken of, he said: "I cannot pretend to advise, but I do sincerely hope that all may be accomplished with as little bloodshed as possible."

Soon after his return to City Point the President started back to Washington. His visit to the army had been a memorable event. General Grant and he had had so much delightful intercourse that they parted from each other with unfeigned regret, and both felt that their acquaintance had already ripened into a genuine friendship.

General Grant, having decided that it would be inexpedient to attempt to carry the works at Petersburg by assault, now began to take measures looking to the investment of that place by leaving a portion of his forces to defend our works, while he moved out with the other portion against the railroads, with the design of cutting off Lee's communications in that direction. Wright's entire corps had been sent back from Butler's front to the Army of the Potomac, and Martindale's command had been returned to Butler, so that Meade's and Butler's armies were again complete. Meade's corps were disposed as follows, from right to left of the line: Burnside, Warren, Birney (Hancock's), Wright.

On the morning of June 22, Wright's and Birney's corps moved westward with a view to crossing the Weldon Railroad and swinging around to the left; but they were vigorously attacked and forced back some distance. They advanced again in the evening, but nothing important was gained.

On June 23, Birney and Wright again moved out. There was great difficulty in preserving the alinement of the troops, as they had to pass through dense woods and almost impenetrable thickets, which made the movement a slow and difficult process. About four o'clock in the afternoon, while a portion of Wright's troops were at work destroying the Weldon Railroad, a large force of the enemy struck his left and drove it back. Darkness soon came on, and nothing of importance was accomplished. Wright was now given authority to withdraw his corps to the position occupied the night before, which was more advantageous. Meade had sent frequent messages to Grant, who was this day at Bermuda Hundred, keeping him advised of the movements in his front; and that night he telegraphed: "I think you had better come up here to-morrow if convenient." General Grant felt considerably annoyed about the operations that day at Petersburg, and regarded the position of the Army of the Potomac as somewhat vulnerable. In extending to the left the center had been depleted, while the left flank was out in the air, and would consequently be weak if a heavy and determined attack should be made upon it. The enemy had made his intrenchments so strong that he could afford to move a large portion of his force to his right for the purpose of such an attack. Hancock was much missed from the command of the Second Corps. It was quite natural that Meade should ask Grant to come in person to the lines in front of Petersburg, and it was another indication of the confidence which his subordinate commanders reposed in him.

At eight o'clock on the morning of June 24 the general rode to the headquarters of the Army of the Potomac, accompanied by Rawlins, myself, and two others of the staff. In discussing with Meade and some of the corps commanders the events of the two previous days, he gave particular instructions for operations on that part of the line. The guns of the siege-train which he had ordered now began to arrive from Washington. Meade was told that they would be sent to him immediately, and it was decided to spend the next few days in putting the guns and mortars into commanding positions, in the meanwhile permitting the troops to desist from active operations. The heat was now intense, and the men were in much need of rest. Meade gave Grant and his staff a comfortable lunch, and late in the afternoon our party started for City Point.

Owing to the heat and dust, the long ride was exceedingly uncomfortable. My best horse had been hurt, and I was mounted on a bay cob that had a trot which necessitated no end of "saddle-pounding" on the part of the rider; and if distances are to be measured by the amount of fatigue endured, this exertion added many miles to the trip. The general was riding his black pony "Jeff Davis." This smooth little pacer shuffled along at a gait which was too fast for a walk and not fast enough for a gallop, so that all the other horses had to move at a brisk trot to keep up with him. When we were about five miles from headquarters the general said to me in a joking way: "You don't look comfortable on that horse. Now I feel about as fresh as when we started out." I replied: "It makes all the difference in the world, general, what kind of horse one rides." He remarked: "Oh, all horses are pretty much alike, as far as the comfort of their gait is concerned." "In the present instance," I answered, "I don't think you would like to swap with me, general." He said at once, "Why, yes; I'd just as lief swap with you as not"; and threw himself off his pony and mounted my uncomfortable beast, while I put myself astride of "Jeff." The general had always been a famous rider, even when a cadet at West Point. When he rode or drove a strange horse, not many minutes elapsed before he and the animal seemed to understand each other perfectly. In my experience I have never seen a better rider, or one who had a more steady seat, no matter what sort of horse he rode; but on this occasion it soon became evident that his body and that of the animal were not always in touch, and he saw that all the party were considerably amused at the jogging to which he was subjected. In the mean time "Jeff Davis" was pacing along with a smoothness which made me feel as if I were seated in a rocking-chair. When we reached headquarters the general dismounted in a manner which showed that he was pretty stiff from the ride. As he touched the ground he turned and said with a quizzical look, "Well, I must acknowledge that animal *is* pretty rough."

Sheridan had arrived on June 20 at White House, on his return from the expedition to the north side of the North Anna River, upon which he had been sent on the 7th. As soon as Lee learned of Hunter's success he sent Breckinridge's troops to oppose him; and hearing that Sheridan had started, he ordered Hampton's and Fitzhugh Lee's cavalry commands to move against our cavalry. They were to attack Sheridan during the night of the 10th and surprise him; but that officer was not to be caught napping. He advanced promptly toward Trevilian's Station, and in a well-conceived and brilliantly executed battle defeated the Confederate cavalry, and then effectually destroyed several miles of the Virginia Central Railroad. He now obtained information from the prisoners he had captured that Hunter was in the vicinity of Lynchburg and not likely to reach Charlottesville; and as the enemy had thrown a large force of infantry and cavalry between Hunter and him, and as he was encumbered with a large number of prisoners and wounded, and his supply of ammunition was nearly exhausted, he felt that it would be useless to try to make a junction with Hunter, and decided to return to the Army of the Potomac by way of White House, where ample and much-needed supplies were awaiting him. On his arrival, orders were given that this depot should be broken up on the 22d, and the train of nine hundred wagons which had been left there was crossed to the south side of the James River, having been gallantly and successfully defended on its way by Sheridan's cavalry.

On the 26th Sheridan came in person to Grant's headquarters, and had an interview with him in regard to
the results of his expedition and the further operations
which he was expected to undertake at once on the
south side of Petersburg.   Sheridan was cordially
greeted on his arrival by the general-in-chief.   He was
at all times a welcome visitor at headquarters, as his
boundless enthusiasm, buoyant spirits, and cheery conversation were always refreshing.

The general, after learning all the details of Sheridan's
expedition, told him that he fully approved his judgment in not attempting, under the contingencies which
had arisen, to reach Hunter; but, as usual, the general
did not dwell at length upon the past, and promptly
began the discussion of the plans he had in view for the
cavalry in the future.

A day or two afterward, Grant paid a visit to Butler's
lines; and while he and the staff were riding out to the
front they came to the place where, according to tradi-
tion, Pocahontas had saved the life of Captain John
Smith.   Whether it was the exact spot or not, it was
regarded in that locality as historic ground; and Virginians, who take a particular pride in well-known family
names, seemed to honor Pocahontas especially, no doubt
because she was largely instrumental in preserving the
Smith family to posterity.   In the efforts to account
for the attempted execution of the prisoner, there is a
story told, about the truth of which there is a lingering
uncertainty.   It is to the effect that, when the captain
fell into the hands of the Indian chief, he was rash
enough to state, in reply to questions as to his identity,
that his name was "John Smith"; and that the noble
red man thought he was trying to perpetrate a practical
joke on him, and was roused to swift vengeance by such
an ill-timed pleasantry.

In climbing a rather steep hill at this point, the party had to move along a narrow bridle-path. The general was riding in the lead, followed by the staff in single file, with Badeau bringing up the rear. The trees were soon found to be so near together that a horse and rider could not pass between them when keeping in the path, and we turned out to the left, where the woods were more open. Badeau's near-sightedness prevented him from seeing very far ahead, and he was not paying much attention to his horse, but simply letting him go along as he pleased. Suddenly we heard a cry from him: " I 'm going off! I say, I 'm going off!" On looking round, we found his horse climbing up the path with a tree on each side, between which he could scarcely squeeze. When Badeau's knees reached the trees his saddle was forced back, and as the horse struggled on his rider finally slid off over the animal's tail. Then came the cry, "See here, I 'm off!" and Badeau and the saddle were seen lying on the ground. The horse stepped out of the girth and quietly continued his march up the hill as if nothing had happened. General Grant stopped, and looking back at the ludicrous sight presented, fairly screamed with laughter, and did not recover his equanimity during the remainder of the ride. Nothing could have been more amusing to him than such an accident; for, as he was an exceptionally expert horseman, awkwardness on the part of a rider was more laughable to him than to most people. Badeau, with the assistance of an orderly, had his horse resaddled, and, mounting again, soon joined the cavalcade. General Grant cracked jokes at his expense all the rest of the ride; and for two or three days afterward, when he would be sitting quietly in front of his tent, he would suddenly begin to shake with laughter, and say: "I can't help thinking how that horse succeeded in sneaking out from under Badeau at Bermuda Hundred."

While the enemy's cavalry was north of the James, and the probabilities were that it would be detained there by Sheridan for some days, it was decided to send Wilson's division of cavalry, which had remained with the Army of the Potomac, and four regiments of the cavalry of the Army of the James under Kautz, to the south of Petersburg, with a view to striking both the South Side and the Danville railroads. This cavalry command started out on the morning of June 22. It was composed of nearly 6000 men and several batteries of horse-artillery. It first struck the Weldon, then the South Side Railroad, and afterward advanced as far as Roanoke Station on the Danville road, inflicting much damage. On the 29th, after severe fighting, it found itself confronted and partly surrounded by such a heavy force of the enemy that there was no means of cutting a way through with success; and it was decided to issue all the remaining ammunition, destroy the wagons and caissons, and fall back to the Union lines. The troops were hard pressed by greatly superior numbers, and suffered severely upon their march, but by untiring energy and great gallantry succeeded in reaching the Army of the Potomac on July 1. The expedition had been absent ten days. It had marched three hundred miles, and destroyed a large quantity of rolling-stock and about fifty miles of railroad. The loss in killed, wounded, and missing amounted to about 1500 men. All the guns and wagons were destroyed or abandoned. The cavalry supposed that the infantry of the Army of the Potomac would be in possession of Reams's Station at the time of their return, but that station was still in the hands of the enemy.

The destruction of communications by Hunter, Sheri-

dan, and Wilson gave the enemy serious alarm; but by
dint of great effort he in time made the necessary re-
pairs, and was again able to bring supplies to Richmond
by rail.   In the mean time the siege of Petersburg had
begun, and it was now Grant's intention to make the
investment as complete as possible, and to take advantage of every opportunity to inflict damage on the enemy, and give him battle whenever he could do so under
circumstances that would be justifiable.

On June 29, Grant felt anxious about the fate of the
cavalry and the progress of Wright's corps, which had
been sent to Reams's Station to Wilson's relief, but did
not reach there in time.   He rode out to the Petersburg
front with his staff, held interviews with Meade, Burnside, and Smith, and visited the lines to make a personal
inspection of the principal batteries.   He became impressed with the idea that more field-artillery could be
used to advantage at several points, and when we returned to headquarters that evening he telegraphed to
Washington for five or six additional batteries.

From the 4th of May until the end of June there had
not been a day in which there was not a battle or a skirmish.   The record of continuous and desperate fighting
had far surpassed any campaign in modern or ancient
military history.

In view of the important operations which were to
be conducted from City Point, General Grant made
some changes in the organization of the staff.   General
Rufus Ingalls, who had distinguished himself by the
exhibition of signal ability as chief quartermaster of
the Army of the Potomac, was assigned to duty as chief
quartermaster upon the staff of the general-in-chief.
Grant and he had been classmates at West Point, and
were on terms of extreme intimacy.   Ingalls was exceedingly popular in the army, and both officially and per-

sonally was regarded as an important acquisition to the staff. Lieutenant-colonel M. R. Morgan, an efficient and experienced officer of the commissary department, was added to the staff of the general-in-chief as chief commissary; thirty years after he became commissary-general of the army. Soon after General M. R. Patrick was made provost-marshal-general, and General George H. Sharpe was assigned to duty as his assistant. The latter officer rendered invaluable service in obtaining information regarding the enemy by his employment of scouts and his skill in examining prisoners and refugees. Captain Amos Webster was placed on duty as assistant quartermaster. Assistant Surgeon E. D. W. Breneman, U. S. A., was assigned to look after the health of those at headquarters; but the particularly robust condition of nearly all the officers he was prepared to attend made his work exceedingly light.

In discussing at this time the large amount of rations which had to be supplied by the subsistence department, and the system required in its management, General Grant said: "When I first had an independent command there were so few experienced men about me that I had to sit down at night and teach officers of the staff departments how to make requisitions for supplies, and fill out the blank forms furnished by the government when such blanks could be procured. I had acted at times as quartermaster and commissary in the old army, and was of course familiar with all the forms used in preparing papers. Word was brought to me one day that a new regimental commissary had gone aboard a commissary boat on the Mississippi and presented a requisition for rations for his men. The officer in charge looked at it in amazement, and exclaimed: 'Why, there are not half enough rations aboard this entire steamer to fill that requisition.' The commissary, who thought he had made only an ordinary demand, said: 'Why, you 're filling requisitions for all the other regiments in our brigade!' 'Regiment!' cried the commissary. 'You mean a corps.' The regimental commissary then discovered that he had made out his requisition on a corps blank."

A hospital had been established at City Point large enough to accommodate 6000 patients, and served a very useful purpose. The general manifested a deep interest in this hospital, frequently visited it, and constantly received verbal reports from the surgeons in charge as to the care and comfort of the wounded.

A telegraph-line had been established on the south side of the James which connected by cable across Hampton Roads with Fort Monroe. From that place there was direct telegraphic communication with Washington. This line was occasionally broken, but by dint of great effort it was generally well maintained and made to perform excellent service.

The general headquarters had become an intensely interesting spot. Direct communication was kept open as far as possible with the various armies throughout the country, all of which the general-in-chief was directing, and information of an exciting nature was constantly received and important orders were issued. The officers on duty had an opportunity to watch the great war drama from behind the scenes, from which point they witnessed not only the performance of the actors, but the workings of the master mind that gave the directions and guided all the preparations.

CHAPTER XVI

A DISAPPOINTED BAND-MASTER — HUNTER'S RAID — EARLY'S RAID ON WASHINGTON — GRANT AS A WRITER — GRANT DEVOTES ATTENTION TO SHERMAN — GRANT'S TREATMENT OF HIS GENERALS — GRANT'S EQUANIMITY — GRANT AS A THINKER — WHY GRANT NEVER SWORE — MEADE AND WARREN — SEWARD VISITS GRANT

EARTHWORKS had been thrown across the neck of land upon which City Point is located. This intrenched line ran from a point on the James to a point on the Appomattox River. A small garrison had been detailed for its defense, and the commanding officer, wishing to do something that would afford the general-in-chief special delight, arranged to send the band over to the headquarters camp to play for him while he was dining. The garrison commander was in blissful ignorance of the fact that to the general the appreciation of music was a lacking sense and the musician's score a sealed book. About the third evening after the band had begun its performances, the general, while sitting at the mess-table, remarked: "I 've noticed that that band always begins its *noise* just about the time I am sitting down to dinner and want to talk." I offered to go and make an effort to suppress it, and see whether it would obey an order to "cease firing," and my services were promptly accepted. The men were gorgeously uniformed, and the band seemed to embrace every sort

234

of brass instrument ever invented, from a diminutive cornet-à-pistons to a gigantic double-bass horn. The performer who played the latter instrument was encaged within its ample twists, and looked like a man standing inside the coils of a whisky-still. The broad-belted band-master was puffing with all the vigor of a quack-medicine advertisement, his eyes were riveted upon the music, and it was not an easy task to attract his attention. Like a sperm-whale, he had come up to blow, and was not going to be put down till he had finished; but finally he was made to understand that, like the hand-organ man, he was desired to move on. With a look of disinheritance on his countenance, he at last marched off his band to its camp. On my return the general said: "I fear that band-master's feelings have been hurt, but I did n't want him to be wasting his time upon a person who has no ear for music." A staff-officer remarked: "Well, general, you were at least much more considerate than Commodore ——, who, the day he came to take command of his vessel, and was seated at dinner in the cabin, heard music on deck, and immediately sent for the executive officer and said to him: 'Have the instruments *and men* of that band thrown overboard at once!'"

Hunter's bold march and destruction of military stores had caused so much alarm that Lee, as has been said before, was compelled to send Breckinridge's force and Early's corps to the valley of Virginia. Hunter continued to drive back the troops he encountered till he reached Lynchburg. There he found that the strength of the works and the combined forces brought against him would prevent the further success of his raid. On June 18 he decided to exercise the discretion which had been left to him in such a contingency and retire toward his base. The result of the campaign, besides compelling Lee to detach troops from his own army, was the burning of Confederate cloth-mills, gun-stock and harness factories, and foundries engaged in the manufacture of ammunition, the destruction of about fifty miles of railroad, and the capture of three thousand muskets, twenty pieces of artillery, and a quantity of ammunition. The stringent orders given by Grant to Sigel, and by him turned over to Hunter, who had succeeded him, were prepared with a view to preventing all wanton destruction. They were in part as follows: " Indiscriminate marauding should be avoided. Nothing should be taken not absolutely necessary for the troops, except when captured from an armed enemy. Impressments should be made under orders from the commanding officer and by a disbursing officer. Receipts should be given for all property taken, so that the loyal may collect pay and the property be accounted for." Notwithstanding these orders, there were some houses burned and damage done to individual property during this raid.

Hunter having been compelled to fall back into West Virginia, the roads to Washington were left uncovered, and the enemy now advanced into Maryland. Sigel's small force retreated precipitately across the Potomac, followed by the enemy. It had been impossible for General Grant to obtain any reliable news for a number of days in regard to these movements, and it was not until the 4th of July that he received definite information.

We did not find many leisure moments to indulge in patriotic demonstrations at headquarters on Independence day, for the directions for executing the plans for checkmating the enemy in his present movement fully occupied every one on duty. Grant telegraphed to Halleck to concentrate all the troops about Washington,

Baltimore, Cumberland, and Harper's Ferry, bring up Hunter's troops, and put Early to flight. While Grant was thinking only of punishing Early, there was great consternation in Washington, and the minds of the officials there seemed to be occupied solely with measures for defending the capital. Hunter's troops had fallen back to Charleston, West Virginia, and a drought had left so little water in the Ohio River that the ascent of the vessels on which his troops had embarked was greatly delayed.

All eyes were, as usual, turned upon Grant to protect the capital and drive back the invading force. On July 5, seeing, as he thought, another opportunity for cutting off and destroying the troops that Lee had detached from his command, Grant ordered one division of Wright's corps and some dismounted cavalry to Washington by steamers. Under subsequent orders the infantry division (Rickett's) proceeded via Baltimore to reinforce General Lew Wallace, at the Monocacy. General Grant had been very much dissatisfied with all of Sigel's movements, and now that the situation was becoming somewhat serious, he determined to make an effort to have him removed from his command. On the 7th he sent Halleck a despatch, saying: " I think it advisable to relieve him [Sigel] from all duty, at least until present troubles are over." Sigel was immediately removed, and General Howe put in command of his forces until Hunter's arrival. By means of the telegraphic communications which he constantly received Grant was able to time pretty well the movements of the enemy, and to make preparations for meeting him before he could attempt the capture of Washington. He had been planning some important offensive operations in front of Richmond, but he now decided to postpone these and turn his chief attention to Early.

The Nineteenth Corps, which had been ordered from New Orleans by sea, and which was now arriving at Fort Monroe, and the remainder of Wright's Sixth Corps from in front of Petersburg, were instructed to proceed at once to Washington. Instead of sympathizing with the alarming messages from the capital and the many rash suggestions made from there, the general telegraphed on July 9: "Forces enough to defeat all that Early has with him should get in his rear, south of him, and follow him up sharply, leaving him to go north, defending depots, towns, etc., with small garrisons and the militia. If the President thinks it advisable that I should go to Washington in person, I can start in an hour after receiving notice." The President answered, saying that he thought it would be well for the general to come to Washington, but making it only as a suggestion. General Grant replied to this: "I think, on reflection, it would have a bad effect for me to leave here, and, with Ord at Baltimore, and Hunter and Wright with the forces following the enemy up, could do no good. I have great faith that the enemy will never be able to get back with much of his force." The general said, in conversation with his staff on the 10th: "One reason why I do not wish to go to Washington to take personal direction of the movement against Early is that this is probably just what Lee wants me to do, in order that he may transfer the seat of war to Maryland, or feel assured that there will be no offensive operations against Petersburg during my absence, and detach some of his forces and send them against Sherman. Sherman is at a long distance from his base of supplies, and I want to be able to have him feel that I shall take no step that will afford an opportunity of detaching troops from here to operate against him."

General Lew Wallace, in command of what was called

the Middle Department, made a gallant stand at the Monocacy, and effected a delay in the enemy's movements toward Washington; but his small force was of course defeated. Early now moved directly on Washington, and on July 11 advanced upon the outer line of fortifications; but, to the surprise of his troops, they saw the well-known banners of the Sixth Corps, and found that Washington, instead of being weakly defended, was now guarded by veterans of the Army of the Potomac. Early discovered that he had been outmanœuvered, and on the night of the 12th began a retreat. Grant had now but one anxiety, which was to have an efficient head selected for the command of the troops that he was collecting to operate against Early. He sent a despatch to Halleck, saying: "Give orders assigning Major-general Wright to supreme command of all troops moving out against the enemy, regardless of the rank of other commanders. He should get outside the trenches with all the force he possibly can, and should push Early to the last moment, supplying himself from the country." The next day (July 13) Wright moved forward with his command, following up Early.

There had been several days of serious perplexity and annoyance at headquarters. The commanders had to be changed, and the best results possible obtained with the material at hand. Twice the wires of the telegraph-line were broken, and important messages between Washington and City Point had to be sent a great part of the way by steamboat. It was rumored at one time that Hill's corps had been detached from Lee's front, and there was some anxiety to know whether it had been sent to Early or to Johnston, who was opposing Sherman; but the rumor was soon found to be groundless. Grant's orders now were to press the enemy in

Maryland with all vigor, to make a bold campaign against him, and destroy him if possible before he could return to Lee. Early, however, had gained a day's start, and although a number of his wagons and animals and some prisoners had been captured, no material damage was inflicted upon him. On July 20 he reached Snicker's Ferry, and the chase was abandoned. Early continued his march to Strasburg, where he arrived July 22.

The general had occupied himself continually during this anxious and exciting period in giving specific instructions by wire and messengers to meet the constantly changing conditions which were taking place from day to day and from hour to hour in the theater of military operations; and no despatches were ever of greater importance than those which were sent from headquarters at this time. His powers of concentration of thought were often shown by the circumstances under which he wrote. Nothing that went on around him, upon the field or in his quarters, could distract his attention or interrupt him. Sometimes, when his tent was filled with officers, talking and laughing at the top of their voices, he would turn to his table and write the most important communications. There would then be an immediate "Hush!" and abundant excuses offered by the company; but he always insisted upon the conversation going on, and after a while his officers came to understand his wishes in this respect, to learn that noise was apparently a stimulus rather than a check to his flow of ideas, and to realize that nothing short of a general attack along the whole line could divert his thoughts from the subject upon which his mind was concentrated. In writing his style was vigorous and terse, with little of ornament; its most conspicuous characteristic was perspicuity. General Meade's chief of staff once said: "There is one striking feature about Grant's orders: no matter how hurriedly he may write them on the field, no one ever has the slightest doubt as to their meaning, or ever has to read them over a second time to understand them." The general used Anglo-Saxon words much more frequently than those derived from the Greek and Latin tongues. He had studied French at West Point, and picked up some knowledge of Spanish during the Mexican war; but he could not hold a conversation in either language, and rarely employed a foreign word in any of his writings. His adjectives were few and well chosen. No document which ever came from his hands was in the least degree pretentious. He never laid claim to any knowledge he did not possess, and seemed to feel, with Addison, that "pedantry in learning is like hypocrisy in religion—a form of knowledge without the power of it." He rarely indulged in metaphor, but when he did employ a figure of speech it was always expressive and graphic, as when he spoke of the commander at Bermuda Hundred being "in a bottle strongly corked," or referred to our armies at one time moving "like horses in a balky team, no two ever pulling together." His style inclined to the epigrammatic without his being aware of it. There was scarcely a document written by him from which brief sentences could not be selected fit to be set in mottos or placed upon transparencies. As examples may be mentioned: "I propose to move immediately upon your works"; "I shall take no backward steps"; the famous "I propose to fight it out on this line if it takes all summer," and, later in his career, "Let us have peace"; "The best means of securing the repeal of an obnoxious law is its vigorous enforcement"; "I shall have no policy to enforce against the will of the people"; and "Let no guilty man escape." He wrote with the first pen he

happened to pick up, and never stopped to consider
whether it was sharp-pointed or blunt-nibbed, good or
bad.   He was by no means as particular in this regard
as General Zachary Taylor, of whom an old army rumor
said that the only signature he ever made which was
entirely satisfactory to him was written with the butt-
end of a ramrod dipped in tar.   General Grant's desk
was always in a delirious state of confusion; pigeon-
holes were treated with a sublime disregard, and he left
his letters piled up in apparently inextricable heaps;
but, strange to say, he carried in his mind such a distinct recollection of local literary geography as applied
to his writing-table that he could go to it and even in
the dark lay his hand upon almost any paper he wanted.
His military training had educated him to treat purely
official documents with respect, and these were always
handed over to Colonel Bowers, the adjutant-general, to
be properly filed; but as to his private letters, he made
his coat-pockets a general depository for his correspondence until they could hold no more, and then he discharged their contents upon his desk in a chaotic mass.
The military secretaries made heroic struggles to bring
about some order in this department, and generally saw
that copies were kept of all letters of importance which
the chief wrote.   Whatever came from his pen was
grammatically correct, well punctuated, and seldom
showed an error in spelling.   In the field he never had
a dictionary in his possession, and when in doubt about
the orthography of a word, he was never known to
write it first on a separate slip of paper to see how it
looked.   He spelled with heroic audacity, and "chanced
it" on the correctness.   While in rare instances he made
a mistake in doubling the consonants where unnecessary, or in writing a single consonant where two were
required, he really spelled with great accuracy.   His

pronunciation was seldom, if ever, at fault, though in two words he had a peculiar way of pronouncing the letter *d*: he always pronounced corduroy "corjuroy," and immediately "immejetly."

While planning means for the defeat of Early, General Grant was still giving constant attention to the movements of Sherman. That officer had been repulsed in making his attack on Kenesaw Mountain, but by a successful flank movement had turned the enemy's very strong position, and compelled him to fall back over the Chattahoochee River on July 4. On the 17th Sherman crossed that river and drove the enemy into his defenses about Atlanta. It now looked as if Sherman would be forced to a siege of that place; and as he was many hundreds of miles from his base, and there was only a single line of railroad to supply him, it was more than ever important that no troops should be allowed to leave Virginia to be thrown against his lines.

Grant was frequently in consultation with Meade in regard to preventing the enemy from withdrawing troops from Petersburg. The Southern papers received through the lines gave very conflicting accounts of the operations on Sherman's front, and indicated that there was a great demand for the reinforcement of Johnston, and expressed the belief that there would be vigorous movements made to break Sherman's communications. In a despatch to Halleck Grant said: "If he [Sherman] can supply himself with ordnance and quartermaster's stores, and partially with subsistence, he will find no difficulty in staying until a permanent line can be opened with the south coast." The general directed a large quantity of the stores at Nashville to be transferred to Chattanooga. There was another contingency which he mentioned, and which he had to devise steps to guard against—a determination on the part of the enemy to withdraw the troops in front of Sherman and move them quickly by rail to Petersburg, and in the mean time march Early's corps back to Lee, and make a combined attack upon the Army of the Potomac. This, Grant believed, would be done only in some extreme emergency, and in case the enemy felt convinced that Sherman was so far from his base of supplies that he could not move much farther into the interior. One means which the general-in-chief had in contemplation at this time for preventing troops from being sent from Virginia was to start Sheridan on a raid to cut the railroads southwest of Richmond.

Important news reached headquarters on July 17 to the effect that General Joe Johnston had been relieved from duty, and General Hood put in command of the army opposed to Sherman. General Grant said when he received this information: "I know very well the chief characteristics of Hood. He is a bold, dashing soldier, and has many qualities of successful leadership, but he is an indiscreet commander, and lacks cool judgment. We may look out now for rash and ill-advised attacks on his part. I am very glad, from our standpoint, that this change has been made. Hood will prove no match for Sherman." He waited with some curiosity to know just what policy Hood would adopt. As was anticipated, he came out of his lines and made an attack on July 20, but was repulsed with great loss. He made another offensive movement on the 22d, and fought the celebrated battle of Atlanta, but was again driven back. On the 28th he made another bold dash against Sherman, but in this also he was completely defeated, and fell back within the defenses at Atlanta. In the battle of the 22d General McPherson was killed. When this news reached General Grant he was visibly affected, and dwelt upon it in his conversations for the next two or three days. "McPherson," he said, "was one of my earliest staff-officers, and seemed almost like one of my own family. At Donelson, Shiloh, Vicksburg, and Chattanooga he performed splendid service. I predicted from the start that he would make one of the most brilliant officers in the service. I was very reluctant to have him leave my staff, for I disliked to lose his services there, but I felt that it was only fair to him to put him in command of troops where he would be in the line of more rapid promotion. I was very glad to have him at the head of my old Army of the Tennessee. His death will be a terrible loss to Sherman, for I know that he will feel it as keenly as I. McPherson was beloved by everybody in the service, both by those above him and by those below him."

In the midsummer of 1864 General Grant had an increasing weight of responsibility thrown upon him every day. While he was requiring his commanders to sleep with one foot out of bed and with one eye open, lest Lee might make some unexpected movement which would require a prompt change in the general plan of operations, he had to devise new methods almost daily to check raids in different parts of the country, protect the capital, save the North from invasion, and lay vigorous siége to Petersburg, which had been rendered as nearly impregnable by the enemy as the art of the military engineer was capable of making it. He was constantly embarrassed, too, by some of his subordinates. An acrimonious personal warfare was progressing between Butler and W. F. Smith, and the latter's severe criticisms of Meade had aroused the resentment of that officer, which added a new phase to the general quarrel. General Grant finally made up his mind to relieve General Smith from duty; he was given a leave of absence, and never recalled.

As a commander General Butler had not been General Grant's choice. The general-in-chief, when he assumed command of the armies, found Butler in charge of the Department of Virginia and North Carolina, and utilized him to the best advantage possible. He had always found him subordinate, prompt to obey orders, possessed of great mental activity, and clear in his conception of the instructions given him. He was a good administrative officer, though often given to severe and unusual methods in enforcing discipline and in dealing with the dissatisfied element of the population living within his department; yet he did not possess the elements necessary to make an efficient officer in the field. As he was inexperienced in fighting battles, Grant felt reluctant to give him charge of any important military movement. One embarrassment was that he was the senior officer in rank in Virginia, and if General Grant should be called away temporarily, Butler would be in supreme command of the operations against Petersburg. The general struggled along under this embarrassment by keeping matters under his own direction when Butler's forces were employed in actual battle, and by sending an experienced corps commander to handle the troops in the immediate presence of the enemy.

General Meade's irritability of temper, and over-sensitiveness to implied censure or criticism on the part of the newspapers, led him at one time to tender his resignation as commander of the Army of the Potomac. General Grant talked to him very kindly on the subject, soothed his feelings, and induced him to reconsider his intention. The general-in-chief did not mention the matter publicly, and was very glad that hasty action had been prevented. If Meade had resigned at this time, Hancock would have succeeded him, and Ingalls, who had shown such signal executive ability, might possibly have been given an important command. Ingalls and I expressed a desire repeatedly to serve in command of troops, as such service gave promise of more rapid promotion and was more in accordance with our tastes; but the general always insisted upon retaining us on his staff.[1]

General Meade was a most accomplished officer. He had been thoroughly educated in his profession, and had a complete knowledge of both the science and the art of war in all its branches. He was well read, possessed of a vast amount of interesting information, had cultivated his mind as a linguist, and spoke French with fluency. When foreign officers visited the front they were invariably charmed by their interviews with the commander of the Army of the Potomac. He was a disciplinarian to the point of severity, was entirely subordinate to his superiors, and no one was more prompt than he to obey orders to the letter. In his intercourse with his officers the bluntness of the soldier was always conspicuous, and he never took pains to smooth any one's ruffled feelings.

There was an officer serving in the Army of the Potomac who had formerly been a surgeon. One day he appeared at Meade's headquarters in a high state of in-

[1] A reference to this subject occurs in "Around the World with General Grant," by the Hon. John Russell Young, who accompanied him upon his tour. The language used by General Grant in one of his interviews with Mr. Young is reported as follows: "Ingalls in command of troops would, in my opinion, have become a great and famous general. . . . Horace Porter was lost in the staff. Like Ingalls, he was too useful to be spared. But as a commander of troops Porter would have risen, in my opinion, to a high command."—EDITOR.

dignation, and said: "General, as I was riding over here some of the men in the adjoining camps shouted after me and called me 'Old Pills,' and I would like to have it stopped." Meade just at that moment was not in the best possible frame of mind to be approached with such a complaint. He seized hold of the eye-glasses, conspicuously large in size, which he always wore, clapped them astride of his nose with both hands, glared through them at the officer, and exclaimed: "Well, what of that? How can I prevent it? Why, I hear that, when I rode out the other day, some of the men called me a 'd—d old goggle-eyed snapping-turtle,' and I can't even stop that!" The officer had to content himself with this explosive expression of a sympathetic fellow-feeling, and to take his chances thereafter as to obnoxious epithets.

In view of the want of harmony which often prevailed, the service would have suffered severely if an officer of a different character had been in supreme command; but Grant was so complacent in his manner, so even in temper, and so just in his method of dealing with the conflicting interests and annoying questions which arose, that whatever his subordinates may have thought of one another, to him they were at all times well disposed and perfectly loyal.

Throughout this memorable year, the most important as well as the most harassing of his entire military career, General Grant never in any instance failed to manifest those traits which were the true elements of his greatness. He was always calm amid excitement, and patient under trials. He looked neither to the past with regret nor to the future with apprehension. When he could not control he endured, and in every great crisis he could "convince when others could not advise." His calmness of demeanor and unruffled temper were often a marvel even to those most familiar with him. In the midst of the most exciting scenes he rarely raised his voice above its ordinary pitch or manifested the least irritability. Whether encountered at noonday or awakened from sleep at midnight, his manner was always the same; whether receiving the report of an army commander or of a private soldier serving as a courier or a scout, he listened with equal deference and gave it the same strict attention. He could not only discipline others, but he could discipline himself. If he had lived in ancient days he might, in his wrath, have broken the two tables of stone: he never would have broken the laws which were written on them. The only manifestation of anger he had indulged in during the campaign was upon the occasion, hereinbefore mentioned, when he found a teamster beating his horses near the Totopotomoy. He never criticized an officer harshly in the presence of others. If fault had to be found with him, it was never made an occasion to humiliate him or wound his feelings. The only pointed reprimand he ever administered was in the instance mentioned in the battle of the Wilderness, when an officer left his troops and came to him to magnify the dangers which were to be feared from Lee's methods of warfare. The fact that he never "nagged" his officers, but treated them all with consideration, led them to communicate with him freely and intimately; and he thus gained much information which otherwise he might not have received. To have a well-disciplined command he did not deem it necessary to have an unhappy army. His ideas of discipline did not accord with those of the Russian officer who, one night in the Moscow campaign, reprimanded a soldier for putting a ball of snow under his head for a pillow, for the reason that indulgence in such uncalled-for luxuries would destroy the high character of the army.

It was an interesting study in human nature to watch

the general's actions in camp. He would sit for hours in front of his tent, or just inside of it looking out, smoking a cigar very slowly, seldom with a paper or a map in his hands, and looking like the laziest man in camp. But at such periods his mind was working more actively than that of any one in the army. He talked less and thought more than any one in the service. He studiously avoided performing any duty which some one else could do as well or better than he, and in this respect demonstrated his rare powers of administration and executive methods. He was one of the few men holding high position who did not waste valuable hours by giving his personal attention to petty details. He never consumed his time in reading over court-martial proceedings, or figuring up the items of supplies on hand, or writing unnecessary letters or communications. He held subordinates to a strict accountability in the performance of such duties, and kept his own time for thought. It was this quiet but intense thinking, and the well-matured ideas which resulted from it, that led to the prompt and vigorous action which was constantly witnessed during this year, so pregnant with events.

He changed his habits somewhat at this period about going to bed early, and began to sit up later; and as he preferred to have some one keep him company and discuss matters with him of an evening, one of the staff-officers always made it a point not to retire until the chief was ready for bed. Many a night now became a sort of "watch-night" with us; but the conversations held upon these occasions were of such intense interest that they amply compensated for the loss of sleep they caused, even after a hard day's ride at the front. The general, however, did not always curtail the eight hours of rest which his system seemed to require; for he often pieced out the time by lying in bed later in the morning when there was no stirring movement afoot.

While sitting with him at the camp-fire late one night, after every one else had gone to bed, I said to him: " General, it seems singular that you have gone through all the rough and tumble of army service and frontier life, and have never been provoked into swearing. I have never heard you utter an oath or use an imprecation." " Well, somehow or other, I never learned to swear," he replied. " When a boy I seemed to have an aversion to it, and when I became a man I saw the folly of it. I have always noticed, too, that swearing helps to rouse a man's anger; and when a man flies into a passion his adversary who keeps cool always gets the better of him. In fact, I could never see the use of swearing. I think it is the case with many people who swear excessively that it is a mere habit, and that they do not mean to be profane; but, to say the least, it is a great waste of time." His example in this respect was once quoted in my hearing by a member of the Christian Commission to a teamster in the Army of the Potomac, in the hope of lessening the volume of rare oaths with which he was italicizing his language, and upon which he seemed to be placing his main reliance in moving his mule-team out of a mud-hole. The only reply evoked from him was: " Then thar 's one thing sart'in: the old man never druv mules."

On July 22 General Grant called upon the aides to go with him to Meade's headquarters. Soon after our arrival there, Meade mounted his horse and rode out with us to visit Warren. The meeting between Meade and Warren was not very cordial, in consequence of a rather acrimonious discussion and correspondence which had just taken place between them; but they were both such good soldiers that they did not make any display of their personal feelings while engaged in their official duties. A Pittsburg newspaper had stated that Meade had preferred charges against Warren for disobedience and tardy execution of orders. Warren at once wrote to Meade, asking him what truth there was in it, and if the rumor was correct that he had told General Grant that he had threatened him (Warren) with a court martial if he did not resign. Meade replied, denying the statement of the newspaper, but said he had been offended by the temper and ill feeling that Warren had manifested against him recently in the presence of subordinates, and the want of harmony and coöperation which he had exhibited, and that he had spoken to Grant about this, and had gone so far as to write a letter to him asking that Warren might be relieved; but that, in the hope that disagreements might not occur in future, and in order to avoid doing him so serious an injury, he had withheld the letter.

A thorough examination of Warren's front and other parts of the line was made. Sharp firing occurred in front of Burnside, which was thought to indicate something of importance; but it was only a random fusillade on the part of the troops, kept up between the parts of the lines which were quite close together.

Saturday, July 23, William H. Seward, the Secretary of State, came down from Washington to visit General Grant and see the armies. He arrived at seven o'clock in the morning on the steamer *City of Hudson*, and came at once to General Grant's quarters. The general had seen but little of the distinguished Secretary of State previous to this time, and was very glad to welcome him to City Point, and make his more intimate acquaintance. He presented the officers of the staff who were in camp at the time, and invited them to take seats under the tent-fly in front of his quarters, where he and the Secretary were sitting. Mr. Seward was profuse in his expressions of congratulation at the progress which had been made by the Union armies in the East, and their successes generally throughout the country. We soon began to realize that he fully merited his reputation as a talker. He spoke very freely in reference to the progress of the war, and more particularly about our foreign relations. He had conducted our many delicate negotiations with foreign nations with such consummate ability that every one was anxious to draw him out in regard to them. The first topic of conversation which came up was the unfriendliness of our relations with England the first year of the war, and especially how near we came to an open break with that power in regard to the " *Trent* affair," in which Commodore Wilkes, commanding the U. S. S. *San Jacinto*, had taken Slidell and Mason, the Confederate emissaries, from the English vessel *Trent*, upon which they were passengers. Mr. Seward said : " The report first received from the British government gave a most exaggerated account of the severity of the measures which had been employed ; but I found from Commodore Wilkes's advices that the vessel had not been endangered by the shots fired across her bows, as charged ; that he had simply sent a lieutenant and a boat's crew to the British vessel ; that none of the crew even went aboard ; that the lieutenant used only such a show of force as was necessary to convince the ' contraband ' passengers he wanted that they would have to go with him aboard the *San Jacinto*. The books on international law were silent on the subject as to exactly how an act such as this should be treated ; and as our relations abroad were becoming very threatening, we decided, after a serious discussion, that whatever was to be done should be done promptly, and that, under all the circumstances, it would be wise and prudent to release the prisoners captured, rather than contend for a principle which might not have been sound, and run the risk of becoming involved in a war with Great Britain at that critical period. The great desire of the Davis government was to have this incident embroil us in such a war, and we were not anxious to please it in that respect. Our decision in the matter was the severest blow the Confederacy received in regard to its hope of 'assistance from abroad.'"

This naturally led to the mention of a more recent event upon the seas—the destruction of the *Alabama* by the *Kearsarge*. General Grant had rejoiced greatly at this triumph of our sister service the navy, and admired immensely the boldness and pluck exhibited by Winslow, the commander of the *Kearsarge*, in forcing the fight with the Confederate cruiser. The general was naturally delighted, for it showed that Winslow was a man after his own heart, who acted upon the commendable military maxim, "When in doubt, fight." Mr. Seward was asked whether he had in contemplation any steps to take England to task for the action of the British yacht *Deerhound* for picking up and carrying off our prisoners. He said: "I have communicated with our minister at London, directing him to lay before the British government our grievance in this matter. I feel pretty well convinced that the captain of the *Deerhound* had arranged with Semmes, the captain of the *Alabama*, previous to the fight, to transfer to the yacht certain moneys and valuables which Semmes had aboard, so as to carry them to England for him, and to occupy a position during the fight near enough to render assistance under certain contingencies. It was reported that Captain Winslow asked the captain of the *Deerhound* to rescue the crew of the *Alabama*, who were drowning when that vessel was sinking; but that did not seem to be necessary, as Winslow was able with his boats to rescue all the men.   It appears that many of Semmes's guns were manned by British gunners, and the wounded who were picked up were carried to England and cared for in a British naval hospital.   The circumstance is a most aggravating one, and we have given Great Britain to understand that such acts will not be tolerated in future by this nation."

General Grant then brought up the subject of the empire in Mexico, which was supported by Louis Napoleon.   The general's services in the Mexican war had made him thoroughly well acquainted with Mexico, and he not only had deep sympathy for her people in their present struggle, but was a stanch supporter of the Monroe doctrine generally, and was opposed on principle to any European monarchy forcing its institutions upon an American republic.   Mr. Seward expressed himself at great length upon this subject, saying among other things: " I have had a very exhaustive correspondence on this subject with Louis Napoleon's ministry. He has tried by every form of argument to justify his acts; but I have insisted from the start that when an American state has established republican institutions, no foreign power has the right to use force in attempting to subvert the government formed by its people and set up a monarchy in its place.   When an American republic becomes a monarchy by the voluntary act of its people, the matter is no affair of ours, as the people are always the rightful source of authority; but in the present instance a European emperor has stepped in to deprive the Mexicans of the right of republican freedom. I have been insisting very forcibly that Louis Napoleon must withdraw his army from Mexico.   Why, rumors have reached us from time to time that his forces were to advance across the Rio Grande, by an understanding

with the Davis government, and take possession of the
State of Texas.   We shall never feel easy until those
troops are withdrawn."

General Grant said: "While we don't want another
war on our hands before we finish the present one, yet
I feel that the reëstablishment of republican government
in Mexico would really be a part of our present struggle.
As soon as the war of secession ends, and I think it is
coming to a close pretty rapidly, we will have a veteran
army in the West ready to make a demonstration upon
the Rio Grande with a view to enforcing respect for our
opinions concerning the Monroe doctrine.   I regard this
expedition to Mexico not as a movement of the French
people, but as one of the ambitious schemes of Louis
Napoleon, which shows that he has as little respect for
the French people's opinions as for our own.   The French
people are our old allies; it is natural that we should
have a great regard for them, and there is a very close
bond of sympathy between the two countries; but Louis
Napoleon does not represent the people of France.   I
hope that his power may some day cease, and that France
may become a republic, and I do not think that day is
far distant."   Mr. Seward remarked, "Yes; we want to
get Napoleon out of Mexico, but we don't want any war
over it; we have certainly had enough of war."

One of the party remarked to Mr. Seward that he
always seemed to have an abiding faith in the triumph
of the Union cause.   The Secretary replied: "Yes;
though we have passed through many gloomy periods
since the breaking out of the war, I have always felt
confident that the integrity of the Union would be preserved.   It is a part of my philosophy to believe that
the American republic has now, and will have for many
years to come, enough virtue in its people to insure the

safety of the state. Sometimes there does not seem to be any virtue to spare, but there 's always enough."

After some further conversation, Mr. Seward, by invitation of General Grant, visited some of the nearest camps; and in the afternoon General Butler accompanied the Secretary on his steamer on a trip up the James River as far as it was safe to go. Mr. Seward was urged to prolong his visit, but as he had an engagement to be in Norfolk in the evening, he felt compelled to start for that place in the afternoon, as soon as his steamer returned from the excursion up the James.

CHAPTER XVII

PREPARING THE PETERSBURG MINE—EXPLODING THE MINE
—GRANT'S ADVENTURE BETWEEN THE LINES—FAILURE
OF THE ASSAULT AT THE MINE—A NEW COMMAND FOR
SHERIDAN—AN INFERNAL MACHINE EXPLODED NEAR
HEADQUARTERS

AT this time the general-in-chief was devoting much
of his attention to the planning of an important
movement in connection with the explosion of the famous Petersburg mine, which had now been completed.
The operations attending it were novel and interesting,
though the result was the greatest disaster which occurred during the siege of Petersburg. After the assaults on the 17th and 18th of June, Burnside's corps
established a line of earthworks within one hundred
yards of those of the enemy. In rear of his advanced
position was a deep hollow. In front the ground rose
gradually until it reached an elevation on which the
Confederate line was established. Colonel Pleasants,
commanding the 48th Pennsylvania Regiment, composed
largely of miners, conceived the idea of starting a gallery
from a point in the hollow which was concealed from the
enemy's view, pushing it forward to a position under his
earthworks, and there preparing a mine large enough to
blow up the parapets and make a sufficiently wide opening for assaulting columns to rush through. Before the
end of June he communicated the project to Burnside,

who talked the matter over with General Meade. It was
then submitted to General Grant for his action. This
point of the line was in some respects unfavorable for
an assault; but it was not thought well to check the
zeal of the officer who had proposed the scheme, and so
an authorization was given for the undertaking to continue. There was a main gallery, 511 feet long and 4½
feet square, and two lateral galleries. The terminus was
under the enemy's parapet, and at a depth of about 23
feet below the surface of the ground. These preparations were completed July 23, and the mine was soon
after charged with eight thousand pounds of powder,
and made ready for use. A movement preliminary to
its explosion was begun on July 26, that required the
exercise of much ingenuity and good generalship, and
which the general-in-chief had planned with great care.
It involved making a feint against Richmond, which
should be conducted with such a show of serious intention that it would induce Lee to throw a large portion
of his command to the north side of the James, and
leave the works at Petersburg so depleted that the movement on Burnside's front would have in its favor many
chances of success. Hancock's corps drew out from its
position on the afternoon of the 26th, and made a rapid
night march to Deep Bottom, on the north side of the
James, and was followed by Sheridan with the cavalry.
This entire force was placed under Hancock's command.
On the morning of the 27th it advanced and captured
a battery of rifled guns. I had been sent to Hancock
that morning, and found him with his troops, lying upon
the grass with some of his staff during a lull in the firing.
I threw myself on the ground beside him while we conversed in regard to the situation, and informed him that
General Grant would be with him some hours later.
Suddenly firing broke out again in front, and we all

sprang to our feet to mount our horses. Hancock wore a thin blue flannel blouse, and as I rose up one of my spurs caught in the sleeve, and ripped it open from wrist to elbow. I felt not a little chagrined to find that I was the means of sending this usually well-dressed corps commander into battle with his sleeve slit open and dangling in the air, and made profuse apologies. There was not much time for words, but Hancock treated the matter so good-naturedly in what he said in reply that he at once put my mind at ease.

General Grant rode out on the field in the afternoon, arriving there at half-past three o'clock, for the purpose of determining upon the spot what the possibilities were on that side of the river before giving directions for carrying out the rest of his plans. Lee was now rushing troops to the north side of the James to reinforce the defenses of Richmond. The next morning (July 28) Sheridan, while moving around the enemy's left, was vigorously assaulted by a large body of infantry, and driven back a short distance; but he promptly dismounted his men, made a determined counter-attack, and drove the enemy back in confusion, capturing two hundred and fifty prisoners and two stands of colors. This engagement was called the battle of Darbytown. Now that Grant had satisfied himself that more than half of Lee's command had been sent to the north side of the James, he made preparations to throw Hancock's corps again in front of Petersburg, and carry out his intended assault upon that front.

It was decided that the attack should be made at daylight on the morning of the 30th. In the mean time, in order to keep up the deception and detain the enemy on the north side of the river, many clever ruses were resorted to, in which the general-in-chief's ingenuity and rare powers of invention were displayed to the greatest advantage. Meade and Ord were directed to cease all artillery-firing on the lines in front of Petersburg, and to conceal their guns, with a view to convincing the enemy that the troops were moving away from that position. Hancock withdrew one of his divisions quietly on the night of the 28th, and moved it back, while he remained with his two other divisions north of the James until the night of the 29th, so as still to keep up the feint. On the 28th Sheridan had the pontoon-bridge covered with moss, grass, and earth to prevent the tramping of horses from being heard, and quietly moved a division of his cavalry to the south side of the James. He then dismounted his men, concealed his horses, and marched back by daylight, so that the enemy would suppose that infantry was still moving to the north side. A train of empty wagons was also crossed to that side in sight of the enemy. Steamboats and tugs were sent up the river at night to the pontoon-bridges, and ordered to show their lights and blow their whistles for the purpose of making the enemy believe that we were transferring troops to the north side. These manœuvers were so successful that they detained the enemy north of the James all day on the 29th. Immediately after dark that evening the whole of Hancock's corps withdrew stealthily from Deep Bottom, followed by the cavalry. On the morning of the 30th Lee was holding five eighths of his army on the north side of the James, in the belief that Grant was massing the bulk of his troops near Deep Bottom, while he had in reality concentrated his forces in the rear of Burnside at a point fifteen miles distant, ready to break through the defenses at Petersburg.

On the afternoon of July 29 the general-in-chief proceeded with his staff to Burnside's front, and bivouacked near the center of his line, to give final instructions, and to be upon the spot when the assault should be made. Burnside had been carefully instructed to prepare his parapets and abatis in advance for the passage of his assaulting columns, so that when daylight came the troops would have no obstacles in their way in moving to the attack rapidly and with a strong formation. Ord had been moved to a position in Burnside's rear. Burnside had proposed to put Ferrero's colored troops in advance, but Meade objected to this, as they did not have the experience of the white troops; and in this decision he was sustained by Grant, and white troops were assigned to make the assault. Burnside, of course, was allowed to choose the division commander who was to lead the attack; but instead of selecting the best officer for the purpose, he allowed the division commanders to draw straws for the choice, and the lot fell, unfortunately, upon Ledlie, who was by far the least fitted for such an undertaking. Meade had joined Grant at his bivouac near Burnside's headquarters, and every one was up long before daylight, aiding in communicating final instructions and awaiting the firing of the mine.

Now came the hour for the explosion—half-past three o'clock. The general-in-chief was standing, surrounded by his officers, looking intently in the direction of the mine; orderlies were holding the saddled horses near by; not a word was spoken, and the silence of death prevailed. Some minutes elapsed, and our watches were anxiously consulted. It was found to be ten minutes past the time, and yet no sound from the mine. Ten minutes more, and still no explosion. More precious minutes elapsed, and it became painfully evident that some neglect or accident had occurred. Daylight was now breaking, and the formation of the troops for the assault would certainly be observed by the enemy. Officers had been sent to find out the cause of the delay,

and soon there came the information that the match had
been applied at the hour designated, but that the fuse
had evidently failed at some point along the gallery.
Another quarter of an hour passed, and now the minutes
seemed like ages; the suspense was agonizing; the whole
movement depended upon that little spark which was
to fire the mine, and it had gone out.   The general-in-
chief stood with his right hand placed against a tree;
his lips were compressed and his features wore an expression of profound anxiety, but he uttered few words.
There was little to do but to wait.   Now word came that
the men of the 48th Pennsylvania were not going to
permit a failure.   Not knowing whether the fuse had
gone out or was only "holding fire," a search through
the long gallery meant the probability of death to those
who undertook it; but Lieutenant Jacob Douty and
Sergeant Henry Reese, of the 48th Pennsylvania, undertook to penetrate the long passageway and discover
the cause of the failure.   They found that the fire had
been interrupted at a point at which two sections of the
fuse had been defectively spliced.   They promptly renewed the splice, and as soon as they emerged from the
gallery the match was again applied.   It was now twenty
minutes to five, over an hour past the appointed time.
The general had been looking at his watch, and had just
returned it to his pocket when suddenly there was a
shock like that of an earthquake, accompanied by a dull,
muffled roar; then there rose two hundred feet in the
air great volumes of earth in the shape of a mighty
inverted cone, with forked tongues of flame darting
through it like lightning playing through the clouds.
The mass seemed to be suspended for an instant in the
heavens; then there descended great blocks of clay, rock,
sand, timber, guns, carriages, and men whose bodies
exhibited every form of mutilation.   It appeared as if

part of the debris was going to fall upon the front line of our troops, and this created some confusion and a delay of ten minutes in forming them for the charge. The crater made by the explosion was 30 feet deep, 60 feet wide, and 170 feet long. One hundred and ten cannon and fifty mortars opened fire from our lines. Soon fatal errors in carrying out the orders became painfully apparent. The abatis had not been removed in the night, and no adequate preparations had been made at the parapets for the troops to march over them; the débouchés were narrow, and the men had to work their way out slowly. When they reached the crater they found that its sides were so steep that it was almost impossible to climb out after once getting in. Ledlie remained under cover in the rear; the advance was without superior officers, and the troops became confused. Some stopped to assist the Confederates who were struggling out of the debris, in which many of them were buried up to their necks.

The crater was soon filled with our disorganized men, who were mixed up with the dead and dying of the enemy, and tumbling aimlessly about, or attempting to scramble up the other side. The shouting, screaming, and cheering, mingled with the roar of the artillery and the explosion of shells, created a perfect pandemonium, and the crater had become a caldron of hell.

When it was found that the troops were accomplishing so little, and that matters were so badly handled, General Grant quickly mounted his horse, and calling to me, said, " Come with me." I was soon in the saddle, and, followed by a single orderly, we moved forward through some intervening woods, to make our way as far as we could on horseback to the front of the attack. It was now a little after half-past five. We soon came to a brigade lying upon its arms. The general said to an officer near by, who proved to be General Henry G. Thomas, a brigade commander, "Who commands this brigade?" "I do," he replied, springing up from the ground suddenly, and manifesting no little surprise to find that the voice of the person addressing him was that of the general-in-chief. "Well," remarked the general, "why are you not moving in?" The officer replied, "My orders are to follow that brigade," pointing to the one in front of him. Then, after a pause, he added, "Will you give me the order to go in now?" "No," said General Grant, not wishing to interfere with the instructions of the division commander, "you may keep the orders you have," and moved on to the front. A Pennsylvania regiment was now met with knapsacks piled on the ground, and about to move to the attack. The commanding officer made a salute, and the general returned it by lifting his hat. The men now recognized him, and it was all the commander of the regiment could do to keep them from breaking out into a cheer, although all noise had been forbidden. The officer said to me some years after: "If the general had given me only a slight nod of the head that morning I should have been delighted; but when I saw him, at such a trying moment, look at me and politely take off his hat, it brought the tears to my eyes and sent a big lump into my throat."

The enemy had now rallied his men upon the line in the rear of the crater, and there was heavy fighting going on between them and our advanced troops. After proceeding a short distance I said: "General, you cannot go much farther on horseback, and I do not think you ought to expose yourself in this way. I hope you will dismount, as you will then be less of a target for the enemy's fire." Without saying a word, he threw himself from his horse and handed the reins to the orderly, who was then directed to take our animals back to the edge of the woods, while we proceeded to the front on foot. The general had by this time taken in the situation pretty fully, and his object was to find the corps commander, to have him try to bring some order out of the chaos which existed. Upon inquiry it was ascertained that Burnside was on our left and some distance farther in advance. General Grant now began to edge his way vigorously to the front through the lines of the assaulting columns as they poured out of the rifle-pits and crawled over the obstructions. It was one of the warmest days of the entire summer, and even at this early hour of the morning the heat was suffocating. The general wore his blue blouse and a pair of blue trousers—in fact, the uniform of a private soldier, except the shoulder-straps. None of the men seemed to recognize him, and they were no respecters of persons as they shoved and crowded to the front. They little thought that the plainly dressed man who was elbowing his way past them so energetically, and whose face was covered with dust and streaked with perspiration, was the chief who had led them successfully from the Wilderness to Petersburg. Some officers were now seen standing in a field-work to the left, about three hundred yards distant, and Burnside was supposed to be one of the number. To reach them by passing inside of our main line of works would have been a slow process, as the ground was covered with obstacles and crowded with troops; so, to save valuable time, the general climbed nimbly over the parapet, landed in front of our earthworks, and resolved to take the chances of the enemy's fire. Shots were now flying thick and fast, and what with the fire of the enemy and the heat of the midsummer Southern sun, there was an equatorial warmth about the undertaking. The very recollection of it, over thirty years after, starts the perspiration.

Scarcely a word was spoken in passing over the distance crossed.   Sometimes the gait was a fast walk, sometimes a dog-trot.   As the shots shrieked through the air, and plowed the ground, I held my breath in apprehension for the general's safety.   Burnside was in the earthwork for which we were heading, and was not a little aston ished to see the general approach on foot from such a direction, climb over the parapet, and make his way to where the corps commander was stationed.   Grant said, speaking rapidly: " The entire opportunity has been lost. There is now no chance of success.   These troops must be immediately withdrawn.   It is slaughter to leave them here."   Burnside was still hoping that something could be accomplished; but the disobedience of orders and the general bungling had been so great that Grant was convinced that the only thing to do now to stop the loss of life was to abandon the movement which a few hours before had promised every success.   The general then made his way on foot, with no little difficulty, to where our horses had been left, mounted, and returned to where we had parted from Meade.

Instructions were reiterated to Burnside to withdraw the troops; but he came to Meade in person and insisted that his men could not be drawn out of the crater with safety; that the enemy's guns now bore upon the only line of retreat; and that there must be a passageway dug to protect them in crossing certain dangerous points. Both of these officers lost their tempers that morning, although Burnside was usually the personification of amiability, and the scene between them was decidedly peppery, and went far toward confirming one's belief in the wealth and flexibility of the English language as a medium of personal dispute.   Meade had sent Burnside a note saying: " Do you mean to say your officers and men will not obey your orders to advance ?   If not, what is the obstacle? I wish to know the truth." Burnside replied: "I have never, in any report, said anything different from what I conceive to be the truth. Were it not insubordinate, I would say that the latter remark of your note was unofficerlike and ungentlemanly." It was quite evident that the conference was not going to resolve itself into a "peace congress." However, both officers were manly enough afterward to express regret for what they had written and said under the excitement of the occasion. Although Ledlie had proved a failure, other division commanders made gallant efforts to redeem the fortunes of the day, but their men became disorganized, and huddled together inextricably in the crater. When the confusion was at its worst Burnside threw in his division of colored troops, who rushed gallantly into the crater, but only added greater disorder to the men already crowded together there. As a colored regiment was moving to the front in the midst of this scene of slaughter, a white sergeant, who was being carried to the rear with his leg shot off, cried out: "Now go in with a will, boys. There's enough of you to eat 'em all up." A colored sergeant replied: "Dat may be all so, boss; but the fac' is, we hab n't got jis de bes' kind ob an appetite for 'em dis mornin'."

The enemy soon brought to bear upon the crater a mortar fire, which did serious execution. There were many instances of superb courage, but the most heroic bravery could not make amends for the utter inefficiency with which the troops had been handled by some of their officers. It was two o'clock before all the survivors could be withdrawn. The total losses amounted to about thirty-eight hundred, nearly fourteen hundred of whom were prisoners.

Thus ended an operation conceived with rare ingenuity, prepared with unusual forethought, and executed up to the moment of the final assault with consummate skill, and which yet resulted in absolute failure from sheer incapacity on the part of subordinates. Burnside had given written orders which were excellent in themselves, but he failed entirely to enforce them. When the general-in-chief and staff rode back to Petersburg that day, the trip was anything but cheerful. For some time but little was said by him, owing to his aversion to indulging in adverse criticisms of individuals, which could not mend matters. He did not dwell long upon the subject in his conversation, simply remarking: " Such an opportunity for carrying a fortified line I have never seen, and never expect to see again. If I had been a division commander or a corps commander, I would have been at the front giving personal directions on the spot. I believe that the men would have performed every duty required of them if they had been properly led and skilfully handled." He had no unkind words for Burnside, but he felt that this disaster had greatly impaired that officer's usefulness. Two weeks afterward Burnside was granted a leave of absence, and did not serve again in the field. General Parke, one of his division commanders, and an officer of eminent ability, was placed in command of the Ninth Corps. Grant and Burnside, however, did not break their amicable relations on account of this official action, and their personal friendship continued as long as they both lived.

A surgeon told us a story, one of the many echoes of the mine affair, about a prisoner who had been dug out of the crater and carried to one of our field-hospitals. Although his eyes were bunged and his face covered with bruises, he was in an astonishingly amiable frame of mind, and looked like a pugilistic hero of the prize-ring coming up smiling in the twenty-seventh round. He said: " I 'll jest bet you that after this I 'll be the most unpopular man in my regiment. You see, I appeared to get started a little earlier than the other boys that had taken passage with me aboard that volcano; and as I was comin' down I met the rest of 'em a-goin' up, and they looked as if they had kind o' soured on me, and yelled after me, 'Straggler!'"

General Grant ordered the cavalry and a corps of infantry to start south at daylight the next morning, before the enemy could recross the James River, with instructions to destroy fifteen or twenty miles of the Weldon Railroad. That night, however, information of the crossing of the Potomac by Early's troops compelled the general to change his plans and send Sheridan to Washington with two divisions of his cavalry.

Early, finding that pursuit had been abandoned, and that the Union forces had returned to Washington, put his army in motion and started to return to Maryland. His advance reached Chambersburg, Pennsylvania, on July 30; and finding no troops to oppose them, burned the defenseless town, and left three thousand women, children, and unarmed men homeless. A week afterward this force, while retreating, was overtaken by Averell, and completely routed.

General Grant now expressed himself as determined not only to prevent these incursions into Maryland, but to move a competent force down the valley of Virginia, and hold permanently that great granary, upon which Lee was drawing so largely for his supplies. The most important thing was to find a commander equal to such an undertaking. No one had commended himself more thoroughly to the general-in-chief for such a mission than Sheridan, and he telegraphed Halleck to put Sheridan in command of all the troops in the field, and to give him instructions to pursue the enemy to the death. Sheridan reached Washington on August 3. Halleck telegraphed expressing some other views in regard to the disposition to be made of Sheridan, but they did not prevail. On the evening of the 3d the President sent to General Grant the following remarkable telegram, which is so characteristic that it is given in full:

"I have seen your despatch in which you say: 'I want Sheridan put in command of all the troops in the field, with instructions to put himself south of the enemy and follow him to the death; wherever the enemy goes, let our troops go also.' This, I think, is exactly right as to how our forces should move; but please look over the despatches you may have received from here even since you made that order, and discover, if you can, that there is any idea in the head of any one here of 'putting our army south of the enemy,' or of 'following him to the death' in any direction. I repeat to you, it will neither be done nor attempted unless you watch it every day and hour, and force it.

"A. LINCOLN, President."

It will be seen from this that the President was undoubtedly possessed of more courage than any of his advisers at Washington, and that he did not call for assistance to protect the capital, but for troops and a competent leader to go after Early and defeat him. It is the language of a man who wanted an officer of Grant's aggressiveness to force the fighting and send the troops after the enemy, even if the capital had to be left temporarily without defense.

General Grant received the President's despatch at noon of August 4, and he left City Point that night for Hunter's headquarters at Monocacy Station in Maryland, reaching there the next evening, August 5. He ordered all the troops in the vicinity to move that night to the valley of Virginia. The general had now a deli-

cate duty to perform. He had decided to put General
Sheridan in command of the active forces in the field;
but he was junior in rank to General Hunter, and in
order to spare the feelings of Hunter, and not subject
him to the mortification of being relieved from duty, the
general-in-chief suggested that he remain in command
of the military department, and that Sheridan be given
supreme control of the troops in the field. Hunter removed all embarrassment by saying that, under the circumstances, he deemed it better for the service that he
should be relieved entirely from duty. This unselfish
offer was accepted, and Sheridan was telegraphed to
come at once from Washington to Monocacy by a special
train. Grant met him at the station, and explained to
him what was expected of him. His present army consisted of nearly thirty thousand men, including eight
thousand cavalry. Early's army was about equal in
numbers. Grant said to Sheridan in his instructions:
" Do not hesitate to give commands to officers in whom
you have confidence, without regard to claims of others
on account of rank. What we want is prompt and active movements after the enemy in accordance with the
instructions you already have. I feel every confidence
that you will do the best, and will leave you as far as
possible to act on your own judgment, and not embarrass you with orders and instructions." This despatch
was eminently characteristic of Grant; it affords a key
to his method of dealing with his subordinates, and ex-
plains one of the chief reasons why his commanders were
so loyal to him. They felt that they would be left to the
exercise of an intelligent judgment; that if they did
their best, even if they did not succeed, they would never
be made scapegoats; and if they gained victories they
would be given the sole credit for whatever they accomplished.

As soon as Sheridan moved south the enemy was compelled to concentrate in front of him, and the effect was what Grant had predicted—the termination of incursions into Maryland. The general returned to City Point on August 8.

Rawlins had broken down in health from the labors and exposures of the campaign, and had been given a leave of absence on August 1, in the hope that he might soon recuperate and return to duty; but he was not able to join headquarters for two months. Already the seeds of consumption had been sown, from which he died while Secretary of War, five years afterward. He was greatly missed by every one at headquarters, and his chief expressed no little anxiety about his illness, although no one then thought that it was the beginning of a fatal disease.

An event occurred in the forenoon of August 9 which looked for an instant as if the general-in-chief had returned to headquarters only to meet his death. He was sitting in front of his tent, surrounded by several staff-officers. General Sharpe, the assistant provost-marshal-general, had been telling him that he had a conviction that there were spies in the camp at City Point, and had proposed a plan for detecting and capturing them. He had just left the general when, at twenty minutes to twelve, a terrific explosion shook the earth, accompanied by a sound which vividly recalled the Petersburg mine, still fresh in the memory of every one present. Then there rained down upon the party a terrific shower of shells, bullets, boards, and fragments of timber. The general was surrounded by splinters and various kinds of ammunition, but fortunately was not touched by any of the missiles. Babcock of the staff was slightly wounded in the right hand by a bullet, one mounted orderly and several horses were instantly killed, and three orderlies were wounded. In a moment all was consternation. On rushing to the edge of the bluff, we found that the cause of the explosion was the blowing up of a boat loaded with ordnance stores which lay at the wharf at the foot of the hill. Much damage was done to the wharf, the boat was entirely destroyed, all the laborers employed on it were killed, and a number of men and horses near the landing were fatally injured. The total casualties were forty-three killed and forty wounded. The general was the only one of the party who remained unmoved; he did not even leave his seat to run to the bluff with the others to see what had happened. Five minutes afterward he went to his writing-table and sent a telegram to Washington, notifying Halleck of the occurrence. No one could surmise the cause of the explosion, and the general appointed me president of a board of officers to investigate the matter. We spent several days in taking the testimony of all the people who were in sight of the occurrence, and used every possible means to probe the matter; but as all the men aboard the boat had been killed, we could obtain no satisfactory evidence. It was attributed by most of those present to the careless handling of the ammunition by the laborers who were engaged in unloading it; but there was a suspicion in the minds of many of us that it was the work of some emissaries of the enemy sent into the lines.

Seven years after the war, when I was serving with President Grant as secretary, a Virginian called to see me at the White House, to complain that the commissioner of patents was not treating him fairly in the matter of some patents he was endeavoring to procure. In the course of the conversation, in order to impress me with his skill as an inventor, he communicated the fact that he had once devised an infernal machine which had been used with some success during the war; and went on to say that it consisted of a small box filled with explosives, with a clockwork attachment which could be set so as to cause an explosion at any given time; that, to prove the effectiveness of it, he had passed into the Union lines in company with a companion, both dressed as laborers, and succeeded in reaching City Point, knowing this to be the base of supplies. By mingling with the laborers who were engaged in unloading the ordnance stores, he and his companion succeeded in getting aboard the boat, placing their infernal machine among the ammunition, and setting the clockwork so that the explosion would occur in half an hour. This enabled them to get to a sufficient distance from the place not to be suspected. I told him that his efforts, from his standpoint, had been eminently successful. At last, after many years, the mystery of the explosion was revealed.

This occurrence set the staff to thinking of the various forms of danger to which the general-in-chief was exposed, and how easily he might be assassinated; and we resolved that in addition to the ordinary guard mounted at the headquarters camp, we would quietly arrange a detail of "watchers" from the members of the staff, so that one officer would go on duty every night and keep a personal lookout in the vicinity of the general's tent. This was faithfully carried out. It had to be done secretly, for if he had known of it he would without doubt have broken it up and insisted upon the staff-officers going to bed after their hard day's work, instead of keeping these vigils throughout the long, dreary nights of the following winter. The general never knew of this action until his second term of the Presidency, when he made the discovery through an accidental reference to it in his presence by a visitor who had heard of it. He then expressed himself as feeling very much touched by the service which had been performed with a view to his personal protection.

CHAPTER XVIII

THE STORMING OF NEWMARKET HEIGHTS — A DRAFT OR-
DERED — BATTLE OF THE WELDON RAILROAD — BATTLE
OF REAMS'S STATION — GENERAL GRANT'S FAMILY VISIT
HIM — THE RELATIONS BETWEEN GRANT AND SHERMAN
— A MISSION TO SHERMAN — THE CAPTOR OF ATLANTA —
AN EVENING WITH GENERAL THOMAS

IT was found that Lee had sent a division of infantry
and cavalry as far as Culpeper to coöperate with
Early's forces, and on August 12, 1864, Grant began a
movement at Petersburg intended to force the enemy to
return his detached troops to that point. Hancock's
corps was marched from Petersburg to City Point, and
there placed on steamboats. The movement was to
create the impression that these troops were to be sent
to Washington. Butler relaid the pontoon-bridge, and
his forces crossed to Deep Bottom. The same night,
August 13, the boats which carried Hancock's corps
were sent up the river, and the troops disembarked on
the north side of the James. Hancock was put in command of the movement.

General Grant said, in discussing the affair: "I am
making this demonstration on the James, not that I expect it to result in anything decisive in the way of crippling the enemy in battle; my main object is to call
troops from Early and from the defenses of Petersburg.
If Lee withdraws the bulk of his army from Meade's

front, Meade will have a good opportunity of making a
movement to his left with one of his corps." The 14th
and 15th were spent in reconnoitering and manœuvuer-
ing and in making one successful assault. On August
16 I was directed to go to Hancock with important instructions, and remain with his command that day.
This gave me an opportunity to participate in the engagements which took place. Early in the morning the
movement began by sending out Miles's brigade and
Gregg's cavalry, which drove back a body of the enemy
to a point only seven miles from Richmond. At ten
o'clock a vigorous attack was made by Birney's corps
upon the works at Fussell's Mills. The intrenchments
were handsomely carried, and three colors and nearly
three hundred prisoners taken; but the enemy soon returned in large force, made a determined assault, and
compelled Birney to abandon the works he had captured. He succeeded, however, in holding the enemy's
intrenched picket-line. In the mean time the enemy
brought up a sufficient force to check the advance of
Gregg and Miles and compel them to withdraw from
their position. Our troops fell back in perfect order,
retiring by successive lines. Gregg took up a line on
Deep Creek. That evening the enemy made a heavy attack on him, but only succeeded in forcing him back a
short distance. The fighting had been desperate, and
all the officers present had suffered greatly from their
constant exposure to the heavy fire of the enemy in their
efforts to hold the men to their work and add as much
as possible to the success of the movements. This day's
fighting was known as the battle of Newmarket Heights.
In these engagements I was fortunate enough to be able
to render service which was deemed to be of some importance by the general-in-chief, who wrote to Washington asking that I be breveted a lieutenant-colonel in

the regular army for "gallant and meritorious services
in action"; and the appointment to that rank was made
by the President.   As a result of these operations, Hill's
command had been withdrawn from Petersburg and
sent to Hancock's front, and a division of Longstreet's
corps, which had been under marching orders for the
Valley, was detained.

General Grant was now giving daily watchfulness and
direction to four active armies in the field—those of
Meade, Butler, Sheridan, and Sherman.   They constituted a dashing four-in-hand, with Grant holding the
reins.   These armies no longer moved "like horses in a
balky team, no two ever pulling together."   While some
of them were at long distances from the others, they
were acting in harmony, and coöperating with one another for the purpose of keeping the enemy constantly
employed in their respective fronts, to prevent him from
concentrating his force against any particular army.
The enemy had short interior lines upon which to move,
and railroads for the prompt transportation of troops;
and it was only by these vigorous coöperative movements on the part of the Union armies that the enemy
was kept from practising the fundamental principle of
war—namely, concentrating the bulk of his forces against
a fraction of those of the enemy.

The affairs of the country were now like a prairie in
the season of fires: as soon as the conflagration was ex-
tinguished in one place it immediately broke out in
another.   While General Grant was hourly employed
in devising military movements to meet the situation
in the field, his advice and assistance were demanded
for a grave state of affairs which had now arisen in the
Northern States.   A draft had been ordered by the
President for the purpose of filling up our depleted regiments, and the disloyal element at home was making

it a pretext to embarrass the government in its prosecution of the war. On August 11 Halleck sent Grant a confidential letter, in which he said, among other things of a disturbing nature: "Pretty strong evidence is accumulating that there is a combination formed, or forming, to make a forcible resistance to the draft. . . . To enforce it may require the withdrawal of a very considerable number of troops from the field. . . . The evidence of this has increased very much within the last few days. . . . Are not the appearances such that we ought to take in sail and prepare the ship for a storm?" General Grant replied, suggesting means for enforcing the draft without depleting the armies in the field, and saying he was not going to break his hold where he was on the James.

On the evening of August 17 General Grant was sitting in front of his quarters, with several staff-officers about him, when the telegraph operator came over from his tent and handed him a despatch. He opened it, and as he proceeded with the reading his face became suffused with smiles. After he had finished it he broke into a hearty laugh. We were curious to know what could produce so much merriment in the general in the midst of the trying circumstances which surrounded him. He cast his eyes over the despatch again, and then remarked: "The President has more nerve than any of his advisers. This is what he says after reading my reply to Halleck's despatch." He then read aloud to us the following:

"'I have seen your despatch expressing your unwillingness to break your hold where you are. Neither am I willing. Hold on with a bulldog grip, and chew and choke as much as possible.

"'A. LINCOLN.'"

Throughout this period of activity at headquarters General Grant was not unmindful of the rewards which were due to his generals for their achievements. On August 10 he had written to the Secretary of War: "I think it but a just reward for services already rendered that General Sherman be now appointed a major-general, and W. S. Hancock and Sheridan brigadiers, in the regular army. All these generals have proved their worthiness for this advancement." Sherman and Hancock received their appointments on the 12th, and Sheridan on the 20th. General Grant was very much gratified that their cases had been acted upon so promptly.

Warren moved out at dawn on August 18, in accordance with orders, to a point three miles west of the left of the Army of the Potomac, and began the work of tearing up the Weldon Railroad. Hard fighting ensued that day, in which the enemy suffered severely. Lee hurried troops from north of the James to Petersburg, and in the afternoon of the 19th a large force turned a portion of Warren's command and forced it to retire. Two divisions of Parke's corps had been ordered to support Warren; our troops were now reformed, the lost ground was soon regained, the enemy fell back in great haste to his intrenchments, and the position on the railroad was firmly held by Warren's men. General Grant remained at City Point this day in order to be in constant communication with Hancock and Butler as well as with Meade. When he heard of Warren's success he telegraphed at once to Meade: "I am pleased to see the promptness with which General Warren attacked the enemy when he came out. I hope he will not hesitate in such cases to abandon his lines and take every man to fight every battle, and trust to regaining them afterward, or to getting better." He said after writing this despatch: "Meade and I have had to criticize Warren pretty severely on several occasions for being slow, and I wanted to be prompt to compliment him now that he has acted vigorously and handsomely in taking the offensive." His corps being greatly exposed in its present position, and knowing that the enemy would use all efforts to save the railroad, Warren on August 20 took up a position in rear of his line of battle the day before, and intrenched. All of Hancock's corps was withdrawn from the north side of the James. Lee soon discovered this, and hurried more troops back to Petersburg. On the morning of August 21 Hill's whole corps, with a part of Hoke's division and Lee's cavalry, attacked Warren. Thirty pieces of artillery opened on him, and at ten o'clock vigorous assaults were made; but Warren repulsed the enemy at all points, and then advanced and captured several hundred prisoners. The enemy had failed in his desperate efforts to recover the Weldon Railroad, and he was now compelled to haul supplies by wagons around the break in order to make any use of that line of supplies.

On August 22 Gregg's division of cavalry and troops from Hancock's corps were sent to Reams's Station, seven miles south of Warren's position, and tore up three miles of the Weldon Railroad south of that place. Hancock discovered the enemy massing heavily in his front on the 25th, and concentrated his force at the station, and took possession of some earthworks which had been constructed before at that place, but which were badly laid out for the purpose of defense. That afternoon several formidable assaults were directed against Miles, who was in command of Barlow's division, but they were handsomely repulsed. At 5 P. M. Hill's corps made a vigorous attack. Owing to the faulty construction of the earthworks, Hancock's command was exposed to a reverse fire, which had an unfortunate effect upon the

morale of the men. A portion of Miles's line finally
gave way, and three of our batteries of artillery were
captured. Our troops were now exposed to attack both
in flank and reverse, and the position of Hancock's command had become exceedingly critical; but the superb
conduct displayed by him and Miles in rallying their
forces saved the day. By a gallant dash the enemy was
soon swept back, and one of our batteries and a portion
of the intrenchments were retaken. Gibbon's divison
was driven from its intrenched position, but it took up
a new line, and after hard fighting the further advance
of the enemy was checked. As the command was now
seriously threatened in its present position, and none of
the reinforcements ordered up had arrived, Hancock's
troops were withdrawn after dark.

Hancock's want of success was due largely to the condition of his troops. They had suffered great fatigue;
there had been heavy losses during the campaign, particularly in officers, and the command was composed
largely of recruits and substitutes. The casualties in
this engagement, in killed, wounded, and missing, were
2742; the number of guns lost, 9. The enemy's loss
was larger than ours in killed and wounded, but less
in prisoners. General Miles, who thirty-one years
thereafter became general-in-chief of the army, in all
his brilliant career as a soldier never displayed more
gallantry and ability than in this memorable engagement, which is known in history as the battle of Reams's
Station.

The enemy had subjected himself to heavy loss in a
well-concerted attempt to regain possession of the Weldon Railroad, which was of such vital importance to
him, but in this he had signally failed. Lee had been
so constantly threatened, or compelled to attack around
Petersburg and Richmond, that he had been entirely

prevented from sending any forces to Hood to be used against Sherman.

Mrs. Grant had come East with the children, and Colonel Dent, her brother, was sent to meet them at Philadelphia, and bring them to City Point to pay a visit to the general. The children consisted of Frederick D., then fourteen years old; Ulysses S., Jr., twelve; Nellie R., nine; and Jesse R., six. Nellie was born on the 4th of July, and when a child an innocent deception had been practised upon her by her father in letting her believe that all the boisterous demonstrations and display of fireworks on Independence day were in honor of her birthday. The general was exceedingly fond of his family, and his meeting with them afforded him the happiest day he had seen since they parted. They were comfortably lodged aboard the headquarters steamboat, but spent most of their time in camp. The morning after their arrival, when I stepped into the general's tent, I found him in his shirt-sleeves engaged in a rough-and-tumble wrestling-match with the two older boys. He had become red in the face, and seemed nearly out of breath from the exertion. The lads had just tripped him up, and he was on his knees on the floor grappling with the youngsters, and joining in their merry laughter, as if he were a boy again himself. I had several despatches in my hand, and when he saw that I had come on business, he disentangled himself after some difficulty from the young combatants, rose to his feet, brushed the dust off his knees with his hand, and said in a sort of apologetic manner: "Ah, you know my weaknesses —my children and my horses." The children often romped with him, and he joined in their frolics as if they were all playmates together. The younger ones would hang about his neck while he was writing, make a terrible mess of his papers, and turn everything in his

tent into a toy: but they were never once reproved for
any innocent sport; they were governed solely by an
appeal to their affections.   They were always respectful,
and never failed to render strict obedience to their father
when he told them seriously what he wanted them to do.

Mrs. Grant, formerly Miss Julia Dent, was four years
younger than the general.   She had been educated in
Professor Moreau's finishing-school in St. Louis, one of
the best institutions of instruction in its day, and was a
woman of much general intelligence, and exceedingly
well informed upon all public matters.   She was noted
for her amiability, her cheerful disposition, and her extreme cordiality of manner.   She was soon upon terms
of intimacy with all the members of the staff, and was
quick to win the respect and esteem of every one at headquarters.   She visited any officers or soldiers who were
sick, went to the cook and suggested delicacies for their
comfort, took her meals with the mess, kept up a pleasant run of conversation at the table, and added greatly
to the cheerfulness of headquarters.   She had visited
her husband several times at the front when he was
winning his victories in the West, and had learned perfectly how to adapt herself to camp life.   She and the
general were a perfect Darby and Joan.   They would
seek a quiet corner of his quarters of an evening, and sit
with her hand in his, manifesting the most ardent devotion; and if a staff-officer came accidentally upon them,
they would look as bashful as two young lovers spied
upon in the scenes of their courtship.   In speaking of
the general to others, his wife usually referred to him as
"Mr. Grant," from force of habit formed before the war.
In addressing him she said "Ulyss," and when they
were alone, or no one was present except an intimate
friend of the family, she applied a pet name which she
had adopted after the capture of Vicksburg, and called

him "Victor." Sometimes the general would tease the children good-naturedly by examining them about their studies, putting to them all sorts of puzzling mathematical questions, and asking them to spell tongue-splitting words of half a dozen syllables. Mrs. Grant would at times put on an air of mock earnestness, and insist upon the general telling her all of the details of the next movement he intended to make. He would then proceed to give her a fanciful description of an imaginary campaign, in which he would name impossible figures as to the number of the troops, inextricably confuse the geography of the country, and trace out a plan of marvelously complicated movements in a manner that was often exceedingly droll. No family could have been happier in their relations; there was never a selfish act committed or an ill-natured word uttered by any member of the household, and their daily life was altogether beautiful in its charming simplicity and its deep affection.

A little before nine o'clock on the evening of September 4, while the general was having a quiet smoke in front of his tent, and discussing the campaign in Georgia, a despatch came from Sherman announcing the capture of Atlanta, which had occurred on September 2. It was immediately read aloud to the staff, and after discussing the news for a few minutes, and uttering many words in praise of Sherman, the general wrote the following reply: "I have just received your despatch announcing the capture of Atlanta. In honor of your great victory I have ordered a salute to be fired with shotted guns from every battery bearing upon the enemy. The salute will be fired within an hour, amid great rejoicing."

In the mean time the glad tidings had been telegraphed to Meade and Butler, with directions to fire the salute, and not long afterward the roar of artillery communicated the joyful news of victory throughout our army, and bore sad tidings to the ranks of the enemy. An answer was received from Sherman, in which he said: "I have received your despatch, and will communicate it to the troops in general orders. . . . I have always felt that you would take personally more pleasure in my success than in your own, and I reciprocate the feeling to the fullest extent." Grant then wrote to Sherman: "I feel that you have accomplished the most gigantic undertaking given to any general in this war with a skill and ability which will be acknowledged in history as unsurpassed, if not unequaled. It gives me as much pleasure to record this in your favor as it would in favor of any living man, myself included." This correspondence, and the unmeasured praise which was given to Sherman at this time by the general-in-chief in his despatches and conversations, afford additional evidences of his constant readiness to give all due praise to his subordinates for any successful work which they accomplished. He was entirely unselfish in his relations with them, and never tired of taking up the cudgels in their defense if any one criticized them unjustly.

The above correspondence with Sherman recalls the letters which were interchanged between them after General Grant's successes in the West. The general wrote to Sherman at that time: "What I want is to express my thanks to you and McPherson as the men to whom, above all others, I feel indebted for whatever I have had of success. How far your advice and assistance have been of help to me you know. How far your execution of whatever has been given you to do entitles you to the reward I am receiving, you cannot know as well as I. I feel all the gratitude this letter would express, giving it the most flattering construction." Sherman wrote a no less manly letter in reply. After insisting that

General Grant assigned to his subordinates too large a share of merit, he went on to say: "I believe you to be as brave, patriotic, and just as the great prototype, Washington; as unselfish, kind-hearted, and honest as a man should be; but the chief characteristic is the simple faith in success you have always manifested, which I can liken to nothing else than the faith a Christian has in the Saviour. . . . I knew, wherever I was, that you thought of me, and if I got in a tight place you would help me out if alive." The noble sentiments expressed in this and similar correspondence were the bright spots which served to relieve the gloomy picture of desolating war.

Now that Sherman had captured Atlanta, the question at once arose as to what his next move should be; and a discussion took place at General Grant's headquarters as to the advisability of a march to the sea. Such a movement had been referred to in a despatch from Grant to Halleck as early as July 15, saying: "If he [Sherman] can supply himself once with ordnance and quartermaster's stores, and partially with subsistence, he will find no difficulty in staying until a permanent line can be opened with the south coast." On August 13 Sherman communicated with Grant about the practicability of cutting loose from his base and shifting his army to the Alabama River, or striking out for St. Mark's, Florida, or for Savannah. Further correspondence took place between the two generals after Sherman had entered Atlanta. The subject was one in which the members of the staff became deeply interested. Maps were pored over daily, and most intelligent discussions were carried on as to the feasibility of Sherman's army making a march to the sea-coast, and the point upon which his movement should be directed.

On September 12 General Grant called me into his tent, turned his chair around from the table at which he had been sitting, lighted a fresh cigar, and began a conversation by saying: "Sherman and I have exchanged ideas regarding his next movement about as far as we can by correspondence, and I have been thinking that it would be well for you to start for Atlanta to-morrow, and talk over with him the whole subject of his next campaign. We have debated it so much here that you know my views thoroughly, and can answer any of Sherman's questions as to what I think in reference to the contemplated movement, and the action which should be taken in the various contingencies which may arise. Sherman's suggestions are excellent, and no one is better fitted for carrying them out. I can comply with his views in regard to meeting him with ample supplies at any point on the sea-coast which it may be decided to have him strike for. You can tell him that I am going to send an expedition against Wilmington, North Carolina, landing the troops on the coast north of Fort Fisher; and with the efficient coöperation of the navy we shall no doubt get control of Wilmington harbor by the time he reaches and captures other points on the sea-coast. Sherman has made a splendid campaign, and the more I reflect upon it the more merit I see in it. I do not want to hamper him any more in the future than in the past with detailed instructions. I want him to carry out his ideas freely in the coming movement, and to have all the credit of its success. Of this success I have no doubt. I will write Sherman a letter, which you can take to him." The general then turned to his writing-table, and retaining between his lips the cigar which he had been smoking, wrote the communication. After reading it over aloud, he handed it to me to take to Atlanta. It said, among other things: "Colonel Porter will explain to you the exact condition of affairs here better than I can do in the limits of a letter. . . . My object now in sending a staff-officer is not so much to suggest operations for you as to get your views and have plans matured by the time everything can be got ready. It will probably be the 5th of October before any of the plans herein indicated will be executed. . . ."

I started the next day on this mission, going by way of Cincinnati and Louisville; and after many tedious interruptions from the crowded state of traffic by rail south of the latter place, and being once thrown from the track, I reached Chattanooga on the afternoon of September 19. From there to Atlanta is one hundred and fifty miles. Guerrillas were active along the line of the road, numerous attempts had recently been made to wreck the trains, and they were run as far as practicable by daylight. Being anxious to reach General Sherman with all despatch, I started forward that night on a freight-train. Rumors of approaching guerrillas were numerous; but, like many other campaign reports, they were unfounded, and I arrived in Atlanta safely the next forenoon. Upon this night trip I passed over the battle-field of Chickamauga on the anniversary of the sanguinary engagement in which I had participated the year before, and all of its exciting features were vividly recalled.

Upon reaching Atlanta, I went at once to General Sherman's headquarters. My mind was naturally wrought up to a high pitch of curiosity to see the famous soldier of the West, whom I had never met. He had taken up his quarters in a comfortable brick house belonging to Judge Lyons, opposite the Court-house Square. As I approached I saw the captor of Atlanta on the porch, sitting tilted back in a large arm-chair, reading a newspaper. His coat was unbuttoned, his black felt hat slouched over his brow, and on his feet were a pair of slippers very much down at the heels. He was in the prime of life and in the perfection of physical health.

He was just forty-four years of age, and almost at the summit of his military fame. With his large frame, tall, gaunt form, restless hazel eyes, aquiline nose, bronzed face, and crisp beard, he looked the picture of "grim-visaged war." My coming had been announced to him by telegraph, and he was expecting my arrival at this time. I approached him, introduced myself, and handed him General Grant's letter. He tilted forward in his chair, crumpled the newspaper in his left hand while with his right he shook hands cordially, then pushed a chair forward and invited me to sit down. His reception was exceedingly cordial, and his manner exhibited all the personal peculiarities which General Grant, in speaking of him, had so often described.

After reading General Grant's letter, he entered at once upon an animated discussion of the military situation East and West, and as he waxed more intense in his manner the nervous energy of his nature soon began to manifest itself. He twice rose from his chair, and sat down again, twisted the newspaper into every conceivable shape, and from time to time drew first one foot and then the other out of its slipper, and followed up the movement by shoving out his leg so that the foot could recapture the slipper and thrust itself into it again. He exhibited a strong individuality in every movement, and there was a peculiar energy of manner in uttering the crisp words and epigrammatic phrases which fell from his lips as rapidly as shots from a magazine-gun. I soon realized that he was one of the most dramatic and picturesque characters of the war. He asked a great deal about the armies of the East, and spoke of the avidity with which he read all accounts of the desperate campaigns they were waging. He said: "I knew Grant would make the fur fly when he started down through Virginia. Wherever he is the enemy will never find any

trouble about getting up a fight.   He has all the tenacity
of a Scotch terrier.   That he will accomplish his whole
purpose I have never had a doubt.   I know well the
immense advantage which the enemy has in acting on
the defensive in a peculiarly defensive country, falling
back on his supplies when we are moving away from
ours, taking advantage of every river, hill, forest, and
swamp to hold us at bay, and intrenching every night
behind fortified lines to make himself safe from attack.
Grant ought to have an army more than twice the size
of that of the enemy in order to make matters at all
equal in Virginia.   When Grant cried 'Forward!' after
the battle of the Wilderness, I said: ' This is the grandest
act of his life; now I feel that the rebellion will be
crushed.'   I wrote him, saying it was a bold order to
give, and full of significance; that it showed the mettle
of which he was made, and if Wellington could have
heard it he would have jumped out of his boots.   The
terms of Grant's despatch in reply to the announcement
of the capture of Atlanta gave us great gratification here.
I took that and the noble letter written by President
Lincoln, and published them in general orders; and they
did much to encourage the troops and make them feel
that their hard work was appreciated by those highest
in command."

After a while lunch was announced, and the general
invited me to his mess, consisting of himself and his
personal staff.   Among the latter I met some of my old
army friends, whom I was much gratified to see again.
The general's mess was established in the dining-room
of the house he occupied, and was about as democratic
as Grant's.   The officers came and went as their duties
required, and meals were eaten without the slightest
ceremony.   After we were seated at the table the general said: "I don't suppose we have anything half as

good to eat out here as you fellows in the East have. You have big rivers upon which you can bring up shell-fish, and lots of things we don't have here, where every-thing has to come over a single-track railroad more than three hundred miles long, and you bet we don't spare any cars for luxuries. It is all we can do to get the ne-cessaries down this far. However, here is some pretty fair beef, and there are plenty of potatoes," pointing to the dishes; "and they are good enough for anybody. We did get a little short of rations at times on the march down here, and one of my staff told me a good story of what one of the men had to say about it. An officer found him eating a persimmon that he had picked up, and cried out to him, 'Don't eat that; it's not good for you.' 'I'm not eatin' it because it's good,' was the re-ply; 'I'm tryin' to pucker up my stomach so as to fit the size of the rations Uncle Billy Sherman's a-givin' us.'"

After lunch we repaired to a room in the house which the general used for his office, and there went into an elaborate discussion of the purpose of my visit. He said: "I am more than ever of the opinion that there ·ought to be some definite objective point or points de-cided upon before I move farther into this country; sweeping around generally through Georgia for the pur-pose of inflicting damage would not be good generalship; I want to strike out for the sea. Now that our people have secured Mobile Bay, they might be able to send a force up to Columbus. That would be of great assis-tance to me in penetrating farther into this State; but unless Canby is largely reinforced, he will probably have as much as he can do at present in taking care of the rebels west of the Mississippi. If after Grant takes Wil-mington he could, with the coöperation of the navy, get hold of Savannah, and open the Savannah River up to the neighborhood of Augusta, I would feel pretty safe in picking up the bulk of this army and moving east, subsisting off the country. I could move to Milledgeville, and threaten both Macon and Augusta, and by making feints I could manœuver the enemy out of Augusta. I can subsist my army upon the country as long as I can keep moving; but if I should have to stop and fight battles the difficulty would be greatly increased. There is no telling what Hood will do, whether he will follow me and contest my march eastward, or whether he will start north with his whole army, thinking there will not be any adequate force to oppose him, and that he can carry the war as far north as Kentucky. I don't care much which he does. I would rather have him start north, though; and I would be willing to give him a free ticket and pay his expenses if he would decide to take that horn of the dilemma. I could send enough of this army to delay his progress until our troops scattered through the West could be concentrated in sufficient force to destroy him; then with the bulk of my army I could cut a swath through to the sea, divide the Confederacy in two, and be able to move up in the rear of Lee, or do almost anything else that Grant might require of me. Both Jeff Davis, according to the tone of his recent speeches, and Hood want me to fall back. That is just the reason why I want to go forward."

The general then went into a long discussion of the details which would have to be carried out under the several contingencies which might occur. He said: "In any emergency I should probably want to designate a couple of points on the coast where I could reach the sea as compelled by circumstances; and a fleet of provisions ought to be sent to each one of the points, so that I would be sure of having supplies awaiting me." I told him that this had been discussed by General Grant, and it was his intention to make ample provisions of that nature. The general said further: "You know when I cut loose from my communications you will not hear anything from me direct, and Grant will have to learn of my whereabouts, and the points where I reach the coast, by means of scouts, if we can get any through the country, and possibly depend largely upon the news obtained from rebel newspapers. I suppose you get these papers through the lines just as we do here." I said: "Yes; and I think more readily. The enemy is always eager to get the New York papers, and as we receive them daily, we exchange them for Richmond and Petersburg papers, and obtain in that way much news that is valuable. There will be no difficulty in hearing of your movements almost daily." At the close of the conversation I told the general I was anxious to get back to headquarters as soon as it would suit his convenience. He asked me to stay a couple of days, saying he would talk matters over further, and would write some communications for General Grant, a report, and also a list of the names of officers whom he wished to have promoted, if it could be prepared in time. I was invited to share the quarters of one of the staff-officers, and spent a couple of days very advantageously in looking over the captured city, and learning many points of interest regarding the marvelous campaign which had secured it.

That evening I paid a visit to my old commanding officer, General George H. Thomas, who had quartered himself in a house on Peachtree street, now known as the Leyden House, and passed a very pleasant hour with him. The house was surrounded by a broad porch supported by rows of fluted columns, and was very commodious. The meeting revived a great many stories of the

Chickamauga campaign.   The general said in the course
of the conversation: " Do you remember that jackass
that looked over the fence one day when we were passing
along a road near the Tennessee River?   He pricked up
his ears and brayed until he threatened to deafen everybody within a mile of him; and when he stopped, and
a dead silence followed, a soldier quietly remarked,
'Boys, did you hear him purr?'   I thought that was
about the loudest specimen of a purr I had ever heard."
Then the general lay back in his chair and shook with
laughter at the recollection.   While grave in manner and
leonine in appearance, he had a great deal more fun in
him than is generally supposed.   When quartered at Murfreesboro, Tennessee, the year before, a piano had been
secured, and it was the custom to have musical entertainments in the evening at general headquarters.   There
were some capital voices among the officers, and no end
of comic songs at hand; and these, with the recitations
and improvisations which were contributed, made up a
series of variety performances which became quite celebrated.   General Thomas was a constant attendant, and
would nod approval at the efforts of the performers, and
beat time to the music, and when anything particularly
comical took place he would roll from side to side and
nearly choke with merriment.

That day Sherman wrote to Grant: " I have the honor
to acknowledge, at the hands of Lieutenant-colonel
Porter of your staff, your letter of September 12, and
accept with thanks the honorable and kindly mention
of the services of this army in the great cause in which
we are all engaged."   Then followed three or four pages,
closing with the sentence: " I will have a long talk with
Colonel Porter, and tell him everything that may occur
to me of interest to you.   In the mean time, know that
I admire your dogged perseverance and pluck more than

ever.   If you can whip Lee, and I can march to the Atlantic, I think Uncle Abe will give us a twenty days' leave of absence to see the young folks."   Two days later I started back to City Point, and reached there September 27.

CHAPTER XIX

GRANT VISITS SHERIDAN — GOOD NEWS FROM WINCHESTER —
GRANT UNDER FIRE AT FORT HARRISON — CONSTERNA-
TION IN RICHMOND — SECRETARY STANTON VISITS
GRANT — HOW GRANT RECEIVED THE NEWS FROM
CEDAR CREEK

GENERAL GRANT listened with manifest interest
to the report which I brought of the situation at
Atlanta, and of Sherman's feelings and intentions, and
asked many questions as to the condition of the great
army of the West. I found that during my absence the
general-in-chief had paid a visit to Sheridan. He had
started from City Point on the 15th of September, had
passed through Washington without stopping, and had
gone directly to Charlestown, where Sheridan then had
his headquarters. He went from there to Burlington,
New Jersey, where it was arranged to place his children
at school, and returned to City Point on the 19th. He
spoke with much pleasure and satisfaction of his visit
to Sheridan, and said: "I was so anxious not to have
the movement made in the Valley unless I felt assured
of its success that I thought I would go and have a talk
with Sheridan before giving a decided answer as to
what should be done. I had written out a plan of campaign for his guidance, and did not stop at Washington
for the reason that I thought there might be a disposition there to modify it and make it less aggressive. I

first asked Sheridan if he had a plan of his own, and if so, what it was. He brought out his maps, and laid out a plan so complete, and spoke so confidently about his ability to whip the enemy in his front, that I did not take my plan out of my pocket, but let him go ahead. I also decided not to remain with him during the movement, which was to begin in a day or two, for fear it might be thought that I was trying to share in a success which I wished to belong solely to him."

In speaking of his visit to the Middle Military Division, General Grant said: "I ordered Sheridan to move out and whip Early." An officer present ventured the remark: "I presume the actual form of the order was to move out and attack him." "No," answered the general; "I mean just what I say: I gave the order to whip him."

Sheridan advanced promptly on September 19, and struck Early's army at Winchester, where he gained a signal victory, capturing five guns and nine battle-flags. He pursued the enemy the next day as far as Fisher's Hill, and on the 22d attacked him again in front and flank, carried his earthworks at every point, captured sixteen guns and eleven hundred prisoners, put him to flight, and completed his destruction. This left Sheridan in possession of the valley of Virginia. He had obeyed to the letter his orders to whip Early.

General Grant sent cordial congratulations to the victorious commander, and ordered a salute of one hundred guns in honor of each of his victories. No events had created more rejoicing in the mind of the general-in-chief than these brilliant triumphs of Sheridan. The general had taken the sole responsibility of bringing Sheridan East and placing him in command of a separate, important army, amid the doubts of some of the principal officials at Washington, and these victories on the part of the young commander were an entire vindication of Grant's judgment. The spirits of the loyal people of the North were beginning to droop, and the disloyal element had become still more aggressive, and such victories just at this time were of inestimable value.

During Grant's visit to Sheridan the enemy's cavalry had made a bold dash round the left of Meade's line, and captured over two thousand head of cattle. One evening after Grant's return, at the close of a conversation upon this subject, a citizen from Washington, who was stopping at City Point, inquired of him, "When do you expect to starve out Lee and capture Richmond?" "Never," replied the general, significantly, "if our armies continue to supply him with beef-cattle."

The general-in-chief was still planning to keep the enemy actively engaged in his own immediate front, so as to prevent him from detaching troops against distant commanders. He telegraphed Sherman September 26: "I will give them another shake here before the end of the week." On the 27th he sent a despatch to Sheridan, saying: ". . . No troops have passed through Richmond to reinforce Early. I shall make a break here on the 29th." All these despatches were of course sent in cipher. Definite instructions were issued on the 27th for the "break" which was in contemplation. Birney's and Ord's corps of Butler's army were to cross on the night of September 28 to the north side of the James River at Deep Bottom, and attack the enemy's forces there. If they succeeded in breaking through his lines they were to make a dash for Richmond. While the general did not expect to capture the city by this movement, he tried to provide for every emergency, thinking that if the enemy's line should be found weak, there would be a bare chance, after having once broken through, of creating a panic in Richmond, and getting inside of its inner works.

Ord and Birney moved out promptly before daylight
on September 29. General Grant left a portion of his
staff at City Point to communicate with him and Meade,
and rode out, taking the rest of us with him, to Butler's
front. Ord moved directly against Fort Harrison, a
strong earthwork occupying a commanding position,
carried it by assault, captured fifteen guns and several
hundred prisoners, and secured possession of an entire
line of intrenchments. Everything promised further
success, when Ord was wounded so severely in the leg
that he had to leave the field, and proper advantage was
not taken of the important success which had been gained.
Birney moved with his colored troops against the line of
intrenchments on the New Market road, promptly carried it, and drove the enemy back in great confusion.
General Grant was with Birney's command in the early
part of the day. His youngest son, Jesse, had obtained
permission that morning to go up the river on the boat
which carried his father, and had taken along his black
Shetland pony called "Little Reb." The boy was then
only a little over six years old, and was dressed in kilts,
probably in honor of his Scotch ancestors. When the
party reached the north side of the river, and mounted
and rode out to the front, Jesse got on "Little Reb" and
followed along. His father was so busy in supervising
the movement that he did not notice the boy until he
got under fire, when, on looking around, he saw his en-
terprising heir moving about as coolly as any of the
others of the group, while the shots were striking the
earth and stirring up the dust in every direction.
"What's that youngster doing there?" cried the general, manifesting no little anxiety; and turning to the
junior aide, added, "Dunn, I wish you would take him
to the rear, and put him where he will be safe." But
Jesse had too much of his sire's blood in his veins to

yield a prompt compliance, and at first demurred. Dunn, however, took hold of "Little Reb's" bridle, and started him on a gallop toward the river; and the boy, much to his mortification, had to beat an ignominious retreat. Dunn was more troubled than any one else over this masterly retrograde movement, for he was afraid that the troops who saw him breaking for the rear under fire might think that he had suddenly set too high a value on his life, and was looking out for a safe place.

After the capture of the works by Birney's troops, the general-in-chief rode over to Fort Harrison to push matters in that direction. He was greatly gratified at the handsome manner in which the fort had been carried, and the pluck which had been shown by the troops. The fort was an inclosed work, and formed a salient upon the enemy's line. There were batteries in its rear, however, which still commanded it. The general rode up to a point near the ditch, and there dismounted, and made his way into the work on foot. The ground gave ample evidence of the effects of the assault, and was so torn with shot and shell and covered with killed and wounded in some places that the general had to pick his way in stepping over the dead bodies that lay in his path. He turned his looks upward to avoid as much as possible the ghastly sight, and the expression of profound grief impressed upon his features told, as usual, of the effect produced upon him by the sad spectacle. Upon entering the fort, he climbed up and looked over the parapet on the north side, and remained there for some time, viewing the surrounding works and taking a look at Richmond, while the enemy's batteries continued to shell us. This was the nearest view of the city he had yet obtained, and the church spires could be indistinctly seen. He made up his mind that both corps should move forward promptly, and sat down on the ground, tucked his legs under him, and wrote the following despatch to Birney, dating it 10: 35 A. M.: "General Ord has carried the very strong works and some fifteen pieces of artillery, and his corps is now ready to advance in conjunction with you. General Ord was wounded, and has returned to his headquarters, leaving General Heckman in command of the corps. Push forward on the road I left you on." The enemy's projectiles were still flying in our direction, and when the general had reached the middle of the despatch a shell burst directly over him. Those standing about instinctively ducked their heads, but he paid no attention to the occurrence, and did not pause in his writing, or even look up. The handwriting of the despatch when finished did not bear the slightest evidence of the uncomfortable circumstances under which it was indited.

General Butler had ridden up to the fort, his face flushed with excitement; and in an interview which followed with General Grant, the commander of the Army of the James grew enthusiastic in lauding the bravery of the colored troops, who had carried so handsomely the work which Birney had assaulted that morning.

General Grant had not heard from Meade since early in the morning, and feeling somewhat anxious, he now made his way out of the fort, mounted his horse, and rode over to Deep Bottom, at which point he could communicate by a field telegraph-line with the commander of the Army of the Potomac. About half-past one o'clock the general received a telegram at Deep Bottom from the President, saying: "I hope it will lay no constraint on you, nor do harm any way, for me to say I am a little afraid lest Lee sends reinforcements to Early, and thus enables him to turn upon Sheridan." It will be seen that the President did not pretend to thrust military advice upon his commander, but only modestly suggested his views. The general replied immediately: "Your despatch just received. I am taking steps to prevent Lee sending reinforcements to Early, by attacking him here"; and closed with an account of the successes of the morning.

But little further progress was made during the day north of the James. General Grant remained on the north side of the river until after 4 P. M., and then returned to City Point so as to be within easy communication with Meade, and to determine what should be done the next day. It was long after midnight before any one at headquarters went to bed, and then only to catch a nap of a couple of hours. General Grant set out again for Deep Bottom at five o'clock the next morning; and after consulting with Butler, and finding everything quiet on the part of the enemy, he decided that no movement should be made on that front at present, and returned to City Point, starting back at 8 A. M.

The activity this day was on Meade's front. His troops moved out two miles west of the Weldon Railroad, and captured two redoubts, a line of rifle-pits, a gun, and over one hundred prisoners. Three times that afternoon the enemy made vigorous efforts to recover the works which had been captured by Butler's army the day before, for they commanded the shortest road to Richmond. So important was the movement deemed for their recapture that Lee was present in person with the troops who made the attack. Every assault, however, was handsomely repulsed. Meade threw up a strong line of intrenchments from the Weldon Railroad to the advanced position which he had captured, and his left was now only about two miles from the South Side Railroad.

In these movements no little advantage had been gained. The ability to carry strong works had encouraged the troops, and the circle had been closed in still further upon Lee, both on our right and left, and the effect upon the enemy was shown by the consternation and excitement which prevailed in Richmond. From refugees, scouts, and other sources of information it was learned that there was a feeling prevailing among the inhabitants that the city would very soon have to be abandoned. Provost-marshal's guards seized all available citizens, young and old, and impressed them into the service, whether sick or well—government clerks, and even the police, being put in line in Butler's front. All business was suspended, as there was no one left to attend to it; publication of the newspapers was interrupted; shops were closed; and alarm-bells were rung from all the churches.

In the mean time the enemy was having no rest in the Shenandoah Valley. On the 9th of October, Sheridan's cavalry, under Torbert, had an engagement with the enemy's cavalry, which it completely routed, capturing eleven guns and a number of wagons, and taking over three hundred prisoners. Our loss did not exceed sixty men. The enemy was pursued about twenty-six miles.

In the forenoon of October 16 a steamer arrived from Washington, having aboard the Secretary of War, Mr. Stanton; the new Secretary of the Treasury, Mr. Fessenden, who had succeeded Chase; and several of their friends. They came at once to headquarters, were warmly received by General Grant, and during their short stay of two days were profuse in their expressions of congratulation to the general upon the progress he had made with his armies. They wanted to see as much as they could of the positions occupied by our forces, and the general proposed that they should visit the Army of the James that afternoon, and offered to accompany them. He telegraphed Butler to this effect, and the party started up the river by boat. I was invited to

join the excursion, and was much interested in the conversations which occurred. Stanton did most of the
talking. He began by saying: "In getting away from
my desk, and being able to enjoy the outdoor air, I feel
like a boy out of school. I have found much relief in
my office from the use of a high desk, at which I at
times stand up and sign papers. It has been said that
the best definition of rest is change of occupation, and
even a change of attitude is a great rest to those who
have to work at desks."

He then gave a graphic description of the anxieties
which had been experienced for some months at Washington on account of the boldness of the disloyal element in the North and the emissaries sent there from
the South. Sheridan's name was mentioned in terms of
compliment. General Grant said: "Yes; Sheridan is
an improvement upon some of his predecessors in the
valley of Virginia. They demonstrated the truth of the
military principle that a commander can generally retreat successfully from almost any position—if he only
starts in time." Stanton laughed heartily at the general's
way of putting it, and remarked: "But in all retreats
I am told that there is another principle to be observed:
a man must not look back. I think it was Cæsar who
said to an officer in his army who had retreated repeatedly, but who afterward appeared before his commander
and pointed with pride to a wound on his cheek: 'Ah!
I see you are wounded in the face; you should not have
looked back.'" At Aiken's Landing General Butler
joined the party, and pointed out the objects of interest
along his lines. Mr. Stanton then spoke with much
earnestness of the patient labors and patriotic course of
the President. There had been rumors of disagreements
and unpleasant scenes at times between the distinguished
Secretary of War and his chief; but there evidently was

little, if any, foundation for such reports, and certainly upon this occasion the Secretary manifested a genuine personal affection for Mr. Lincoln, and an admiration for his character which amounted to positive reverence.

Mr. Stanton wore spectacles, and had a habit of removing them from time to time when he was talking earnestly, and wiping the glasses with his handkerchief. His style of speech was deliberate, but his manner at times grew animated, and he presented a personality which could not fail to interest and impress all who came in contact with the great Carnot of our war.

The next morning, after breakfast, the Secretary's party went by the military railroad to our lines about Petersburg, where they had pleasant interviews with Meade, Hancock, Warren, and Parke, and returned in the afternoon to City Point. After some further consultation with General Grant about the military situation, particularly in the valley of Virginia, the Secretary, with his friends, started back to Washington.

Sheridan had been ordered to Washington to consult with the authorities there; and as no immediate attack on the part of the enemy was expected, he started for that city on October 16. Early, however, had concentrated all the troops that could be brought to his assistance, and was determined to make a desperate effort to retrieve the defeats which he had suffered in the Valley. Sheridan arrived in Washington on the 17th, and started back to his command at noon of that day. The next day he reached Winchester, which was twenty miles from his command, and remained there that night.

At three o'clock on the afternoon of October 20 General Grant was sitting at his table in his tent, writing letters. Several members of the staff who were at headquarters at the time were seated in front of the tent discussing some anticipated movements. The telegraph operator came across the camp-ground hurriedly, stepped into the general's quarters, and handed him a despatch. He read it over, and then came to the front of the tent, put on a very grave look, and said to the members of the staff: "I'll read you a despatch I have just received from Sheridan." We were all eager to hear the news, for we felt that the telegram was of importance. The general began to read the despatch in a very solemn tone. It was dated 10 P. M. the night before: "'I have the honor to report that my army at Cedar Creek was attacked this morning before daylight, and my left was turned and driven in confusion; in fact, most of the line was driven in confusion, with the loss of twenty pieces of artillery. I hastened from Winchester, where I was on my return from Washington, and joined the army between Middletown and Newtown, having been driven back about four miles.'" Here the general looked up, shook his head solemnly, and said, "That's pretty bad, is n't it?" A melancholy chorus replied, "It's too bad, too bad!" "Now just wait till I read you the rest of it," added the general, with a perceptible twinkle in his eye. He then went on, reading more rapidly: "'I here took the affair in hand, and quickly united the corps, formed a compact line of battle just in time to repulse an attack of the enemy's, which was handsomely done at about 1 P. M. At 3 P. M., after some changes of the cavalry from the left to the right flank, I attacked with great vigor, driving and routing the enemy, capturing, according to last reports, forty-three pieces of artillery and very many prisoners. I do not yet know the number of my casualties or the losses of the enemy. Wagon-trains, ambulances, and caissons in large numbers are in our possession. They also burned some of their trains. General Ramseur is a prisoner in our hands, severely, and perhaps mortally, wounded. I have to regret the loss of General Bidwell, killed, and Generals Wright, Grover, and Ricketts, wounded—Wright slightly wounded. Affairs at times looked badly, but by the gallantry of our brave officers and men disaster has been converted into a splendid victory. Darkness again intervened to shut off greater results. . . .'" By this time the listeners had rallied from their dejection, and were beside themselves with delight. The general seemed to enjoy the bombshell he had thrown among the staff almost as much as the news of Sheridan's signal victory. In these after years, when this victory is recorded among the most brilliant battles of the war, and "Sheridan's Ride" has been made famous in song and story, one cannot help recalling the modesty with which he spoke of his headlong gallop to join his command, and snatch victory from defeat. He dismissed it with the sentence: "I hastened from Winchester, where I was on my return from Washington, and joined the army. . . ." Further news brought the details of the crushing blow he had struck the enemy. General Grant, in referring to the matter at headquarters, commented at great length upon the triumph which Sheridan had achieved, and the genius he had displayed. He telegraphed to Washington: "Turning what bid fair to be a disaster into a glorious victory stamps Sheridan what I have always thought him—one of the ablest of generals"; and said in conversation: "Sheridan's courageous words and brilliant deeds encourage his commanders as much as they inspire his subordinates. While he has a magnetic influence possessed by few other men in an engagement, and is seen to best advantage in battle, he does as much beforehand to contribute to victory as any living commander. His plans are always well matured, and in every movement he strikes with a definite purpose in view. No man would be better fitted to command all the armies in the field." He ordered one hundred guns to be fired in honor of Sheridan's decisive victory.

CHAPTER XX

EVEN before the completion of Sheridan's victory in the Valley, Grant was planning another movement for the purpose of threatening Lee's position, keeping him occupied, and attacking his communications. On October 24 he directed both Meade and Butler to prepare for a movement which was to be made on the 27th. Meade was to move against the South Side road, while Butler was to go to the north side of the James again, and make a demonstration there against the enemy.

Early on the morning of October 27 General Grant, with his staff, started for the headquarters of the Army of the Potomac, and rode out to the front, accompanied by Meade. The morning was dark and gloomy, a heavy rain was falling, the roads were muddy and obstructed, and tangled thickets, dense woods, and swampy streams confronted the troops at all points. The difficulties of the ground made the movements necessarily slow. After a conference with Warren, Grant and Meade rode over to Hancock's front, and found that the enemy was there disputing the passage of Hatcher's Run at Burgess's Mill. His troops were strongly posted, with a battery in position directly in front of the head of Hancock's corps, and another about eight hundred yards to our left.   Unless this force on the opposite side of the stream could be driven back, our lines could not be thrown forward for the purpose of making the contemplated movement.   Prompt action had to be taken, and General Grant rode out farther to the front, accompanied by General Meade and the members of their staffs, to give orders on the spot.   As this group of mounted officers formed a conspicuous target, the enemy was not slow to open upon it with his guns; and soon the whistling of projectiles and the explosion of shells made the position rather uncomfortable.   One of our orderlies was killed, and two were wounded.   It looked at one time as if the explosion of a shell had killed General Meade, but fortunately he escaped untouched.   A little speck of blood appeared on Hancock's cheek after the bursting of a shell.   It was probably caused by a bit of gravel being thrown in his face.   Staff-officers were sent forward to the principal points to reconnoiter.   General Grant, as was his constant practice, wished to see the exact position of the enemy with his own eyes.   He stopped the officers who were riding with him, called on one aide-de-camp, Colonel Babcock, to accompany him, and rode forward rapidly to within a few yards of the bridge.   Before he had gone far a shell exploded just under his horse's neck.   The animal threw up his head and reared, and it was thought that he and his rider had both been struck, but neither had been touched.   The enemy's batteries and sharp-shooters were both firing, and the situation was such that all the lookers-on experienced intense anxiety, expecting every moment to see the general fall.   The telegraph-lines had been cut, and the twisted wires were lying about in confusion upon the ground.   To make matters more critical, the general's horse got his foot caught in a loop of the wire,

and as the animal endeavored to free himself the coil
became twisted still tighter.   Every one's face now began to wear a still more anxious look.   Babcock, whose
coolness under fire was always conspicuous, dismounted,
and carefully uncoiled the wire and released the horse.
The general sat still in his saddle, evidently thinking
more about the horse than of himself, and in the most
quiet and unruffled manner cautioned Babcock to be sure
not to hurt the animal's leg.   The general soon succeeded
in obtaining a clear view of the enemy's line and the
exact nature of the ground, and then, much to our relief, retired to a less exposed position.   The advance of
the troops was impeded by the dense underbrush, the
crookedness of the Run, the damming of its waters, the
slashed trees, and other obstacles of every conceivable
description which had been placed in the line of march.
It was seen by afternoon that an assault under the circumstances would not promise favorable results, and it
was abandoned.   The success of the operation depended
upon reaching the objective point by a rapid movement;
and as unexpected obstacles were presented by the character of the country and by the weather, instructions
were now given to suspend operations, and Grant and
Meade rode to Armstrong's Mill.   General Grant then
took a narrow cross-road leading down to the Run to the
right of Hancock's corps; but it was soon found that
there were no troops between our party and the enemy,
and that if we continued along this road it would probably not be many minutes before we should find ourselves prisoners in his lines.   There was nothing to do
but to turn around and strike a road farther in the rear.
This, as usual, was a great annoyance to the general,
who expressed his objections, as he had done many a
time before, to turning back.   We paused for a few
minutes, and tried to find some cross-cut; but there was

not even a pathway leading in the proper direction, and the party had to retrace its steps for some distance.

General Grant was now becoming anxious to get in telegraphic communication with Butler, and he rode on to a point on the military railroad called Warren Station, reaching there about half-past five P. M.

After giving some further instructions to General Meade, he started back to City Point. On the way to general headquarters he discussed the events which had just taken place, and said: " To-day's movement has resulted, up to the time I left, only in a reconnaissance in force. I had hoped to accomplish more by means of it, but it has at least given us a much more thorough knowledge of the country, which, with its natural and artificial obstacles, is stronger than any one could have supposed. This movement has convinced me of the next course which will have to be pursued. It will be necessary for the Army of the Potomac to cut loose from its base, leaving only a small force at City Point and in front of Petersburg to hold those positions. The whole army can then swing completely round to the left and make Lee's present position untenable." There was some doubt in his mind as to what action the enemy would take in front of Hancock and Warren. News came that evening, showing that Lee had assumed the offensive, and that severe fighting had occurred. Between four and five o'clock a heavy force of the enemy passed between Hancock and Warren, and made a vigorous assault on the right and rear of Hancock's corps; but Hancock struck the enemy in flank, threw him into confusion, and captured nine hundred prisoners and a number of colors. The enemy was unable to reform his troops, and did not attempt any further offensive operations. This day's engagement is known as the battle of Hatcher's Run.

Butler had sent a force to the north side of the James; but the enemy retired to his intrenched works whenever our troops advanced against him, and only one attack was made.

These operations closed for the winter the series of battles in front of Petersburg and Richmond, cold weather and the condition of the roads rendering further important movements impracticable. While there was much skirmishing and some spirited fighting, no more general engagements occurred until spring.

Since my return from Atlanta a number of communications had been exchanged between Grant and Sherman regarding the contemplated "march to the sea." Jefferson Davis had visited Hood's headquarters, and at different points on his trip had made speeches, assuring the people that Atlanta was to be retaken, that Sherman's communications were to be cut, and that his retreat would be as disastrous as Napoleon's retreat from Moscow. When General Grant received the reports of these speeches, which were widely published in the Southern newspapers, he remarked: "Mr. Davis has not made it quite plain who is to furnish the snow for this Moscow retreat through Georgia and Tennessee. However, he has rendered us one good service at least in notifying us of Hood's intended plan of campaign." In a short time it was seen that Hood was marching his army against the railroad which constituted Sherman's only line of communication with his base of supplies. Sherman now called for reinforcements, and Grant directed all recruits in the West to be sent to him.

On September 29 Hood crossed the Chattahoochee River. This was the day on which Grant made the movements hereinbefore described against Richmond and Petersburg, with a view to preventing Lee from detaching any troops. There were some who thought

Grant manifested unnecessary anxiety on this subject: but it must be remembered that just one year before, Lee had sent Longstreet's whole corps to northern Georgia; that it was not discovered until it was well on its way to join Bragg's forces against Rosecrans's army at Chickamauga; and that it accomplished the reverse which occurred to our arms on that field. Besides, Grant's mind seemed always more concerned about preventing disasters to the armies of his distant commanders than to the troops under his own personal direction. He was invariably generous to others, and his self-reliance was so great that he always felt that he could take ample care of himself.

General Rawlins had now returned, and it was very gratifying to see that while his health was not restored, it was greatly improved. He still, however, was troubled with a cough. The day he arrived General Grant saw that he was still far from well, and said with much distress, when Rawlins was out of earshot, "I do not like that cough." When Rawlins learned the plan proposed in regard to Sherman's future movements, he was seriously opposed to it, and presented every possible argument against it. Rawlins always talked with great force. He had a natural taste for public speaking, and when he became particularly earnest in the discussion of a question, his speech often took the form of an oration; and as he grew more excited, and his enthusiasm increased, he would hold forth in stentorian tones, and emphasize his remarks with vehement gesticulation and no end of expletives. As I had been sent to confer with Sherman, and had studied the subject in all its bearings, and felt absolute faith in the success of the movement, I became the chief spokesman in its favor; and many evenings were occupied in discussing the pros and cons of the contemplated movement. The staff had in fact resolved itself into an animated debating society. The general-in-chief would sit quietly by, listening to the arguments, and sometimes showed himself greatly amused by the vehemence of the debaters. One night the discussion waxed particularly warm, and was kept up for some time after the general had gone to bed. About one o'clock he poked his head out of his tent, and interrupted Rawlins in the midst of an eloquent passage by crying out: "Oh, do go to bed, all of you! You 're keeping the whole camp awake."

Rawlins had convinced himself that if Hood kept his army in front of Sherman to bar his progress, Sherman, having cut loose from his base, would not be able to supply himself, and his army would be destroyed; and that, on the other hand, if Hood turned north, Sherman's army would be unavailable, and it would be difficult to assemble sufficient force to prevent Hood from reaching the Ohio River. Against this view it was argued that if Hood decided to confront Sherman to prevent his passage across the country, Sherman would always have a force large enough to whip him in a pitched battle, or so threaten him as to compel him to keep his forces concentrated, while Sherman could throw detachments out from his flanks and rear and obtain plenty of provisions in a country which had never been ravaged by contending armies; or, if Hood started north, that Sherman could detach a large force to send against him, which, when reinforced by the troops that could be hurried from Missouri and other points, would be amply able to take care of Hood, while Sherman, with the bulk of his army, could cut the Confederacy in two, sever all its lines of communication, and destroy its principal arsenals and factories. In fact, Sherman was so far away from his base, with only a single-track railroad, liable constantly to be broken by raiders, that it became a necessity for him either to fall back or to go ahead. Rawlins was possessed of an earnest nature, and was devoted to General Grant's interests, and his urgency against this movement was not a factious opposition, for he had really convinced himself that nothing but an absolute calamity would be the result. In this case General Grant, as usual, paid but little attention to the opinions of others upon a purely military question about the advisability of which he really had no doubt in his own mind.

It was suggested, one evening, that he instruct Sherman to hold a council of war on the subject of the next movement of his army.   To this General Grant replied: "No; I will not direct any one to do what I would not do myself under similar circumstances. I never held what might be called formal councils of war, and I do not believe in them. They create a divided responsibility, and at times prevent that unity of action so necessary in the field. Some officers will in all likelihood oppose any plan that may be adopted; and when it is put into execution, such officers may, by their arguments in opposition, have so far convinced themselves that the movement will fail that they cannot enter upon it with enthusiasm; and might possibly be influenced in their actions by the feeling that a victory would be a reflection upon their judgment. I believe it is better for a commander charged with the responsibility of all the operations of his army to consult his generals freely but informally, get their views and opinions, and then make up his mind what action to take, and act accordingly. There is too much truth in the old adage, ' Councils of war do not fight.'"

On October 6 General Grant went to Washington to consult with the authorities in regard to the raising of additional troops, and to learn upon what number of reinforcements he could rely before deciding definitely upon the course to be pursued in the West. Hood had now turned north, and was operating against Sherman's railroad in his rear. Sherman had left the Twentieth Corps in Atlanta to hold that place, and had marched with the rest of his army as far north as Marietta. On October 10 Sherman telegraphed Grant: "Hood is now crossing the Coosa, twelve miles below Rome, bound west. If he passes over to the Mobile and Ohio road, had I not better execute the plan of my letter sent by Colonel Porter, and leave General Thomas with the troops now in Tennessee to defend the State?" The situation was such, however, that General Grant disliked to see a veteran army like Sherman's marching away from Hood without first crippling him; and he replied to Sherman the next day (the 11th), saying, among other things: ". . . If you were to cut loose, I do not believe you would meet Hood's army, but would be bushwhacked by all the old men, little boys, and such railroad guards as are still left at home. Hood would probably strike for Nashville, thinking by going north he could inflict greater damage upon us than we could upon the rebels by going south. If there is any way of getting at Hood's army, I would prefer that, but I must trust to your own judgment. . . ."

It will be seen from the above despatch that Grant's military foresight had enabled him to predict at this time precisely what afterward took place as to Sherman's army not meeting Hood's. At the same hour at which Grant wrote this despatch at City Point, Sherman had sent a telegram to him, saying that he would prefer to start on his march to the sea, and that he believed Hood would be forced to follow him. A little before midnight on the 11th, Grant sent Sherman the following reply: "Your despatch of to-day received. If you are satisfied the trip to the sea-coast can be made, holding the line of the Tennessee firmly, you may make it, destroying all the railroads south of Dalton or Chattanooga, as you think best."

General Sherman informed me long after the war that he did not receive this reply, which was accounted for, no doubt, by the fact that his telegraph-wires were cut at that time. He was ignorant of the existence of this despatch when he wrote in his "Memoirs," in 1875, that November 2 was " the first time that General Grant ordered the march to the sea."

General Grant was now actively engaged in making additional preparations for Sherman's reception on the sea-coast. He directed that vessels should be loaded with abundant supplies, and sail as soon as it became known that Sherman had started across Georgia, and rendezvous at Ossabaw Sound, a short distance below the mouth of the Savannah River.

On October 29, finding that the movement of the troops ordered from Missouri to Tennessee was exceedingly slow, the general directed Rawlins to go in person to St. Louis, and confer with Rosecrans, the department commander, and see that all haste was made. The Secretary of War now sent a telegram to General Grant, wishing him to reconsider his order authorizing the march to the sea. In fact, the President and the Secretary had never been favorably impressed with Sherman's contemplated movement, and as early as October 2 Halleck had written to General Grant advocating a different plan. Grant felt that as there was so much hesitation in Washington, he ought once more to impress upon Sherman the importance of dealing a crushing blow to Hood's army, if practicable, before starting on his march eastward, and telegraphed him accordingly. To this Sherman replied that if he pursued Hood he would have to give up Atlanta, and that he preferred to strike out for the sea.

At 11 : 30 A. M., November 2, before Grant had received the above reply from Sherman, he sent another message to that officer, closing with the words: "I really do not see that you can withdraw from where you are to follow Hood without giving up all we have gained in territory. I say, then, go as you propose."

Several additional despatches were interchanged, and at 10 : 30 P. M., November 7, Grant telegraphed Sherman: "I see no present reason for changing your plan; should any arise, you will see it; or if I do, will inform you. I think everything here favorable now. Great good fortune attend you. I believe you will be eminently successful, and at worst can only make a march less fruitful of results than is hoped for." The telegraph-wires were soon after cut, and no more despatches could be sent. It was not until the 15th that Sherman was entirely ready to move. On the morning of that day Atlanta was abandoned, and the famous march to the sea was begun.

Extracts from the correspondence between the general-in-chief and the distinguished commander of the armies of the West, and the views expressed by them regarding the conception and execution of this memorable movement, are given in some detail in order to correct many erroneous impressions upon the subject. Over-zealous partizans of General Grant have claimed that he originated and controlled the entire movement; while enthusiastic admirers of Sherman have insisted that Grant was surprised at the novelty of the suggestion, and was at first opposed to the march, and that Sherman had to exert all his force of character to induce Grant to consent to the campaign. The truth is that the two generals were in perfect accord in this, as in all other movements undertaken while Grant was in supreme command of the armies. These two distinguished officers acted in entire

harmony, and the movement reflects lasting credit upon
both.   Long before Sherman's army started upon his
Atlanta campaign it was clear to Grant, and others with
whom he discussed the matter, that after that army
reached a point in the interior of the South too far from
its base to maintain a line of supplies, communication
would have to be opened up with the sea-coast, and a
new base established there.   Sherman, however, is entitled to the exclusive credit of the plan of cutting loose
entirely from his source of supplies, moving a long distance through the enemy's country without a base, and
having in view several objective points upon which to
direct his army, his selection to depend upon the contingencies of the campaign.   It was the same sort of
campaigning as that which Grant had undertaken when
operating in the rear of Vicksburg.   General Grant said
more than once: "I want it to be recorded in history
that Sherman is entitled to the entire credit of the detailed plan of cutting loose from his base at Atlanta and
marching to Savannah.   As to the brilliancy of the execution of the plan on Sherman's part there can never
be any dispute.   The plan was entirely in accord with
my views as to the general coöperation of our widely
separated armies."   He approved the suggestions at the
start, in spite of the doubts expressed by army officers
about him and by some of the authorities at Washington; he encouraged and aided Sherman in all the work
of preparation; and when the time for final action came
he promptly gave his consent to the undertaking.   About
the only point upon which their military judgments differed was as to the action of Hood, Grant being firmly
convinced that he would turn north, while Sherman
thought their armies might encounter each other.

CHAPTER XXI

GRANT SUGGESTS A PLAN FOR VOTING IN THE FIELD—
GRANT VISITS NEW YORK—A PHILADELPHIA OVATION
TO GRANT—GRANT AND LINCOLN IN CONFERENCE—
GRANT'S WINTER QUARTERS AT CITY POINT—GENERAL
INGALLS'S SPOTTED DOG—GRANT'S INTERCOURSE WITH
HIS ASSOCIATES—CORRESPONDENCE WITH GENERAL
THOMAS

THE Presidential election was now approaching, and
provisions were being carried out for receiving the
ballots of the soldiers who came from those States which
had passed laws authorizing their soldiers in the field to
cast their votes. General Grant had been consulted in
regard to the propriety and practicability of permitting
the soldiers to vote, and he had written a letter which
contains such broad principles of statesmanship, and ex-
hibits so much foresight as to the checks and restraints
with which the matter should be guarded, and produced
so profound an impression at the time, that it is given
in full:

CITY POINT, VA., September 27, 1864.
THE HON. E. M. STANTON,
Secretary of War, Washington, D. C.
The exercise of the right of suffrage by the officers and soldiers of armies in the field is a novel thing. It has, I believe,
generally been considered dangerous to constitutional liberty
and subversive of military discipline. But our circumstances

321

are novel and exceptional. A very large proportion of the legal voters of the United States are now either under arms in the field, or in hospitals, or otherwise engaged in the military service of the United States. Most of these men are not regular soldiers in the strict sense of that term; still less are they mercenaries who give their services to the government simply for its pay, having little understanding of political questions, or feeling little or no interest in them. On the contrary, they are American citizens, having still their homes and social and political ties binding them to the States and districts from which they come and to which they expect to return. They have left their homes temporarily, to sustain the cause of their country in the hour of its trial. In performing this sacred duty, they should not be deprived of a most precious privilege. They have as much right to demand that their votes shall be counted in the choice of their rulers as those citizens who remain at home —nay, more; for they have sacrificed more for their country.

I state these reasons in full, for the unusual thing of allowing armies in the field to vote, that I may urge, on the other hand, that nothing more than the fullest exercise of this right should be allowed; for anything not absolutely necessary to this exercise cannot but be dangerous to the liberties of the country.

The officers and soldiers have every means of understanding the questions before the country. The newspapers are freely circulated, and so, I believe, are the documents prepared by both parties to set forth the merits and claims of their candidates.

Beyond this, nothing whatever should be allowed—no political meetings, no harangues from soldiers or citizens, and no canvassing of camps or regiments for votes.

I see not why a single individual not belonging to the armies should be admitted into their lines to deliver tickets. In my opinion, the tickets should be furnished by the chief provost-marshal of each army, by them to the provost-marshal (or some other appointed officer) of each brigade or regiment, who shall, on the day of election, deliver tickets, irrespective of party, to whoever may call for them. If, however, it shall be deemed expedient to admit citizens to deliver tickets, then it should be most positively prohibited that such citizens should electioneer, harangue, or canvass the regiments in any way. Their business should be, and only be, to distribute on a certain fixed day tickets to whoever may call for them.

In the cases of those States whose soldiers vote by proxy, proper State authority could be given to officers belonging to regiments so voting to receive and forward votes.

As it is intended that all soldiers entitled to vote shall exercise that privilege according to their own convictions of right, unmolested and unrestricted, there will be no objection to each party sending to armies easy of access a number of respectable gentlemen to see that these views are fully carried out. To the army at Atlanta, and those armies on the sea-coast from New Berne to New Orleans, not to exceed three citizens of each party should be admitted.

U. S. GRANT,
Lieutenant-general.

Fourteen of the loyal States authorized their troops in the field to vote. General Grant felt that he was simply a soldier, and he took no active part in the political campaign, although he never failed to let it be known that he ardently desired the triumph of the party which was in favor of vigorously prosecuting the war to a successful termination. He had been exceedingly annoyed by the fact that the Missouri State Convention had instructed its delegates to the National Convention which nominated Lincoln to " cast their twenty-two votes for Ulysses S. Grant," and exerted what influence he could not to have his name mentioned in any way in the convention; but as the delegates had received instructions, they felt that they could not disobey them. The Hon. John F. Hume, chairman of the Missouri delegation, therefore cast the votes of his State for General Grant; but before the result of the ballot was announced he changed them to Mr. Lincoln. General Grant did not have an opportunity to vote at the election, as his State (Illinois) had made no provision for allowing her soldiers at the front to cast their ballots.

On the 8th of November the Presidential election took place. The voting passed off very quietly in the camps. Every soldier was allowed absolute freedom in the choice of candidates, and perhaps no election had ever been conducted with greater fairness. The soldiers' vote in favor of Lincoln over McClellan was in the proportion of more than three to one. General Grant strolled through some of the neighboring camps while the voting was going on, and watched with interest how quietly and effectively the system for depositing the ballots worked. On the 10th of November enough was known at headquarters to make it plain that Lincoln was elected. That night Grant telegraphed to Halleck: ". . . Congratulate the President for me for the double victory. The election having passed off quietly, no bloodshed or riot throughout the land, is a victory worth more to the country than a battle won. . . ."

General Grant had a marked aversion to interfering in any matters which pertained to the civil administration of the government. He had contented himself with sending to points in the North such troops as were really necessary as precautionary steps, and had left it entirely to the War Department to carry out measures for arresting and punishing the Confederate emissaries in the loyal States, and breaking up the bands of conspirators who were plotting against the government.

Considering the positions of the armies of Sherman and Thomas, General Grant was still anxious that Lee should send no troops to the West; and he determined to watch him closely, but not to make any move which might have the effect of inducing him to evacuate Richmond and Petersburg.

As the apprehension throughout the North had been allayed, and as there were no operations in contemplation in Virginia, General Grant started on the 17th of November, and made a short trip to Burlington, New Jersey, to see his children, who had been placed at school there, and his wife, who was with them. There went with the party an expert telegraph operator, familiar with the cipher used in official despatches, who was used in keeping up telegraphic communication with the front. On November 19 news was received at headquarters, through Confederate sources, that Lee had recalled Early's command from the valley of Virginia. This was instantly communicated to the general-in-chief. He telegraphed at once to Sheridan, mentioning this news, and saying that if he was satisfied that it was so, to send Wright's corps to City Point without delay, and move with his cavalry to cut the Virginia Central Railroad. There was destined to be no respite for the general-in-chief. Even while snatching a couple of days' rest in the quiet of his little family, he was still called on to direct important movements in the field.

Finding that there was no immediate need of his presence at the front, he decided to run over to New York for a couple of days. He had promised Mrs. Grant to go there on a shopping expedition, and he also felt some curiosity to take a look at the city, as he had not seen it since he was graduated from the Military Academy, twenty-one years before. He went with Mrs. Grant to the Astor House, quietly and unannounced, being particularly desirous of avoiding any public demonstrations. He did not realize, however, the sensation which his arrival in the metropolis would create. The news spread rapidly throughout the city, and the greatest eagerness was manifested on the part of the people to get a sight of the famous commander. The foremost citizens presented themselves at the hotel to pay their respects to him, and enthusiastic crowds filled the streets and stood for hours gazing at the windows of his rooms, in the hope of catching a glimpse of him. Entertainments of every kind were tendered him, and invitations poured in from every quarter. He received many prominent citizens in his rooms, and had a great many interesting talks with them; but the invitations to entertainments were declined, and all public demonstrations avoided as much as possible. The next morning after his arrival the general strolled out into the streets with a former staff-officer then living in New York, and being in plain citizen's clothes, was for some time unobserved; but finally his features, which had been made known by means of the portraits everywhere displayed, were recognized, and finding a crowd surrounding him, he stepped into a street-car. The gentleman with him, finding no vacant seat, asked the conductor to have the people sit closer together and make room for General Grant. The conductor put on a broad grin, and quietly winked one eye, as much as to say, "You can't fool me with such a cock-and-bull story as that"; and the general quietly took hold of a strap, and rode throughout the trip standing with a number of others who had crowded into the car.

After remaining two days in the city, seeing what little he could in that time of the vast improvements which had taken place since he was last there, he started for Washington, but on the way decided to remain over a day in Philadelphia. After he had spent a little while at the Continental Hotel, he attempted to take a walk down Chestnut street; but his features had become as familiar to the people of the Quaker City as to the New-Yorkers, and he was promptly recognized, and his name was passed from mouth to mouth in the street. Soon the people rushed out in crowds from the stores on both sides of the way, and curiosity was on tiptoe to see him. First those near by took off their hats to him; then they crowded up to shake hands; then applause was started along the sidewalks, and soon cheer after cheer arose. He was now near Independence Hall, and the crowd, in its good nature and enthusiasm, pressed upon him so vigorously that he was compelled to take refuge in the building. His presence was then announced to the mayor, who set to work hurriedly to improvise a reception. The news of the commander's presence had spread in the mean time like wild-fire, and a dense mass of people had crowded into the hall. In their eagerness to shake hands with him, they soon lost all restraint, and many were in danger of being injured in the crush. His friends now induced him to consent to an act which his enemies had never succeeded in compelling him to perform — to beat a retreat. He was conducted from the hall by a private exit, placed in a carriage, and the coachman was directed to drive rapidly back to the hotel. In this flank movement, however, the general did not meet with the success which had crowned his efforts in the field. The admiring crowd of people soon discovered his change of base, and those in front, being pressed on by those in rear, surged up against the carriage, checking its movement, breaking some of the windows, and nearly toppling it over. Never had there been a greater necessity for the prayer, " Save me from my friends! " Finally, however, the hotel was safely reached. The general treated the matter throughout with his accustomed good nature and his usual calmness. In the entire mass of people he was perhaps the only one unexcited and unruffled. The only feeling he exhibited was one of intense surprise that he should attract so much attention.

He then proceeded to Washington, and on November

23 called upon the President and the Secretary of War, and had extended interviews with them. One object in his going to Washington was to make a determined effort to obtain promotion for his officers who had made themselves conspicuous for their gallantry and efficiency in the field. In order to create the necessary vacancies, he recommended that the inefficient general officers be mustered out of service, and gave a list of eight major-generals and thirty-three brigadiers whose services the government could dispense with to advantage. In the matter of relieving these useless officers the general was entirely impartial, as the list contained a number of his warm personal friends. The President said to him: " Why, I find that lots of the officers on this list are very close friends of yours; do you want them all dropped?" The general replied: " That 's very true, Mr. President; but my personal friends are not always good generals, and I think it but just to adhere to my recommendation."

The Secretary of War had impaired his health by his incessant labors, and by his positive and sometimes arbitrary conduct had created an opposition to himself in many quarters, and there were rumors at this time that he might retire from his position. This subject was brought up by the President in his conversation with the general-in-chief, and he was considerate enough to say that in case such a change should occur, he would not appoint another secretary without giving the general an opportunity to express his views as to the selection. General Grant took occasion to say to Mr. Lincoln at this interview: " I doubt very much whether you could select as efficient a Secretary of War as the present incumbent. He is not only a man of untiring energy and devotion to duty, but even his worst enemies never for a moment doubt his personal integrity and the purity of his motives; and it tends largely to reconcile the peo-

ple to the heavy taxes they are paying when they feel
an absolute certainty that the chief of the department
which is giving out contracts for countless millions of
dollars is a person of scrupulous honesty." The general
now returned to City Point, feeling much gratified with
his visit to Washington, and well satisfied with what he
had accomplished while there.

General Hancock was suffering so intensely from his
wounds that he was given a leave of absence for twenty
days, it being hoped that at the end of that time he
might be better; but he was unable to return, and General A. A. Humphreys thereafter commanded the Second
Corps. His assignment was dated November 25. He
was a most accomplished officer, and by his talents and
his personal gallantry had already won great distinction.
His appointment was recognized as eminently fitting,
and met with favor throughout the entire army.

The camp at City Point had now given place to winter
quarters; for in view of the character of the campaigns
that were to be conducted by our armies in the West
and South, it was decided to make no immediate attempt
to dislodge Lee's army from Petersburg and Richmond,
and preparations were made by the general-in-chief to
pass the winter months at City Point. The tents, which
were much worn, had become very uncomfortable as the
cold weather set in; and they were removed, and log
huts were erected in their stead. Each hut contained
space enough for bunks for two officers, and had a small
door in front, a window on each side, and an open fireplace at the rear end. General Grant's hut was as plain
as the others, and was constructed with a sitting-room
in front, and a small apartment used as a bedroom in
rear, with a communicating door between them. An
iron camp-bed, an iron wash-stand, a couple of pine
tables, and a few common wooden chairs constituted

the furniture.   The floor was entirely bare.   There were many comments in the newspapers about this time upon the preparations for winters quarters.   One comic paper had a picture of the general's hut, with smoke curling out of the chimney, and under it the words: "Grant fought it out on this line, though it took him all summer, and has now sent for his stove."   Papers inimical to the cause gave the establishment of winter quarters as a proof that the oldest inhabitant would not be likely to live long enough to see Grant enter Richmond.   Some of the jocose remarks referring to this subject displayed no little wit, and many of them were a source of considerable amusement to the general and those about him.

General Ingalls had just returned from a trip to Washington, and brought with him an English spotted coach-dog, which followed him everywhere through camp, and attracted no end of attention.   A dog of any kind was rather an unusual sight in an army in the field, and an animal of the peculiar marks and aristocratic bearing of Ingalls's companion excited wide-spread remark.   Every time the dog came to headquarters, General Grant was certain to comment upon the animal, and perpetrate some good-natured joke at the expense of his classmate. The dog followed the usual canine custom, and expressed his feelings by an agitation of his caudal appendage.   To describe his actions astronomically, it may be said that he indicated anger by imparting to his tail a series of longitudinal vibrations, and pleasure by giving it a gentle "motion in azimuth" — familiarly known as a wag.   One evening, as the general was sitting in front of his quarters, Ingalls came up to have a chat with him, and was followed by the dog, which sat down in the usual place at its master's feet.   The animal squatted upon its hind quarters, licked its chops, pricked up its ears, and looked first at one officer and then at the other,

as if to say: "I am General Ingalls's dog; whose pup
are you?" In the course of his remarks General Grant
took a look at the animal, and said: "Well, Ingalls, what
are your real intentions in regard to that dog? Do you
expect to take it into Richmond with you?" Ingalls,
who was noted for his dry humor, replied with mock
seriousness and an air of extreme patience: "I hope to;
it is said to come from a long-lived breed." This retort,
coupled with the comical attitude of the dog at the time,
turned the laugh upon the general, who joined heartily
in the merriment, and seemed to enjoy the joke as much
as any of the party.

While the general's manners were simple and uncon-
strained, and his conversation with his staff was of the
most sociable nature, yet he always maintained a dignity
of demeanor which set bounds to any undue familiarity
on the part of those who held intercourse with him.
However close they were to him in their relations, there
was never any obtrusive intimacy. He always addressed
his chief of staff as "Rawlins," General Sherman as
"Sherman," and usually called his cavalry leader "Sheridan"; but in addressing Meade and nearly all the other
commanders he invariably employed the title "general."
Sherman always called the general-in-chief "Grant" in
public and private conversation. Ingalls and other
classmates used this term in talking with him alone,
but when others were present they gave him his military title. All other officers in the service addressed
him invariably as "general." In conversation with his
personal aides, who had served intimately with him, he
would call them sometimes by their last names, and at
other times by their military titles. He was scrupulously careful under all circumstances not to neglect the
little courtesies which are the stamp of genuine politeness. When a general officer came to his headquarters,

the general-in-chief always rose to receive him, shook hands, and invited him to sit down. If smoking at the time, he offered the visitor a cigar, and if it was near the hour for a meal, invited him to be a guest at the mess. He never made any remarks in criticism of a person who had called on him after the visitor had left, and by his manner always showed an objection to hearing others talk about people behind their backs. He never had the slightest fondness for gossip of any kind. Whenever any one attempted to whisper to him in the presence of others, while he did not openly rebuke the offender, he always managed in some way to make it evident that the practice was distasteful to him. Usually when any one came close to him and started to communicate with him in a whisper before company, he drew slightly back, and at once began to reply in a loud tone of voice, which was a sufficient indication that he regarded the whispering as an impoliteness. If there was really any reason for a confidential interview, he would proceed to his back room and hold it there. His conduct was particularly courteous in the presence of ladies, and he never neglected those little attentions to their sex which constitute true politeness. If he were reclining on a bench or sitting in a lounging attitude in a chair after a fatiguing day, when any lady approached, whether a visitor or a person of his own household, he would at once assume a more deferential position, and show her every possible courtesy.

The general's mind was much absorbed at this time in the movements of Sherman and Thomas. Sherman was marching rapidly into the interior of Georgia, cut off from all communication. The general, in speaking of the movement one evening, said: "Sherman's army is now somewhat in the condition of a ground-mole when he disappears under a lawn. You can here and there trace his track, but you are not quite certain where he will come out till you see his head." Hood had abandoned Georgia to Sherman, and was moving north with his whole force against Thomas. His army now consisted of about 45,000 men. Schofield, who, under Thomas's orders, was in advance watching Hood's movements and endeavoring to delay him, had less than 25,000 troops. On November 30 Hood closed up on Schofield and attacked him. This brought on the desperate battle of Franklin, and the fighting continued until long after nightfall. The enemy was handsomely repulsed, with a loss of over 6000 men, while Schofield lost only 2326. This day was made still more eventful by reason of Sherman's capturing Millen, Georgia, at the same time that Schofield was achieving his signal victory in Tennessee. The night of the battle of Franklin, Thomas was reinforced at Nashville by two divisions from Missouri, and the next day by two divisions of his own troops that he had brought in from the front. The day after the battle of Franklin (December 1), General Thomas reported that he had retired to the fortifications around Nashville until he could get his cavalry equipped, which was then outnumbered by that of the enemy four to one, adding that if Hood attacked that position he would be seriously damaged, and if he made no attack until our cavalry could be equipped, he or Schofield would move against him at once. General Grant telegraphed Thomas on December 2: "If Hood is permitted to remain quietly about Nashville, you will lose all the road back to Chattanooga, and possibly have to abandon the line of the Tennessee. Should he attack you, it is all well; but if he does not, you should attack him before he fortifies. Arm and put in the trenches your quartermaster's employees, citizens, etc." Nashville was a large military depot where there were nearly 10,000 employees, mainly quartermaster's men.

The same day the Secretary of War telegraphed Grant: "The President feels solicitous about the disposition of General Thomas to lay in fortifications for an indefinite period 'until Wilson gets equipments.' This looks like the McClellan and Rosecrans strategy of do nothing and let the rebels raid the country. The President wishes you to consider the matter." That afternoon the general sent a second despatch to General Thomas, urging him to dispose of Hood as speedily as possible, and if he got him to retreating to give him no peace. General Thomas replied at some length, stating his weak condition, and recalling the fact that his command was made up of Sherman's two weakest corps and all his dismounted cavalry except one brigade; and he also called his attention to the delays made necessary by the task of reorganization and equipment. He said that his cavalry was still outnumbered four to one, but that he had just received reinforcements of infantry, and now had infantry enough, though not sufficient cavalry, to assume the offensive, but that he expected more cavalry, and in a few days more should be able to give Hood another fight. General Grant's instructions had been put in the form of suggestions thus far, as he was reluctant to give positive orders. He entertained a high regard for General Thomas personally, and the greatest respect for his military capacity. Thomas was a conspicuous representative of the loyal Virginians. At the breaking out of the war he had shown great strength of character and determination of purpose in deciding to remain loyal to the country which had educated him as a soldier, and to defend the flag which he had sworn to uphold. No one had displayed greater devotion to the cause, and few officers in the service stood higher in the affection of their associates or in the confidence of their superior officers. General Thomas, being in command of only a single army, looked naturally to the means of securing the largest measure of success in his immediate front, and it was not likely that he would regard time as of so much importance as the general-in-chief of all the armies. With Grant, the movements of Thomas's army were a part of a series of coöperative campaigns, and unnecessary delays in the movements of any one army might seriously affect contemplated operations on the part of the others. Canby was expected to send a force into the interior, but he could not do so until Thomas had assumed the offensive against Hood; and he was compelled to postpone his expedition, and to hold Vicksburg and Memphis, and patrol the Mississippi to try to prevent troops from crossing from the Trans-Mississippi Department to relieve Hood. On December 3 General Thomas described the situation further, and closed by saying that he would feel able to march against Hood in less than a week. The seat of war in the West had been transferred from Atlanta as far north as Nashville, and General Grant now became apprehensive that Hood would cross the Cumberland River, move into Kentucky, and cut Thomas's railroad communications, and that the theater of operations in that region might be transferred even to the Ohio River, the disastrous moral effect of which would be beyond calculation. General Thomas telegraphed, December 6, that he thought he ought to have 6000 cavalry mounted before attacking Hood, and hoped to have such a mounted force in three days. General Grant's anxiety was increased by the fact that he realized that the inclement season was at hand, and feared that the winter storms might appear at any time and prove unfavorable for attack. Thomas had concentrated the forces in his department, troops had been hurried forward from Missouri, and the cavalry was being remounted by General James H. Wilson with great energy.

CHAPTER XXII

PLANNING THE FIRST FORT FISHER EXPEDITION—GRANT'S
AVERSION TO LIARS—REMINISCENCES OF GRANT'S CA-
DET LIFE—GRANT ORDERS THOMAS TO MOVE AGAINST
HOOD—THOMAS CRUSHES HOOD

DECISIONS of the utmost importance had to be made at this time in regard to movements on foot in other directions. The enemy was found to be making desperate efforts to collect troops to stay the progress of Sherman, whose march was creating the greatest consternation in the State of Georgia. News received from prisoners and spies, as well as from Southern newspapers, all confirmed the rumor that Sherman was destroying large quantities of supplies essential to the enemy, and striking terror at all points on his line of march. The governors of five Southern States were sending their reserves to confront Sherman, and the garrison of Fort Fisher, near Wilmington, North Carolina, was largely reduced for the same purpose. The latter news now made the general-in-chief anxious to start the expedition which he had in contemplation against Wilmington. This port had become the principal resort for vessels running the blockade, and was of incalculable importance to the enemy on account of the supplies received from foreign countries. A large fleet of naval vessels had been put under the command of Admiral Porter, and a force of 6500 men of Butler's army was held in readiness to be placed upon transports and sent to the mouth of the Cape Fear River, under the command of General Weitzel, to coöperate with the fleet in capturing Fort Fisher, the formidable earthwork which constituted the main defense of the mouth of the Cape Fear River and the city of Wilmington. General Butler, who was always prolific in ideas, made an original suggestion in regard to this expedition, which he believed would accomplish immensely important results. His proposition was to load a vessel with powder, tow it up as near as possible to Fort Fisher, and explode it, in the hope of shaking up the fort so seriously that its parapet would be sufficiently injured greatly to weaken its defense. Admiral Porter and other naval authorities seemed to favor the project, and General Grant finally agreed to let the experiment be tried, although his own judgment was decidedly against it. He said, in speaking of it: " Whether the report will be sufficient even to wake up the garrison in the fort, if they happen to be asleep at the time of the explosion, I do not know. It is at least foolish to think that the effect of the explosion could be transmitted to such a distance with enough force to weaken the fort. However, they can use an old boat which is not of much value, and we have plenty of damaged powder which is unserviceable for any other purpose, so that the experiment will not cost much, at any rate." Mr. Lincoln, in assenting to it, said facetiously: " We might as well explode the notion with powder as with anything else."

On December 3 General Grant wrote Sherman a letter, which he sent down the coast, to be delivered as soon as the Western commander reached the sea in the vicinity of Savannah, in which he said: " Bragg has gone from Wilmington. I am trying to take advantage of his absence to get possession of that place. Owing to some preparations that Admiral Porter and General Butler are making to blow up Fort Fisher, and which, while I hope for the best, I do not believe a particle in, there is a delay in getting the expedition off. . . ."

As Thomas's army was now larger than Hood's, and splendidly officered, Grant was much disturbed at the delay in striking Hood; and his anxiety had become so great that at 4 P. M. on December 6 he telegraphed Thomas: "Attack Hood at once, and wait no longer for a remount of your cavalry. There is great danger of delay resulting in a campaign back to the Ohio River." Thomas replied at 9 o'clock that night: ". . . I will make the necessary dispositions and attack Hood at once, agreeably to your order, though I believe it will be hazardous with the small force of cavalry now at my service." News had been received that Hood was moving a force toward Harpeth Shoals on the Cumberland.

That night Weitzel's troops embarked for the Fort Fisher expedition. Butler came over to headquarters, and announced his purpose of accompanying the expedition. This was the first intimation the general had that Butler was ambitious to go in person with the troops, as it was not the intention that he should command. Grant had selected in Weitzel an officer whom he regarded as peculiarly qualified for the management of such a delicate undertaking. However, it would have been, under the circumstances, a mortal affront to prevent the commander of the troops and of the department in which they were operating from accompanying them; and the alternative was presented to General Grant's mind of either letting Butler go on the expedition or relieving him from duty altogether. Butler placed great reliance upon the explosion of the powder-boat, and had counted upon being present at the attack; and finally the general-in-chief, rather than wound his feelings at such a crisis, did not order him to remain behind. He felt that Weitzel would have immediate command of the attacking party.

General Grant now wrote instructions to Sherman directing him to move his army by sea to Richmond, it appearing to him, under all the circumstances at that time, that it would be the means of dealing a death-blow to the Confederacy, and prove the quickest method of bringing the war to a close.

Late that night the general, Rawlins, Ingalls, and I, with one or two others, were sitting by the camp-fire. The general was seated on a rustic bench as usual, and was wrapped in his blue overcoat. He loved the open air, and nothing but a rain-storm could drive him into his hut. Some camp rumors had just been received which bore on their face the assurance that they were manufactured out of whole cloth. The discussion which ensued led the general to relate a story which was particularly well told. He said: "There was a man at the same post with me who had such a propensity for lying that his example taught every one a lesson as to the evil and absurdity of the practice. He seemed to believe that a lie told with particularity was more convincing than a general truth; but he frequently tripped himself up on account of his bad memory, for in order to be a successful liar a man ought to have a good memory. One day there were some strangers invited to dinner, and the champion was urged to try and keep as far within reasonable bounds in his statements as possible, so as not to mortify the company more than was necessary. This he promised, and evidently in good faith; for he asked an officer to touch his foot under the table if he told anything that might to unimaginative persons appear to be an exaggeration. Before the soup was finished, however, he began to indulge in his Munchausenisms. A person at the table mentioned the existing tendency to build hotels larger and larger every year. The champion joined in the conversation by saying: 'But it's not a new thing, after all. As long ago as when I was a mere boy, my father built a bigger hotel in our place than anybody has ever attempted since.' 'About how big was it?' asked one of the strangers. 'Why,' was the answer, 'it was two hundred and ninety-six feet high, five hundred and eighty feet long, and—' here the officer kicked his foot under the table, and he continued in a more subdued tone of voice—'and five feet and a half wide.'" After the laughter which followed this story had ceased, the general arose from his seat, threw away the stump of his cigar, and said: "Well, I think I'll turn in. Good night," and retired to his sleeping-apartment. After he had gone, Rawlins remarked: "The general always likes to tell an anecdote that points a moral on the subject of lying. He hates only two kinds of people, liars and cowards. He has no patience with them, and never fails to show his aversion for them." Ingalls added: "Such traits are so foreign to his own nature that it is not surprising that he should not tolerate them in others. As man and boy he has always been the most absolutely truthful person in the whole range of my acquaintance. I never knew him to run into the slightest exaggeration or to borrow in the least degree from his imagination in relating an occurrence." One of the party remarked: "I was amused one day to hear an officer say that the general was 'tediously truthful.' He explained that what he meant by that was that the general, in mentioning something that had taken place, would direct his mind so earnestly to stating unimportant details with entire accuracy that he would mar the interest of the story. For instance, after returning from a walk around camp he would say: 'I was told so and so about the wounded by Dr. —— while we were talking this morning inside of his tent'; and a half-hour afterward he would take the trouble to come back and say, as if it were a matter of the greatest importance: 'I was mistaken when I told you that my conversation with Dr. —— occurred inside his tent; that was not correct: it took place while we were standing in front of his tent.'" There was much truth in this comment. No one who had served any time with the general could fail to be struck with his excellent memory, and the pains he invariably took to state occurrences with positive accuracy, even in the most unimportant particulars. When he became President, an usher brought him a card one day while he was in a private room writing a message to Congress. " Shall I tell the gentleman you are not in?" asked the usher. "No," answered the President; "you will say nothing of the kind. I don't lie myself, and I won't have any one lie for me."

A staff-officer inquired of Ingalls whether General Grant, when at West Point, gave any promise of his future greatness. Ingalls replied: "Grant was such a quiet, unassuming fellow when a cadet that nobody would have picked him out as one who was destined to occupy a conspicuous place in history; and yet he had certain qualities which attracted attention and commanded the respect of all those in the corps with him. He was always frank, generous, and manly. At cavalry drill he excelled every one in his class. He used to take great delight in mounting and breaking in the most intractable of the new horses that were purchased from time to time and put in the squad. He succeeded in this, not by punishing the animal he had taken in hand, but by patience and tact, and his skill in making the creature know what he wanted to have it do. He was a particularly daring jumper. In jumping hurdles, when Grant's turn came the soldiers in attendance would, at an indication from him, raise the top bar a foot or so higher than usual, and he would generally manage to clear it. In his studies he was lazy and careless. Instead of studying a lesson, he would merely read it over once or twice; but he was so quick in his perceptions that he usually made very fair recitations even with so little preparation. His memory was not at all good in an attempt to learn anything by heart accurately, and this made his grade low in those branches of study which required a special effort of the memory. In scientific subjects he was very bright, and if he had labored hard he would have stood very high in them. Our class had sixty members the first year, but eight failed to pass the examinations, and the number was reduced to fifty-two. The second year's course had in it the hardest mathematics; Grant's grade in that branch was number ten. The next year he stood fifteen in natural philosophy, which stumped so many of us, and in the graduating year he was sixteen in engineering, the principal study in the first-class course. He was rather slouchy and unmilitary at infantry drills, and received about the average number of demerits. The principal reputation he gained among his fellow-cadets was for common sense, good judgment, entire unselfishness, and absolute fairness in everything he did. When we would get into an excited dispute over any subject, it was a very common thing to say, 'Well, suppose we see what Sam Grant has to say about it,' and leave it to his decision. He had been given the nickname of 'Uncle Sam' from his initials, and this was often shortened into 'Sam.' As I said, while he was not by any means conspicuous in the class, and never sought to be, he had enough marked characteristics to prevent him from being considered commonplace, and every one associated with him was sure to remember him and retain a high regard for him."

The anxiety of the authorities at Washington had now become so intense regarding Thomas's delay that Grant became more anxious than ever to have prompt action taken in Tennessee. On the morning of December 7 Stanton sent a despatch to City Point, saying: ". . . Thomas seems unwilling to attack, because it is hazardous—as if all war was anything but hazardous. . . ." The government was throwing the entire responsibility upon General Grant, and really censuring him in its criticisms of Thomas. Grant telegraphed to Washington: "There is no better man to repel an attack than Thomas, but I fear he is too cautious to take the initiative." On the 8th he sent a long despatch to General Thomas, urging him strenuously to attack, picturing the consequences which might follow longer delay, and appealing to his pride and patriotism. He wound up by saying: "Now is one of the finest opportunities ever presented of destroying one of the three armies of the enemy. If destroyed, he can never replace it. Use the means at your command, and you can do this, and cause a rejoicing that will resound from one end of the land to another." The next morning Halleck, too, telegraphed Thomas, urging him to wait no longer, and saying that if he delayed till all the cavalry was mounted he would wait till doomsday, as the waste was equaling the supply. On the 8th Grant learned that there was still no certainty as to when an attack would be made; and he telegraphed to Halleck, though with much reluctance, saying that if Thomas had not struck yet he ought to be ordered to hand over his command to Schofield. To this Halleck replied: "If you wish General Thomas relieved, give the order. No one here will, I think, interfere. The responsibility, however, will be yours, as no one here, so far as I am informed, wishes General Thomas's removal." Grant replied to Halleck that he would not ask to have Thomas relieved until he heard further from him. While the authorities at Washington were prodding Grant, demanding of him an immediate and vigorous movement in Tennessee, and shaping a correspondence which would have thrown all the blame on him if Hood had passed around Thomas and moved north, yet when severe measures were to be taken General Grant was promptly informed that he must assume all responsibility for any seemingly harsh treatment. He was, however, the last man to be timid about shouldering responsibilities, however disagreeable, and he was not acting upon the goadings received from Washington, but upon his own military judgment. On December 9, at 1 P. M., Thomas sent a telegram to Grant, saying: "Your despatch of 8:30 P. M. of the 8th is just received. I had nearly completed my preparations to attack the enemy to-morrow morning, but a terrible storm of freezing rain has come on to-day, which will make it impossible for our men to fight to any advantage. I am therefore compelled to wait for the storm to break, and make the attack immediately after. Admiral Lee is patrolling the river above and below the city, and, I believe, will be able to prevent the enemy from crossing. There is no doubt but that Hood's forces are considerably scattered along the river, with the view of attempting a crossing; but it has been impossible for me to organize and equip the troops for an attack at an earlier time. Major-general Halleck informs me that you are very much dissatisfied with my delay in attacking. I can only say I have done all in my power to prepare, and if you should deem it necessary to relieve me I shall submit without a murmur."

Nothing could better illustrate the nobility of Thomas's character, and his unselfishness and devotion to duty, than the words of this despatch. It was dignified in tone, and entirely subordinate in spirit. While the general fully appreciated the manly character of the despatch, it was nevertheless a grievous disappointment to him. He had felt that in war delays are always dangerous, and there is no telling what adverse circumstances may occur meanwhile. His worst apprehensions were now realized. The season was far into the winter, and a freezing storm had set in, which might prove a serious disadvantage to General Thomas's army. Rumors were abroad that Hood confidently expected reinforcements from the Trans-Mississippi Department, and these might now reach him before the coming battle. General Grant replied to General Thomas, at 7:30 P. M. that day: "I have as much confidence in your conducting a battle rightly as I have in any other officer; but it has seemed to me that you have been slow, and I have had no explanation of affairs to convince me otherwise. Receiving your despatch of 2 P. M. from General Halleck before I did the one to me, I telegraphed to suspend the order relieving you until we should hear further. I hope most sincerely that there will be no necessity of repeating the order, and that the facts will show that you have been right all the time." Notwithstanding the radical difference in judgment between the general and his distinguished subordinate, he was willing to give every reasonable consideration to his views, and even to express the hope that events might prove that he was wrong and Thomas right. That night Thomas telegraphed to both Grant and Halleck, explaining his condition, and saying that the storm continued. Still no attack was made, and General Grant curbed his impatience, and hoped to hear from hour to hour that his orders would be obeyed without further urging. He forbore from further suggestions until 4 P. M. on the 11th, when he telegraphed Thomas the following: " If you delay attack longer, the mortifying spectacle will be witnessed of a rebel army moving for the Ohio River, and you will be forced to act, accepting such weather as you find. Let there be no further delay. Hood cannot stand even a drawn battle so far from his supplies of ordnance stores. If he retreats, and you follow, he must lose his material and much of his army. I am in hopes of receiving a despatch from you to-day announcing that you have moved. Delay no longer for weather or reinforcements."

To add to General Grant's discomfort, Butler's expedition had not yet got off from Fort Monroe for Fort Fisher. This gave the general-in-chief anxiety for the reason that news was received this day, from the Richmond papers of the day before, that Sherman's advance was within twenty-five miles of Savannah, and that he was approaching at the rate of about eighteen miles a day. Grant felt that if the enemy were driven from Savannah, troops would be sent back to Fort Fisher, and that garrison strengthened sufficiently to make the success of any assault upon it doubtful; besides, by this delay our expedition was losing the chance of surprise. He therefore telegraphed Butler, urging him to start immediately.

The only good news received at headquarters upon this important day was the information that a movement made by Warren had been successful. He had destroyed the Weldon Railroad from Nottoway River to Hicksford, with but little loss, and his troops were now on their return to the Army of the Potomac. Grant promptly telegraphed the situation to Sheridan, and impressed upon him the importance of destroying the roads north of Richmond, in furtherance of the plan of cutting off the supplies of that city.

The next morning a reply came from Thomas to Grant's last despatch, saying that he would obey the orders as promptly as possible, but the country was covered with a sheet of ice and sleet, and the attack would be made under every disadvantage. About four hours afterward he telegraphed again that the condition of the country was no better, and it was impossible for cavalry, or even infantry, to move in anything like order, and he thought that an attack would result only in a useless sacrifice of life. Another day of anxiety passed, and another telegram came, saying there was no change in the weather. At 12:30 P. M. on the 14th Halleck telegraphed Thomas from Washington, reiterating that it was felt that every delay on his part seriously interfered with the general plans.

The past week had been the most anxious period of Grant's entire military career, and he suffered mental torture. On the one hand, he felt that he was submitting to delays which might seriously interfere with his general plans; that he was placed in an attitude in which he was virtually incapable of having his most positive orders carried out; and that he was occupying a position of almost insubordination to the authorities at Washington. On the other hand, he realized that nothing but the most extreme case imaginable should lead him to do even a seeming injustice to a distinguished and capable commander by relieving him when he was on the eve of a decided victory; for his military instincts convinced him that nothing but victory could follow the moment that Thomas moved, and he wished that loyal and devoted army commander to reap all the laurels of such a triumph. However, there was yet no time named for the attack, and Grant felt himself compelled to take some further steps. General John A. Logan happened to be at this time on a visit to headquarters at City Point. Logan had served under General Grant in the West, and held a high place in his estimation as a vigorous fighter. The general talked over the situation with Logan, and finally directed him to start at once for Nashville, with a view to putting him in command of the operations there, provided, upon his arrival, it was still found that no attack had been made. He gave him the requisite order in writing, to be used if necessary; and told him to say nothing about it, but to telegraph his arrival at Nashville, and if it was found that Thomas had already moved, not to deliver it or act upon it. Logan started promptly for the West. It was now December 14; and General Grant, being still more exercised in mind over the situation, determined to carry out a design which he had had in view for several days —to proceed to Nashville and take command there in person. The only thing which had prevented him from doing this earlier was the feeling which always dominated him in similar cases, and made him shrink from having even the appearance of receiving the credit of a victory the honor of which he preferred to have fall upon a subordinate. He now thought that his taking command in person would avoid the necessity of relieving Thomas, and be much less offensive to that officer than superseding him by some one else.

General Grant therefore started for Washington that night, the 14th. When he arrived there the next evening, as soon as the steamboat touched the wharf a despatch of the night before was shown him from Thomas to Halleck, saying that the enemy would be attacked in the morning; and also a telegram of the 15th from Van Duzer, a superintendent of the military telegraph-lines, announcing that Thomas had attacked the enemy early that morning, driving him back at all points. This was an incalculable relief to the general, and lifted a heavy load from his mind. He at once telegraphed Thomas: "I was just on my way to Nashville, but receiving a despatch from Van Duzer detailing your splendid success of to-day, I shall go no farther. Push the enemy now, and give him no rest until he is entirely destroyed. Your army will cheerfully suffer many privations to break up Hood's army and render it useless for future operations. Do not stop for trains or supplies, but take them from the country, as the enemy has done. Much is now expected."

The general had scarcely arrived at his hotel when a despatch came in from Thomas, saying: "I attacked the enemy's left this morning and drove it from the river, below the city, very nearly to the Franklin Pike, distance about eight miles. . . ." Before the general went to bed he sent a reply to Thomas, dated midnight, as follows: "Your despatch of this evening just received. I congratulate you and the army under your command for to-day's operations, and feel a conviction that tomorrow will add more fruits to your victory." Mr. Lincoln, on hearing the news, telegraphed Thomas: "You have made a magnificent beginning. A grand consummation is within your easy reach. Do not let it slip."

Logan had proceeded as far as Louisville when he heard the news of Thomas's first day's fight. Grant received a telegram from him there, saying: "People here jubilant over Thomas's success. Confidence seems to be restored. . . . All things going right. It would seem best that I return to join my command with Sherman." The general sent him a reply, saying: "The news from Thomas so far is in the highest degree gratifying. You need not go farther."

General Grant was now a much happier man than he

had been for many weeks—happy not only over the victory, but because it had at last come in time to spare him from resorting to extreme measures regarding one of his most trusted lieutenants. He went from Washington to Burlington, spent a day with his family, where a general rejoicing took place over the good news from Tennessee, and then returned to City Point.

It was not until the 17th that the full details of Thomas's victory were received. His army from the very outset of the battle had charged the enemy so vigorously at all points that his lines were completely broken and his troops thrown into confusion, which, upon the second day, resulted in a panic. The most heroic defense the enemy could make did not enable him to stay the impetuosity of Thomas's troops. Battery after battery fell into the hands of our forces, and prisoners were captured by the thousand. All the enemy's dead and wounded were abandoned on the field, and the line of his retreat was covered with abandoned wagons, gun-carriages, knapsacks, blankets, and small arms. In two days Thomas had captured over 4000 prisoners and 53 pieces of artillery, and left Hood's army a wreck. The pursuit of the enemy was continued for several days, and much additional damage inflicted. On the 18th General Grant telegraphed to Thomas: "The armies operating against Richmond have fired two hundred guns in honor of your great victory. . . ." One hundred guns had been the salute fired in honor of other victories.

Hood's army was pursued and driven south of the Tennessee River. In this campaign he had suffered ignominious defeat, with the loss of half his army. Thomas's captures amounted to more than 13,000 prisoners and 72 pieces of artillery; 2000 deserters had also given themselves up to the Union forces, and taken the oath of allegiance to the United States government. The remnant of Hood's demoralized and disorganized troops were no longer held together in one army. Some of them were furloughed and allowed to return to their homes, and the rest were transferred to the East, and joined the forces there for the purpose of opposing Sherman. Thomas's entire loss in this campaign was about 10,000 men in killed, wounded, and missing.

General Grant's predictions that Hood would turn north, and not follow Sherman when the latter cut loose from Atlanta, and that Thomas's army would crush Hood's as soon as it was led against it, were completely fulfilled. There has been so much discussion in regard to the actions of General Grant and General Thomas during the two weeks preceding the battle of Nashville that a synopsis of the correspondence between them has been given in order that the reader may form his own conclusions. General Grant has been charged with being inimical to Thomas, allowing himself to become unduly irritated over the delay of the latter, and ordering an ill-advised advance of the army, against Thomas's expressed judgment. The general-in-chief had had a larger experience with Confederate armies than any one else, and felt that the urgent orders he gave were necessary; and as he was held responsible by the government and by the country for the operations of all the armies, and the success of the coöperative movements which he had planned, he certainly exercised a perfectly proper authority in giving the orders he issued. When General Thomas did not obey the instructions repeatedly sent him, the general-in-chief did not treat the case as one of insubordination or defiance, and act hastily or arbitrarily in taking steps immediately to enforce his orders, but exercised a patience which he would not have done under other circumstances or toward any other army com-

mander. He felt while sending his urgent despatches for
an advance of the army that he was doing Thomas a positive service; for he knew better than any one else could
know that as soon as Thomas launched his army against
Hood's forces he would win triumphantly, and demonstrate to the country what was already known to his
fellow-officers—that the "Rock of Chickamauga" was
worthy of being placed in the front rank of the great
commanders of the war. It was because he felt entire
confidence in Thomas's ability to whip Hood that he
urged Thomas to strike, and not because he doubted
him. When General Grant made his report of the
operations, he stated, in referring to General Thomas,
substantially what he had said in conversation at headquarters after the victory of Nashville: " His final defeat
of Hood was so complete that it would be accepted as
a vindication of that distinguished officer's judgment."
On the other hand, there were those who criticized General Thomas severely for disobedience of orders of his
superior officer, and manifesting a spirit of insubordination at a critical crisis of the war. Such insinuations,
when all the circumstances are taken into consideration,
would attribute to General Thomas traits of character
which were certainly foreign to his nature. He believed that he was right, and that he was acting for the
best interests of the service, and evidently felt so thoroughly convinced of this that he was willing to run
the risk of assuming all responsibility, and to submit
to being displaced from his command, rather than yield
his judgment. There is very little doubt that if any
other two general officers in the service had been placed
in the same trying circumstances there would have been
an open rupture; but both being men of patience as
well as firmness, their correspondence was conducted
without acrimony, the services of both were utilized for

the benefit of the country, and each was prompt to acknowledge the high qualifications of the other.

Their personal relations were not broken, as has been alleged, by this circumstance, as far as an observer could judge. General Thomas, when he came to Washington after the close of the war, dined with General Grant at his house, and at the table with him at the houses of common friends, where I was present, and their intercourse never seemed to be marked by any lack of cordiality on either side.

CHAPTER XXIII

UPON the return of General Ingalls from another
trip to Washington, he brought with him on a visit
to City Point Senator Nesmith of Oregon, who had been
an intimate acquaintance of Generals Grant and Ingalls
when these two officers were stationed at Fort Vancouver, Oregon, in 1853. Nesmith was a great wag, and
used to sit by the headquarters camp-fire in the evening,
and tell no end of Pacific-coast stories. By the way in
which he elaborated all the incidents, and led up with
increasing humor to the climax of an anecdote, he
stamped himself a true artist as a raconteur. One evening he told General Grant of a trip he had made on the
Pacific coast with a number of politicians just after his
election by the Democratic legislature of Oregon to the
United States Senate. In the party was the Republican
governor of California. Nesmith said: " The governor
got to deviling me about my election, and rather got the
laugh on me by inquiring: ' Now, Nesmith, make a clean
breast of it, and tell us just how much money it costs to
get run into the Senate by an Oregon legislature.' To
strike back at him, I replied: ' Well, I 'll give you a little
account of my experience in dealing with the boys, and
leave you to judge. I found, on counting noses, that I

had corralled a majority of one certain on joint ballot of the two houses; but that did n't make things quite safe, and I told my friends that we ought to have still another fellow persuaded of what was due to my eminence as a statesman; that it was altogether likely that if we relied on the one man, he would be shot, or landed in jail, or get blind drunk about the time the vote was to be taken, and we were playing too big a game to take any such chances. Well, they said there was a man that had recently come into the State from California, and had managed to get himself elected to our legislature, and they thought, from what they had heard of him, that he would n't be stubborn enough to hold on blindly to the candidate of his choice if argument sufficiently convincing in favor of some one else were laid before him; that he was a great fellow to "coincide" if it was made an object for him to do it. You see, times were hard, and the price of everything was high. Two years before Bibles were given away free, and now jack-rabbits were selling at two dollars and a half a pair. Most men's possessions were reduced to a hair-brush and a tooth-brush, though they never had time to use either. I said: "Send the man to my hotel to-night; there 's no time to be lost. I intend to handle this rooster myself." When he came to my room, I shoved him into a chair, locked the door, seated myself in front of him, folded my arms, looked him square in the face, and said: "See here! I want your vote. How much?" He glued his eyes on me, and remarked: "Now, pard, yer talkin' business. I don't know just what the state of the market is in Oregon, but what would you propose as a kind o' starter?" I continued: "How would a hundred and fifty dollars strike you?" He rose up out of his chair, looking as if he actually felt hurt by my evident lack of appreciation, and roared out in a tone of voice calculated to wake the dead: "A hundred and fifty hells! I paid the governor of California twice that much last year to pardon me out of the penitentiary, or else I would n't be up here in your blank old legislature to vote for anybody!"'" We were assured that after the recital of this story, which Nesmith had, of course, invented for the purpose of retaliating upon the California governor, there were no further questions from that official as to the methods pursued in Oregon elections.

"I was n't at all surprised, Nes, to see you go to the Senate," said Ingalls; "I always believed old Vancouver could furnish talent enough to supply both the civil and military branches of the government." "Well, you may not have been surprised, but I was," remarked the senator. "I said to the members of our committee one day: 'When I came here from the wilds of Oregon as senator of the United States I could n't realize it; I felt that it was a greater honor than to have been a Roman senator; I could n't help wondering how I ever got here.' 'Well,' said Preston King of New York, 'now that you have been here a couple of weeks, and have got the "hang of the school-house," how do you feel about it?' My answer was, 'Well, since I 've had time to look round and size things up, my wonder now is, how in thunder the rest of you fellows ever got here.'"

Upon this, as upon one or two other occasions, some stories were attempted which were too broad to suit the taste of the general-in-chief, but they were effectually suppressed. He believed that stories, like diamonds, are always of greater value when they are not "off color." If reference were made to subjects which warred against his notions of propriety, while he seldom checked them by words, he would show immediately, by the blush which mantled his cheek, and by his refusal to smile at a joke which depended for its success upon its coarseness, that such things were objectionable to him. The same evening a citizen who had come to camp with Nesmith said he would tell a story, and began by looking around significantly and saying, "I see there are no ladies present." The general interrupted him with the remark, "No; but there are gentlemen"; and the subject was at once changed, and the story was not attempted.

The senator, after seeing the lines around Petersburg, expressed a desire to pay a visit to General Butler, and Ingalls and I volunteered to take him to that officer's headquarters by boat. Butler greeted the senator warmly, and the two soon began to discuss the war, and to banter each other on the subject of politics, one being a radical Republican, and the other a war Democrat. Nesmith drew an amusing picture of Butler's propensity for confiscation and destruction of property. In the course of the conversation Butler referred to some pranks played in his boyish days, and said: "There was a cake-peddler who used to come by our school-house every day, and during recess we would 'play cakes' with him; that is, he would set his basket on the ground, and a boy, by paying twenty-five cents, could have the privilege of starting from a certain distance, and by a series of designated hops, skips, and jumps, trying to land in the basket and break as many cakes as he could. If he succeeded he had a right to take all the cakes he had damaged. The game was pretty difficult, and the cakeman generally came out ahead; but one day I strained every nerve to win, and succeeded in landing in the middle of the basket with both feet, and breaking every cake the fellow had." Nesmith's comment upon this story was: "Well, that 's just like you, general; you seem to have spent all your life in trying to break other people's cakes." The joke, which had been rather in Butler's favor up to that time, was now turned against him, but he took it all in good part.   In discussing General Grant's popularity, Butler remarked: "Grant first touched the popular chord when he gained his signal victory at Donelson."   "No," said Nesmith, who always went round with a huge joke concealed somewhere about his person; "I think he first touched the popular cord when he hauled wood from his farm and sold it at full measure in St. Louis."

That night Nesmith told General Grant the story of the cipher correspondence he and Ingalls had carried on the year before.   He said: "One day the Secretary of War sent me a message that he would like to see me at the War Department, at the earliest moment, on a matter of public importance.   Well, I was rather flattered by that.   I says to myself: 'Perhaps the whole Southern Confederacy is moving on Stanton, and he has sent for a war Democrat to get between him and them and sort of whirl 'em back.'   I hurried up to his office, and when I got in he closed the door, looked all around the room like a stage assassin to be sure that we were alone, then thrust a telegram under my nose, and cried, 'Read that!'   I suppose I ought to have appeared scared, and tried to find a trap-door in the floor to fall through, but I did n't.   I ran my eye over the despatch, seeing that it was addressed to me and signed by Ingalls, and read: 'Klat-a-wa ni-ka sit-kum mo-litsh weght o-coke kon-a-mox lum.'   Stanton, who was glaring at me over the top of his spectacles, looking as savage as a one-eyed dog in a meat-shop, now roared out, 'You see I have discovered everything!'   I handed back the despatch, and said, 'Well, if you 've discovered everything, what do you want with me?'   He cried: 'I 'm determined, at all hazards, to intercept every cipher despatch from officers at the front to their friends in the North, to enable them to speculate in the stock-markets upon early information as to the movements of our armies.' I said: 'Well, I can't help but admire your pluck; but it seems to me you omitted one little matter: you forgot to read the despatch.' 'How can I read your incomprehensible hieroglyphics?' he replied. 'Hieroglyphics—thunder!' I said; 'why that 's Chinook.' 'And what 's Chinook?' he asked. 'What! you don't know Chinook? Oh, I see your early education as a linguist has been neglected,' I answered. 'Why, Chinook is the court language of the Northwestern Indian tribes. Ingalls and I, and all the fellows that served out in Oregon, picked up that jargon. Now I 'll read it to you in English: " Send me half barrel more that same whisky." You see, Ingalls always trusts my judgment on whisky. He thinks I can tell the quality of the liquor by feeling the head of the barrel in the dark.' That was too much for the great War Secretary, and he broke out with a laugh such as I don't believe the War Department had ever heard since he was appointed to office; but I learned afterward that he took the precaution, nevertheless, to show the despatch to an army officer who had served in the Northwest, to get him to verify my translation." As General Grant knew a good deal of Chinook, he was able to appreciate the joke fully, and he enjoyed the story greatly. Nesmith had served to enliven the camp for several days with his humorous reminiscences of life in the West, and when he left every one parted with him with genuine regret.

On December 13 Sherman reached Ossabaw Sound, southeast of Savannah, just a month after he had left Atlanta, and communicated with the fleet which had been sent to meet him. His 65,000 men and half that number of animals had been abundantly fed, and his losses had been only 103 killed, 428 wounded, and 278 missing. The destruction of the enemy's property has been estimated as high as one hundred millions of dollars. On December 15 General Sherman received General Grant's letter of the 3d. In this he said, among other things: "Not liking to rejoice before the victory is assured, I abstain from congratulating you and those under your command until bottom has been struck. I have never had a fear of the result." The next day Sherman received General Grant's orders outlining the plan of transferring the greater part of Sherman's army by sea to join the armies in front of Petersburg, and end the war. As the enemy's troops were now nearly all in Virginia, it was thought that as the railroads in the South had been pretty well destroyed, it would bring hostilities to a close quicker to move Sherman by sea than to consume the time and subject the men to the fatigue of marching by land. General Grant said this would be the plan unless Sherman saw objections to it. A prompt and enthusiastic letter was written by Sherman, saying his army could join Grant before the middle of January if sent on transports by sea, and that he expected to take Savannah meanwhile. When General Grant visited the capital he consulted as to the means of ocean transportation, and became convinced that with all the sea-going vessels that could be procured it would take two months to move Sherman's army, with its artillery and trains, to the James River; and he therefore wrote him from Washington: "I did think the best thing to do was to bring the greater part of your army here and wipe out Lee. The turn affairs now seem to be taking has shaken me in that opinion. I doubt whether you may not accomplish more toward that result where you are than if brought here, especially as I am informed since my arrival in the city [Washington] that it would take about two months to get you here, with all the other calls there are for ocean transportation. I want to get your views about what ought to be done. . . . My own opinion is that Lee is averse to going out of Virginia, and if the cause of the South is lost, he wants Richmond to be the last place surrendered. If he has such views, it may be well to indulge him until we get everything else in our hands. Congratulating you and the army again upon the splendid result of your campaign, the like of which is not read of in past history, I subscribe myself more than ever, if possible, your friend."

Sherman now invested Savannah on the south side, but the enemy evacuated the city on the night of December 20. Sherman's army then entered, and on the 22d the general sent his famous despatch to the President, which reached him on Christmas eve: "I beg to present you as a Christmas gift the city of Savannah, with 150 heavy guns and plenty of ammunition, and also about 25,000 bales of cotton."

On December 8 General Butler had come over to see General Grant at headquarters, and said that as his troops would be aboard the transports at Fort Monroe the next day, he would start in the afternoon for that place, and see that the expedition was promptly started. They had a general conversation in regard to what would be required of the expedition, which was merely a reiteration of the written orders which had been carefully prepared. It was decided that one of General Grant's staff should accompany the expedition, and Colonel Comstock was designated for that duty. Delay in taking aboard additional supplies, and severe storms, prevented the expedition from beginning operations against Fort Fisher before December 24. The navy had converted a gunboat, the *Louisiana*, into a powder-boat. She was filled with two hundred and fifty tons of powder, and disguised as a blockade-runner. This vessel was run in toward the beach, anchored about five hundred yards from the fort, and exploded about 2 A. M. on the 24th. The report was not much greater than the discharge of a piece of heavy artillery; no damage was done to the enemy's earthworks, and no result accomplished. A negro on shore was afterward reported to have said when he heard the sound: "I reckon de Yankees hab done bu'st one ob dah b'ilers."

At daylight on the 24th the naval fleet of fifty vessels moved forward and began the bombardment of the fort. About noon on the 25th General Ames's division landed, and a skirmish-line was pushed to within a few yards of the fort. It was reported that the fort had not been materially damaged, and that Hoke's command had been sent south from Lee's army, and was approaching to reinforce the garrison. Butler now decided not to make an attack, and reëmbarked all of his troops, except Curtis's brigade, on the transports, and steamed back to Fort Monroe, reaching there on the 27th. Curtis's brigade also reëmbarked on the 27th, and followed the other forces. On the 28th General Butler came to headquarters, and had an interview with General Grant, in which he sought to explain the causes of the failure. General Grant expressed himself very positively on the subject. He said he considered the whole affair a gross and culpable failure, and that he proposed to make it his business to ascertain who was to blame for the want of success. The delays from storms were, of course, unavoidable. The preparation of the powder-boat had caused a loss of several weeks. It was found that the written orders which General Grant had given to General Butler to govern the movements of the expedition had not been shown to Weitzel. An important part of these instructions provided that under certain contingencies the troops were expected to intrench and hold themselves in readiness to coöperate with the navy for the reduction of the fort, instead of reëmbarking on the

transports. General Grant had not positively ordered
an assault, and would not have censured the commander
if the failure to assault had been the only error; but he
was exceedingly dissatisfied that the important part of
his instructions as to gaining and holding an intrenched
position had been disobeyed, and the troops withdrawn,
and all further efforts abandoned.

Mrs. Grant, Fred, and Jesse came to City Point to
spend the Christmas holidays with the general. Rawlins
always called Fred the "Veteran," for the reason that he
had been with his father in the fight which took place
in rear of Vicksburg the year before, when he was only
thirteen years of age.   One evening Rawlins said, in referring to that campaign: "Fred crossed the Mississippi
with his father on the gunboat *Price*. Early in the
morning the general went ashore to direct the movement
of the troops, leaving the boy coiled up on the forward
deck fast asleep. When he woke up the youngster insisted on following his father, but was told by a staff-
officer to stay where he was and keep out of danger;
but he happened just then to see some troops chasing a
rabbit, and jumped ashore and joined in the fun. Thinking the men were a pretty jolly set of fellows, he followed
along with the regiment in its march to the front, thinking he would meet his father somewhere on the road.
The troops soon encountered the enemy, and Fred found
himself suddenly participating in the battle of Port Gib-
son. That night he recognized a mounted orderly belonging to headquarters, and hailed him. The orderly
gave him a blanket, and he rolled himself up in it and
managed to get several hours' sleep. About midnight
his father came across him, and his surprise may be
imagined when he discovered that the boy had left the
boat and turned amateur soldier. The general had
crossed the river in true light-marching order, for he

had no encumbrances but an overcoat and a tooth-brush. A couple of horses were soon captured. The general took one, and gave the other to Fred. They were ungainly, ragged-hipped nags, and the general was greatly amused at seeing the figure the boy cut when mounted on his raw-boned war-charger. At the battle of Black River Bridge, Fred saw Lawler's brigade making its famous charge which broke the enemy's line, and rode forward and joined in the pursuit of the foe; but he had not gone far when a musket-ball struck him on the left thigh. A staff-officer rode up to him, and asked him how badly he was hurt; and Fred, not being an expert in gunshot wounds, said he rather thought his leg was cut in two. 'Can you work your toes?' asked the officer. The boy tried, and said he could. 'Then,' cried the officer, 'you 're all right'; and taking him to a surgeon, it was found that the ball had only clipped out a little piece of flesh, so that he was not damaged enough to have to join the ranks of the disabled.

"Speaking of the charge of Lawler's brigade," continued Rawlins, "while the general was watching the preparations for it an officer came up bearing a despatch from Halleck, written six days before, which had been forwarded through General Banks. It ordered General Grant to withdraw at once from where he was, march to Grand Gulf, and coöperate with Banks against Port Hudson, and then return with the combined forces and besiege Vicksburg. The general read the communication, and just as he had finished it he saw Lawler charging through the enemy's broken lines and heard the men's cheers of victory. Turning to the officer who had brought the message, he said: 'I 'll have to say, in this case, what the Irishman said to the chicken that was in the egg he swallowed, and which peeped as it was going down his throat: "You spoke too late."' Then,

putting spurs to his horse, he galloped off to join the
advancing lines. The enemy's forces were in full retreat, hurrying on to shut themselves up in Vicksburg,
and the general, under such circumstances, had no hesitation in disobeying orders six days old, and written
without any knowledge of the circumstances."

Soon after Fred's arrival at City Point he took it into
his head that he must go duck-shooting. The general
was no sportsman himself, and never shot or fished; but
he liked to see the youngsters enjoy the Christmas holidays, and he readily gave his consent to anything they
proposed in the way of amusement. He never gave a
reason for not hunting, but it was evident that he felt
that certain forms of it furnished a kind of sport which
was too cruel to suit his tastes. He described the only
bull-fight he ever attended as presenting "a most sickening sight," and never seemed to take any pleasure in
sports which caused suffering on the part of either animals or human beings. As sporting-guns are not found
among army supplies, Fred had to content himself with
an infantry rifled musket. The general's colored servant, Bill, accompanied the boy. Bill was not much of
a shot himself. He usually shot as many a man votes,
with his eyes shut. But he was a good hand to take the
place of the armor-bearer of the ancients, and carry the
weapons. Taking a boat, they paddled down the river
in search of game. They had not gone far when they
were brought to by the naval pickets who had been
posted on the river-bank by the commander of one of
the vessels. A picket-boat was sent after them, and
they were promptly arrested as rebel spies, and taken
aboard a gunboat. The declaration by the white prisoner, who, it was supposed, was plotting death and
destruction to the Union, that he was the son of the
general-in-chief, was at first deemed too absurd to be

entertained by sailors, and fit only to be told to the marines; but after a time Fred succeeded in convincing the officers as to his identity, and was allowed to return to headquarters. When he arrived he wore a rueful expression of countenance at the thought of the ingratitude of republics to their "veterans." His father was greatly amused by the account of his adventure, teased him good-naturedly, and told him how fortunate it was that he had not been hanged at the yard-arm as an enemy of the republic, and his body consigned to the waters of the Potomac.

CHAPTER XXIV

CAPTURE OF FORT FISHER — THE DUTCH GAP CANAL —
GRANT RECEIVES UNASKED ADVICE — GRANT RELIEVES
BUTLER — SHERMAN'S LOYALTY TO GRANT — A "GOOD
SHOT" — NIGHT ATTACK OF THE ENEMY'S IRONCLADS —
HOW GRANT BECAME A CONFIRMED SMOKER — GRANT
OFFERS HIS PURSE TO HIS ENEMY — GRANT RECEIVES
THE "PEACE COMMISSIONERS"

AS soon as General Grant obtained accurate information in regard to the circumstances and conditions at Fort Fisher, he decided to send another expedition, and to put it in charge of an efficient officer, and one who could be trusted implicitly to carry out his instructions. As there had been a lack of precaution on the part of the officers engaged in the previous expedition to keep the movement secret, the general-in-chief at first communicated the facts regarding the new expedition to only two persons at headquarters. Of course he had to let it be known to the Secretary of War; but as the Secretary was always reticent about such matters, there was a reasonable probability that the secret could be kept. Directions were given which tended to create the impression that the vessels were being loaded with supplies and reinforcements for Sherman's army, and studious efforts were made to throw the enemy off his guard. Of course every one who knew the general's tenacity of purpose felt sure that he would never relinquish his determination to take Fort Fisher, and would immediately take steps to retrieve the failure which had been made in the first attempt; and as soon as Butler returned I suggested to the general that, in case another expedition should be sent, General A. H. Terry would be, for many reasons, the best officer to be placed in command. We had served together in the Sherman-Du-pont expedition which in 1861 took Hilton Head and captured Fort Pulaski and other points on the Atlantic coast, and I knew him to be the most experienced officer in the service in embarking and disembarking troops upon the sea-coast, looking after their welfare on trans-ports, and intrenching rapidly on shore. General Grant had seldom come in contact with Terry personally, but had been much pleased at the manner in which he had handled his troops in the movements on the James River. A suggestion, too, was made that as Terry was a volun-teer officer, and as the first expedition had failed under a volunteer, it would only be fair that another officer of that service, rather than one from the regular army, should be given a chance to redeem the disaster. The general seemed to listen with interest to what was said about Terry, particularly as to his experience in sea-coast expeditions, but gave no hint at the time of a dis-position to appoint him; nor did he even say whether he would send another expedition to Fort Fisher: but on January 2 he telegraphed to Butler, "Please send Major-general Terry to City Point to see me this morn-ing." Grant considered the propriety of going in person with the expedition, but his better judgment did not approve such a course, for he would be too far out of reach of communication with City Point, and as Butler was the senior army commander, it would leave him in supreme command of the armies operating against Petersburg and Richmond.

When Terry came the general-in-chief told him simply that he had been designated to take command of a transfer by sea of eight thousand men, and that he was to sail under sealed orders. Terry felt much complimented that he should be singled out for such a command, but had no idea of his destination, and was evidently under the impression that he was to join Sherman. On January 5 Terry was ready to proceed to Fort Monroe, and Grant accompanied him down the James River for the purpose of giving him his final instructions. After the boat had proceeded some distance from City Point, the general sat down with Terry in the after-cabin of the steamer, and there made known to him the real destination and purposes of the expedition. He said: "The object is to renew the attempt to capture Fort Fisher, and in case of success to take possession of Wilmington. It is of the greatest importance that there should be a complete understanding and harmony of action between you and Admiral Porter. I want you to consult the admiral fully, and to let there be no misunderstanding in regard to the plan of coöperation in all its details. I served with Admiral Porter on the Mississippi, and have a high appreciation of his courage and judgment. I want to urge upon you to land with all despatch, and intrench yourself in a position from which you can operate against Fort Fisher, and not to abandon it until the fort is captured or you receive further instructions from me." Full instructions were carefully prepared in writing, and handed to Terry on the evening of January 5; and captains of the transports were given sealed orders, not to be opened until the vessels were off Cape Henry. The vessels soon appeared off the North Carolina coast. A landing was made on January 13, and on the morning of the 14th Terry had fortified a position about two miles from the fort. The navy, which had been firing upon the fort for two days, began another bombardment at daylight on the 15th. That afternoon Ames's division made an assault on the work. Two thousand sailors and marines were also landed for the purpose of making a charge. They had received an order from the admiral, in the wording of which facetiousness in nautical phraseology could go no further. It read: "Board the fort in a seamanlike manner."

They made a gallant attack, but were met with a murderous fire, and did not gain the work. Ames's division, with Curtis's brigade in advance, overcame all efforts of the defenders, and the garrison was driven from one portion of the fort to another in a series of hand-to-hand contests, in which individual acts of heroism surpassed almost anything in the history of assaults upon well-defended forts. The battle did not close until ten o'clock at night. Then the formidable work had been fairly won. The garrison was taken prisoners, the mouth of the Cape Fear River was closed, and Wilmington was at the mercy of our troops. The trophies were 169 guns, over 2000 stands of small arms, large quantities of ammunition and commissary stores, and more than 2000 prisoners. About 600 of the garrison were killed or wounded. Terry's loss was 110 killed, 536 wounded, and 13 missing. After the news of the capture of the fort was received, I was sent there by General Grant with additional instructions to Terry; and upon my arrival I could not help being surprised at the formidable character of the work. No one without having seen it could form an adequate conception of the almost insurmountable obstacles which the assaulting columns encountered.

During the summer General Butler, who was always fertile in ideas, had conceived the notion that there were many advantages to be gained by making a canal across

W. T. SHERMAN.

From a photograph.

GRANT UNDER FIRE AT FORT HARRISON.

A. Lincoln

FROM AN ORIGINAL, UNRETOUCHED NEGATIVE, MADE IN 1864, AT THE TIME THE PRESI-
DENT COMMISSIONED ULYSSES S. GRANT LIEUTENANT-GENERAL AND COMMANDER OF
ALL THE ARMIES OF THE REPUBLIC. IT IS STATED THAT THIS NEGATIVE, "WITH
ONE OF GENERAL U. S. GRANT," WAS MADE IN COMMEMORATION OF THAT EVENT.

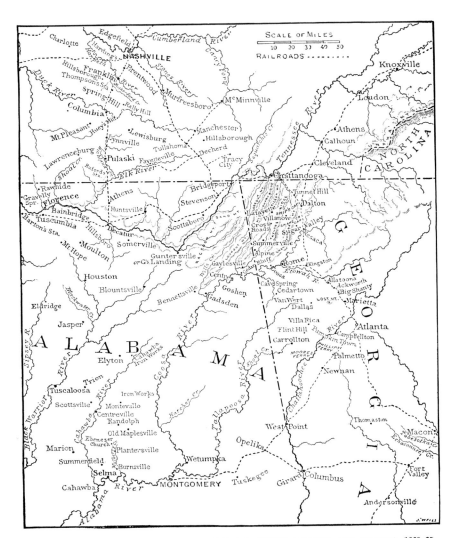

MAP OF OPERATIONS IN MIDDLE TENNESSEE AND NORTH ALABAMA AND GEORGIA, 1863–65.

MAJOR-GENERAL GEORGE H. THOMAS.

From a photograph.

GRANT'S WINTER HEADQUARTERS AT CITY POINT.

GENERAL GRANT'S CABIN, FORMERLY HEADQUARTERS AT CITY POINT; REMOVED IN 1865 TO EAST PARK, PHILADELPHIA, WHERE IT NOW STANDS.

ELIHU B. WASHBURNE.

PRESIDENT LINCOLN AND GENERAL GRANT INSPECT A BODY OF PRISONERS CAPTURED ON THE PETERSBURG FRONT.

P H Sheridan

SHERIDAN AND HIS GENERALS RECONNOITERING AT FIVE FORKS.

VISIT OF PRESIDENT LINCOLN, ADMIRAL PORTER, AND TAD LINCOLN, TO GENERAL
GRANT AT THE WALLACE HOUSE IN PETERSBURG.

GENERAL ROBERT E. LEE.

From a photograph taken after the war.

Porter.   Marshall.   Sheridan.
                                                         Ingalls.
                                                           Babcock.   Custer.

Lee.   Grant.   Merritt.
                                         Parker.

GRANT AT APPOMATTOX.

Photograph taken in the field at City Point, Va., by H. F. Warren, March 15, 1865. The original photograph is in the possession of the Bostonian Society, and hangs in the Memorial Hall, Old State House, Boston, Mass.

a narrow neck of land, known as Dutch Gap, on the James River, which would cut off four and three-quarter miles of river navigation. This neck was about one hundred and seventy-four yards wide. The name originated from the fact that a Dutchman had many years before attempted a similar undertaking, but little or no progress had been made. The enterprise involved the excavation of nearly eighty thousand cubic feet of earth. Butler had been somewhat reluctantly authorized to dig the canal, and work upon it had been begun on August 10. The enemy soon erected heavy rifle-guns, and afterward put mortars in positions which bore upon it; and our men were subjected to a severe fire, and frequently had to seek shelter in "dugouts" constructed as places of refuge. Under the delays and difficulties which arose, the canal was not finished until the end of the year. On the 31st of December General Grant received a message from Butler saying: "We propose to explode the heading of Dutch Gap at 11 A. M. to-morrow. I should be happy to see yourself and friends at headquarters. We must be near the time because of the tide." The general-in-chief replied: "Do not wait for me in your explosion. I doubt my ability to be up in the morning." After the bulkhead wall of earth had been blown out, the debris at the north end was partly removed by means of steam dredges. The canal was not of any service during the war, but it has since been enlarged and improved, and has become the ordinary channel for the passage of vessels plying on the James River.

General Grant had become very tired of discussing methods of warfare which were like some of the problems described in algebra as "more curious than useful," and he was not sufficiently interested in the canal to be present at the explosion which was expected to complete it. About this time all the cranks in the country, besides men of real inventive genius, were sending extraordinary plans and suggestions for capturing Richmond. A proposition from an engineer was received one day, accompanied by elaborate drawings and calculations, which had evidently involved intense labor on the part of the author. His plan was to build a masonry wall around Richmond, of an elevation higher than the tallest houses, then to fill the inclosure with water pumped from the James River, and drown out the garrison and people like rats in a cage. The exact number of pumps required and their capacity had been figured out to a nicety. Another inventive genius, whose mind seemed to run in the direction of the science of chemistry and the practice of sternutation, sent in a chemical formula for making an all-powerful snuff. In his communication he assured the commanding general that after a series of experiments he had made with it on people and animals, he was sure that if shells were filled with it and exploded within the enemy's lines, the troops would be seized with such violent fits of sneezing that they would soon become physically exhausted with the effort, and the Union army could walk over at its leisure and pick them up as prisoners without itself losing a man. A certain officer had figured out from statistics that the James River froze over about once in seven years, and that this was the seventh year, and advised that troops be massed in such a position that when the upper part of the James changed from a liquid to a solid, columns could be rushed across it on the ice to a position in rear of the enemy's lines, and Richmond would be at our mercy. A sorcerer in Rochester sent the general word that he had cast his horoscope, and gave him a clear and unclouded insight into his future, and added to its general attractiveness by telling him how gloriously he was going to succeed in taking Richmond.

One evening the general referred to these emanations of the prolific brains of our people, and the many novel suggestions made to him, beginning with the famous powder-boat sent against Fort Fisher, and closed the conversation by saying: " This is a very suggestive age. Some people seem to think that an army can be whipped by waiting for rivers to freeze over, exploding powder at a distance, drowning out troops, or setting them to sneezing; but it will always be found in the end that the only way to whip an army is to go out and fight it."

On January 4 General Grant had written to the Secretary of War asking that Butler might be relieved, saying: " I am constrained to request the removal of General Butler from the command of the Department of Virginia and North Carolina. I do this with reluctance, but the good of the service requires it. In my absence General Butler necessarily commands, and there is a lack of confidence felt in his military ability, making him an unsafe commander for a large army. His administration of the affairs of his department is also objectionable." Learning that the Secretary of War had gone to Savannah to visit General Sherman, and could not receive this letter in due time, on January 6 the general telegraphed to the President, asking that prompt action be taken in the matter. The order was made on the 7th, and on the morning of the 8th General Grant directed Colonel Babcock and me to go to General Butler's headquarters, announce the fact to him, and hand him the written order relieving him from command. We arrived there about noon, found the general in his camp, and by his invitation went with him into his tent. He opened the communication, read the order, and was silent for a minute; then he began to manifest considerable nervousness, and turning to his desk, wrote " Received" on the envelop, dated it 1864 instead of 1865,

and handed it back.   It was the custom in the army to
return envelop receipts in case of communications delivered by enlisted men, but this was omitted when the
instructions were transmitted by staff-officers.   He was
politely reminded that a written receipt was not necessary.   Thereupon, in a somewhat confused manner, he
uttered a word or two of apology for offering it, and
after a slight pause added: " Please say to General Grant
that I will go to his headquarters, and would like to
have a personal interview with him."

General Grant was in constant correspondence with
Sherman in regard to the movements in the Carolinas.
Sherman was to move north, breaking up all lines of
communication as he advanced.   If Lee should suddenly
abandon Richmond and Petersburg, and move with his
army to join the Confederate forces in the Carolinas
with a view to crushing Sherman, that officer was to
whip Lee if he could, and if not to fall back upon the
sea-coast.   Grant was to hold Lee's army where it was,
if possible, and if not to follow it up with vigor.   Sherman's triumphant march to the sea had gained him
many admirers in the North, and it was believed about
this time that a bill might be introduced in Congress
providing for his promotion to the grade of lieutenant-
general, which would make him eligible to command the
armies in case he should be assigned to such a position.
On January 21 he said in a letter to General Grant: " I
have been told that Congress meditates a bill to make
another lieutenant-general for me.   I have written to
John Sherman to stop it if it is designed for me.   It
would be mischievous, for there are enough rascals who
would try to sow differences between us, whereas you
and I now are in perfect understanding.   I would rather
have you in command than anybody else; for you are
fair, honest, and have at heart the same purpose that

should animate all.   I should emphatically decline any
commission calculated to bring us into rivalry. . . ."
General Grant replied: "No one would be more pleased
at your advancement than I, and if you should be placed
in my position and I put subordinate, it would not change
our relations in the least.   I would make the same exertions to support you that you have ever done to support
me, and I would do all in my power to make our cause
win."   On January 31 Sherman wrote: "I am fully aware
of your friendly feeling toward me, and you may always
depend on me as your steadfast supporter.   Your wish
is law and gospel to me, and such is the feeling that
pervades my army."

In all the annals of history no correspondence between men in high station furnishes a nobler example
of genuine, disinterested personal friendship and exalted
loyalty to a great cause.

Admiral Porter had withdrawn nearly all the naval
vessels from the James River in order to increase his
fleet for the Fort Fisher expedition.   Only three or four
light gunboats were left, and one ironclad, the *Onondaga*,
a powerful double-turreted monitor carrying two 15-inch
smooth-bores and two 150-pound Parrott rifles.   This
vessel was commanded by Captain William A. Parker
of the navy.   Captain Parker would occasionally pay a
visit to General Grant at City Point, and he usually
brought with him a junior officer who afforded the general-in-chief no little amusement by the volubility of his
conversation.   When the general asked the captain a
question, before he could venture a reply his sub would
volunteer an answer, and frequently make it the occasion of an elaborate lecture upon the intricate science of
marine warfare.   The captain could rarely get in a
word edgewise.   In fact, he seemed to accept the situation, and did not often make the attempt.   It might

have been said of this young officer what Talleyrand said of a French diplomat: "Clever man, but he has no talent for dialogue."

There had been so much talk about the formidable character of the double-turreted monitors that General Grant decided one morning to go up the James and pay a visit to the *Onondaga*, and invited me to accompany him. The monitor was lying above the pontoon-bridge in Trent's Reach. After looking the vessel over, and admiring the perfection of her machinery, the general said to the commander: "Captain, what is the effective range of your 15-inch smooth-bores?" "About eighteen hundred yards, with their present elevation," was the reply. The general looked up the river, and added: "There is a battery which is just about that distance from us. Suppose you take a shot at it, and see what you can do." The gun was promptly brought into position by revolving the turret, accurate aim taken, and the order given to fire. There was a tremendous concussion, followed by a deafening roar as the enormous shell passed through the air; and then all eyes were strained to see what execution would be done by the shot. The huge mass struck directly within the battery, and exploded. A cloud of smoke arose, earth and splintered logs flew in every direction, and a number of the garrison sprang over the parapet. The general took another puff at the cigar he was smoking, nodded his head, and said, "Good shot!" The naval officers indulged in broad smiles of triumph, and tried to look as if this was only one of the little things they always did with equal success when they tried hard.

On the night of January 23 a naval officer, at General Grant's suggestion, was sent up to plant torpedoes at the obstructions which had been placed in the river at Trent's Reach, as he was apprehensive that our depleted

naval force might be attacked by the enemy's fleet,
which was lying in the river near Richmond. The officer
made the discovery that the Confederate ironclads were
quietly moving down the river. News of their approach
was promptly given, and at once telegraphed to headquarters. The enemy's fleet consisted of six vessels, and
by half-past ten o'clock they had passed the upper end
of Dutch Gap Canal. The general directed me and another staff-officer to take boats and communicate with
all despatch with certain naval vessels, warn them of
the character of the anticipated attack, and direct them
to move up and make a determined effort to prevent
the enemy's fleet from reaching City Point. The officer
whom I was to take with me got a little rattled in the
hurry of the departure, and started, from force of habit,
to put on his spurs. It took me some time to persuade
him that these appendages to his heels would not particularly facilitate his movements in climbing aboard
gunboats. A third officer, Lieutenant Dunn, was sent
to communicate with a gunboat stationed at some distance from the others. In the mean time orders were
given to tow coal-schooners up the river, ready to sink
them in the channel if necessary; and instructions were
issued to move all heavy guns within reach down to the
river shore, where their fire could command the channel.
There was an enormous accumulation of supplies at
City Point, and their destruction at this time would
have been a serious embarrassment. The night was
pitch-dark, but our naval vessels were promptly reached
by means of steam-tugs; and their commanders, who
displayed that cordial spirit of coöperation always manifested by our sister service, expressed an eagerness to
obey General Grant's orders as implicitly as if he had
been their admiral. Most of these vessels were out of
repair and almost unserviceable, but their officers were

determined to make the best fight they could. When I
returned to headquarters, the general, Mrs. Grant, and
Ingalls were talking the matter over in the front room
of the general's quarters. "Well, now that we 've got
all ready for them," said Ingalls, "why don't their old
gunboats come down?" "Ingalls, you must have patience," remarked the general; " perhaps they don't know
that you 're in such a hurry for them, or they would
move faster; you must give them time." "Well, if
they 're going to postpone their movement indefinitely,
I 'll go to bed," continued Ingalls, and started for his
quarters. News now came that it was thought the
vessels could not pass the obstructions, and would not
make the attempt; and the general and Mrs. Grant retired to their sleeping-apartment, orders being left that
the general was to be wakened if there should be any
change in the situation. Soon after one o'clock word
came that the enemy's vessels had succeeded at high
water in getting through the obstructions. A loud knock
was now given upon the door of the general's sleeping-
room. He called out instantly: "Yes. What have you
heard?" The reply was: "The gunboats have passed
the obstructions, and are coming down." In about two
minutes the general came hurriedly into the office. He
had drawn on his top-boots over his drawers, and put
on his uniform frock-coat, the skirt of which reached
about to the tops of the boots and made up for the absence of trousers. He lighted a cigar while listening to
the reports, and then sat down at his desk and wrote
out orders in great haste. The puffs from the cigar
were now as rapid as those of the engine of an express-
train at full speed. Mrs. Grant soon after came in, and
was anxious to know about the situation. It was certainly an occasion upon which a woman's curiosity was
entirely justifiable. Dunn had returned with a report

about the movement of the gunboat with which he had been sent to communicate, and Ingalls had also rejoined the party.   Mrs. Grant, in the midst of the scene, quietly said, "Ulyss, will those gunboats shell the bluff?" "Well, I think all their time will be occupied in fighting our naval vessels and the batteries ashore," he replied.   "The *Onondaga* ought to be able to sink them, but I don't know what they would do if they should get down this far."   Just then news came in that upon the approach of the enemy's vessels the *Onondaga* had retired down the river.   The captain had lost his head, and under pretense of trying to obtain a more advantageous position, had turned tail with his vessel, and moved down-stream below the pontoon-bridge.   General Grant's indignation knew no bounds when he heard of this retreat.   He said: "I have been thrown into close contact with the navy, both on the Mississippi River and upon the Atlantic coast.   I entertain the highest regard for the intrepidity of the officers of that service, and it is an inexpressible mortification to think that the captain of so formidable an ironclad, and the only one of its kind we have in the river, should fall back at such a critical moment.   Why, it was the great chance of his life to distinguish himself."   Additional instructions were at once telegraphed to the shore batteries to act with all possible vigor.

Mrs. Grant, who was one of the most composed of those present, now drew her chair a little nearer to the general, and with her mild voice inquired, "Ulyss, what had I better do?"   The general looked at her for a moment, and then replied in a half-serious and half-teasing way, "Well, the fact is, Julia, you ought n't to be here."   Dunn now spoke up and said: "Let me have the ambulance hitched up, and drive Mrs. Grant back into the country far enough to be out of reach of the shells." "Oh, their gunboats are not down here yet," answered the general; "and they must be stopped at all hazards." Additional despatches were sent, and a fresh cigar was smoked, the puffs of which showed even an increased rapidity. In about two hours it was reported that only one of the enemy's boats was below the obstructions, and the rest were above, apparently aground. More guns had by this time been placed in the shore batteries, and the situation was greatly relieved. Ingalls, whose dry humor always came to his rescue when matters were serious, again assumed an air of disappointment, and said: "I tell you, I 'm getting out of all patience, and I 've about made up my mind that these boats never intended to come down here anyhow—that they 've just been playing it on us to keep us out of bed."

A little while after matters had so quieted down that the general-in-chief and Mrs. Grant retired to finish their interrupted sleep. At daylight the *Onondaga* moved up within nine hundred yards of the Confederate ironclad *Virginia*, the flag-ship, and opened fire upon her. Some of the shore guns were also trained upon her, and a general pounding began. She was struck about one hundred and thirty times, our 15-inch shells doing much damage. Another vessel, the *Richmond*, was struck a number of times, and a third, the *Drewry*, and a torpedo-launch were destroyed. At flood-tide the enemy succeeded in getting their vessels afloat, and withdrew up the river. That night they came down again, and attacked the *Onondaga*, but retired after meeting with a disastrous fire from that vessel and our batteries on the river banks. This was the last service performed by the enemy's fleet in the James River.

On the morning of January 24 breakfast in the messroom was a little later than usual, as every one had been trying to make up for the sleep lost the previous night. When the chief had lighted his cigar after the morning meal, and taken his place by the camp-fire, a staff-officer said: "General, I never saw cigars consumed quite so rapidly as those you smoked last night when you were writing despatches to head off the ironclads." He smiled, and remarked: "No; when I come to think of it, those cigars did n't last very long, did they?" An allusion was then made to the large number he had smoked the second day of the battle of the Wilderness. In reply to this he said: "I had been a very light smoker previous to the attack on Donelson, and after that battle I acquired a fondness for cigars by reason of a purely accidental circumstance. Admiral Foote, commanding the fleet of gunboats which were coöperating with the army, had been wounded, and at his request I had gone aboard his flag-ship to confer with him. The admiral offered me a cigar, which I smoked on my way back to my headquarters. On the road I was met by a staff-officer, who announced that the enemy were making a vigorous attack. I galloped forward at once, and while riding among the troops giving directions for repulsing the assault I carried the cigar in my hand. It had gone out, but it seems that I continued to hold the stump between my fingers throughout the battle. In the accounts published in the papers I was represented as smoking a cigar in the midst of the conflict; and many persons, thinking, no doubt, that tobacco was my chief solace, sent me boxes of the choicest brands from everywhere in the North. As many as ten thousand were soon received. I gave away all I could get rid of, but having such a quantity on hand, I naturally smoked more than I would have done under ordinary circumstances, and I have continued the habit ever since."

General Grant never mentioned, however, one incident in connection with the battle of Donelson, and no one ever heard of it until it was related by his opponent in that battle, General Buckner. In a speech made by that officer at a banquet given in New York on the anniversary of General Grant's birthday, April 27, 1889, he said: ". . . Under these circumstances, sir, I surrendered to General Grant. I had at a previous time befriended him, and it has been justly said that he never forgot an act of kindness. I met him on the boat, and he followed me when I went to my quarters. He left the officers of his own army and followed me, with that modest manner peculiar to himself, into the shadow, and there tendered me his purse. It seems to me, Mr. Chairman, that in the modesty of his nature he was afraid the light would witness that act of generosity, and sought to hide it from the world. We can appreciate that, sir."

On the morning of the 31st of January General Grant received a letter sent in on the Petersburg front the day before, signed by the Confederates Alexander H. Stephens, J. A. Campbell, and R. M. T. Hunter, asking permission to come through our lines. These gentlemen constituted the celebrated "Peace Commission," and were on their way to endeavor to have a conference with Mr. Lincoln. The desired permission to enter our lines was granted, and Babcock was sent to meet them and escort them to City Point. Some time after dark the train which brought them arrived, and they came at once to headquarters. General Grant was writing in his quarters when a knock came upon the door. In obedience to his "Come in!" the party entered, and were most cordially received, and a very pleasant conversation followed. Stephens was the Vice-President of the Confederacy; Campbell, a former justice of the Supreme Court of the United States, was Assistant Secretary of War; and Hunter was president *pro tempore*

of the Confederate Senate. As General Grant had been
instructed from Washington to keep them at City Point
until further orders, he conducted them in person to the
headquarters steamer, the *Mary Martin*, which was lying
at the wharf, made them his guests, and had them provided with well-furnished state-rooms and comfortable
meals during their stay. They were treated with every
possible courtesy; their movements were not restrained,
and they passed part of the time upon the boat, and
part of it at headquarters. Stephens was about five feet
five inches in height; his complexion was sallow, and
his skin seemed shriveled upon his bones. He possessed
intellect enough, however, for the whole commission.
Many pleasant conversations occurred with him at headquarters, and an officer once remarked, after the close
of an interview: "The Lord seems to have robbed that
man's body of nearly all its flesh and blood to make
brains of them."

The commissioners twice endeavored to draw General
Grant out as to his ideas touching the proper conditions
of the proposed terms of peace; but as he considered
himself purely a soldier, not intrusted with any diplo-
matic functions, and as the commissioners spoke of
negotiations between the two governments, while the
general was not willing to acknowledge even by an in-
ference any government within our borders except that
of the United States, he avoided the subject entirely,
except to let it be known by his remarks that he would
gladly welcome peace if it could be secured upon proper
terms. Mr. Lincoln had directed Mr. Seward, the Secretary of State, on January 31, to meet the commissioners at Fort Monroe on February 2. General Grant
telegraphed the President that he thought the gentlemen
were sincere in their desire to restore peace and union,
and that it would have a bad effect if they went back

without any expression from one who was in authority, and said he would feel sorry if Mr. Lincoln did not have an interview with them, or with some of them. This changed the President's mind, and he started at once for Fort Monroe. The commissioners were sent down the James River that afternoon, and were met at Fort Monroe by the President and Mr. Seward on the 3d, and had a conference lasting several hours aboard the President's steamer. Mr. Lincoln stated that peace could be secured only by a restoration of the national authority over all the States, a recognition of the position assumed by him as to the abolition of slavery, and an understanding that there should be no cessation of hostilities short of an end of the war and a disbanding of all forces hostile to the government. The commissioners, while they did not declare positively that they would not consent to reunion, avoided giving their assent; and as they seemed to desire to postpone that important question, and adopt some other course first which might possibly lead in the end to union, but which Mr. Lincoln and Mr. Seward thought would amount simply to an indefinite postponement, the conference ended without result. After stopping at City Point and having another conversation with General Grant, principally in reference to an exchange of prisoners, the Confederate commissioners were escorted through our lines on their way back to Richmond. I accompanied the escort part of the way, and had an interesting talk with Mr. Stephens. He was evidently greatly disappointed at the failure of the conference, but was prudent enough not to talk much about it. He spoke freely in regard to General Grant, saying: " We all form our preconceived ideas of men of whom we have heard a great deal, and I had certain definite notions as to the appearance and character of General Grant; but I was never so completely surprised in all my life as when I met him and found him a person so entirely different from my idea of him. His spare figure, simple manners, lack of all ostentation, extreme politeness, and charm of conversation were a revelation to me, for I had pictured him as a man of a directly opposite type of character, and expected to find in him only the bluntness of the soldier. Notwithstanding the fact that he talks so well, it is plain that he has more brains than tongue." He continued by saying what he said several times in Washington after the war, and also wrote in his memoirs: "He is one of the most remarkable men I ever met. He does not seem to be aware of his powers, but in the future he will undoubtedly exert a controlling influence in shaping the destinies of the country."

Mr. Stephens was wrapped from his eyes to his heels in a coarse gray overcoat about three sizes too large for him, with a collar so high that it threatened to lift his hat off every time he leaned his head back. This coat, together with his complexion, which was as yellow as a ripe ear of corn, gave rise to a characterization of the costume by Mr. Lincoln which was very amusing. The next time he saw General Grant at City Point, after the "Peace Conference," he said to him, in speaking on the subject, "Did you see Stephens's greatcoat?" "Oh, yes," answered the general. "Well," continued Mr. Lincoln, "soon after we assembled on the steamer at Hampton Roads, the cabin began to get pretty warm, and Stephens stood up and pulled off his big coat. He peeled it off just about as you would husk an ear of corn. I could n't help thinking, as I looked first at the coat and then at the man, 'Well, that 's the biggest shuck and the littlest nubbin I ever did see.'" This story became one of the general's favorite anecdotes, and he often related it in after years with the greatest zest.

CHAPTER XXV

GRANT PLANS THE SPRING CAMPAIGNS—THE PRESIDENT'S
SON JOINS GRANT'S STAFF—LEE ASKS A PERSONAL IN-
TERVIEW—A VISIONARY PEACE PROGRAM—HIGH PRICES
IN RICHMOND—GRANT RECEIVES A MEDAL FROM CON-
GRESS—SHAVING UNDER DIFFICULTIES—ARRIVAL OF
SHERIDAN'S SCOUTS

GENERAL GRANT was at this time employing
all his energies in maturing his plans for a comprehensive campaign on the part of all the armies, with
a view to ending the war in the early spring. Sheridan
was to move down the valley of Virginia for the purpose
of destroying the railroads, the James River Canal, and
the factories in that section of country used for the pro-
duction of munitions of war. Stoneman was to start
upon a raid from east Tennessee with 4000 men, with a
view to breaking up the enemy's communications in that
direction. Canby, who was in command at New Orleans,
was to advance against Mobile, Montgomery, and Selma.
In the movement on Mobile, Canby had at least 45,000
men. Thomas was to send a large body of cavalry under
Wilson into Alabama. The movements of our forces
in the West were intended not only to destroy communications, but to keep the Confederate troops there from
being sent East to operate against Sherman. Sherman
was to march to Columbia, South Carolina, thence to
Fayetteville, North Carolina, and afterward in the di-

rection of Goldsborough. Schofield was to be transferred from Tennessee to Annapolis, Maryland, and thence by steamer to the Cape Fear River, for the purpose of moving inland from there and joining Sherman in North Carolina. Schofield's orders were afterward changed, and he rendezvoused at Alexandria, Virginia, instead of Annapolis. The Army of the Potomac and the Army of the James were to watch Lee, and at the proper time strike his army a crushing blow, or, if he should suddenly retreat, to pursue him and inflict upon him all damage possible, and to endeavor to head off and prevent any portion of his army from reaching North Carolina as an organized force capable of forming a junction with Johnston and opposing Sherman. Some of these operations were delayed longer than was expected, and a few changes were made in the original plan; but they were all carried into effect with entire success, and the military ability of the general-in-chief never appeared to better advantage than in directing these masterly movements, which covered a theater of war greater than that of any campaigns in modern history, and which required a grasp and comprehension which have rarely been possessed even by the greatest commanders. He was at this period indefatigable in his labors, and he once wrote in a single day forty-two important despatches with his own hand.

In the latter part of January, General Grant went with Schofield down the coast, and remained there a short time to give personal directions on the ground. Sherman entered Columbia February 17, and the garrison of Charleston evacuated that place on the 18th without waiting to be attacked. When this news was received, Dr. Craven, a medical officer who was in the habit of drawing all his similes from his own profession, commended the movement by saying: "General Sher-

man applied a remedial agency which is in entire accord
with the best medical practice. Charleston was suffering from the disease known as secession, and he got
control of it by means of counter-irritation." Wilmington was captured on the 22d of February.

An addition was now made to our staff in the person
of Captain Robert T. Lincoln, the President's eldest son.
He had been graduated at Harvard University in 1864,
and had at once urged his father to let him enter the
army and go to the front; but Mr. Lincoln felt that this
would only add to his own personal anxieties, and Robert was persuaded to remain at Harvard and take a
course of study in the law-school. The fact is not generally known that Mr. Lincoln already had a personal
representative in the army. He had procured a man to
enlist early in the war, whom he always referred to as
his " substitute." This soldier served in the field to the
end with a good record, and the President watched his
course with great interest, and took no little pride in
him.

In the spring of 1865 Robert renewed his request to
his father, who mentioned the subject to General Grant.
The general said to the President that if he would let
Robert join the staff at headquarters, he would be glad
to give him a chance to see some active service in the
field. The President replied that he would consent to
this upon one condition : that his son should serve as a
volunteer aide without pay or emoluments; but Grant
dissuaded him from adhering to that determination,
saying that it was due to the young man that he should
be regularly commissioned, and put on an equal footing
with other officers of the same grade. So it was finally
settled that Robert should receive the rank of captain
and assistant adjutant-general; and on February 23 he
was attached to the staff of the general-in-chief. The

new acquisition to the company at headquarters soon
became exceedingly popular. He had inherited many
of the genial traits of his father, and entered heartily
into all the social pastimes at headquarters. He was
always ready to perform his share of hard work, and
never expected to be treated differently from any other
officer on account of his being the son of the Chief
Executive of the nation. The experience acquired by
him in the field did much to fit him for the position
of Secretary of War, which he afterward held. This
month had brought me another promotion. I received
a commission as brevet colonel of volunteers, dated
February 24, for "faithful and meritorious services."

On the evening of March 3, just as the general was
starting to the mess-hut for dinner, a communication
was handed to him from General Lee, which had come
through our lines, and was dated the day before. After
referring to a recent meeting under a flag of truce between Ord and Longstreet, from which the impression
was derived that General Grant would not refuse to see
him if he had authority to act for the purpose of attempting to bring about an adjustment of the present
difficulties by means of a military convention, the letter went on to say : " Sincerely desiring to leave nothing
untried which may put an end to the calamities of war,
I propose to meet you at such convenient time and
place as you may designate, with the hope that, upon
an interchange of views, it may be found practicable to
submit the subjects of controversy between the belliger-
ents to a convention of the kind mentioned. In such
event, I am authorized to do whatever the result of the
proposed interview may render necessary or advisable."
There came inclosed with this letter another stating that
General Lee feared there was some misunderstanding
about the exchange of political prisoners, and saying

that he hoped that at the interview proposed some satisfactory solution of that matter might be arrived at. General Grant, not being vested with any authority whatever to treat for peace, at once telegraphed the contents of the communication to the Secretary of War, and asked for instructions. The despatch was submitted to Mr. Lincoln at the Capitol, where he had gone, according to the usual custom at the closing hours of the session of Congress, in order to act promptly upon bills presented to him. He consulted with the Secretaries of State and War, and then wrote with his own hand a reply, dated midnight, which was signed by Stanton, and forwarded to General Grant. It was received the morning of the 4th, and read as follows: "The President directs me to say to you that he wishes you to have no conference with General Lee, unless it be for the capitulation of General Lee's army, or on some minor and purely military matter. He instructs me to say that you are not to decide, discuss, or confer upon any political question. Such questions the President holds in his own hands, and will submit them to no military conferences or conventions. Meantime you are to press to the utmost your military advantages." The general thought that the President was unduly anxious about the manner in which the affair would be treated, and replied at once: ". . . I can assure you that no act of the enemy will prevent me from pressing all advantages gained to the utmost of my ability; neither will I, under any circumstances, exceed my authority or in any way embarrass the government. It was because I had no right to meet General Lee on the subject proposed by him that I referred the matter for instructions." He then replied to Lee: "In regard to meeting you on the 6th instant, I would state that I have no authority to accede to your proposition for a conference on the subject proposed.

Such authority is vested in the President of the United States alone. General Ord could only have meant that I would not refuse an interview on any subject on which I have a right to act, which, of course, would be such as are purely of a military character, and on the subject of exchanges, which has been intrusted to me."

It was learned afterward that an interesting but rather fanciful program had been laid out by the enemy as a means to be used in restoring peace, and that this contemplated interview between Grant and Lee was to be the opening feature. Jefferson Davis had lost the confidence of his people to such an extent as a director of military movements that Lee had been made generalissimo, and given almost dictatorial powers as to war measures. As the civilians had failed to bring about peace, it was resolved to put Lee forward in an effort to secure it upon some terms which the South could accept without too great a sacrifice of its dignity, by means of negotiations, which were to begin by a personal interview with General Grant. One proposition discussed was that after the meeting of Grant and Lee, at which peace should be urged upon terms of granting amnesty, making some compensation for the emancipated slaves, etc., by the national government, it should be arranged to have Mrs. Longstreet, who had been an old friend of Mrs. Grant, visit her at City Point, and after that to try and induce Mrs. Grant to visit Richmond. It was taken for granted that the natural chivalry of the soldiers would assure such cordial and enthusiastic greetings to these ladies that it would arouse a general sentiment of good will, which would everywhere lead to demonstrations in favor of peace between the two sections of the country. General Longstreet says that the project went so far that Mrs. Longstreet, who was at Lynchburg, was telegraphed to come on to Richmond. The plan outlined in this order of procedure was so visionary that it seems strange that it could ever have been seriously discussed by any one; but it must be remembered that the condition of the Confederacy was then desperate, and that drowning men catch at straws.

It was seen that Grant, by his operations, was rapidly forcing the fight to a finish. The last white man in the South had been put into the ranks, the communications were broken, the supplies were irregular, Confederate money was at a fabulous discount, and hope had given place to despair. The next evening one of our scouts returned from a trip to Richmond, and was brought to headquarters in order that the general-in-chief might question him in person. The man said: "The depreciation in the purchasing power of 'graybacks,' as we call the rebel treasury notes, is so rapid that every time I go into the enemy's lines I have to increase my supply of them. On my last trip I had to stuff my clothes full of their currency to keep myself going for even a couple of days. A barrel of flour in Richmond now costs over a thousand dollars, and a suit of clothes about twelve hundred. A dollar in gold is equal in value to a hundred dollars in graybacks. Then so much counterfeit Confederate money has been shoved in through our lines that in the country places they don't pretend to make any difference between good and bad money. A fellow that had come in from the western part of the State told me a pretty tough yarn about matters out there. He said: 'Everything that has a picture on it goes for money. If you stop at a hotel, and the bill of fare happens to have an engraving of the house printed at the top, you can just tear off the picture and pay for your dinner with it.'"

On the 10th of March the Hon. Elihu B. Washburne, who had paid one or two visits before to headquarters, arrived at City Point, and brought with him the medal which had been struck, in accordance with an act of Congress, in recognition of General Grant's services, and which Mr. Washburne had been commissioned to present. A dozen prominent ladies and gentlemen from Washington came at the same time. On the afternoon of the next day General Grant went with them to the lines of the Army of the Potomac, and gave orders for a review of some of the troops. That evening some simple arrangements were made for the presentation of the medal, which took place at 8 P. M. in the main cabin of the steamer which had brought the visitors, and which was lying at the City Point wharf. General Meade suggested that he and the corps commanders would like to witness the ceremony, and in response to an invitation they came to City Point for the purpose, accompanied by a large number of their staff-officers. Mr. Washburne arose at the appointed hour, and after delivering an exceedingly graceful speech eulogistic of the illustrious services for which Congress had awarded this testimonial of the nation's gratitude and appreciation, he took the medal from the handsome morocco case in which it was inclosed, and handed it to the general-in-chief. The general, who had remained standing during the presentation speech, with his right hand clasping the lapel of his coat, received the medal, and expressed his appreciation of the gift in a few well-chosen words, but uttered with such modesty of manner, and in so low a tone of voice, that they were scarcely audible. A military band was in attendance, and at the suggestion of Mrs. Grant a dance was now improvised. The officers soon selected their partners from among the ladies present, and the evening's entertainment was continued to a late hour. The general was urged to indulge in a waltz, but from this he begged off. However, he finally agreed to compromise the matter by dancing a square dance. He went through the cotillion, not as gracefully as some of the beaux among the younger officers present, but did his part exceedingly well, barring the impossibility of his being able to keep exact time with the music. He did not consider dancing his forte, and in after life seldom indulged in that form of amusement, unless upon some occasion when he attended a ball given in his honor. In such case he felt that he had to take part in the opening dance to avoid appearing impolite or unappreciative.

Mr. Washburne was assigned quarters in camp next to General Grant. The next day was Sunday. The congressman was the first one up, and when he went to shave he found there was no looking-glass in his quarters; so he stepped across to the general's office in his shirt-sleeves, and finding a glass there, proceeded to lather his face and prepare for the delicate operation of removing his beard. Just as he had taken hold of his nose with his left thumb and forefinger, which he had converted into a sort of clothes-pin for the occasion, and had scraped a wide swath down his right cheek with the razor, the front door of the hut was suddenly burst open, and a young woman rushed in, fell on her knees at his feet, and cried: "Save him! oh, save him! He's my husband." The distinguished member of Congress was so startled by the sudden apparition that it was with difficulty that he avoided disfiguring his face with a large gash. He turned to the intruder, and said: "What's all this about your husband? Come, get up, get up! I don't understand you." "Oh, general, for God's sake, do save my husband!" continued the woman. "Why, my good woman, I'm not General Grant," the congressman insisted. "Yes, you are; they told me this was your room. Oh, save him, general; they're to shoot him this very day for desertion if you don't stop them." Mr. Washburne now began to take in the situation, and led the woman to a seat, and tried to comfort her, while she began to tell how her young husband had been led, through his fondness for her, to desert in order to go home and see her, and how he had been captured and court-martialed, and was to be executed that day, and how she had heard of it only in time to reach headquarters that morning to plead for his life. By this time the general was up, and hearing from his sleeping-apartment an excited conversation in the front room, dressed hurriedly, and stepped upon the scene in time to hear the burden of the woman's story. The spectacle presented partook decidedly of the serio-comic. The dignified member of Congress was standing in his shirt-sleeves in front of the pleading woman, his face covered with lather, except the swath which had been made down his right cheek; the razor was uplifted in his hand, and the tears were starting out of his eyes as his sympathies began to be worked upon. The woman was screaming and gesticulating frantically, and was almost hysterical with grief. I appeared at the front door about the same time that the general entered from the rear, and it was hard to tell whether one ought to laugh or cry at the sight presented. The general now took a hand in the matter, convinced the woman that he was the commanding general, assured her that he would take steps at once to have her husband reprieved and pardoned, and sent her away rejoicing. His interposition saved the man's life just in the nick of time. He cracked many a joke with Mr. Washburne afterward about the figure he cut on the morning of the occurrence.

Sheridan had started out from Winchester on the 27th of February with nearly 10,000 cavalry. On March 5 news was received that he had struck Early's forces between Staunton and Charlottesville, and crushed his entire command, compelling Early and other officers to take refuge in houses and in the woods. For some time thereafter only contradictory reports were heard from Sheridan, through the Richmond papers which came into our hands; and as he was in the heart of the enemy's country, and direct communication was cut off, it was difficult to ascertain the facts. General Grant felt no apprehension as to the result of Sheridan's movements, but was anxious to get definite reports. On Sunday evening, March 12, the members of the mess sat down to dinner about dark. Mrs. Grant and Mrs. Rawlins, who was also visiting headquarters, were at the table. Toward the end of the meal the conversation turned upon Sheridan, and all present expressed the hope that we might soon hear something from him in regard to the progress of his movements. Just then a colored waiter stepped rapidly into the mess-room, and said to the general: "Thah's a man outside dat say he want to see you right away, and he don't 'pear to want to see nobody else." "What kind of looking man is he?" asked the general. "Why," said the servant, "he's de mos' dreffle-lookin' bein' I ebber laid eyes on; he 'pears to me like he was a' outcast." With the general's consent, I left the table and went to see who the person was. I found a man outside who was about to sink to the ground from exhaustion, and who had scarcely strength enough to reply to my questions. He had on a pair of soldier's trousers three or four inches too short, and a blouse three sizes too large; he was without a hat, and his appearance was grotesque in the extreme. With him was another man in about the same condition. After giving them some whisky they gathered strength enough to state that they were scouts sent by Sheridan from Columbia on the James River, had passed through the enemy's lines, bringing with them a long and important despatch from their commander, had ridden hard for two days, and had had a particularly rough experience in getting through to our lines. Their names were J. A. Campbell and A. H. Rowand, Jr. As Campbell had the despatch in his possession, I told him to step into the mess-room with me, and hand it to the general in person, so as to comply literally with his instructions, knowing the general's anxiety to have the news at once. The message was written on tissue-paper and inclosed in a ball of tin-foil, which the scout had carried in his mouth. The general glanced over it, and then read it aloud to the party at the dinner-table. It consisted of about three pages, and gave a vivid account of Sheridan's successful march, and the irreparable damage he had inflicted upon the enemy's communications, saying that he had captured twenty-eight pieces of artillery, destroyed many mills and factories, the James River Canal for a distance of fifteen miles, and the bridges on the Rivanna River, and stating that he was going to destroy the canal still further the next day, and then move on the Central and the Fredericksburg railroads, tear them up, and afterward march to White House, where he would like to have forage and rations sent him; and notifying the general that his purpose, unless otherwise ordered, was then to join the Army of the Potomac. The general proceeded to interrogate Campbell, but the ladies, who had now become intensely interested in the scout, also began to ply him with questions, which were directed at him so thick and fast that he soon found himself in the situation of the outstretched human figure in the almanac, fired at with arrows from every sign of the zodiac. The general soon rose from his seat, and said good-naturedly: " Well, I will never get the information I want from this scout as long as you ladies have him under cross-examination, and I think I had better take him over to my quarters, and see if I cannot have him to myself for a little while." By this time the dinner-party was pretty well broken up, and by direction of the general several members of the staff accompanied him and the scouts to the general's quarters. It was learned from them that Sheridan, deeming it very important to get a despatch through to headquarters, selected two parties, consisting each of two scouts. To each party was given a copy of the despatch, and each was left to select its own route. Campbell and Rowand started on horseback from Columbia on the evening of the 10th, following the roads on the north side of Richmond. They were twice overhauled by parties of the enemy, but they represented themselves as belonging to Imboden's cavalry, and being in Confederate uniforms and skilled in the Southern dialect, they escaped without detection. When they approached the Chickahominy they were met by two men and a boy, with whom they fell into conversation, and were told by them that they had better not cross the river, as there were Yankee troops on the other side. Before the scouts were out of earshot they heard one of the men say to the other, " I believe those fellows are d—d Yankees," and soon they found that the alarm had been given, and the Confederate cavalry were pursuing them. They rode forward to the Chickahominy as rapidly as they could proceed in the jaded condition of their horses, and when they reached the stream they took off everything except their undershirts, tied their clothes on the pommels of their saddles, and swam their horses across the river. Campbell had taken the roll of tin-foil which contained the despatch from the lining of his boot, and put it in his mouth. On the other side of the stream they found a steep, muddy bank and a row of piles. As the horses could not struggle out, the men abandoned them, and got into a canoe which providentially happened to be floating past, and by this means got ashore. The Confederates by this time had opened fire on them from the opposite bank. The scouts made their way on foot for eleven miles, in their almost naked condition, to Harrison's Landing on the James River, where they met a detachment of our troops. The soldiers supplied them with trousers and blouses such as they could spare, and took them by boat to City Point. They had ridden one hundred and forty-five miles without sleep and with but little food. The second pair of scouts sent by Sheridan made their way by canal and on foot to the south of Richmond. After six unsuccessful attempts to get across the lines, one of them reached headquarters several days later. The scouts were given a meal of the best food of which the headquarters mess could boast, and put into a comfortable hut, where they lost no time in making up for lost sleep. The next day General Grant made all preparation for sending supplies and troops to meet Sheridan at White House. The general complimented the scouts warmly upon their success, directed that they be supplied with two good horses and an outfit of clothing, and sent them around to White House on a steamer to await Sheridan there; but on their arrival they could not restrain their spirit of adventure, and rode out through the enemy's country in the direction of the South Anna River until they met their commander.

Campbell was only nineteen years of age. Sheridan always addressed him as " Boy," and the history of his many hairbreadth escapes that year would fill a volume. Campbell has always remained a scout and is still in the employ of the government in that capacity at Fort

Custer; Rowand is now a prominent lawyer in Pittsburg, Pennsylvania.

This day (March 13) possesses a peculiar personal
interest for me, for the reason that it is the date borne
by two brevet appointments I received—one of colonel
and the other of brigadier-general in the regular army
—for "gallant and meritorious services in the field
during the rebellion."

CHAPTER XXVI

SHERIDAN reached White House on March 19, after having made a campaign seldom equaled in activity, through a difficult country and during incessant rains. He had whipped the enemy at all points, captured 17 pieces of artillery and 1600 prisoners, and destroyed 56 canal-locks, 5 aqueducts, 23 railroad bridges, 40 canal and road bridges, together with 40 miles of railroad, numerous warehouses and factories, and vast quantities of military supplies.

On March 20 Stoneman advanced toward east Tennessee, and on the same day Canby moved his forces against Mobile. Sherman had whipped all the troops opposed to him in his march through the Carolinas, and destroyed communications in all directions. He and Schofield met with their armies at Goldsboro', North Carolina, on the 23d of March, and about all the points on the Atlantic coast were now in our possession.

When Sheridan started to join Grant, Hancock had been put in command of the Middle Military Division. The various armies were all working successfully with

401

a common purpose in view, and under one watchful, guiding mind the web was being woven closer and closer about the Confederate capital, and the cause of secession was every day drawing nearer to its doom.

General Grant's only anxiety now was to prevent the escape of the enemy from Richmond before he could be struck a crushing blow. No campaign in force could be made at this time by moving around to the west of Lee's army and heading it off in that direction, for the reason that the rainy season still continued, and rendered the roads difficult for infantry and impassable for wagons and artillery, and because Sheridan's cavalry had not yet joined our army in front of Petersburg. Every possible precaution was taken meanwhile to prevent Lee from withdrawing his army. Scouts and spies were more active than ever before; about 30,000 men were kept virtually on the picket-line, and all the troops were equipped and supplied, ready to make a forced march at a moment's notice in case Lee should be found moving. It was now ascertained that Sheridan could start from White House on March 25 to join the Army of the Potomac, and on the 24th orders were issued for a general movement of the armies operating against Petersburg and Richmond, to begin on the night of the 28th, for the purpose of marching around Lee's right, breaking up his last remaining railroads, the Danville and the South Side, and giving, if possible, the final blow to the Confederacy.

On March 20 General Grant had telegraphed the President: "Can you not visit City Point for a day or two? I would like very much to see you, and I think the rest would do you good." This invitation was promptly accepted, and on the 24th word came that he was on his way up the James aboard the *River Queen*. About nine o'clock that evening the steamer approached the wharf, and General Grant, with those of us who were with him at the moment, including Robert Lincoln, went down to the landing and met the President, Mrs. Lincoln, their youngest son, "Tad," and several ladies who had come from Washington with the Presidential party.   The meeting was very cordial.   It lasted but a short time, however, as Mr. Lincoln and his family were evidently fatigued by the trip, and it was thought that they might want to retire at an early hour.   His steamer was escorted by a naval vessel named the *Bat*, commanded by Captain John S. Barnes, an accomplished officer of the navy.

Grant, with his usual foresight, had predicted that Lee would make a determined assault at some point on our lines in an endeavor to throw our troops into confusion, and then make his escape before our men could recover from their consternation and be prepared to follow him closely.   As early as February 22 the general-in-chief sent a very characteristic despatch to Parke, who was temporarily in command of the Army of the Potomac during Meade's absence: "As there is a possibility of an attack from the enemy at any time, and especially an attempt to break your center, extra vigilance should be kept up both by the pickets and the troops on the line.   Let commanders understand that no time is to be lost awaiting orders, if an attack is made, in bringing all their resources to the point of danger.   With proper alacrity in this respect, I would have no objection to seeing the enemy get through."

On the evening of the 24th of March, General Meade came to headquarters to meet Mrs. Meade, who had arrived by steamer at City Point, and General Grant suggested to him that he had better remain over till the next day, which he did.   General Ord also stayed at headquarters that night.

About six o'clock the next morning, March 25, the camp was awakened and was soon all astir by reason of a message from the Petersburg front saying that the enemy had broken through our lines near Fort Stedman and was making a heavy attack. Soon after it was found that the telegraph-line had been broken, and as messages would now have to come most of the distance by couriers, there was increased anxiety as to the movement. General Grant saw at once that his prediction of a month before had been fulfilled, but believed that the cautions given would be observed, so that he did not experience much apprehension. We had wakened him the moment the announcement came by rapping upon the door of the room occupied by him and Mrs. Grant; and in reply to his questions the despatch was read loud enough for him to hear it without opening the door. He dressed at once, and as this was a process which never occupied many minutes, he was soon out in front of his quarters, where he was met by Meade and others. Meade was greatly nettled by the fact that he was absent from his command at such a time, and was pacing up and down with great strides, and dictating orders to his chief of staff, General Webb, who was with him, in tones which showed very forcibly the intensity of his feelings. The President, who was aboard his boat anchored out in the river, soon heard of the attack, and he was kept informed of the events which were taking place by his son Robert, who carried the news to him.

General Grant, with his usual aggressiveness, telegraphed to the Army of the James: "This may be a signal for leaving. Be ready to take advantage of it." It was nearly two hours before any very definite information could be obtained, but the news began to be favorable, and by half-past eight o'clock it was learned that our whole line had been recaptured, many prisoners taken, and that everything was again quiet. Mr. Lincoln now sent a telegram to the Secretary of War, winding up with the words: "Robert just now tells me there was a little rumpus up the line this morning, ending about where it began." Generals Meade and Ord returned as soon as they could to their respective commands, and took vigorous measures against the enemy.

It seems that the Richmond authorities had come to the conclusion that their position was no longer tenable, and that their army must retreat as soon as possible. A successful attack on our right, it was hoped, would throw our troops into confusion, and while we were maturing plans for the recapture of the lost portion of our lines, and drawing in troops from our left for this purpose, Lee would find an opportunity to make a forced march with his army toward the Carolinas.

This attack was one of the most dramatic events of the siege of Petersburg. It was commanded by General J. B. Gordon. There had been placed at his disposal for the purpose about one half of Lee's entire army. For some time men had been leaving the ranks of the enemy and making their way to us through the lines at night. The arms which they brought in were purchased from them at a fair price, and everything possible was done to encourage these desertions. The attacking party, knowing of this practice, took advantage of it, and succeeded in having his skirmishers gain an entrance to our lines in the guise of deserters, and suddenly make prisoners of our pickets. Just before dawn our trench guards were overpowered, our main line was broken between two of our batteries, and Fort Stedman, after a brief but gallant resistance, was captured, and its guns turned against our own troops. Several more batteries to the right and left were soon taken, and as friends could not be distinguished from foes, owing to the darkness, it was for a time difficult for our troops to use artillery. Further assaults, however, were handsomely repulsed; as soon as there was sufficient light a heavy artillery fire was concentrated on the enemy, and at a quarter to eight o'clock Hartranft advanced against Fort Stedman, and recaptured it with comparatively small loss.

The movement was well planned, and carried out with skill and boldness, but it proved a signal failure. It was a desperate military gamble, with very few chances of winning. It was a curious coincidence that on the same day that Lee was preparing for his assault on our right, Grant was writing his orders for a general movement of the Union armies against the enemy's right.

General Grant proposed to the President that forenoon that he should accompany him on a trip to the Petersburg front. The invitation was promptly accepted, and several hours were spent in visiting the troops, who cheered the President enthusiastically. He was greatly interested in looking at the prisoners who had been captured that morning; and while at Meade's headquarters, about two o'clock, sent a despatch to Stanton, saying: ". . . I have nothing to add to what General Meade reports, except that I have seen the prisoners myself, and they look like there might be the number he states—1600." The President carried a map with him, which he took out of his pocket and examined several times. He had the exact location of the troops marked on it, and he exhibited a singularly accurate knowledge of the various positions.

Upon the return to headquarters at City Point, he sat for a while by the camp-fire; and as the smoke curled about his head during certain shiftings of the wind, and he brushed it away from time to time by waving his right hand in front of his face, he entertained the general-in-chief and several members of the staff by talking in a most interesting manner about public affairs, and illustrating the subjects mentioned with his incomparable anecdotes. At first his manner was grave and his language much more serious than usual. He spoke of the appalling difficulties encountered by the administration, the losses in the field, the perplexing financial problems, and the foreign complications; but said they had all been overcome by the unswerving patriotism of the people, the devotion of the loyal North, and the superb fighting qualities of the troops. After a while he spoke in a more cheerful vein, and said: "England will live to regret her inimical attitude toward us. After the collapse of the rebellion John Bull will find that he has injured himself much more seriously than us. His action reminds me of a barber in Sangamon County in my State. He had just gone to bed when a stranger came along and said he must be shaved; that he had a four days' beard on his face, and was going to take a girl to a ball, and that beard must come off. Well, the barber got up reluctantly and dressed, and seated the man in a chair with a back so low that every time he bore down on him he came near dislocating his victim's neck. He began by lathering his face, including his nose, eyes, and ears, stropped his razor on his boot, and then made a drive at the man's countenance as if he had practised mowing in a stubble-field. He cut a bold swath across the right cheek, carrying away the beard, a pimple, and two warts. The man in the chair ventured to remark: 'You appear to make everything level as you go.' 'Yes,' said the barber; 'and if this handle don't break, I guess I'll get away with most of what's there.' The man's cheeks were so hollow that the barber could n't get down into the valleys with the razor, and the ingenious idea occurred to him to stick his finger in the man's mouth and press out the cheeks. Finally he cut clear through the cheek and into his own finger. He pulled the finger out of the man's mouth, snapped the blood off it, glared at him, and cried: 'There, you lantern-jawed cuss, you 've made me cut my finger!' And so England will discover that she has got the South into a pretty bad scrape by trying to administer to her, and in the end she will find that she has only cut her own finger."

After the laugh which followed this story had exhausted itself, General Grant asked: "Mr. President, did you at any time doubt the final success of the cause?" "Never for a moment," was the prompt and emphatic reply, as Mr. Lincoln leaned forward in his camp-chair and enforced his words by a vigorous gesture of his right hand. "Mr. Seward, when he visited me last summer, gave a very interesting account of the complications and embarrassments arising from the Mason and Slidell affair, when those commissioners were captured on board the English vessel *Trent*," remarked General Grant. "Yes," said the President; "Seward studied up all the works ever written on international law, and came to cabinet meetings loaded to the muzzle with the subject. We gave due consideration to the case, but at that critical period of the war it was soon decided to deliver up the prisoners. It was a pretty bitter pill to swallow, but I contented myself with believing that England's triumph in the matter would be short-lived, and that after ending our war successfully we would be so powerful that we could call her to account for all the embarrassments she had inflicted upon us. I felt a good deal like the sick man in Illinois who was told he probably had n't many days longer to live, and he ought to make his peace with any enemies he might have. He said the man he hated worst of all was a fellow named Brown, in the next village, and he guessed he had better begin on him. So Brown was sent for, and when he came the sick man began to say, in a voice as meek as Moses's, that he wanted to die at peace with all his fellow-creatures, and he hoped he and Brown could now shake hands and bury all their enmity. The scene was becoming altogether too pathetic for Brown, who had to get out his handkerchief and wipe the gathering tears from his eyes. It was n't long before he melted, and gave his hand to his neighbor, and they had a regular love-feast of forgiveness. After a parting that would have softened the heart of a grind-stone, Brown had about reached the room door when the sick man rose up on his elbow and called out to him: 'But see here, Brown; if I should happen to get well, mind, that old grudge stands.' So I thought that if this nation should happen to get well we might want that old grudge against England to stand."

It was a singular sequel to this conversation that the officer to whom he was then speaking became Mr. Lincoln's successor in the Presidential chair, and carried out this determination by securing a settlement of the account known in history as the "*Alabama* claims," and the payment from England of fifteen and a half millions of dollars as compensation for damages inflicted upon our commerce.

The President now went aboard his boat to spend the night. The next morning he wandered into the tent of the headquarters telegraph operator, where several of us were sitting. He pulled out of his pocket a telegram which he had received from the Secretary of War, and his face assumed a broad smile as he said: "Well, the serious Stanton is actually becoming facetious. Just listen to what he says in his despatch: 'Your telegram and Parke's report of the scrimmage this morning are received. The rebel rooster looks a little the worse, as he could not hold the fence. We have nothing new here. Now you are away, everything is quiet and the tormentors vanished. I hope you will remember General Harrison's advice to his men at Tippecanoe, that they can "see as well a little farther off."'"

Three tiny kittens were crawling about the tent at the time. The mother had died, and the little wanderers were expressing their grief by mewing piteously. Mr. Lincoln picked them up, took them on his lap, stroked their soft fur, and murmured: "Poor little creatures, don't cry; you 'll be taken good care of," and turning to Bowers, said: "Colonel, I hope you will see that these poor little motherless waifs are given plenty of milk and treated kindly." Bowers replied: "I will see, Mr. President, that they are taken in charge by the cook of our mess, and are well cared for." Several times during his stay Mr. Lincoln was found fondling these kittens. He would wipe their eyes tenderly with his handkerchief, stroke their smooth coats, and listen to them purring their gratitude to him. It was a curious sight at an army headquarters, upon the eve of a great military crisis in the nation's history, to see the hand which had affixed the signature to the Emancipation Proclamation, and had signed the commissions of all the heroic men who served the cause of the Union, from the general-in-chief to the lowest lieutenant, tenderly caressing three stray kittens. It well illustrated the kindness of the man's disposition, and showed the childlike simplicity which was mingled with the grandeur of his nature.

General Grant had sent word to Sheridan, whose troops were now crossing the James, to come in person to headquarters, and early on the morning of March 26 he arrived. Rawlins and several other officers were in front of our quarters at the time, and upon seeing Sheridan, who had been separated from us for so long a time, we hurried forward to greet him. Rawlins, in his enthusiasm, seized both of Sheridan's hands in his own, wrung them vigorously, and then went to patting him on the back. Sheridan returned all the greetings warmly, and Rawlins now informed him that General Grant had made up his mind to send the cavalry through to join Sherman, destroying all communications as they went. Sheridan looked greatly annoyed at this information, and Rawlins agreed with him that such a move ought not to be made. Sheridan was told that the general-in-chief was awaiting him in his quarters, and went in and had a long talk. The general showed him the written instructions which he had prepared, and to which Rawlins had just referred. They directed him to proceed with his cavalry around Lee's right, and then to move independently under other instructions. Sheridan felt convinced, from what was said verbally, that he was expected to cut loose and move down to Sherman's army. Some of the staff now entered the room, and found Sheridan arguing against the policy of such a move. When he rose up to go, the general followed him out and had a few words of private conversation. We learned afterward that he told Sheridan that the part of the instructions to which he objected was merely a blind; that he intended to end the contest at once where we were, and that Sheridan was to operate against Lee's right, and be in at the death. He said: " In case the operations of the cavalry should not be an entire success, the people would take it for granted that a definite movement which they had been expecting had been a complete failure, and they would be greatly discouraged. So I wanted the impression to prevail that a different movement had been contemplated. I really have no intention of sending you to Sherman." This was the general's little secret, which he had kept from all of the staff, and revealed to the cavalry commander Sheridan only at the last moment. Sheridan was made happy by this conversation, and immediately told it to Rawlins, who was as much delighted as Sheridan himself.

It was decided that upon this day Mr. Lincoln would review a portion of the Army of the James on the north side of the James River, and Sheridan was invited to join the party from headquarters who were to accompany the President. The boat started from City Point at eleven o'clock.

At breakfast General Grant said to me: "I shall accompany the President, who is to ride 'Cincinnati,' as he seems to have taken a fancy to him. I wish you would take Mrs. Lincoln and Mrs. Grant to the reviewing-ground in our headquarters ambulance." I expressed my pleasure at being selected for so pleasant a mission, and arranged to have the ambulance and two good horses put aboard the headquarters boat, which was to carry the party up the river. Captain Barnes, who commanded the vessel which had escorted the President's steamer, was to be one of the party, and I loaned him my horse. This was a favor which was usually accorded with some reluctance to naval officers when they came ashore; for these men of the ocean at times tried to board the animal on the starboard side, and often rolled in the saddle as if there was a heavy sea on; and if the horse, in his anxiety to rid himself of a sea-monster, tried to scrape his rider off by rubbing against a tree, the officer attributed the unseaman-like conduct of the animal entirely to the fact that his steering-gear had become unshipped. A naval hero not long before had borrowed a horse ashore, and attempted to make his seat firmer on deck by grappling the animal's beam-ends with his spurs, which caused the horse to run a little too free before the wind; and when the officer could not succeed in making him shorten sail by hauling in on the reins, he took out his jack-knife and dug it in the animal's flanks, swearing that if he could not bring the craft to in any other way he would scuttle it. Navy officers were about as reluctant to lend their boats to army people, for fear they would knock holes in the bottom when jumping in, break the oars in catching crabs, and stave in the bows through an excess of modesty which manifested itself in a reluctance to give the command, "Way enough!" in time when approaching a wharf.

The President was in a more gloomy mood than usual on the trip up the James. He spoke with much seriousness about the situation, and did not attempt to tell a single anecdote. As the boat passed the point where Sheridan's cavalry was crossing the river on the pontoon-bridge, he manifested considerable interest in watching the troopers, and addressed a number of questions to their commander. When the boat reached the landing on the north side of the river, I helped the two distinguished ladies who had been intrusted to my care into the ambulance, and started for the reviewing-ground, about two miles distant. The horsemen got the start of us and made good time; but as the road was swampy, and part of it corduroyed with the trunks of small trees, without much reference to their relative size or regularity of position, the ambulance could make but slow progress. Some additional springs had been put under it, and cross-seats arranged so as to make it ride more easily than the ordinary army ambulance; but the improved springs only served to toss the occupants higher in the air when the wheels struck a particularly aggravating obstacle. Mrs. Lincoln, finding we were losing time, and fearing we would miss part of the review, expressed a wish to move faster, and I reluctantly gave the order to the driver. We were still on a corduroyed portion of the road, and when the horses trotted the mud flew in all directions, and a sudden jolt lifted the party clear off the seats, jammed the ladies' hats against the top of the wagon, and bumped their heads as well. Mrs. Lincoln now insisted on getting out and walking; but as the mud was nearly hub-deep, Mrs. Grant and I persuaded her that we had better stick to the wagon as our only ark of refuge. Finally we reached our destination, but it was some minutes after the review had begun. Mrs. Ord, and the wives of several of the officers who had come up from Fort Monroe for the purpose, appeared on horseback as a mounted escort to Mrs. Lincoln and Mrs. Grant. This added a special charm to the scene, and the review passed off with peculiar brilliancy. Mrs. Grant enjoyed the day with great zest, but Mrs. Lincoln had suffered so much from the fatigue and annoyances of her overland trip that she was not in a mood to derive much pleasure from the occasion. I made up my mind that ambulances, viewed as vehicles for driving distinguished ladies to military reviews, were not a stupendous success, and that thereafter they had better be confined to their legitimate uses of transporting the wounded and attending funerals.

Upon the return trip on the boat, the President seemed to recover his spirits. Perhaps the manifestation of strength on the part of the splendid Army of the James which he had witnessed at the review had served to cheer him up. He told one excellent story on the way back. In speaking of a prominent general, and the failure of the numerous attempts on the President's part to make the officer's services useful to the country, and the necessity finally of relieving him from all command, he said: "I was not more successful than the blacksmith in our town, in my boyhood days, when he tried to put to a useful purpose a big piece of wrought-iron that was in the shop. He heated it, put it on the anvil, and said: 'I'm going to make a sledge-hammer out of you.' After a while he stopped hammering it, looked at it, and remarked: 'Guess I've drawed you out a little too fine for a sledge-hammer; reckon I'd better make a clevis of you.' He stuck it in the fire, blew the bellows, got up a good heat, then began shaping the iron again on the anvil. Pretty soon he stopped, sized it up with his eye, and said: 'Guess I've drawed you out too thin for a clevis; suppose I better make a clevis-bolt of you.' He put it in the fire, bore down still harder on the bellows, drew out the iron, and went to work at it once more on the anvil. In a few minutes he stopped, took a look, and exclaimed: 'Well, now I've got you down a leetle too thin even to make a clevis-bolt out of you.' Then he rammed it in the fire again, threw his whole weight on the bellows, got up a white heat on the iron, jerked it out, carried it in the tongs to the water-barrel, held it over the barrel, and cried: 'I've tried to make a sledge-hammer of you, and failed; I've tried to make a clevis of you, and failed; I've tried to make a clevis-bolt of you, and failed; now, darn you, I'm going to make a fizzle of you'; and with that he soused it in the water and let it fizz."

It was nearly dark when the party returned to City Point. After dinner the band was brought down to the steamboat, and a dance was improvised. Several ladies were aboard, and they and the officers danced till midnight.   Neither the President nor General Grant joined, even in a square dance, but sat in the after part of the boat conversing.   Sheridan stayed overnight at City Point, and started early in the morning for the cavalry headquarters on the Petersburg front.

CHAPTER XXVII

MEETING OF GRANT AND SHERMAN AT CITY POINT—AMUS-
ING COLLOQUY BETWEEN MRS. GRANT AND SHERMAN
—MEETING OF SHERMAN AND SHERIDAN—THE FAMOUS
CONFERENCE ABOARD THE "RIVER QUEEN"—GRANT
STARTS ON HIS LAST CAMPAIGN — STORM-BOUND —
GRANT AND SHERIDAN CONFER—GRANT ON WARREN'S
FRONT—CARRYING INSTRUCTIONS TO SHERIDAN

SHERMAN, in his correspondence, had intimated
a desire to have a personal conference with his
chief before the general movement of all the armies took
place; and it was learned on March 27 that he had arrived at Fort Monroe, and was on his way up the James.
Grant telegraphed to several prominent officers to meet
Sherman that evening at headquarters. Late in the
afternoon the *Russia*, a captured steamer, arrived with
Sherman aboard, and General Grant and two or three
of us who were with him at the time started down to
the wharf to greet the Western commander. Before we
reached the foot of the steps, Sherman had jumped
ashore and was hurrying forward with long strides to
meet his chief. As they approached Grant cried out,
"How d' you do, Sherman!" "How are you, Grant!"
exclaimed Sherman; and in a moment they stood upon
the steps, with their hands locked in a cordial grasp,
uttering earnest words of familiar greeting. Their encounter was more like that of two school-boys coming

417

together after a vacation than the meeting of the chief actors in a great war tragedy. Sherman walked up with the general-in-chief to headquarters, where Mrs. Grant extended to the illustrious visitor a cordial greeting. Sherman then seated himself with the others by the camp-fire, and gave a most graphic description of the stirring events of his march through Georgia. The story was the more charming from the fact that it was related without the manifestation of the slightest egotism. His field of operations had covered more than half of the entire theater of war; his orders always spoke with the true bluntness of the soldier; he had fought from valley depths to mountain heights, and marched from inland rivers to the sea. Never were listeners more enthusiastic; never was a speaker more eloquent. The story, told as he alone could tell it, was a grand epic related with Homeric power. At times he became humorous, and in a nervous, offhand, rattling manner recounted a number of amusing incidents of the famous march. He said, among other things: "My old veterans got on pretty familiar terms with me on the march, and often used to keep up a running conversation with me as I rode along by their side. One day a man in the ranks had pulled off his shoes and stockings, and rolled up his trousers as far as they would go, to wade across a creek we had struck. I could n't help admiring his magnificently developed limbs, which might have served as models for a sculptor, and I called out to him: 'A good stout pair of legs you 've got there, my man.' 'Yes, general; they 're not bad underpinning,' he replied, looking down at them with evident pride. 'I would n't mind exchanging mine for them, if you don't object,' I continued. He sized up my legs with his eye, and evidently considered them mere spindle-shanks compared with his, and then looked up at me and said: 'General, if it 's all the same to you, I guess I 'd rather not swap.' "

Sherman then went on to talk about his famous " bummers," saying : " They are not stragglers or mere self-constituted foragers, as many have been led to suppose, but they are organized for a very useful purpose from the adventurous spirits who are always found in the ranks.   They serve as ' feelers ' who keep in advance and on the flanks of the main columns, spy out the land, and discover where the best supplies are to be found. They are indispensable in feeding troops when compelled, like my army, to live off the country, and in destroying the enemy's communications.   The bummers are, in fact, a regular institution.   I was amused at what one of Schofield's officers told me at Goldsboro'. He said Schofield's army was maintaining a telegraph-line to keep up communication with the sea-coast, and that one of my men, who was a little more ' previous ' than the rest, and was far in advance of my army, was seen up a telegraph-pole hacking away at the wires with a hatchet.   The officer yelled out to him : ' What are you doing there ? You 're destroying one of our own telegraph-lines.'   The man cast an indignant look at his questioner, and said, as he continued his work of destruction : ' I 'm one o' Billy Sherman's bummers ; and the last thing he said to us when we started out on this hunt was : " Be sure and cut all the telegraph-wires you come across, and don't go to foolin' away time askin' who they belong to." ' "

After the interview had continued nearly an hour, Grant said to Sherman : " I 'm sorry to break up this entertaining conversation, but the President is aboard the *River Queen*, and I know he will be anxious to see you.   Suppose we go and pay him a visit before dinner." " All right," cried Sherman ; and the generals started down the steps, and were soon after seated in the cabin of the steamer with the President.

In about an hour the two commanders came back and entered the general-in-chief's hut. I was there talking to Mrs. Grant at the time. She, with her usual thoughtfulness, had prepared some tea, and was awaiting the return of the generals. She at once inquired, in her womanly way: "Did you see Mrs. Lincoln?" "Oh," replied her husband, "we went rather on a business errand, and I did not ask for Mrs. Lincoln." "And I did n't even know she was aboard," added Sherman. "Well, you are a pretty pair!" exclaimed Mrs. Grant. "I do not see how you could have been so neglectful." "Well, Julia," said her husband, "we are going to pay another visit in the morning, and we 'll take good care then to make amends for our conduct to-day." "And now, let us talk further about the immediate movements of my army," said Sherman. "Perhaps you don't want me here listening to all your secrets," remarked Mrs. Grant. "Do you think we can trust her, Grant?" exclaimed Sherman, casting a sly glance at Mrs. Grant. "I 'm not so sure about that, Sherman," said the commander, entering into the spirit of fun which had now taken possession of the trio. "Public documents, in disseminating items of information, are accustomed to say, 'Know all men by these presents.' I think it would be just as effective to say, 'Know one woman,' for then all men would be certain to hear of it." Sherman laughed heartily at this way of putting it, and said: "Now, Mrs. Grant, let me examine you, and I can soon tell whether you are likely to understand our plans well enough to betray them to the enemy." "Very well," she answered; "I 'm ready for all your questions." Then Sherman turned his chair squarely toward her, folded his arms, assumed the tone and look of a first-class pedagogue, and, in a manner which became more and more amusing as the conversation went on, proceeded to ask all sorts of geographical questions about the Carolinas and Virginia. Mrs. Grant caught the true essence of the humor, and gave replies which were the perfection of drollery. When asked where a particular river in the South was, she would locate it a thousand miles away, and describe it as running up stream instead of down; and when questioned about a Southern mountain she would place it somewhere in the region of the north pole. Railroads and canals were also mixed up in interminable confusion. She had studied the maps in camp very carefully, and had an excellent knowledge of the geography of the theater of war, and this information stood her in good stead in carrying on the little comedy which was being enacted. In a short time Sherman turned to his chief, who had been greatly amused by the by-play, and exclaimed: "Well, Grant, I think we can trust her"; and then, speaking again to the general's wife, he said: "Never mind, Mrs. Grant; perhaps some day the women will vote and control affairs, and then they will take us men in hand and subject us to worse cross-examinations than that." "Not if my plan of female suffrage is ever adopted," remarked the chief. "Why, Ulyss, you never told me you had any plans regarding that subject," said Mrs. Grant. "Oh, yes," continued the general; "I would give each married woman two votes; then the wives would all be represented at the polls, without there being any divided families on the subject of politics."

Dinner was now announced, and Sherman escorted Mrs. Grant to the mess-room, and occupied a seat beside her at the table.

In the evening several officers came to pay their respects to Sherman. Sheridan had been telegraphed to come to headquarters, but he did not appear until nearly midnight, and after all the others had left. He had been delayed several hours by his train running off the track on the military railroad. Sherman had been told by Grant about the plans he had discussed with Sheridan for the operations of the cavalry, and Sherman urged that it should join him after destroying the railroads on the way. Sheridan became a good deal nettled at this, and argued earnestly against it; but General Grant soon cut short the discussion by saying that it had been definitely decided that Sheridan was to remain with our army, then in front of Petersburg. Sheridan's command was made separate from the Army of the Potomac, and was to be subject only to direct orders from the general-in-chief. The cavalry commander had cheerfully given up the command of the Middle Military Division to take the field at the head of the cavalry corps, and General Grant felt that he was entitled to every consideration which could be shown him.

The next morning (March 28) Admiral Porter came to headquarters, and in the course of his conversation said to Sherman: "When you were in the region of those swamps and overflowed rivers, coming through the Carolinas, did n't you wish you had my gunboats with you?" "Yes," answered Sherman; "for those swamps were very much like that Western fellow's Fourth of July oration, of which a newspaper said, 'It was only knee-deep, but spread out over all creation.' One day, on the march, while my men were wading a river which was surrounded for miles by swamps on each side, after they had been in the water for about an hour, with not much prospect of reaching the other side, one of them cried out to his chum: 'Say, Tommy, I 'm blowed if I don't believe we 've struck this river lengthways!'"

After spending a quarter of an hour together, General Grant said that the President was expecting them aboard his boat, and the two generals and the admiral started for the *River Queen*. No one accompanied them. There now occurred in the upper saloon of that vessel the celebrated conference between these four magnates, the scene of which has been so faithfully transferred to canvas by the artist Healy. It was in no sense a council of war, but only an informal interchange of views between the four men who, more than any others, held the destiny of the nation in their hands. Upon the return of the generals and the admiral to headquarters, they entered the general-in-chief's hut, where Mrs. Grant and one or two of us were sitting. The chief said to his wife: "Well, Julia, as soon as we reached the boat this morning I was particular to inquire after Mrs. Lincoln, and to say that we desired to pay our respects to her. The President went to her state-room, and soon returned, saying that she was not well, and asking us to excuse her." General Grant afterward told us the particulars of the interview. It began by his explaining to the President the military situation and prospects, saying that the crisis of the war was now at hand, as he expected to move at once around the enemy's left and cut him off from the Carolinas, and that his only apprehension was that Lee might move out before him and evacuate Petersburg and Richmond, but that if he did there would be a hot pursuit. Sherman assured the President that in such a contingency his army, by acting on the defensive, could resist both Johnston and Lee till Grant could reach him, and that then the enemy would be caught in a vise and have his life promptly crushed out. Mr. Lincoln asked if it would not be possible to end the matter without a pitched battle, with the attendant losses and suffering; but was informed that that was a matter not within the control of our commanders, and must rest necessarily with the enemy. Lincoln spoke about the course which he thought had better be pursued after the war, and expressed an inclination to lean toward a generous policy. In speaking about the Confederate political leaders, he intimated, though he did not say so in express terms, that it would relieve the situation if they should escape to some foreign country. Sherman related many interesting incidents which occurred in his campaign. Grant talked less than any one present. The President twice expressed some apprehension about Sherman being away from his army; but Sherman assured him that he had left matters safe in Schofield's hands, and that he would start back himself that day.

That afternoon Sherman took leave of those at headquarters, and returned to his command in the *Bat*, as that vessel was faster than the one which had brought him up the coast.

The troops had been in motion the previous night, and the general had decided that headquarters should be moved on the morning of the 29th. The horses were to be put aboard the train which was to take the general and staff to the Petersburg front. About 8:30 Mr. Lincoln came ashore to say good-by. We had the satisfaction of hearing one good story from him before parting. General Grant was telling him about the numerous ingenious and impracticable suggestions that were made to him almost daily as to the best way of destroying the enemy, and said: "The last plan proposed was to supply our men with bayonets just a foot longer than those of the enemy, and then charge them. When they met, our bayonets would go clear through the enemy, while theirs would not reach far enough to touch our men, and the war would be ended."

Mr. Lincoln laughed, and remarked: "Well, there is

a good deal of terror in cold steel. I had a chance to test it once myself. When I was a young man, I was walking along a back street in Louisville one night about twelve o'clock, when a very tough-looking citizen sprang out of an alleyway, reached up to the back of his neck, pulled out a bowie-knife that seemed to my stimulated imagination about three feet long, and planted himself square across my path. For two or three minutes he flourished his weapon in front of my face, appearing to try to see just how near he could come to cutting my nose off without quite doing it. He could see in the moonlight that I was taking a good deal of interest in the proceeding, and finally he yelled out, as he steadied the knife close to my throat: 'Stranger, kin you lend me five dollars on that?' I never reached in my pocket and got out money so fast in all my life. I handed him a bank-note, and said: 'There's ten, neighbor; now put up your scythe.'"

The general soon after bade an affectionate good-by to Mrs. Grant, kissing her repeatedly as she stood at the front door of his quarters. She bore the parting bravely, although her pale face and sorrowful look told of the sadness that was in her heart. The party, accompanied by the President, then walked down to the railroad-station. Mr. Lincoln looked more serious than at any other time since he had visited headquarters. The lines in his face seemed deeper, and the rings under his eyes were of a darker hue. It was plain that the weight of responsibility was oppressing him. Could it have been a premonition that with the end of this last campaign would come the end of his life? Five minutes' walk brought the party to the train. There the President gave the general and each member of the staff a cordial shake of the hand, and then stood near the rear end of the car while we mounted the platform. As the train was about to start we all raised our hats respectfully. The salute was returned by the President, and he said in a voice broken by an emotion he could ill conceal: "Good-by, gentlemen. God bless you all! Remember, your success is my success." The signal was given to start; the train moved off; Grant's last campaign had begun.

The general sat down near the end of the car, drew from his pocket the flint and slow-match that he always carried, struck a light, and was soon wreathed in the smoke of the inevitable cigar. I took a seat near him, with several other officers of the staff, and he at once began to talk over his plans. Referring to Mr. Lincoln, he said: "The President is one of the few visitors I have had who have not attempted to extract from me a knowledge of my movements, although he is the only one who has a right to know them. He intends to remain at City Point for the present, and he will be the most anxious man in the country to hear from us, his heart is so wrapped up in our success; but I think we can send him some good news in a day or two." I never knew the general to be more sanguine of victory than in starting out on this campaign.

When we reached the end of the railroad, we mounted our horses, started down the Vaughan road, and went into camp for the night in an old corn-field just south of that road, close to Gravelly Run. That night (March 29) the army was disposed in the following order from right to left: Weitzel in front of Richmond, with a portion of the Army of the James; Parke and Wright holding our works in front of Petersburg; Ord extending to the intersection of Hatcher's Run and the Vaughan road; Humphreys stretching beyond Dabney's Mill; Warren on the extreme left, reaching as far as the junction of the Vaughan road and the Boydton plank-road;

and Sheridan still farther west at Dinwiddie Court-
house. The weather had been fair for several days, and
the roads were getting in as good condition for the
movement of troops as could be expected; for in that
section of country in summer the dust was usually so
thick that the army could not see where to move, and
in winter the mud was so deep that it could not move
anywhere. The weather had now become cloudy, and
toward evening rain began to fall. It descended in torrents all night, and continued with but little interruption during the next day. The country was densely
wooded, and the ground swampy, and by the evening
of the 30th whole fields had become beds of quicksand,
in which the troops waded in mud above their ankles,
horses sank to their bellies, and wagons threatened to
disappear altogether. The men began to feel that if any
one in after years should ask them whether they had
been through Virginia, they could say, " Yes; in a number of places." The roads soon became sheets of water,
and it looked as if the saving of that army would require the services, not of a Grant, but of a Noah.
Soldiers would call out to officers as they rode by: "I
say, fetch along the pontoons." "When are the gunboats coming up?" The buoyancy of the day before
was giving place to gloom; men lost their tempers, and
those who employed profanity on such occasions as a
means of mental relaxation wanted to set up a mark
and go to swearing at it. Some began to be apprehensive that the whole movement was premature. This led
to an animated debate at headquarters. General Rawlins expressed the opinion around the camp-fire, on the
morning of the 30th, that no forage could be hauled out
to our cavalry; that Joe Johnston might come up in our
rear if we remained long in our present position; that
the success of turning Lee's right depended on our ce-

lerity; that now he had been given time to make his dispositions to thwart us; and that it might be better to fall back, and make a fresh start later on. General Grant replied by saying that if Johnston could move rapidly enough in such weather to reach us, he (Grant) would turn upon him with his whole command, crush him, and then go after Lee; and that as soon as the weather cleared up the roads would dry rapidly, and the men's spirits would recover all their former buoyancy. The general then entered his tent, and Rawlins followed him.

Just then we saw Sheridan turning in from the Vaughan road, with a staff-officer and an escort of about a dozen cavalrymen, and coming toward our headquarters camp. He was riding his white pacer named "Breckinridge," a horse which had been captured from General Breckinridge in the valley of Virginia. But instead of striking a pacing gait now, it was at every step driving its legs knee-deep into the quicksand with the regularity of a pile-driver. As soon as Sheridan dismounted he was asked with much eagerness about the situation on the extreme left. He took a decidedly cheerful view of matters, and entered upon an animated discussion of the coming movements. He said: "I can drive in the whole cavalry force of the enemy with ease, and if an infantry force is added to my command, I can strike out for Lee's right, and either crush it or force him to so weaken his intrenched lines that our troops in front of them can break through and march into Petersburg." He warmed up with the subject as he proceeded, threw the whole energy of his nature into the discussion, and his cheery voice, beaming countenance, and impassioned language showed the earnestness of his convictions.

"How do you expect to supply your command with

forage if this weather lasts?" he was asked by one of the group. "Forage!" said Sheridan. "I'll get up all the forage I want. I'll haul it out, if I have to set every man in the command to corduroying roads, and corduroy every mile of them from the railroad to Dinwiddie. I tell you, I'm ready to strike out to-morrow and go to smashing things"; and, pacing up and down, he chafed like a hound in the leash. We told him that this was the kind of talk we liked to hear, and that while General Grant felt no apprehension, it would do his heart good to listen to such words as had just been spoken. Sheridan, however, objected to obtruding his views unbidden upon the general-in-chief. Then we resorted to a stratagem. One of us went into the general's tent, and told him Sheridan had just come in from the left and had been telling us some matters of much interest, and suggested that he be invited in and asked to state them. This was assented to, and Sheridan was told that the general wanted to hear what he had to say. Sheridan then went in, and found Grant and Rawlins still discussing the situation. Several persons soon after came into the tent, and Sheridan, saying he was cold and wet, stepped out to the camp-fire. The general-in-chief remarked that he wanted to have some words with Sheridan in private before parting, and followed him out. Ingalls said his tent was vacant, and Grant and Sheridan entered it and had a talk there, in which a definite understanding was reached as to Sheridan's immediate movements. In about twenty minutes they came out, and Sheridan mounted his horse, waved us a good-by with his hand, and rode off to Dinwiddie.

The next morning (March 31) Sheridan reported that the enemy had been hard at work intrenching at Five Forks and to a point about a mile west of that place.

Lee had been as prompt as Grant to recognize Five Forks, the junction of five roads, as a strategic point of great importance, and to protect his right had sent there a large force of infantry and nearly all his cavalry. The rain had continued during the night of March 30, and on the morning of the 31st the weather was cloudy and dismal.

General Grant had anticipated that Warren would be attacked that morning, and had warned him to be on the alert. Warren advanced his corps to develop with what force the enemy held the White Oak road, and to try and drive him from it; but before he had gone far he was met by a vigorous assault. When news came of the attack, General Grant directed me to go to the spot and look to the situation of affairs there. I found that Warren's troops were falling back, but he was reinforced by Humphreys, and by noon the enemy was checked. As soon as Grant was advised of the situation he directed Meade to take the offensive vigorously, and the enemy was soon driven back. General Grant had now ridden out to the front, and hearing that he was at Mrs. Butler's house near the Boydton plank-road, I joined him there. It was then a little after one o'clock. He had in the mean time ordered the headquarters camp to be moved to Dabney's Mill, about two miles from Meade's camp.

Warren's corps was now ordered to move forward again for the purpose of deterring the enemy from detaching infantry from that portion of the line to send against Sheridan. The advance was made later in the afternoon, and with decided success.

When this movement had been decided upon, General Grant directed me to go to Sheridan and explain what was taking place on Warren's and Humphreys's front, and have a full understanding with him as to future operations in his vicinity. I rode rapidly down the Boydton plank-road, and soon came to Gravelly Run. The bridge was destroyed, but my horse was able to ford the stream, notwithstanding the high water caused by the recent rains. Hearing heavy firing in the direction of the Five Forks road, I hurried on in that direction by way of the Brooks road, and soon saw a portion of our cavalry moving eastward, pressed by a superior force of the enemy, while another portion was compelled to fall back southward toward Dinwiddie. I turned the corner of the Brooks cross-road and the Five Forks road just as the rear of the latter body of cavalry was passing it, and found one of Sheridan's bands with his rear-guard playing " Nellie Bly " as cheerfully as if furnishing music for a country picnic. Sheridan always made an effective use of his bands. They were usually mounted on gray horses, and instead of being relegated to the usual duty of carrying off the wounded and assisting the surgeons, they were brought out to the front and made to play the liveliest airs in their repertory, which produced excellent results in buoying up the spirits of the men. After having several of their instruments pierced by bullets, however, and the drums crushed by shells, as often happened, it must be admitted that the music, viewed purely in the light of an artistic performance, was open to adverse criticism.

I found Sheridan a little north of Dinwiddie Courthouse, and gave him an account of matters on the left of the Army of the Potomac. He said he had had one of the liveliest days in his experience, fighting infantry and cavalry with only cavalry, but that he would hold his position at Dinwiddie at all hazards. He did not stop there, but declared his belief that with the corps

of infantry which he expected to be put under his command, he could take the initiative the next morning,
and cut off the whole of the force which Lee had detached. He said: "This force is in more danger than
I am. If I am cut off from the Army of the Potomac,
it is cut off from Lee's army, and not a man in it ought
ever be allowed to get back to Lee. We at last have
drawn the enemy's infantry out of its fortifications, and
this is our chance to attack it." He begged me to go
to General Grant at once, and urge him to send him
Wright's corps, because it had been under his command
in the valley of Virginia, and was familiar with his way
of fighting. I told him, as had been stated to him before, that Wright's corps was next to our extreme right,
and that the only corps which could reach him by daylight was Warren's. I returned soon after to headquarters at Dabney's Mill, a distance of about eight miles,
reaching there at 7 P. M., and gave the general a full
description of Sheridan's operations. He took in the
situation in an instant, and at once telegraphed the
substance of my report to Meade, and preparations soon
began looking to the sending of Warren's corps and
Mackenzie's small division of cavalry to report to Sheridan. It was expected that the infantry would reach its
destination in ample time to take the offensive about
daybreak; but one delay after another was met with,
and Grant, Meade, and Sheridan spent a painfully anxious night in hurrying forward the movement. Ayres's
division of Warren's corps had to rebuild the bridge
over Gravelly Run, which took till 2 A. M. Warren, with
his other two divisions, did not get started from their
position on the White Oak road till 5 A. M., and the hope
of crushing the enemy was hourly growing less. This
proved to be one of the busiest nights of the whole
campaign. Generals were writing despatches and tele-

graphing from dark to daylight. Staff-officers were rushing from one headquarters to another, wading through swamps, penetrating forests, and galloping over corduroy roads, carrying instructions, getting information, and making extraordinary efforts to hurry up the movement of the troops.

CHAPTER XXVIII

THE MOVEMENT AGAINST FIVE FORKS — THE BATTLE OF
FIVE FORKS — CARRYING THE NEWS OF FIVE FORKS TO
GRANT — GRANT PREPARES TO ASSAULT THE PETERS-
BURG LINES — CAPTURING THE WORKS AT PETERSBURG
— GRANT WRITES DESPATCHES UNDER FIRE — CAPTURE
OF FORTS GREGG AND WHITWORTH

EARLY the next morning (April 1) General Grant
said to me: " I wish you would spend the day with
Sheridan's command, and send me a bulletin every half-
hour or so, advising me fully as to the progress made.
You know my views, and I want you to give them to
Sheridan fully. Tell him the contemplated movement
is left entirely in his hands, and he must be responsible
for its execution. I have every confidence in his judgment and ability. I hope that there may now be an
opportunity of fighting the enemy's infantry outside of
their fortifications."

I set out with half a dozen mounted orderlies to act
as couriers in transmitting field bulletins, and met Sheridan about 10 A. M. on the Five Forks road not far from
J. Boisseau's house. Ayres had his division on this road,
having arrived about daylight; and Griffin had reached
J. Boisseau's between 7 and 8 A. M. I had a full conference with Sheridan, in which he told me that the force
in front of him had fallen back early in the morning;
that he had pursued with his cavalry, had had several

brushes with the enemy, and was driving him steadily back; that he had had his patience sorely tried by the delays which had occurred in getting the infantry to him, but that he was going to make every effort to strike a heavy blow with all the infantry and cavalry as soon as he could get them into position, provided the enemy should make a stand behind his intrenchments at Five Forks, which seemed likely. While we were talking, General Warren, who had accompanied Crawford's division, rode up and reported in person to Sheridan. It was then eleven o'clock.

A few minutes before noon Colonel Babcock came over from headquarters, and said to Sheridan: "General Grant directs me to say to you that if, in your judgment, the Fifth Corps would do better under one of its division commanders, you are authorized to relieve General Warren and order him to report to him [General Grant] at headquarters." General Sheridan replied in effect that he hoped such a step as that might not become necessary, and then went on to speak of his plan of battle. We all rode on farther to the front, and soon met General Devin of the cavalry, who was considerably elated by his successes of the morning, and loudly demanded to be permitted to make a general attack on the enemy. Sheridan told him he did n't believe he had ammunition enough. Said Devin: "I guess I 've got enough to give 'em one surge more." Colonel Babcock now left us to return to headquarters. About one o'clock it was reported by the cavalry that the enemy was retiring to his intrenched position at Five Forks, which was just north of the White Oak road and parallel to it, his earthworks running from a point about three quarters of a mile east of Five Forks to a point a mile west, with an angle or "crochet," about one hundred yards long, thrown back at right angles to the left of his line to protect that flank. Orders were at once given to Warren's corps to move up the Gravelly Run Church road to the open ground near the church, and form in order of battle, with Ayres on the left, Crawford on his right, and Griffin in rear as a reserve. The corps was to wheel to the left and make its attack upon the angle, and then, moving westward, sweep down in rear of the enemy's intrenched line. The cavalry, principally dismounted, was to deploy in front of the enemy's line and engage his attention, and as soon as it heard the firing of our infantry to make a vigorous assault upon his works.

The Fifth Corps had borne the brunt of the fighting ever since the army had moved out on March 29; and the gallant men who composed it, and who had performed a conspicuous part in nearly every battle in which the Army of the Potomac had been engaged, seemed eager once more to cross bayonets with their old antagonists. But the movement was slow, the required formation seemed to drag, and Sheridan, chafing with impatience and consumed with anxiety, became as restive as a racer struggling to make the start. He made every possible appeal for promptness, dismounted from his horse, paced up and down, struck the clenched fist of one hand against the palm of the other, and fretted like a caged tiger. He exclaimed at one time: "This battle must be fought and won before the sun goes down. All the conditions may be changed in the morning. We have but a few hours of daylight left us. My cavalry are rapidly exhausting their ammunition, and if the attack is delayed much longer they may have none left." And then another batch of staff-officers was sent out to gallop through the mud and hurry up the columns.

At four o'clock the formation was completed, the order

for the assault was given, and the struggle for Pickett's intrenched line began. The Confederate infantry brigades were posted from left to right as follows: Terry, Corse, Steuart, Ransom, and Wallace. General Fitzhugh Lee, commanding the cavalry, had placed W. H. F. Lee's two brigades on the right of the line, Munford's division on the left, and Rosser's in rear of Hatcher's Run, to guard the trains. I rode to the front, in company with Sheridan and Warren, with the head of Ayres's division, which was on the left. Ayres threw out a skirmish-line and advanced across an open field which sloped down gradually toward the dense woods just north of the White Oak road. He soon met with a fire from the edge of these woods, a number of men fell, and the skirmish-line halted and seemed to waver. Sheridan now began to exhibit those traits which always made him a tower of strength in the presence of an enemy. He put spurs to his horse, and dashed along in front of the line of battle from left to right, shouting words of encouragement, and having something cheery to say to every regiment. "Come on, men," he cried; "go at 'em with a will! Move on at a clean jump, or you'll not catch one of 'em. They're all getting ready to run now, and if you don't get on to them in five minutes they'll every one get away from you! Now go for them!" Just then a man on the skirmish-line was struck in the neck; the blood spurted as if the jugular vein had been cut. "I'm killed!" he cried, and dropped to the ground. "You're not hurt a bit!" cried Sheridan. "Pick up your gun, man, and move right on to the front." Such was the electric effect of his words that the poor fellow snatched up his musket, and rushed forward a dozen paces before he fell, never to rise again. The line of battle of weather-beaten veterans was now moving right along down the slope toward the woods with a steady swing that boded no good for Pickett's command, earthworks or no earthworks. Sheridan was mounted on his favorite black horse, "Rienzi," which had carried him from Winchester to Cedar Creek, and which Buchanan Read made famous for all time by his poem of "Sheridan's Ride." The roads were muddy, the fields swampy, the undergrowth dense, and "Rienzi," as he plunged and curveted, kept dashing the foam from his mouth and the mud from his heels. Had the Winchester pike been in a similar condition, it is altogether likely that he would not have made his famous twenty miles without breaking his own neck as well as Sheridan's. This historic horse derived his name from the fact that he was presented to Sheridan by the Second Michigan Cavalry in the little town of Rienzi, Mississippi, in 1862. After the famous ride he was sometimes called "Winchester." He was of "Blackhawk" blood. He bore Sheridan in nearly all his subsequent battles. When the animal died in 1878, in his twentieth year, his body was stuffed, and now stands in the museum on Governor's Island. The surviving veterans often decorate his body with flowers on Memorial Day.

Mackenzie had been ordered up the Crump road, with directions to turn east on the White Oak road, and whip everything he met on that route. He encountered a small cavalry command, and whipped it, according to orders, and then came galloping back to join in the general scrimmage.

Soon Ayres's men met with a heavy fire on their left flank, and had to change directions by facing more toward the west. As the troops entered the woods, and moved forward over the boggy ground, and struggled through the dense undergrowth, they were staggered by a heavy fire from the angle, and fell back in some confusion. Sheridan now rushed into the midst of the broken lines, and cried out: "Where is my battle-flag?" As the sergeant who carried it rode up, Sheridan seized the crimson-and-white standard, waved it above his head, cheered on the men, and made heroic efforts to close up the ranks. Bullets were now humming like a swarm of bees about our heads, and shells were crashing through the ranks. A musket-ball pierced the battle-flag; another killed the sergeant who had carried it; another wounded an aide, Captain McGonnigle, in the side; others struck two or three of the staff-officers' horses. All this time Sheridan was dashing from one point of the line to another, waving his flag, shaking his fist, encouraging, entreating, threatening, praying, swearing, the true personification of chivalry, the very incarnation of battle. It would be a sorry soldier who could help following such a leader. Ayres and his officers were equally exposing themselves at all points in rallying the men; and soon the line was steadied, for such troops could suffer but a momentary check. Ayres, with drawn saber, rushed forward once more with his veterans, who now behaved as if they had fallen back only to get a "good ready," and with fixed bayonets and a rousing cheer dashed over the earthworks, sweeping everything before them, and killing or capturing every man in their immediate front whose legs had not saved him.

Sheridan spurred "Rienzi" up to the angle, and with a bound the animal carried his rider over the earthworks, and landed among a line of prisoners who had thrown down their arms and were crouching close under the breastworks. Some of them called out: "Wha' do you want us all to go to?" Then Sheridan's rage turned to humor, and he had a running talk with the "Johnnies" as they filed past. "Go right over there," he said to them, pointing to the rear. "Get right along, now. Oh, drop your guns; you'll never need them any more. You'll all be safe over there. Are there any more of you? We want every one of you fellows." Nearly 1500 were captured at the angle.

An orderly here came up to Sheridan, saluted, and said: "Colonel Forsyth of your staff is killed, sir." "It's no such thing!" cried Sheridan. "I don't believe a word of it. You'll find Forsyth's all right." Ten minutes later Forsyth rode up. He had been mistaken for the gallant General Winthrop, who had fallen in the assault. Sheridan did not even seem surprised when he saw Forsyth, and merely said: "There; I told you so." This incident is mentioned as illustrative of a peculiar trait of Sheridan's character, which never allowed him to be disturbed by camp rumors, however disastrous.

The dismounted cavalry had assaulted as soon as they heard the infantry fire open. The natty cavalrymen, with their tight-fitting jackets, and short carbines, swarmed through the pine thickets and dense undergrowth, looking as if they had been especially equipped for crawling through knot-holes.

The cavalry commanded by the gallant Merritt made a final dash, went over the earthworks with a hurrah, captured a battery of artillery, and scattered everything in front of them. Here Custer, Devin, Fitzhugh, and the other cavalry leaders were in their element, and vied with each other in deeds of valor. Crawford's division had moved off in a northerly direction, marching away from Ayres, and leaving a gap between the two divisions. Sheridan became exceedingly annoyed at this circumstance, complained that Warren was not giving sufficient personal supervision to the infantry, and sent nearly all his staff-officers to the Fifth Corps to see that the mistakes made were corrected. After the capture of the angle I started off toward the right to see how matters were going there. I went in the direction of Crawford's division, on our right. Warren, whose personal gallantry was always conspicuous, had had his horse shot while with these troops. I passed around the left of the enemy's works, then rode due west to a point beyond the Ford road. Here I rejoined Sheridan a little before dark. He was laboring with all the energy of his nature to complete the destruction of the enemy's forces, and to make preparations to protect his own detached command from a possible attack by Lee's army in the morning. He said to me that he had just relieved Warren, and placed Griffin in command of the Fifth Corps. I had been sending frequent bulletins to the general-in-chief during the day, and now despatched a courier announcing the change of corps commanders, and giving the general result of the round-up.

Sheridan had that day fought one of the most interesting tactical battles of the war, admirable in conception, brilliant in execution, strikingly dramatic in its incidents, and productive of immensely important results.

I said to him: "It seems to me that you have exposed yourself to-day in a manner hardly justifiable on the part of a commander of such an important movement." His reply gave what seems to be the true key to his uniform success on the field: "I have never in my life taken a command into battle, and had the slightest desire to come out alive unless I won."

About half-past seven o'clock I started for general headquarters. The roads in many places were corduroyed with captured muskets; ammunition-trains and ambulances were still struggling forward; teamsters, prisoners, stragglers, and wounded were choking the roadway; the "coffee-boilers" had kindled their fires in the woods; cheers were resounding on all sides, and everybody was riotous over the victory. A horseman had to pick his way through this jubilant condition of things as best he could, as he did not have a clear right of way by any means. As I galloped past a group of men on the Boydton plank-road, my orderly called out to them the news of the victory. The only response he got was from one of them, who raised his open hand to his face, put his thumb to his nose, and yelled: "No, you don't—April fool!" I then realized that it was the 1st of April. I had ridden so rapidly that I reached headquarters at Dabney's Mill before the arrival of the last courier I had despatched. General Grant was sitting, with most of the staff about him, before a blazing camp-fire. He wore his blue cavalry overcoat, and the ever-present cigar was in his mouth. I began shouting the good news as soon as I got in sight, and in a moment all but the imperturbable general-in-chief were on their feet giving vent to boisterous demonstrations of joy. For some minutes there was a bewildering state of excitement, and officers fell to grasping hands, shouting, and hugging each other like school-boys. The news meant the beginning of the end, the reaching of the "last ditch." It pointed to peace and home. Dignity was thrown to the winds, and every man at that moment was in a fitting mood to dig his elbows into the ribs of the Archbishop of Canterbury, or to challenge the Chief Justice of the Supreme Court to a game of leap-frog. The proprieties of army etiquette were so far forgotten in the enthusiasm of the occasion that as soon as I had thrown myself from my horse I found myself rushing up to the general-in-chief and clapping him on the back with my hand, to his no little astonishment, and to the evident amusement of those about him.[1] The general, as might have been expected, asked his usual question: " How many prisoners have been taken ? " I was happy to report that the prisoners this time were estimated at over five thousand, and this was the only part of my recital that seemed to call forth a responsive expression from his impassive features. After having listened attentively to the description of Sheridan's day's work, the general, with scarcely a word of comment, walked into his tent, and by the light of a flickering candle took up his " manifold writer," and after finishing several despatches handed them to an orderly to be sent over the field wires, came out and joined our group at the camp-fire, and said as coolly as if remarking upon the state of the weather: " I have ordered a general assault along the lines." This was about nine o'clock in the evening.

In his conversation his sense of humor now began to assert itself. During the day I had sent him a bulletin saying: " I have noticed among the prisoners and dead many old men whose heads are quite bald." This was mentioned as an evidence that the enemy in recruiting was " robbing the grave." Ingalls was sitting with us. His hair had become so thin that he used to part it low behind and comb the stray locks forward, trying to make the rear-guard do picket duty at the front. The general delighted in teasing him on this subject, and looking toward him, he now said to me: " When I got

[1] Badeau, in his " Military History of Ulysses S. Grant," says in referring to this scene : " The bearer of the good news was Colonel Horace Porter, one of the most abstemious men in the army ; but he came up with so much enthusiasm, clapping the general-in-chief on the back, and otherwise demonstrating his joy, that the officer who shared his tent rebuked him at night for indulging too freely in drink at this critical juncture. But Porter had tasted neither wine nor spirits that day. He was only drunk with victory." —EDITOR.

your message to-day about the bald-headed men, I
showed it to Ingalls, and told him he had better take
care and not fall into the hands of the enemy, for that
is just the way they would be commenting on his head
in their reports."

Grant was anxious to have the different commands
move against the enemy's lines at once to prevent Lee
from withdrawing troops and sending them against
Sheridan.   Meade was all activity, and so alive to the
situation, and so anxious to carry out the orders of the
general-in-chief, that he sent word that he was going
to have the troops make a dash at the works without
waiting to form assaulting columns.   Grant at 9 : 30 P. M.
sent a message that he did not mean to have the corps
attack without assaulting columns, but to let the batteries open at once, and to feel out with skirmishers,
and if the enemy was found to be leaving to let the
troops attack in their own way.   The corps commanders reported that it would be impracticable to make a
successful assault until morning, but sent back replies
full of enthusiasm, and having in them a ring of the
true soldierly metal.   Ord said he would go into the
enemy's works "as a hot knife goes into butter."
Wright sent word that when he started in he would
"make the fur fly," and said: "If the corps does half
as well as I expect, we will have broken through the
rebel lines in fifteen minutes from the word 'go.'"
Grant was highly pleased with the spirit evinced in
these messages, and said: "I like the way Wright talks;
it argues success.   I heartily approve."

The hour for the general assault was fixed at four
o'clock the next morning.   Miles was ordered to march
with his division at midnight to reinforce Sheridan and
enable him to make a stand against Lee in case he
should move westward in the night.   A little after mid-

night the general tucked himself into his camp-bed, and
was soon sleeping as peacefully as if the next day was
to be devoted to a picnic instead of a decisive battle.
Every one at headquarters had caught as many cat-
naps as he could, so as to be able to keep both eyes open
the next day, in the hope of getting a sight of Petersburg, and possibly Richmond. And now four o'clock
came, but no assault. It was found that to remove
abatis, climb over chevaux-de-frise, jump rifle-pits, and
scale parapets, a little daylight would be of material
assistance.

At 4:45 there was a streak of gray in the heavens,
which soon revealed another streak of gray formed by
Confederate uniforms in the works opposite, and the
charge was ordered. The thunder of hundreds of guns
shook the ground like an earthquake, and soon the
troops were engaged all along the lines. The general
awaited for a while the result of the assault at headquarters, where he could be easily communicated with,
and from which he could give general directions.

At a quarter past five a message came from Wright
that he had carried the enemy's line in his front and
was pushing in. Next came news from Parke that he
had captured the outer works, with 12 pieces of artillery
and 800 prisoners. At 6:40 the general wrote a telegram with his own hand to Mr. Lincoln at City Point,
as follows: "Both Wright and Parke got through the
enemy's line. The battle now rages furiously. Sheridan, with his cavalry, the Fifth Corps, and Miles's
division of the Second Corps, which was sent to him
since one this morning, is now sweeping down from the
west. All now looks highly favorable. Ord is engaged,
but I have not yet heard the result in his front." A
cheering despatch was also sent to Sheridan, winding
up with the words: " I think nothing is now wanting

but the approach of your force from the west to finish up the job on this side."

Soon Ord was heard from as having broken through the intrenchments. Humphreys, too, had been doing gallant work. At half-past seven the line in his front was captured, and half an hour later Hays's division of his corps had carried an important earthwork, with three guns and most of the garrison. At 8:30 A. M. a despatch was brought in from Ord saying that some of his troops had just captured the enemy's works south of Hatcher's Run.

The general and staff now rode out to the front, as it was necessary to give immediate direction to the actual movements of the troops, and prevent confusion from the overlapping and intermingling of the several corps as they pushed forward. He urged his horse over the works which Wright's corps had captured, and suddenly came upon a body of 3000 prisoners marching to our rear. His whole attention was for some time riveted upon them, and we knew that he was enjoying his usual satisfaction in seeing so large a capture. Some of the guards told the prisoners who the general was, and they manifested great curiosity to get a good look at him. Next he came up with a division of Wright's corps, flushed with success, and rushing forward with a dash that was inspiriting beyond description. When they caught sight of the leader whom they had patiently followed from the Rapidan to Petersburg, their cheers broke forth with a will, and their enthusiasm knew no limit. The general galloped along toward the right, and soon met Meade, with whom he had been in constant communication, and who had been urging on the Army of the Potomac with all vigor. Congratulations were rapidly exchanged, and both went to pushing forward the good work. Grant, after taking in the situation, directed both Meade and Ord to face their commands more toward the east, and close up toward the inner lines which covered Petersburg. Lee had been pushed so vigorously that he seemed for a time to be making but little effort to recover any of his lost ground; but now he made a determined fight against Parke's corps, which was threatening his inner line on his extreme left, and the bridge across the Appomattox. Repeated assaults were made, but Parke resisted them all successfully, and could not be stirred from his position. Lee had ordered Longstreet's command from the north side of the James, and with these troops reinforced his extreme right.

General Grant dismounted near a farm-house which stood on a knoll, from which he could get a good view of the field of operations. He seated himself on the ground at the foot of a tree, and was soon busy receiving despatches and writing orders to officers conducting the advance. The position was under fire, and as soon as the group of staff-officers was seen, the enemy's guns began paying their respects to the party. This lasted for about a quarter of an hour, and as the fire became hotter and hotter, several of the officers, apprehensive for the general's safety, urged him to move to some less conspicuous position; but he kept on writing and talking, without the least interruption from the shots falling around him, and apparently not noticing what a target the place was becoming, or paying any heed to the gentle reminders to " move on." After he had finished his despatches he got up, took a view of the situation, and as he started toward the other side of the farm-house said with a quizzical look at the group around him: " Well, they do seem to have the range on us." The staff was now sent to the various points of the advancing lines, and all was activity in pressing forward the good work.

By noon nearly all the outer line of works was in our possession, except two strong redoubts which occupied a commanding position, named respectively Fort Gregg and Fort Whitworth. The general decided that these should be stormed, and about one o'clock three of Ord's brigades swept down upon Fort Gregg. The garrison of 300 men, commanded by Lieutenant-colonel J. H. Duncan, with two rifled cannon, made a desperate defense, and a gallant contest took place. For half an hour after our men had gained the parapet a bloody hand-to-hand struggle continued, but nothing could stand against the onslaught of Ord's troops, flushed with their morning's victory. By half-past two 57 of the brave garrison lay dead, and the rest had surrendered. Fort Whitworth was abandoned, but the guns of Fort Gregg were opened upon the garrison as they marched out, and the commander, Colonel Joseph M. Jayne, and 60 men surrendered.

About this time Miles struck a force of the enemy at Sutherland's Station, on Lee's extreme right, and captured two pieces of artillery and nearly 1000 prisoners. At 4:40 the general, who had been keeping Mr. Lincoln fully advised of the history that was so rapidly being made that day, sent him a telegram inviting him to come out the next day and pay him a visit. A prompt reply was received from the President, saying: " Allow me to tender you, and all with you, the nation's grateful thanks for the additional and magnificent success. At your kind suggestion, I think I will meet you to-morrow."

Prominent officers now urged the general to make an assault on the inner lines, and capture Petersburg that afternoon; but he was firm in his resolve not to sacrifice the lives necessary to accomplish such a result. He said the city would undoubtedly be evacuated during the night, and he would dispose the troops for a parallel march westward, and try to head off the escaping army. And thus ended this eventful Sunday.

CHAPTER XXIX

GRANT ENTERS PETERSBURG — LINCOLN AT PETERSBURG —
IN HOT PURSUIT OF LEE — GRANT MAKES A NIGHT RIDE
TO REACH ·SHERIDAN — GRANT HURRIES ON TO FARM-
VILLE — GRANT AT FARMVILLE — GRANT OPENS A COR-
RESPONDENCE WITH LEE — THE RIDE TO CURDSVILLE —
GRANT SUFFERS AN ATTACK OF ILLNESS — MORE COR-
RESPONDENCE WITH LEE

THE general was up at daylight the next morning, and the first report brought in was that Parke had gone through the lines at 4 A. M., capturing a few skirmishers, and that the city had surrendered at 4:28 to Colonel Ralph Ely. A second communication surrendering the place was sent in to Wright. General Grant's prediction had been fully verified. The evacuation had begun about ten the night before, and was completed on the morning of the 3d. Between 5 and 6 A. M. the general had a conference with Meade, and orders were given to push westward with all haste. About 9 A. M. the general rode into Petersburg. Many of the citizens, panic-stricken, had escaped with the army. Most of the whites who remained stayed indoors; a few groups of negroes gave cheers, but the scene generally was one of complete desertion. Grant rode along quietly until he came to a comfortable-looking brick house with a yard in front, No. 21 Market street, the residence of Mr. Thomas Wallace, and here he and the staff dismounted and took seats on the piazza.   A number of the citizens now gathered on the sidewalk, and stood gazing with eager curiosity upon the features of the commander of the Yankee armies. Soon an officer came with a despatch from Sheridan, who had been reinforced and ordered to strike out along the Danville Railroad, saying he was already nine miles beyond Namozine Creek, and pressing the enemy's trains. The general was anxious to move westward at once with the leading infantry columns, but he prolonged his stay until the President came up.

Mr. Lincoln soon after arrived, accompanied by Robert, who had ridden back to the railroad-station to meet him, and by his little son, "Tad," and Admiral Porter. He dismounted in the street, and came in through the front gate with long and rapid strides, his face beaming with delight. He seized General Grant's hand as the general stepped forward to greet him, and stood shaking it for some time, and pouring out his thanks and congratulations with all the fervor of a heart which seemed overflowing with its fullness of joy. I doubt whether Mr. Lincoln ever experienced a happier moment in his life. The scene was singularly affecting, and one never to be forgotten. He said: "Do you know, general, I had a sort of sneaking idea all along that you intended to do something like this; but I thought some time ago that you would so manœuver as to have Sherman come up and be near enough to coöperate with you." "Yes," replied the general; "I thought at one time that Sherman's army might advance far enough to be in supporting distance of the Eastern armies when the spring campaign against Lee opened; but I had a feeling that it would be better to let Lee's old antagonists give his army the final blow, and finish up the job. If the Western troops were even to put in an appearance against Lee's army, it might give some of our politicians a chance to stir up sectional feeling in claiming everything for the troops from their own section of country. The Western armies have been very successful in their campaigns, and it is due to the Eastern armies to let them vanquish their old enemy single-handed." "I see, I see," said Mr. Lincoln; "but I never thought of it in that light. In fact, my anxiety has been so great that I did n't care where the help came from, so that the work was perfectly done." "Oh," General Grant continued, "I do not suppose it would have given rise to much of the bickering I mentioned, and perhaps the idea would not have occurred to any one else. I feel sure there would have been no such feeling among the soldiers. Of course I would not have risked the result of the campaign on account of any mere sentiment of this kind. I have always felt confident that our troops here were amply able to handle Lee." Mr. Lincoln then began to talk about the civil complications that would follow the destruction of the Confederate armies in the field, and showed plainly the anxiety he felt regarding the great problems in statecraft which would soon be thrust upon him. He intimated very plainly, in a conversation that lasted nearly half an hour, that thoughts of leniency to the conquered were uppermost in his heart.

Meanwhile his son Tad, for whom he always showed a deep affection, was becoming a little uneasy, and gave certain appealing looks, to which General Sharpe, who seemed to understand the mute expressions of small boys, responded by producing some sandwiches, which he offered to him, saying: "Here, young man, I guess you must be hungry." Tad seized them as a drowning man would seize a life-preserver, and cried out: "Yes, I am; that 's what 's the matter with me." This greatly amused the President and the general-in-chief, who had a hearty laugh at Tad's expense.

A gentleman whom we supposed was the proprietor of the house asked the general to go into the parlor; but he declined politely, saying, "Thank you, but I am smoking."

The general hoped that before he parted with Mr. Lincoln he would hear that Richmond was in our possession; but after waiting about an hour and a half, he said he must ride on to the front and join Ord's column, and took leave of the President, who shook his hand cordially, and with great warmth of feeling wished him God-speed and every success.

The general and staff had ridden as far as Sutherland's Station—about nine miles—when a despatch from Weitzel overtook him, which had come by a roundabout way. It read: " We took Richmond at 8:15 this morning. I captured many guns. The enemy left in great haste.' The city is on fire in two places. Am making every effort to put it out. The people received us with enthusiastic expressions of joy." Although the news was expected, there were loud shouts of rejoicing from the group who heard it read. The general, as usual, did not manifest the slightest sign of emotion, and merely remarked: "I am sorry I did not get this information before we left the President. However, I suppose he has heard it by this time"; and then added: " Let the news be circulated among the troops as rapidly as possible."

Grant and Meade both went into camp at Sutherland's Station that evening (April 3). The Army of the Potomac caught but a few hours' sleep, and at three the next morning was again on the march. The pursuit had now become swift, unflagging, relentless. Sheridan, " the inevitable," as the enemy had learned to call him, was in advance, thundering on with his cavalry, followed by Griffin and the rest of the Army of the Potomac; while Ord was swinging along toward Burke- ville to head off Lee from Danville, to which point it was naturally supposed he was pushing in order to unite with Joe Johnston's army. April 4 was another active day; the troops were made to realize that this campaign was to be won by legs; that the great walking-match had begun, and success depended upon which army could make the best distance record. Grant rode this day with Ord's troops. Meade was quite sick, and had to take at times to an ambulance; but his loyal spirit never flagged, and all his orders breathed the true spirit of a soldier. That night General Grant camped at Wil- son's Station on the South Side Railroad, twenty-seven miles west of Petersburg. A railroad engineer who had been brought in as a prisoner reported that Davis and his cabinet had passed through Burkeville, on their way south, early on the morning of the day before. The next morning the general sent a despatch to Sherman in North Carolina, giving him an account of the situa- tion, containing instructions as to his future movements, and winding up with the famous words: "Rebel armies are now the only strategic points to strike at." On the 5th he marched again with Ord's column, and at noon reached Nottoway Court-house, about ten miles east of Burkeville, where he halted with Ord for a couple of hours. A young staff-officer here rode up to Ord in a state of considerable excitement, and said: "Is this a way-station?" The grim old soldier, who was always fond of a quiet joke, replied with great deliberation: "This is Nott-a-way Station." The staff collected around General Grant on the front porch of the old town tavern, and while examining maps and discussing the movements a ringing despatch came in from Sheridan saying he had captured six guns and some wagons, and had intercepted Lee's advance toward Burkeville; that Lee was in person at Amelia Court-house, etc. This news was given to the passing troops, and lusty cheers went up from every throat. They had marched about fifteen miles already that day, and now struck out as if they were good for fifteen more, and vowed that they were going to beat the record of the cavalry.

We continued to move along the wagon-road which runs parallel to the South Side Railroad till nearly dark, and had by that time reached a point about half-way between Nottoway and Burkeville. The road was skirted by a dense woods on the north side — the side toward the enemy. A commotion suddenly arose among the head-quarters escort, and on looking round, I saw some of our men dashing up to a horseman in full Confederate uniform, who had emerged like an apparition from the woods, and in the act of seizing him as a prisoner. I recognized him at once as the scout who had brought the important despatch sent by Sheridan from Columbia to City Point. I said to him, "How do you do, Campbell?" and told our men he was all right, and was one of our people. He said he had had a hard ride from Sheridan's camp, and had brought a despatch for General Grant. By this time the general had also recognized him, and had ridden up to him and halted in the road to see what he had brought. Campbell took from his mouth a small pellet of tin-foil, opened it, and pulled out a sheet of tissue-paper, on which was written the famous despatch, so widely published at the time, in which Sheridan described the situation at Jetersville, and added, "I wish you were here yourself."

The general said he would go at once to Sheridan, and dismounted from his black pony "Jeff Davis," which he had been riding, and called for his horse "Cincinnati."

He stood in the road for a few minutes, and wrote a despatch to Ord, using the pony's back for a desk, and then, mounting the fresh horse, told Campbell to lead the way. It was found that we would have to skirt pretty closely to the enemy's lines, and it was thought that it would be prudent to take some cavalry with us; but there was none near at hand, and the general said he would risk it with our mounted escort of fourteen men. Calling upon me and three other officers to accompany him, he started off. I had in the mean while questioned the scout about the trip, and found that we would have to follow some cross-roads through a wooded country and travel nearly twenty miles. It was now dark, but there was enough moonlight to enable us to see the way without difficulty. After riding for nearly two hours, the enemy's camp-fires were seen in the distance, and it was noticed that the fence-rails were thrown down in a number of places, indicating that cavalry had been moving across this part of the country, though we were certain our cavalry had not been there. Knowing that scouts are seldom trustworthy, and are often in the employ of both sides, and feeling that the general's safety was now entirely in the power of a comparatively unknown man, I, for one, began to grow suspicious. Just then Campbell fell back several paces and suddenly turned his horse into a piece of woods which we were skirting, and seemed to be acting in a manner that indicated either confusion or treachery. I cocked my pistol, and rode close behind him, thinking his feelings would stand that much in the way of precaution anyhow, and determined that if he was caught giving any suspicious signals I would at once arrest him. The scout, however, was thoroughly loyal, and one of Sheridan's most trusted men; no thought of treachery had crossed his mind; he was only looking for a short

cut through the woods. About half-past ten o'clock
we struck Sheridan's pickets. They could hardly be
made to understand that the general-in-chief was
wandering about at that hour with so small an escort,
and so near to the enemy's lines. The cavalry were
sleeping on their arms, and as our little party picked
its way through their ranks, and the troopers woke
up and recognized the general in the moonlight, their
remarks were highly characteristic of the men. One
said: "Why, there 's the old man. Boys, this means
business"; and another: "Great Scott! the old chief 's
out here himself. The rebs are going to get bu'sted
to-morrow, certain"; and a third: "Uncle Sam 's joined
the cavalry sure enough. You can bet there 'll be
lively times here in the morning." Sheridan was
awaiting us, feeling sure that the general would come
after getting his despatch. A good supper of beef, cold
chicken, and coffee was soon prepared, and it was
quickly demonstrated that the night ride had not impaired any one's appetite.

When the general-in-chief had learned fully the situation in Sheridan's front, he first sent a message to
Ord to watch the roads running south from Burkeville
and Farmville, and then went over to Meade's camp
near by. Meade was lying down, and still suffering
from illness. His views differed somewhat from General Grant's regarding the movements of the Army of the
Potomac for the next day, and the latter changed the
dispositions that were being made, so as to have the army
unite with Sheridan's troops in swinging round more
toward the south and heading off Lee in that direction.

The next day (April 6) proved a decided field-day in
the pursuit. It was found in the morning that Lee had
retreated during the night from Amelia Court-house;
and from the direction he had taken, and information

received that he had ordered rations to meet him at
Farmville, it was seen that he had abandoned all hope
of reaching Burkeville, and was probably heading for
Lynchburg. Ord was to try to burn the High Bridge
over the Appomattox, and push on to Farmville. Sheridan's cavalry was to work around Lee's left flank, and
the Army of the Potomac was to make another forced
march, and strike the enemy wherever it could reach
him. I spent a portion of the day with Humphreys's
corps, which attacked the enemy near Deatonsville and
gave his rear-guard no rest. I joined General Grant
later, and rode with him to Burkeville, getting there
some time after dark.

Ord had pushed out to Rice's Station, and Sheridan
and Wright had gone in against the enemy and fought
the battle of Sailor's Creek, capturing 6 general officers
and about 7000 men, and "smashing things" generally.
General Grant broke camp and started from Burkeville
early the next morning (the 7th), and moved rapidly in
the direction of Farmville. The columns were crowding
the roads, and the men, aroused to still greater efforts
by the inspiriting news of the day before, were sweeping
steadily along, despite the rain that fell, like trained
pedestrians on a walking-track. As the general rode
among them he was greeted with shouts and hurrahs
on all sides, and a string of sly remarks, which showed
how familiar swords and bayonets become when victory
furnishes the topic of their talk, such as " Cavalry 's gi'n
out, general. Infantry 's going to crush the rest of the
mud"; and " We 've marched nigh twenty miles on this
stretch, and we 're good for twenty more if the general
says so "; and " We 're not straddlin' any hosses, but
we 'll get there all the same." The general raised his
hat in acknowledgment of the cheers, and gave a pleasant nod to each of the men who addressed him.

A little before noon on April 7, 1865, General Grant, with his staff, rode into the little village of Farmville, on the south side of the Appomattox River, a town that will be memorable in history as the place where he opened the correspondence with Lee which, two days later, led to the surrender of the Army of Northern Virginia. He drew up in front of the village hotel, a comfortable brick building, dismounted, and established headquarters on its broad piazza. News came in that Crook was fighting large odds with his cavalry on the north side of the river, and I was directed to go to his front and see what was necessary to be done to assist him. I found that he was being driven back, the enemy (Munford's and Rosser's cavalry divisions, under Fitzhugh Lee) having made a bold stand north of the river. Humphreys was also on the north side, isolated from the rest of our infantry, confronted by a large portion of Lee's army, and having some heavy fighting. On my return to general headquarters that evening, Wright's corps was ordered to cross the river and move rapidly to the support of our troops there. Notwithstanding their long march that day, the men sprang to their feet with a spirit that made every one marvel at their pluck, and came swinging through the main street of the village with a step that seemed as elastic as on the first day of their toilsome tramp. It was now dark, but they spied the general-in-chief watching them with evident pride from the piazza of the hotel as they marched past. Then was witnessed one of the most inspiring scenes of the campaign. Bonfires were lighted on the sides of the street; the men seized straw and pine-knots, and improvised torches; cheers arose from their throats, already hoarse with shouts of victory; bands played, banners waved, and muskets were swung in the air. A regiment now broke forth with the song of "John Brown's body," and soon a whole division was shouting the swelling chorus of that popular air, which had risen to the dignity of a national anthem.   The night march had become a grand review, with Grant as the reviewing officer.

Ord and Gibbon had visited the general at the hotel, and he had spoken with them, as well as with Wright, about sending some communication to Lee that might pave the way to the stopping of further bloodshed.   Dr. Smith, formerly of the regular army, a native of Virginia, and a relative of General Ewell, now one of our prisoners, had told General Grant the night before that Ewell had said in conversation that their cause was lost when they crossed the James River, and he considered that it was the duty of the authorities to negotiate for peace then, while they still had a right to claim concessions, adding that now they were not in condition to claim anything.   He said that for every man killed after this somebody would be responsible, and it would be little better than murder.   He could not tell what General Lee would do, but he hoped that he would at once surrender his army.   This statement, together with the news that had been received from Sheridan, saying that he had heard that General Lee's trains of provisions, which had come by rail, were at Appomattox, and that he expected to capture them before Lee could reach them, induced the general to write the following communication:

HEADQUARTERS, ARMIES OF THE U. S.,
5 P. M., April 7, 1865.

GENERAL R. E. LEE, Commanding C. S. A.:

The results of the last week must convince you of the hopelessness of further resistance on the part of the Army of Northern Virginia in this struggle.   I feel that it is so, and regard it as my duty to shift from myself the responsibility of any further effusion of blood by asking of you the surrender of that

portion of the Confederate States army known as the Army of
Northern Virginia.

U. S. GRANT,
Lieutenant-general.

This he intrusted to General Seth Williams, adjutant-
general, with directions to take it to Humphreys's front,
as his corps was close up to the enemy's rear-guard, and
see that it reached Lee. Williams's orderly was shot,
and he himself came near losing his life in getting this
communication through the lines. General Grant decided to remain all night at Farmville and await the
reply from Lee, and he was shown to a room in the
hotel in which he was told that Lee had slept the night
before, although this statement could not be verified.
Lee wrote the following reply within an hour after he
received General Grant's letter, but it was brought in by
a rather circuitous route, and did not reach its destination till after midnight:

April 7, 1865.

GENERAL: I have received your note of this date. Though
not entertaining the opinion you express of the hopelessness of
further resistance on the part of the Army of Northern Virginia, I reciprocate your desire to avoid useless effusion of
blood, and therefore, before considering your proposition, ask
the terms you will offer on condition of its surrender.

R. E. LEE,
General.

LIEUTENANT-GENERAL U. S. GRANT,
    Commanding Armies of the U. S.

The next morning, before leaving Farmville, the following reply was given to General Seth Williams, who
again went to Humphreys's front to have it transmitted
to Lee:

April 8, 1865.

GENERAL R. E. LEE, Commanding C. S. A.:

Your note of last evening, in reply to mine of the same date,
asking the conditions on which I will accept the surrender of

the Army of Northern Virginia, is just received. In reply would say that, peace being my great desire, there is but one condition I would insist upon—namely, that the men and officers surrendered shall be disqualified for taking up arms against the Government of the United States until properly exchanged. I will meet you, or will designate officers to meet any officers you may name for the same purpose, at any point agreeable to you, for the purpose of arranging definitely the terms upon which the surrender of the Army of Northern Virginia will be received.

U. S. GRANT,
Lieutenant-general.

The last sentence shows great delicacy of feeling on the part of General Grant, who wished to spare General Lee the mortification of personally conducting the surrender. The consideration displayed has a parallel in the terms accorded by Washington to Cornwallis at Yorktown. Cornwallis took advantage of the privilege, and sent O'Hara to represent him; but Lee rose superior to the British general, and in a manly way came and conducted the surrender in person.

There turned up at this time a rather hungry-looking gentleman in gray, wearing the uniform of a colonel, who proclaimed himself the proprietor of the hotel. He gave us to understand that his regiment had crumbled to pieces; that he was about the only portion of it that had succeeded in holding together, and he thought he might as well "stop off" at home and look after his property. It is safe to say that his hotel had never before had so many guests in it, nor at such reduced rates. His story was significant as indicating the disintegrating process which was going on in the ranks of the enemy.

General Grant had been marching most of the way with the columns which were pushing along south of Lee's line of retreat; but, expecting that a reply to his last letter would soon be received, and wanting to keep within easy communication with Lee, he decided to march this day with the portion of the Army of the Potomac that was pressing Lee's rear-guard. After issuing some further instructions to Ord and Sheridan, he started from Farmville, crossed to the north side of the Appomattox, conferred in person with Meade, and rode with his columns. Encouraging reports came in all day, and that night headquarters were established at Curdsville in a large white farm-house a few hundred yards from Meade's camp. The general and several of the staff had cut loose from the headquarters trains the night he started to meet Sheridan at Jetersville, and had neither baggage nor camp equipage. The general did not even have his sword with him. This was the most advanced effort yet made in moving in "light-marching order," and we billeted ourselves at night in farm-houses, or bivouacked on porches, and picked up meals at any camp that seemed to have something to spare in the way of rations. That night we sampled the fare of Meade's hospitable mess, and once more lay down with full stomachs.

General Grant had been suffering all the afternoon from a severe headache, the result of fatigue, anxiety, scant fare, and loss of sleep, and by night he grew much worse. He was induced to bathe his feet in hot water and mustard, and apply mustard-plasters to his wrists and the back of his neck; but these remedies afforded little relief. The dwelling we occupied was a double house. The general threw himself upon a sofa in the sitting-room on the left side of the hall, while the staff-officers bunked on the floor of the room opposite, to catch what sleep they could. About midnight we were aroused by Colonel Charles A. Whittier of Humphreys's staff, who brought the expected letter from Lee. Raw-

lins took it, and stepped across the hall to the door of
General Grant's room.   He hesitated to knock, not wishing to awake the commander if he were asleep, and
opened the door softly and listened a moment to ascertain whether he could judge by any sound how the
chief was resting.   Soon the general's voice was heard
saying: "Come in; I am awake.   I am suffering too
much to get any sleep."   I had in the mean time brought
a lighted candle, and now stepped into the room with it.
The general, who had taken off only his coat and boots,
sat up on the sofa and read the communication.

The letter was as follows:

April 8, 1865.

GENERAL: I received at a late hour your note of to-day.   In
mine of yesterday I did not intend to propose the surrender of
the Army of Northern Virginia, but to ask the terms of your
proposition.   To be frank, I do not think the emergency has
arisen to call for the surrender of this army; but as the restoration of peace should be the sole object of all, I desired to know
whether your proposals would lead to that end.   I cannot,
therefore, meet you with a view to surrender the Army of
Northern Virginia; but as far as your proposal may effect the
Confederate States forces under my command, and tend to the
restoration of peace, I shall be pleased to meet you at 10 A. M.
to-morrow on the old stage-road to Richmond, between the
picket-lines of the two armies.

R. E. LEE,
General.

LIEUTENANT-GENERAL U. S. GRANT.

The general shook his head, expressive of his disappointment, and remarked, " It looks as if Lee still means
to fight; I will reply in the morning"; and after making
a few more comments, lay down again upon the sofa.
Rawlins and I expressed the hope that the general might
still be able to get some sleep, and then retired from the
room.   About four o'clock on the morning of April 9 I

rose and crossed the hall to ascertain how the general was feeling. I found his room empty, and upon going out of the front door, saw him pacing up and down in the yard, holding both hands to his head. Upon inquiring how he felt, he replied that he had had very little sleep, and was still suffering the most excruciating pain. I said: " Well, there is one consolation in all this, general: I never knew you to be ill that you did not receive some good news before the day passed. I have become a little superstitious regarding these coincidences, and I should not be surprised if some good fortune were to overtake you before night." He smiled, and replied: " The best thing that could happen to me to-day would be to get rid of the pain I am suffering." We were soon joined by some others of the staff, and the general was induced to walk over to Meade's headquarters with us and get some coffee, in the hope that it would do him good. He seemed to feel a little better then, and after writing the following letter to Lee, and despatching it, he prepared to move forward.

April 9, 1865.

GENERAL: Your note of yesterday is received. As I have no authority to treat on the subject of peace, the meeting proposed for 10 A. M. to-day could lead to no good. I will state, however, general, that I am equally anxious for peace with yourself, and the whole North entertains the same feeling. The terms upon which peace can be had are well understood. By the South laying down their arms they will hasten that most desirable event, save thousands of human lives, and hundreds of millions of property not yet destroyed. Sincerely hoping that all our difficulties may be settled without the loss of another life, I subscribe myself, etc.,

U. S. GRANT,
Lieutenant-general.

GENERAL R. E. LEE.

General Grant kept steadily in mind the fact that he was simply a soldier, and could deal only with hostile armies. He could not negotiate a treaty of peace without transcending his authority.

CHAPTER XXX

IT was proposed to the general to ride during the day in a covered ambulance which was at hand, instead of on horseback, so as to avoid the intense heat of the sun; but his soldierly instincts rebelled against such a proposition, and he soon after mounted "Cincinnati," and started from Curdsville toward New Store. From this point he went by way of a cross-road to the south side of the Appomattox, with the intention of moving around to Sheridan's front. While riding along the wagon-road which runs from Farmville to Appomattox Court-house, at a point eight or nine miles east of the latter place, Lieutenant Charles E. Pease of Meade's staff overtook him with a despatch. It was found to be a reply from Lee, which had been sent into our lines on Humphreys's front. It read as follows:

April 9, 1865.

GENERAL: I received your note of this morning on the picket-line, whither I had come to meet you and ascertain definitely what terms were embraced in your proposal of yesterday with reference to the surrender of this army. I now request an

466

interview, in accordance with the offer contained in your letter of yesterday, for that purpose.

> Very respectfully, your obedient servant,
>
> R. E. LEE,
> General.

LIEUTENANT-GENERAL U. S. GRANT,
Commanding U. S. Armies.

Pease also brought a note from Meade saying that, at Lee's request, he had read the communication addressed to Grant, and in consequence of it had granted a short truce.

The general, as soon as he had read these letters, dismounted, sat down on the grassy bank by the roadside, and wrote the following reply to Lee:

> April 9, 1865.

GENERAL R. E. LEE, Commanding C. S. Army:

Your note of this date is but this moment (11 : 50 A. M.) received, in consequence of my having passed from the Richmond and Lynchburg road to the Farmville and Lynchburg road. I am at this writing about four miles west of Walker's Church, and will push forward to the front for the purpose of meeting you. Notice sent to me on this road where you wish the interview to take place will meet me.

> Very respectfully, your obedient servant,
>
> U. S. GRANT,
> Lieutenant-general.

He handed this to Colonel Babcock of the staff, with directions to take it to General Lee by the most direct route. Mounting his horse again, the general rode on at a trot toward Appomattox Court-house. When five or six miles from the town, Colonel Newhall, Sheridan's adjutant-general, came riding up from the direction of Appomattox, and handed the general a communication. This proved to be a duplicate of the letter from Lee that Lieutenant Pease had brought in from Meade's lines. Lee was so closely pressed that he was anxious

to communicate with Grant by the most direct means;
and as he could not tell with which column Grant was
moving, he sent in one copy of his letter on Meade's
front, and one on Sheridan's.   Colonel Newhall joined
our party, and after a few minutes' halt to read the
letter we continued our ride toward Appomattox.   On
the march I had asked the general several times how he
felt.   To the same question now he replied: "The pain
in my head seemed to leave me the moment I got Lee's
letter."   The road was filled with men, animals, and
wagons, and to avoid these and shorten the distance
we turned slightly to the right and began to "cut across
lots"; but before going far we spied men conspicuous
in gray, and it was seen that we were moving toward
the enemy's left flank, and that a short ride farther
would take us into his lines.   It looked for a moment
as if a very awkward condition of things might possibly
arise, and Grant become a prisoner in Lee's lines instead
of Lee in his.   Such a circumstance would have given
rise to an important cross-entry in the system of campaign bookkeeping.   There was only one remedy—to
retrace our steps and strike the right road, which was
done without serious discussion.   About one o'clock the
little village of Appomattox Court-house, with its half-
dozen houses, came in sight, and soon we were entering
its single street.   It is situated on rising ground, and
beyond it the country slopes down into a broad valley.
The enemy was seen with his columns and wagon-trains
covering the low ground.   Our cavalry, the Fifth Corps,
and part of Ord's command were occupying the high
ground to the south and west of the enemy, heading him
off completely.   We saw a group of officers who had dismounted and were standing at the edge of the town, and
at their head we soon recognized the features of Sheridan.   No one could look at Sheridan at such a moment

without a sentiment of undisguised admiration. In this campaign, as in others, he had shown himself possessed of military traits of the highest order. Bold in conception, self-reliant, demonstrating by his acts that "much danger makes great hearts most resolute," fertile in resources, combining the restlessness of a Hotspur with the patience of a Fabius, it is no wonder that he should have been looked upon as the wizard of the battle-field. Generous of his life, gifted with the ingenuity of a Hannibal, the dash of a Murat, the courage of a Ney, the magnetism of his presence roused his troops to deeds of individual heroism, and his unconquerable columns rushed to victory with all the confidence of Cæsar's Tenth Legion. Wherever blows fell thickest, there was his crest. Despite the valor of the defense, opposing ranks went down before the fierceness of his onsets, never to rise again, and he would not pause till the folds of his banners waved above the strongholds he had wrested from the foe. Brave Sheridan! I can almost see him now, his silent clay again quickened into life, once more riding "Rienzi" through a fire of hell, leaping opposing earthworks at a single bound, and leaving nothing of those who barred his way except the fragments scattered in his path. As long as manly courage is talked of, or heroic deeds are honored, the hearts of a grateful people will beat responsive to the mention of the talismanic name of Sheridan.

Ord and others were standing in the group before us, and as our party came up General Grant greeted the officers, and said, "How are you, Sheridan?" "First-rate, thank you; how are you?" cried Sheridan, with a voice and look which seemed to indicate that, on his part, he was having things all his own way. "Is Lee over there?" asked Grant, pointing up the road, having heard a rumor that Lee was in that vicinity. "Yes; he is in that brick house, waiting to surrender to you," answered Sheridan. " Well, then, we 'll go over," said Grant.

The general-in-chief now rode on, accompanied by Sheridan, Ord, and others. Soon Colonel Babcock's orderly was seen sitting on his horse in the street in front of a two-story brick house, better in appearance than the rest of the houses. He said General Lee and Colonel Babcock had gone into this house half an hour before, and he was ordered to post himself in the street and keep a lookout for General Grant, so as to let him know where General Lee was.

Babcock told me afterward that in carrying General Grant's last letter he passed through the enemy's lines, and found General Lee a little more than half a mile beyond Appomattox Court-house. He was lying down by the roadside on a blanket which had been spread over a few fence-rails placed on the ground under an apple-tree which was part of an old orchard. This circumstance furnished the only ground for the wide-spread report that the surrender occurred under an apple-tree, and which has been repeated in song and story. There may be said of that statement what Cuvier said of the French Academy's definition of a crab—" brilliant, but not correct."

Babcock dismounted upon coming near, and as he approached Lee sat up, with his feet hanging over the roadside embankment. The wheels of wagons, in passing along the road, had cut away the earth of this embankment, and left the roots of the tree projecting. Lee's feet were partly resting on these roots. Colonel Charles Marshall, his military secretary, came forward, took the despatch which Babcock handed him, and gave it to General Lee. After reading it the general rose, and said he would ride forward on the road on which Bab-

cock had come, but was apprehensive that hostilities
might begin in the mean time, upon the termination of
the temporary truce, and asked Babcock to write a line
to Meade informing him of the situation.   Babcock
wrote accordingly, requesting Meade to maintain the
truce until positive orders from Grant could be received.
To save time, it was arranged that a Union officer, accompanied by one of Lee's officers, should carry this
letter through the enemy's lines.   This route made the
distance to Meade nearly ten miles shorter than by the
roundabout way of the Union lines.   Lee now mounted
his horse, and directed Colonel Marshall to accompany
him.   They started for Appomattox Court-house in
company with Babcock, followed by a mounted orderly.

When the party
reached the vil-
lage they met one
of its residents,
named   Wilmer
McLean, who was
told that General
Lee wished to oc-

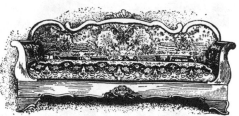

THE SOFA IN THE McLEAN HOUSE.

cupy a convenient room in some house in the town.
McLean ushered them into the sitting-room of one of
the first houses he came to; but upon looking about,
and seeing that it was small and unfurnished, Lee proposed finding something more commodious and better
fitted for the occasion.   McLean then conducted the
party to his own house, about the best one in the town,
where they awaited General Grant's arrival.

The house had a comfortable wooden porch with seven
steps leading up to it.   A hall ran through the middle
from front to back, and upon each side was a room having two windows, one in front and one in rear.   Each
room had two doors opening into the hall.   The build-

ing stood a little distance back from the street, with a yard in front, and to the left on entering was a gate for carriages, and a roadway running to a stable in rear. We entered the grounds by this gate, and dismounted. In the yard were seen a fine, large gray horse, which proved to be General Lee's favorite animal, called "Traveler," and a good-looking, dark-colored mare belonging to Colonel Marshall. An orderly in gray was in charge of them, and had taken off their bridles to let them crop the grass.

General Grant mounted the steps and entered the house. As he stepped into the hall, Colonel Babcock,

TABLE AT WHICH LEE SAT.

who had seen his approach from the window, opened the door of the room on the left, in which he had been sitting with General Lee and Colonel Marshall awaiting General Grant's arrival. The general passed in, and as Lee arose and stepped forward, Grant extended his hand, saying, "General Lee," and the two shook hands cordially. The members of the staff, Generals Sheridan and Ord, and some other general officers who had gathered in the front yard, remained outside, feeling that General Grant would probably prefer his first interview with General Lee to be, in a measure, private. In a few minutes Colonel Babcock came to the front door, and, making a motion with his hat toward the sitting-room, said: "The general says come in." It was then about half-past one on Sunday, the 9th of April. We entered, and found General Grant seated in an old office arm-chair in the center of the room, and Lee sitting in a plain arm-chair with a cane seat beside a square, marble-topped table near the front window, in the corner opposite the door by which we entered, and facing General Grant. Colonel Marshall was standing at his left, with his right elbow resting upon the mantelpiece. We walked in softly, and ranged ourselves quietly about the sides of the room, very much as people enter a sick-chamber when they expect to find the patient dangerously ill. Some found seats on the sofa standing against the wall between the two doors and on the few plain chairs which constituted the furniture, but most of the party stood.

CHAIR IN WHICH LEE SAT.

The contrast between the two commanders was singularly striking, and could not fail to attract marked attention as they sat, six or eight feet apart, facing each other. General Grant, then nearly forty-three years of age, was five feet eight inches in height, with shoulders slightly stooped. His hair and full beard were nut-brown, without a trace of gray in them. He had on his single-breasted blouse of dark-blue flannel, unbuttoned in front and showing a waistcoat underneath. He wore an ordinary pair of top-boots, with his trousers inside, and was without spurs. The boots and portions of his clothes were spattered with mud. He had worn a pair of thread gloves of a dark-yellow color, which he had taken off on entering the room. His felt " sugar-loaf," stiff-brimmed hat was resting on his lap. He had no sword or sash, and a pair of shoulder-straps was all there was about him to designate his rank. In fact, aside from these, his uniform was that of a private soldier.

CHAIR IN WHICH GRANT SAT.

Lee, on the other hand, was six feet and one inch in height, and erect for one of his age, for he was Grant's senior by sixteen years. His hair and full beard were a silver-gray, and thick, except that the hair had become a little thin in front. He wore a new uniform of Confederate gray, buttoned to the throat, and a handsome sword and sash. The sword was of exceedingly fine workmanship, and the hilt was studded with jewels. It had been presented to him by some ladies in England who sympathized with the cause he represented. His top-boots were comparatively new, and had on them near the top some ornamental stitching of red silk. Like his uniform, they were clean. On the boots were handsome spurs with large rowels. A felt hat which in color matched pretty closely that of his uniform, and a pair of long, gray buckskin gauntlets, lay beside him on the table. We endeavored afterward to learn how it was that he wore such fine clothes, and looked so much as if he had turned out to go to church that Sunday afternoon, while with us our outward garb scarcely rose to the dignity even of the "shabby-genteel." One explanation was that when his headquarters wagons had been pressed so closely by our cavalry a few days before, it was found that his officers would have to destroy all their baggage, except the clothes they carried on their backs; and each one naturally selected the newest suit he had, and sought to propitiate the god of destruction by a sacrifice of his second-best. Another reason given was that, in deference to General Grant, General Lee had dressed himself with special care for the purpose of the meeting.

Grant began the conversation by saying: "I met you once before, General Lee, while we were serving in Mexico, when you came over from General Scott's headquarters to visit Garland's brigade, to which I then belonged. I have always remembered your appearance, and I think I should have recognized you anywhere." "Yes," replied General Lee; "I know I met you on that occasion, and I have often thought of it, and tried to recollect how you looked, but I have never been able to recall a single feature." After some further mention of Mexico, General Lee said: "I suppose, General Grant, that the object of our present meeting is fully understood. I asked to see you to ascertain upon what terms you would receive the surrender of my army." General Grant replied: "The terms I propose are those stated substantially in my letter of yesterday; that is, the officers and men surrendered to be paroled and disqualified from taking up arms again until properly exchanged, and all arms, ammunition, and supplies to be delivered up as captured property." Lee nodded

TABLE ON WHICH GRANT WROTE THE ARTICLES OF SURRENDER.

an assent, and said: "Those are about the conditions which I expected would be proposed." General Grant then continued: "Yes; I think our correspondence indicated pretty clearly the action that would be taken at our meeting, and I hope it may lead to a general suspension of hostilities, and be the means of preventing any further loss of life."

Lee inclined his head as indicating his accord with this wish, and General Grant then went on to talk at some length in a very pleasant vein about the prospects of peace. Lee was evidently anxious to proceed to the formal work of the surrender, and he brought the subject up again by saying:

"I presume, General Grant, we have both carefully considered the proper steps to be taken, and I would suggest that you commit to writing the terms you have proposed, so that they may be formally acted upon."

"Very well," replied Grant; "I will write them out." And calling for his manifold order-book, he opened it, laid it on a small oval wooden table which Colonel Parker brought to him from the rear of the room, and proceeded to write the terms. The leaves had been so prepared that three impressions of the writing were made. He wrote very rapidly, and did not pause until he had finished the sentence ending with "officers appointed by me to receive them." Then he looked toward Lee, and his eyes seemed to be resting on the handsome sword that hung at that officer's side. He said afterward that this set him to thinking that it would be an unnecessary humiliation to require the officers to surrender their swords, and a great hardship to deprive them of their personal baggage and horses; and after a short pause he wrote the sentence: "This will not embrace the side-arms of the officers, nor their private horses or baggage."

When he had finished the letter he called Colonel Parker to his side, and looked it over with him, and directed him as they went along to interline six or seven words, and to strike out the word "their," which had been repeated. When this had been done the general took the manifold writer in his right hand, extended his arm toward Lee, and started to rise from his chair to hand the book to him.   As I was standing equally distant from them, with my back to the front window, I stepped forward, took the book, and passed it to General Lee.   The terms were as follows:

APPOMATTOX COURT-HOUSE, VA., April 9, 1865.
GENERAL R. E. LEE, Commanding C. S. A.

GENERAL: In accordance with the substance of my letter to you of the 8th inst., I propose to receive the surrender of the Army of Northern Virginia on the following terms, to wit: Rolls of all the officers and men to be made in duplicate, one copy to be given to an officer to be designated by me, the other to be retained by such officer or officers as you may designate. The officers to give their individual paroles not to take up arms against the Government of the United States until properly [exchanged], and each company or regimental commander to sign a like parole for the men of their commands.   The arms, artillery, and public property to be parked and stacked and turned over to the officers appointed by me to receive them. This will not embrace the side-arms of the officers, nor their private horses or baggage.   This done, each officer and man will be allowed to return to his home, not to be disturbed by the United States authorities so long as they observe their paroles and the laws in force where they may reside.

Very respectfully,
U. S. GRANT,
Lieutenant-general.

Lee pushed aside some books and two brass candlesticks which were on the table, then took the book and laid it down before him, while he drew from his pocket a pair of steel-rimmed spectacles, and wiped the glasses carefully with his handkerchief.   He crossed his legs, adjusted the spectacles very slowly and deliberately, took up the draft of the terms, and proceeded to read them attentively.   They consisted of two pages.   When he reached the top line of the second page, he looked up, and said to General Grant: "After the words 'until properly' the word 'exchanged' seems to be omitted. You doubtless intended to use that word."

"Why, yes," said Grant; "I thought I had put in the word 'exchanged.'"

"I presumed it had been omitted inadvertently," continued Lee; "and, with your permission, I will mark where it should be inserted."

"Certainly," Grant replied.

Lee felt in his pocket as if searching for a pencil, but he did not seem to be able to find one. Seeing this, I handed him my lead-pencil. During the rest of the interview he kept twirling this pencil in his fingers and occasionally tapping the top of the table with it. When he handed it back, it was carefully treasured by me as a memento of the occasion. When Lee came to the sentence about the officers' side-arms, private horses, and baggage, he showed for the first time during the reading of the letter a slight change of countenance, and was evidently touched by this act of generosity. It was doubtless the condition mentioned to which he particularly alluded when he looked toward General Grant, as he finished reading, and said with some degree of warmth in his manner, "This will have a very happy effect upon my army."

General Grant then said: "Unless you have some suggestions to make in regard to the form in which I have stated the terms, I will have a copy of the letter made in ink, and sign it."

"There is one thing I should like to mention," Lee replied, after a short pause. "The cavalrymen and artillerists own their own horses in our army. Its organization in this respect differs from that of the United States." This expression attracted the notice of our officers present, as showing how firmly the conviction was grounded in his mind that we were two distinct countries. He continued: "I should like to understand whether these men will be permitted to retain their horses."

"You will find that the terms as written do not allow this," General Grant replied; "only the officers are permitted to take their private property."

Lee read over the second page of the letter again, and then said: "No, I see the terms do not allow it; that is clear." His face showed plainly that he was quite anxious to have this concession made; and Grant said very promptly, and without giving Lee time to make a direct request:

"Well, the subject is quite new to me. Of course I did not know that any private soldiers owned their animals; but I think we have fought the last battle of the war,— I sincerely hope so,—and that the surrender of this army will be followed soon by that of all the others; and I take it that most of the men in the ranks are small farmers, and as the country has been so raided by the two armies, it is doubtful whether they will be able to put in a crop to carry themselves and their families through the next winter without the aid of the horses they are now riding, and I will arrange it in this way: I will not change the terms as now written, but I will instruct the officers I shall appoint to receive the paroles to let all the men who claim to own a horse or mule take the animals home with them to work their little farms." (This expression has been quoted in various forms, and has been the subject of some dispute. I give the exact words used.)

Lee now looked greatly relieved, and though anything but a demonstrative man, he gave every evidence of his appreciation of this concession, and said: "This will have the best possible effect upon the men. It will be very gratifying, and will do much toward conciliating our people." He handed the draft of the terms back to General Grant, who called Colonel T. S. Bowers of the staff to him, and directed him to make a copy in ink. Bowers was a little nervous, and he turned the matter over to Colonel Parker, whose handwriting presented a better appearance than that of any one else on the staff. Parker sat down to write at the oval table, which he had moved again to the rear of the room. Wilmer McLean's domestic resources in the way of ink now became the subject of a searching investigation, but it was found that the contents of the conical-shaped stoneware ink-stand with a paper stopper which he produced appeared to be participating in the general breaking up, and had disappeared. Colonel Marshall now came to the rescue, and took from his pocket a small boxwood inkstand, which was put at Parker's service, so that, after all, we had to fall back upon the resources of the enemy to furnish the "stage properties" for the final scene in the memorable military drama.

Colonel Marshall then took a seat on the sofa beside Sheridan and Ingalls. When the terms had been copied, Lee directed his military secretary to draw up for his signature a letter of acceptance. Colonel Marshall wrote out a draft of such a letter, making it formal, beginning with, "I have the honor to acknowledge," etc. General Lee took it, and after reading it over very carefully, directed that these formal expressions be stricken out, and that the letter be otherwise shortened. He afterward went over it again, and seemed to change some words, and then told the colonel to make a final copy in ink. When it came to providing the paper, it was found that we had the only supply of that important ingredient in the recipe for surrendering an army, so we gave a few pages to the colonel. The letter when completed read as follows:

HEADQUARTERS, ARMY OF NORTHERN VIRGINIA,
April 9, 1865.

GENERAL: I have received your letter of this date containing the terms of the surrender of the Army of Northern Virginia as proposed by you. As they are substantially the same as those expressed in your letter of the 8th inst., they are accepted. I will proceed to designate the proper officers to carry the stipulations into effect.

Very respectfully, your obedient servant,
R. E. LEE,
General.

LIEUTENANT-GENERAL U. S. GRANT,
Commanding Armies of U. S.

While the letters were being copied, General Grant introduced the general officers who had entered, and each member of the staff, to General Lee. The general shook hands with General Seth Williams, who had been his adjutant when Lee was superintendent at West Point some years before the war, and gave his hand to some of the other officers who had extended theirs; but to most of those who were introduced he merely bowed in a dignified and formal manner. He did not exhibit the slightest change of features during this ceremony until Colonel Parker of our staff was presented to him. Parker being a full-blooded Indian, when Lee saw his swarthy features he looked at him with evident surprise, and his eyes rested on him for several seconds. What was passing in his mind no one knew, but the natural surmise was that he at first mistook Parker for a negro, and was struck with astonishment to find that the commander of the Union armies had one of that race on his personal staff.

Lee did not utter a word while the introductions were going on, except to Seth Williams, with whom he talked cordially. Williams at one time referred in a rather jocose manner to a circumstance which had occurred during their former service together, as if he wished to say something in a good-natured way to thaw the frigidity of the conversation; but Lee was in no mood for pleasantries, and he did not unbend, or even relax the fixed sternness of his features. His only response to the remark was a slight inclination of the head. General Lee now took the initiative again in leading the conversation back into business channels. He said:

"I have a thousand or more of your men as prisoners, General Grant, a number of them officers, whom we have required to march along with us for several days. I shall be glad to send them into your lines as soon as it can be arranged, for I have no provisions for them. I have, indeed, nothing for my own men. They have been living for the last few days principally upon parched corn, and we are badly in need of both rations and forage. I telegraphed to Lynchburg, directing several train-loads of rations to be sent on by rail from there, and when they arrive I should be glad to have the present wants of my men supplied from them."

At this remark all eyes turned toward Sheridan, for he had captured these trains with his cavalry the night before near Appomattox Station. General Grant replied: "I should like to have our men sent within our lines as soon as possible. I will take steps at once to have your army supplied with rations, but I am sorry we have no forage for the animals. We have had to depend upon the country for our supply of forage. Of about how many men does your present force consist?"

"Indeed, I am not able to say," Lee answered, after a slight pause. "My losses in killed and wounded have been exceedingly heavy, and, besides, there have been many stragglers and some deserters. All my reports and public papers, and indeed some of my own private letters, had to be destroyed on the march to prevent them from falling into the hands of your people. Many companies are entirely without officers, and I have not seen any returns for several days, so that I have no means of ascertaining our present strength."

General Grant had taken great pains to have a daily estimate made of the enemy's forces from all the data that could be obtained, and judging it to be about 25,000 at this time, he said: "Suppose I send over 25,000 rations, do you think that will be a sufficient supply?" "I think it will be ample," remarked Lee, and added with considerable earnestness of manner, "and it will be a great relief, I assure you."

General Grant now turned to his chief commissary, Colonel M. R. Morgan, who was present, and directed him to arrange for issuing the rations. The number of officers and men surrendered was over 28,000. As to General Grant's supplies, he had ordered the army, on starting out, to carry twelve days' rations. This was the twelfth and last day of the campaign.

Grant's eye now fell upon Lee's sword again, and it seemed to remind him of the absence of his own, and by way of explanation, and so that it could not be construed as a discourtesy, he said to Lee:

"I started out from my camp several days ago without my sword, and as I have not seen my headquarters baggage since, I have been riding about without any side-arms. I have generally worn a sword, however, as little as possible—only during the active operations of a campaign." "I am in the habit of wearing mine most of the time," remarked Lee, "when I am among my troops moving about through the army."

General Sheridan now stepped up to General Lee, and said that when he discovered some of the Confederate troops in motion during the morning, which seemed to

be a violation. of the truce, he had sent him (Lee) a
couple of notes protesting against this act, and as he
had not had time to copy them, he would like to have
them long enough to make copies.   Lee took the notes
out of the breast pocket of his coat, and handed them
to Sheridan, with a few words expressive of regret that
the circumstance should have occurred, and intimating
that it must have been the result of some misunderstanding.

   After a little general conversation had been indulged
in by those present, the two letters were signed.   Grant
signed the terms on the oval table, which was moved up
to him again for the purpose.   Lee signed his letter of
acceptance on the marble-topped table at which he sat.
Colonel Parker folded up the terms, and gave them to
Colonel Marshall.   Marshall handed Lee's acceptance to
Parker.

CHAPTER XXXI

AFTER THE SURRENDER — GRANT'S FINAL CONFERENCE WITH
LEE — THE DAWN OF PEACE — GRANT AVOIDS A VISIT
TO RICHMOND — HIS RESPECT FOR RELIGION — GRANT'S
ENTHUSIASTIC RECEPTION AT WASHINGTON — HIS LAST
INTERVIEW WITH LINCOLN — JOHN WILKES BOOTH SHAD-
OWS GRANT — GRANT'S INTERRUPTED JOURNEY — LIN-
COLN'S ASSASSINATION

BEFORE parting Lee asked Grant to notify Meade
of the surrender, fearing that fighting might break
out on that front, and lives be uselessly lost. This request was complied with, and two Union officers were
sent through the enemy's lines as the shortest route to
Meade, some of Lee's officers accompanying them to
prevent their being interfered with. A little before
four o'clock General Lee shook hands with General
Grant, bowed to the other officers, and with Colonel
Marshall left the room. One after another we followed,
and passed out to the porch. Lee signaled to his orderly
to bring up his horse, and while the animal was being
bridled the general stood on the lowest step, and gazed
sadly in the direction of the valley beyond, where his
army lay—now an army of prisoners. He thrice smote
the palm of his left hand slowly with his right fist in an
absent sort of way, seemed not to see the group of
Union officers in the yard, who rose respectfully at his
approach, and appeared unaware of everything about

485

him. All appreciated the sadness that overwhelmed him, and he had the personal sympathy of every one who beheld him at this supreme moment of trial. The approach of his horse seemed to recall him from his reverie, and he at once mounted. General Grant now stepped down from the porch, moving toward him, and saluted him by raising his hat. He was followed in this act of courtesy by all our officers present. Lee raised his hat respectfully, and rode off at a slow trot to break the sad news to the brave fellows whom he had so long commanded.

General Grant and his staff then started for the head-quarters camp, which, in the mean time, had been pitched near by. The news of the surrender had reached the Union lines, and the firing of salutes began at several points; but the general sent an order at once to have them stopped, using these words: "The war is over; the rebels are our countrymen again; and the best sign of rejoicing after the victory will be to abstain from all demonstrations in the field." This was in keeping with his order issued after the surrender of Vicksburg: "The paroled prisoners will be sent out of here to-morrow. . . . Instruct the commanders to be orderly and quiet as these prisoners pass, and to make no offensive remarks."

There were present in the room in which the surrender occurred, besides Sheridan, Ord, Merritt, Custer, and the officers of Grant's staff, a number of other officers and one or two citizens, who entered the room at different times during the interview.

Mr. McLean had been charging about in a manner which indicated that the excitement was shaking his nervous system to its center; but his real trials did not begin until the departure of the chief actors in the surrender. Then relic-hunters charged down upon the manor-house, and began to bargain for the numerous pieces of furniture. Sheridan paid the proprietor twenty dollars in gold for the table on which General Grant wrote the terms of surrender, for the purpose of presenting it to Mrs. Custer, and handed it over to her dashing husband, who galloped off to camp bearing it upon his shoulder. Ord paid forty dollars for the table at which Lee sat, and afterward presented it to Mrs. Grant, who modestly declined it, and insisted that Mrs. Ord should become its possessor. General Sharpe paid ten dollars for the pair of brass candlesticks; Colonel Sheridan, the general's brother, secured the stone inkstand; and General Capehart the chair in which Grant sat, which he gave not long before his death to Captain Wilmon W. Blackmar of Boston. Captain O'Farrell of Hartford became the possessor of the chair in which Lee sat. A child's doll was found in the room, which the younger officers tossed from one to the other, and called the "silent witness." This toy was taken possession of by Colonel Moore of Sheridan's staff, and is now owned by his son. Bargains were at once struck for nearly all the articles in the room; and it is even said that some mementos were carried off for which no coin of the republic was ever exchanged. The sofa remains in possession of Mrs. Spillman, Mr. McLean's daughter, who now lives in Camden, West Virginia. Colonel Marshall presented the boxwood inkstand to Mr. Blanchard of Baltimore. Of the three impressions of the terms of surrender made in General Grant's manifold writer, the first and third are believed to have been accidentally destroyed. No trace of them has since been discovered; the second is in the possession of the New York Commandery of the Military Order of the Loyal Legion, which purchased it recently from the widow of General Parker. The headquarters flag which had been used throughout the entire Virginia campaign General Grant

presented to me.   With his assent, I gave a portion of
it to Colonel Babcock.

It is a singular historical coincidence that McLean's
former home was upon a Virginia farm near the battle-
ground of the first Bull Run, and his house was used
for a time as the headquarters of General Beauregard.
When it was found that this fight was so popular that
it was given an encore, and a second battle of Bull Run
was fought the next year on the same ground, Mr.
McLean became convinced that the place was altogether
lacking in repose, and to avoid the active theater of
war he removed to the quiet village of Appomattox,
only to find himself again surrounded by contending
armies.   Thus the first and last scenes of the war drama
in Virginia were enacted upon his property.

Before General Grant had proceeded far toward camp
he was reminded that he had not yet announced the
important event to the government.   He dismounted
by the roadside, sat down on a large stone, and called
for pencil and paper.   Colonel Badeau handed his order-
book to the general, who wrote on one of the leaves the
following message, a copy of which was sent to the
nearest telegraph-station.   It was dated 4:30 P. M.:

Hon. E. M. STANTON, Secretary of War, Washington.

General Lee surrendered the Army of Northern Virginia this
afternoon on terms proposed by myself.   The accompanying
additional correspondence will show the conditions fully.

U. S. GRANT,
Lieutenant-general.

Upon reaching camp he seated himself in front of
his tent, notwithstanding the slight shower which was
then falling, and we all gathered about him, curious to
hear what his first comments would be upon the crown-
ing event of his life.   But our expectations were doomed

to disappointment, for he appeared to have already dismissed the whole subject from his mind, and turning to the chief quartermaster, his first words were: "Ingalls, do you remember that old white mule that So-and-so used to ride when we were in the city of Mexico?" "Why, perfectly," said Ingalls, who was just then in a mood to remember the exact number of hairs in the mule's tail if it would have helped to make matters agreeable. And then the general-in-chief went on to recall the antics played by that animal during an excursion to Popocatepetl. It was not until after supper that he said much about the surrender, when he spoke freely of his entire belief that the rest of the Confederate commanders would follow Lee's example, and that we should have but little more fighting, even of a partizan nature. He then surprised us by announcing his intention of starting for Washington early the next morning. We were disappointed at this, for we wished to see something of the opposing army, now that it had become civil enough, for the first time in its existence, to let us get close up to it, and to meet some of the officers who had been acquaintances in former years. The general, however, had no desire to look at the conquered, — indeed, he had little curiosity in his nature, — and he was anxious above all things to begin the reduction of the military establishment, and diminish the enormous expense attending it, which at this time amounted to nearly four millions of dollars a day. When he considered, however, that the railroad was being rapidly put in condition as far as Burkeville, and that he would lose no time by waiting till noon of the next day, he made up his mind to delay his departure.

About nine o'clock on the morning of April 10, Grant with his staff rode out toward the enemy's lines; but it was found, upon attempting to pass through, that the force of habit is hard to overcome, and that the practice which had so long been inculcated in Lee's army of keeping Grant out of its lines was not to be overturned in a day, and he was politely requested at the picket-lines to wait till a message could be sent to headquarters asking for instructions. As soon as Lee heard that his distinguished opponent was approaching, he was prompt to correct the misunderstanding at the picket-line, and rode out at a gallop to receive him. They met on a knoll that overlooked the lines of the two armies, and saluted respectfully by each raising his hat. The officers present gave a similar salute, and then withdrew out of ear-shot, and grouped themselves about the two chieftains in a semicircle. General Grant repeated to us that evening the substance of the conversation, which was as follows:

Grant began by expressing a hope that the war would soon be over; and Lee replied by stating that he had for some time been anxious to stop the further effusion of blood, and he trusted that everything would now be done to restore harmony and conciliate the people of the South. He said the emancipation of the negroes would be no hindrance to the restoring of relations between the two sections of the country, as it would probably not be the desire of the majority of the Southern people to restore slavery then, even if the question were left open to them. He could not tell what the other armies would do, or what course Mr. Davis would now take; but he believed that it would be best for the other armies to follow his example, as nothing could be gained by further resistance in the field. Finding that he entertained these sentiments, General Grant told him that no one's influence in the South was so great as his, and suggested to him that he should advise the surrender of the remaining armies, and thus exert his influence in

favor of immediate peace.   Lee said he could not take
such a course without first consulting President Davis.
Grant then proposed to Lee that he should do so, and
urge the hastening of a result which was admitted to
be inevitable.   Lee, however, in this instance was averse
to stepping beyond his duties as a soldier, and said the
authorities would doubtless soon arrive at the same
conclusion without his interference.   There was a statement put forth that Grant asked Lee to see Mr. Lincoln
and talk with him as to the terms of reconstruction,
but this was erroneous.   I asked General Grant about
it when he was on his death-bed, and his recollection
was distinct that he had made no such suggestion.   I
am of opinion that the mistake arose from hearing that
Lee had been requested to go and see the " President"
regarding peace, and thinking that this expression referred to Mr. Lincoln, whereas it referred to Mr. Davis.
After the conversation had lasted a little more than half
an hour, and Lee had requested that instructions be
given to the officers left in charge to carry out the details of the surrender, that there might be no misunderstanding as to the form of paroles, the manner of turning
over the property, etc., the conference ended.   The two
commanders lifted their hats and bade each other good-
by.   Lee rode back to his camp to take a final farewell
of his army, and Grant returned to McLean's house,
where he sat on the porch until it was time to take his
final departure.   It will be observed that Grant at no
time actually entered the enemy's lines.

Ingalls, Sheridan, and Williams had asked permission
to visit the enemy's lines and renew their acquaintance
with some old friends, classmates, and former comrades
in arms who were serving in Lee's army.   They now
returned, bringing with them General Cadmus M. Wilcox, who had been one of General Grant's groomsmen;

Longstreet, who had also been at his wedding; Heth, who had been a subaltern with him in Mexico, besides Gordon, Pickett, and a number of others. They all stepped up to pay their respects to General Grant, who received them very cordially, and talked frankly and pleasantly with them until it was time to leave. They manifested a deep appreciation of the terms which had been accorded to them in the articles of surrender, but several of them expressed some apprehension as to the civil processes which might ensue, and the measures which might be taken by the government as to confiscation of property and trial for treason.

The hour of noon had now arrived, and General Grant, after shaking hands with all present who were not to accompany him, mounted his horse, and started with his staff for Burkeville. Lee set out for Richmond, and it was felt by all that peace had at last dawned upon the land. The charges were now withdrawn from the guns, the camp-fires were left to smolder in their ashes, the horses were detached from the cannon to be hitched to the plow, and the Army of the Union and the Army of Northern Virginia turned their backs upon each other for the first time in four long, bloody years.

In this campaign, from March 29 to April 9, the Union loss was 1316 killed, 7750 wounded, and 1714 prisoners—a total of 10,780. The enemy lost about 1200 killed, 6000 wounded, and 75,000 prisoners, including the captures at Appomattox.

The repairers of the railroad had thought more of haste than of solidity of construction, and the special train bearing the general-in-chief from Burkeville to City Point ran off the track three times. These mishaps caused much delay, and instead of reaching City Point that evening, he did not arrive until daylight the next morning, April 11. A telegram had been sent to Mrs.

Grant, who had remained aboard the headquarters steamboat, telling her that we should get there in time for dinner, and she had prepared the best meal which the boat's larder could afford to help to celebrate the victory. She and Mrs. Rawlins and Mrs. Morgan, who were with her, whiled away the long and anxious hours of the night by playing the piano, singing, and discussing the victory; but just before daylight the desire for sleep overcame them, and they lay down to take a nap. Soon after our tired and hungry party arrived. The general went hurriedly aboard the boat, and ran at once up the stairs to Mrs. Grant's state-room. She was somewhat chagrined that she had not remained up to receive her husband, now more than ever her "Victor"; but she had merely thrown herself upon the berth without undressing, and soon joined us all in the cabin, and extended to us enthusiastic greetings and congratulations. The belated dinner now served in good stead as a breakfast for our famished party.

The general was asked whether he was going to run up to Richmond on the steamer, and take a look at the captured city, before starting for Washington. He replied: "No; I think it would be as well not to go. I could do no good there, and my visit might lead to demonstrations which would only wound the feelings of the residents, and we ought not to do anything at such a time which would add to their sorrow"; and then added, "But if any of you have a curiosity to see the city, I will wait till you can take a trip there and back, for I cannot well leave here for Washington anyhow till to-morrow."

Several of us put our horses aboard a boat, and started up the James. As a portion of the river was supposed to be planted with torpedoes, we sat close to the stern, believing that in case of accident the bow would receive the main shock of the explosion.   We reached the lower wharf of Richmond in safety, put our horses ashore, and rode about for an hour, looking at the city upon which we had laid covetous eyes for so many months.   The evacuation had been accompanied by many acts of destruction, and the fire which our troops found blazing when they entered had left a third of the place smoldering in ashes.   The white population were keeping closely to their houses, while the blacks were running wildly about the streets in every direction.

Upon our return that evening to City Point, we found aboard the headquarters boat a clergyman, a member of the Christian Commission, who was personally acquainted with the general.   He had called to see him to tender his congratulations, and during their conversation made the remark: "I have observed, General Grant, that a great many battles in our war have been fought on Sunday.   Shiloh occurred on that day, the surrender of Donelson, Chancellorsville, the capture of Petersburg, the surrender at Appomattox, and, I think, some other important military events.   How has this happened?"   "It is quite true," replied the general. "Of course it was not intentional, and I think that sometimes, perhaps, it has been the result of the very efforts which have been made to avoid it.   You see, a commander, when he can control his own movements, usually intends to start out early in the week so as not to bring on an engagement on Sunday; but delays occur often at the last moment, and it may be the middle of the week before he gets his troops in motion.   Then more time is spent than anticipated in manœuvering for position, and when the fighting actually begins it is the end of the week, and the battle, particularly if it continues a couple of days, runs into Sunday."   "It is unfortunate," remarked the clergyman.   "Yes, very unfortunate," observed the general. "Every effort should be made to respect the Sabbath day, and it is very gratifying to know that it is observed so generally throughout our country." It was always noticeable that he had a strict regard for the Sabbath, and this feeling continued through life. He never played a game of any kind on that day, nor wrote any official correspondence if he could help it. He had been brought up a Methodist, and regularly attended worship in the Methodist Episcopal Church, but he was entirely non-sectarian in his feelings. He had an intimate acquaintance among clergymen, and counted many of them among his closest friends. He rarely, if ever, spoke about his own religious convictions. It was one of those subjects not to be discussed lightly, and was so purely personal that he naturally shrank from dwelling upon it, for he always avoided talking upon any subject which was personal to himself. There was such a total lack of egotism in his nature that he could not see how anything touching his own personality could be of interest to others. He was imbued with a deep reverence, however, for all subjects of a religious nature, and nothing was more offensive to him than an attempt to make light of serious matters, or to show a disrespect for sacred things. His correspondence makes mention of his recognition of an overruling Providence in all the affairs of this world; and in his speech to Mr. Lincoln accepting the commission of lieutenant-general he closed with the words: " I feel the full weight of the responsibilities now devolving on me, and I know that if they are met it will be due to those armies, and, above all, to the favor of that Providence which leads both nations and men." He was always a liberal contributor to church work, and in fact to every good cause. His fault was that he was not sufficiently discriminating.

Every mail brought begging letters, and he gave away sums out of all proportion to his means. When pay-day came, it took all the persuasion of those about him to prevent him from parting in this way with the greater part of his pay, his only source of revenue.

Preparations were made to break up headquarters, and the next afternoon the party started by steamer for Washington, reached there the morning of the 13th, and took up their quarters at Willard's Hotel. It soon became noised about that the conqueror of the rebellion had arrived in the city, and dense crowds thronged the streets upon which the hotel fronted. During the forenoon the general started for the War Department. His appearance in the street was a signal for an improvised reception, in which shouts of welcome rent the air, and the populace joined in a demonstration which was thrilling in its earnestness. He had the greatest difficulty in making his way over even the short distance between the hotel and the department. At one time it was thought he would have to take to a carriage as a means of refuge, but by the interposition of the police he finally reached his destination.

That afternoon the Secretary of War published an order stating that, "after mature consideration and consultation with the lieutenant-general," it was decided to stop all drafting and recruiting, curtail the purchases of supplies, reduce the number of officers, and remove restrictions on commerce as far as consistent with public safety. This was a sort of public declaration of peace, and the city gave itself over to rejoicing. Bands were everywhere heard playing triumphant strains, and crowds traversed the streets, shouting approval and singing patriotic airs. The general was the hero of the hour and the idol of the people; his name was on every lip; congratulations poured in upon him, and blessings were heaped upon him by all.

General Grant visited the President, and had a most pleasant interview with him. The next day (Friday) being a cabinet day, he was invited to meet the cabinet officers at their meeting in the forenoon. He went to the White House, receiving the cordial congratulations of all present, and discussed with them the further measures which should be taken for bringing hostilities to a speedy close. In this interview Mr. Lincoln gave a singular manifestation of the effect produced upon him by dreams. When General Grant expressed some anxiety regarding the delay in getting news from Sherman, the President assured him that favorable news would soon be received, because he had had the night before his usual dream which always preceded favorable tidings, the same dream which he had had the night before Antietam, Murfreesboro, Gettysburg, and Vicksburg. He seemed to be aboard a curious-looking vessel moving rapidly toward a dark and indefinite shore. This time, alas! the dream was not to be the precursor of good news.

The President and Mrs. Lincoln invited the general and Mrs. Grant to go to Ford's Theater and occupy a box with them to see "Our American Cousin." The general said he would be very sorry to have to decline, but that Mrs. Grant and he had made arrangements to go to Burlington, New Jersey, to see their children, and he feared it would be a great disappointment to his wife to delay the trip. The President remarked that the people would be so delighted to see the general that he ought to stay and attend the play on that account. The general, however, had been so completely besieged by the people since his arrival, and was so constantly the subject of outbursts of enthusiasm, that it had become a little embarrassing to him, and the mention of a demonstration in his honor at the theater did not appeal to him as an argument in favor of going. A note was now brought to him from Mrs. Grant expressing increased anxiety to start for Burlington on the four-o'clock train, and he told the President that he must decide definitely not to remain for the play. It was probably this declination which saved the general from assassination, as it was learned afterward that he had been marked for a victim. It was after two o'clock when he shook Mr. Lincoln's hand and said good-by to him, little thinking that it would be an eternal farewell, and that an appalling tragedy was soon to separate them forever. Their final leave-taking was only thirteen months after their first meeting, but during that time their names had been associated with enough momentous events to fill whole volumes of a nation's history.

The general went at once to his rooms at the hotel. As soon as he entered Mrs. Grant said to him: "When I went to my lunch to-day, a man with a wild look followed me into the dining-room, took a seat nearly opposite to me at the table, stared at me continually, and seemed to be listening to my conversation." The general replied: "Oh, I suppose he did so merely from curiosity." In fact, the general by this time had become so accustomed to having people stare at him and the members of his family that such acts had ceased to attract his attention. About half-past three o'clock the wife of General Rucker called with her carriage to take the party to the Baltimore and Ohio railroad-station. It was a two-seated top-carriage. Mrs. Grant sat with Mrs. Rucker on the back seat. The general, with true republican simplicity, sat on the front seat with the driver. Before they had gone far along Pennsylvania Avenue, a horseman who was riding in the same direction passed them, and as he did so peered into the carriage. When Mrs. Grant caught sight of his face she remarked to the general: "That is the same man who sat down at the lunch-table near me. I don't like his looks." Before they reached the station the horseman turned and rode back toward them, and again gazed at them intently. This time he attracted the attention of the general, who regarded the man's movements as singular, but made light of the matter so as to allay Mrs. Grant's apprehensions.

On their arrival at the station, they were conducted to the private car of Mr. Garrett, then president of the Baltimore and Ohio railway company. Before the train reached Baltimore a man appeared on the front platform of the car, and tried to get in; but the conductor had locked the door so that the general would not be troubled with visitors, and the man did not succeed in entering. The general and Mrs. Grant drove across Philadelphia about midnight from the Broad street and Washington Avenue station to the Walnut street wharf on the Delaware River, for the purpose of crossing the ferry and then taking the cars to Burlington. As the general had been detained so long at the White House that he was not able to get luncheon before starting, and as there was an additional ride in prospect, a stop was made at Bloodgood's Hotel, near the ferry, for the purpose of getting supper. The general had just taken his seat with Mrs. Grant at the table in the supper-room when a telegram was brought in and handed to him. His whereabouts was known to the telegraph people from the fact that he had sent a message to Bloodgood's ordering the supper in advance. The general read the despatch, dropped his head, and sat in perfect silence. Then came another, and still another despatch, but not a word was spoken. Mrs. Grant now broke the silence by saying: "Ulyss, what do the telegrams say? Do they bring any bad news?" "I will read them to you," the general replied in a voice which betrayed his emotion;

"but first prepare yourself for the most painful and startling news that could be received, and control your feelings so as not to betray the nature of the despatches to the servants." He then read to her the telegrams conveying the appalling announcement that Mr. Lincoln, Mr. Seward, and probably the Vice-President, Mr. Johnson, had been assassinated, and warning the general to look out for his own safety. A special train was at once ordered to take him back to Washington, but finding that he could take Mrs. Grant to Burlington (less than an hour's ride), and return to Philadelphia nearly as soon as his train could be got ready, he continued on, took her to her destination, returned to Philadelphia, and was in Washington the next morning.

It was found that the President had been shot and killed at Ford's Theater by John Wilkes Booth; that Mr. Seward had received severe but not fatal injuries at the hands of Payne, who attempted his assassination; but that no attack had been made on the Vice-President. When the likenesses of Booth appeared, they resembled so closely the mysterious man who had followed the general and Mrs. Grant on their way to the railroad-station in Washington, that there remained no doubt that he had intended to be the President's assassin, and was bent upon ascertaining the movements of the general-in-chief. An anonymous letter was afterward received by the general saying that the writer had been designated by the conspirators to assassinate him, and had been ordered by Booth to board the train and commit the deed there; that he had attempted to enter the special car for this purpose, but that it was locked, and he was thus baffled; and that he thanked God that this circumstance had been the means of preventing him from staining his hands with the blood of so great and good a man.

Washington, as well as the whole country, was plunged in an agony of grief, and the excitement knew no bounds. Stanton's grief was uncontrollable, and at the mention of Mr. Lincoln's name he would break down and weep bitterly. General Grant and the Secretary of War busied themselves day and night in pushing a relentless pursuit of the conspirators, who were caught, and were brought to trial before a military commission, except Booth, who was shot in an attempt to capture him. John H. Surratt, who escaped from the country, was captured and tried years later, the jury disagreeing as to his guilt.

I was appointed a member of the court which was to try the prisoners. The defense, however, raised the objection that as I was a member of General Grant's military family, and as it was claimed that he was one of the high officials who was an intended victim of the assassins, I was disqualified from sitting in judgment upon them. The court very properly sustained the objection, and I was relieved, and another officer was substituted. However, I sat one day at the trial, which was interesting from the fact that it afforded an opportunity of seeing the assassins and watching their actions before the court. The prisoners, heavily manacled, were marched into the court-room in solemn procession, an armed sentinel accompanying each of them. The men's heads were covered with thickly padded hoods with openings for the mouth and nose. The hoods had been placed upon them in consequence of Powell, *alias* Payne, having attempted to cheat the gallows by dashing his brains out against a beam on a gunboat on which he had been confined. The prisoners, whose eyes were thus bandaged, were led to their seats, the sentinels were posted behind them, and the hoods were then removed. As the light struck their eyes, which for several days had been unaccustomed to its brilliancy, the sudden glare gave them great discomfort. Payne had a wild look in his wandering eyes, and his general appearance stamped him as the typical reckless desperado. Mrs. Surratt was placed in a chair at a little distance from the men. She sat most of the time leaning back, with her feet stretched forward. She kept up a piteous moaning, and frequently called for water, which was given her. The other prisoners had a stolid look, and seemed crushed by the situation.

CHAPTER XXXII

SHERMAN'S TERMS TO JOSEPH E. JOHNSTON — THE END OF
HOSTILITIES — THE GRAND REVIEW AT WASHINGTON —
GRANT'S PLACE IN MILITARY HISTORY

AS soon as the surrender at Appomattox had taken
place, General Grant despatched a boat from City
Point with a message to Sherman announcing the event,
and telling him that he could offer the same terms to
Johnston. On April 18 Sherman entered into an agreement with Johnston which embraced political as well
as merely military questions, but only conditionally,
and with the understanding that the armistice granted
could be terminated if the conditions were not approved
by superior authority. A staff-officer sent by General
Sherman brought his communication to Washington
announcing the terms of this agreement. It was received by General Grant on April 21. Perceiving that
the terms covered many questions of a civil and not of
a military nature, he suggested to the Secretary of War
that the matter had better be referred at once to President Johnson and the cabinet for their action. A cabinet
meeting was called before midnight, and there was a
unanimous decision that the basis of agreement should
be disapproved, and an order was issued directing
General Grant to proceed in person to Sherman's headquarters and direct operations against the enemy. Instead of merely recognizing that Sherman had made an

honest mistake in exceeding his authority, the President
and the Secretary of War characterized his conduct as
akin to treason, and the Secretary denounced him in
unmeasured terms.   At this General Grant grew indignant, and gave free expression to his opposition to an
attempt to stigmatize an officer whose acts throughout
all his career gave ample contradiction to the charge
that he was actuated by unworthy motives.   The form
of the public announcement put forth by the War Department aroused great public indignation against
Sherman, and it was some time before his motives were
fully understood.

Grant started at daybreak on the 22d, proceeded at
once to Raleigh, explained the situation and attitude of
the government fully to Sherman, and directed him to
give the required notice for annulling the truce, and to
demand a surrender of Johnston's army on the same
terms as those accorded to Lee.   Sherman was, as usual,
perfectly loyal and subordinate, and made all haste to
comply with these instructions.   When he went out to
the front to meet Johnston, Grant remained quietly at
Raleigh, and throughout the negotiations kept himself
entirely in the background, lest he might seem to share
in the honor of receiving the surrender, the credit for
which he wished to belong wholly to Sherman.   The
entire surrender of Johnston's forces was promptly
concluded.   Having had a talk with the Secretary of
War soon after General Grant's departure, and finding
him bent upon continuing the denunciation of Sherman
before the public, I started for North Carolina to meet
General Grant and inform him of the situation in Washington.   I passed him, however, on the way, and at once
returned and rejoined him at Washington.

Hostilities were now brought rapidly to a close
throughout the entire theater of war.   April 11, Canby

compelled the evacuation of Mobile. By the 21st our troops had taken Selma, Tuscaloosa, Montgomery, West Point, Columbus, and Macon. May 4, Richard Taylor surrendered the Confederate forces east of the Mississippi. May 10, Jefferson Davis was captured; and on the 26th Kirby Smith surrendered his command west of the Mississippi. Since April 8, 1680 cannon had been captured, and 174,223 Confederate soldiers had been paroled. There was no longer a rebel in arms, the Union cause had triumphed, slavery was abolished, and the National Government was again supreme.

The Army of the Potomac, Sheridan's cavalry, and Sherman's army had all reached the capital by the end of May. Sheridan could not remain with his famous corps, for General Grant sent him post-haste to the Rio Grande to look after operations there in a contemplated movement against Maximilian's forces, who were upholding a monarchy in Mexico, in violation of the Monroe doctrine.

It was decided that the troops assembled at Washington should be marched in review through the nation's capital before being mustered out of service. The Army of the Potomac, being senior in date of organization, and having been for four years the more direct defense of the capital city, was given precedence, and May 23 was designated as the day on which it was to be reviewed.

During the preceding five days Washington had been given over to elaborate preparations for the coming pageant. The public buildings were decked with a tasteful array of bunting; flags were unfurled from private dwellings; arches and transparencies with patriotic mottos were displayed in every quarter; and the spring flowers were fashioned into garlands, and played their part. The whole city was ready for the most imposing fête-day in its history.   Vast crowds of citizens had gathered from neighboring States.   During the review they filled the stands, lined the sidewalks, packed the porches, and covered even the housetops. The weather was superb.

A commodious stand had been erected on Pennsylvania Avenue in front of the White House, on which were gathered a large number of distinguished officials, including the President; the members of his cabinet, who had won renown in the cabinet of Lincoln; the acting Vice-President; justices of the Supreme Court; governors of States; senators and representatives; the general-in-chief of the army, and the captor of Atlanta, with other generals of rank; admirals of the navy; and brilliantly uniformed representatives of foreign powers.

General Grant, accompanied by the principal members of his staff, was one of the earliest to arrive.   With his customary simplicity and dislike of ostentation, he had come on foot through the White House grounds from the headquarters of the army at the corner of 17th and F streets.   Grant's appearance was, as usual, the signal for a boisterous demonstration.   Sherman arrived a few minutes later, and his reception was scarcely less enthusiastic.

At nine o'clock the signal-gun was fired, and the legions took up their march.   They started from the Capitol, and moved along Pennsylvania Avenue toward Georgetown.   The width and location of that street made it an ideal thoroughfare for such a purpose.   Martial music from scores of bands filled the air, and when familiar war-songs were played the spectators along the route joined in shouting the chorus.   Those oftenest sung and most applauded were, "When this cruel war is over," "When Johnny comes marching home," and "Tramp, tramp, tramp! the boys are marching."

At the head of the column rode Meade, crowned with the laurels of four years of warfare. The plaudits of the multitude followed him along the entire line of march; flowers were strewn in his path, and garlands decked his person and his horse. He dismounted after having passed the reviewing-stand, stepped upon the platform, and was enthusiastically greeted by all present. Then came the cavalry, with the gallant Merritt at their head, commanding in the absence of Sheridan. The public were not slow to make recognition of the fame he had won on so many hard-fought fields. Conspicuous among the division commanders was Custer. His long golden locks floating in the wind, his low-cut collar, his crimson necktie, and his buckskin breeches, presented a combination which made him look half general and half scout, and gave him a daredevil appearance which singled him out for general remark and applause. When within two hundred yards of the President's stand, his spirited horse took the bit in his teeth, and made a dash past the troops, rushing by the reviewing officers like a tornado; but he found more than a match in Custer, and was soon checked, and forced back to his proper position. When the cavalryman, covered with flowers, afterward rode by the reviewing officials, the people screamed with delight.

After the cavalry came Parke, who might well feel proud of the prowess of the Ninth Corps, which followed him; then Griffin, riding at the head of the gallant Fifth Corps; then Humphreys and the Second Corps, of unexcelled valor. Wright's Sixth Corps was greatly missed from the list, but its duties kept it in Virginia, and it was accorded a special review on June 8.

The men preserved their alinement and distances with an ease which showed their years of training in the field. Their movements were unfettered, their step was elastic, and the swaying of their bodies and the swinging of their arms were as measured as the vibrations of a pendulum. Their muskets shone like a wall of steel. The cannon rumbled peacefully over the paved street, banks of flowers almost concealing them.

Nothing touched the hearts of the spectators so deeply as the sight of the old war-flags as they were carried by—those precious standards, bullet-riddled, battle-stained, many of them but remnants, often with not enough left of them to show the names of the battles. they had seen. Some were decked with ribbons, and some festooned with garlands. Everybody was thrilled by the sight; eyes were dimmed with tears of gladness, and many of the people broke through all restraint, rushed into the street, and pressed their lips upon the folds of the standards.

The President was kept busy doffing his hat. He had a way of holding it by the brim with his right hand and waving it from left to right, and occasionally passing his right arm across his breast and resting the hat on his left shoulder. This manual of the hat was original, and had probably been practised with good effect when its wearer was stumping east Tennessee. As each commander in turn passed the reviewing-stand, he dismounted and came upon the platform, where he paid his respects to the President, was presented to the guests, and remained during the passage of his command.

A prominent officer of the engineer brigade, while riding by, led to a slight commotion on the platform. He wore a French chasseur cap, which he had had made of a pattern differing from the strict regulation head-gear in having an extra amount of cloth between the lower band and the crown. As he came opposite the President and raised his sword in saluting, he paid an additional mark of respect by bowing his head. At the same moment the horse, as if catching the spirit of its rider, kicked up behind and put down its head. This unexpected participation of the horse in the salute sent the officer's head still lower, and the crown of his cap fell forward, letting out the superfluous cloth till it looked like an accordion extended at full length. The sight was so ludicrous that several of us who were standing just behind the President burst out into a poorly suppressed laugh. This moved him to turn squarely round and glare at us savagely, in an attempt to frown down such a lack of dignity before, or rather behind, the Chief Magistrate of the nation.

For nearly seven hours the pageant was watched with unabated interest; and when it had faded from view the spectators were eager for the night to pass, so that on the morrow the scene might be renewed in the marching of the mighty Army of the West.

The next day the same persons, with a few exceptions, assembled upon the reviewing-stand. At nine o'clock Sherman's veterans started. Howard had been relieved of the command of the Army of the Tennessee to take charge of the Freedmen's Bureau, and instead of leading his old troops he rode with Sherman at the head of the column, his armless right sleeve giving evidence of his heroism in action.

Sherman, unknown by sight to most of the people in the East, was eagerly watched for, and his appearance awoke great enthusiasm. His tall, spare figure, war-worn face, and martial bearing made him all that the people had pictured him. He had ridden but a little way before his body was decorated with flowery wreaths, and his horse enveloped in garlands. As he approached the reviewing-stand the bands struck up "Marching through Georgia," and played that stirring air with a will. This was the signal for renewed demonstrations of delight. When he had passed, he turned his horse into the White House grounds, dismounted, and strode rapidly to the platform. He advanced to where the President was standing, and the two shook hands. The members of the cabinet then stepped up to greet him. He took their extended hands, and had a few pleasant words to say to each of them, until Stanton reached out his hand. Then Sherman's whole manner changed in an instant; a cloud of anger overspread his features, and, smarting under the wrong the Secretary had done him in his published bulletins after the conditional treaty with Johnston, the general turned abruptly away. This rebuff became the sensation of the day. There was no personal intercourse between the two men till some time afterward, when General Grant appeared, as usual, in the rôle of peacemaker, and brought them together. Sherman showed a manly spirit of forgiveness in going to see Stanton in his last illness, manifesting his respect and tendering his sympathy.

Sherman's active mind was crowded with the remembrance of past events, and he spent all the day in pointing out the different subdivisions of his army as they moved by, and recalling in his pithy and graphic way many of the incidents of the stirring campaigns through which they had passed.

Logan, "Black Jack," came riding at the head of the Army of the Tennessee, his swarthy features and long, coal-black hair giving him the air of a native Indian chief. The army corps which led the column was the Fifteenth, commanded by Hazen; then came the Seventeenth, under Frank P. Blair. Now Slocum appeared at the head of the Army of Georgia, consisting of the Twentieth Corps, headed by the gallant Mower, with his bushy whiskers covering his face, and looking the picture of a hard fighter, and the Fourteenth Corps, headed by Jefferson C. Davis.

Each division was preceded by a pioneer corps of negroes, marching in double ranks, with picks, spades,

and axes slung across their brawny shoulders, their
stalwart forms conspicuous by their height.   But the
impedimenta were the novel feature of the march.   Six
ambulances followed each division to represent its bag-
gage-train; and then came the amusing spectacle of
" Sherman's bummers," bearing with them the " spoils
of war." The bummers were men who were the fore-
runners, flankers, and foragers of the army.   Each one
was often his own commanding officer.   If a bummer
was too short-sighted to see the enemy, he would go
nearer; if he was lame, he would make it an excuse to
disobey an order to retreat; if out of reach of supplies,
he would wear his clothes till there was not enough of
his coat left to wad a gun, and not enough of his shirt
to flag a train.   He was always last in a retreat and first
in an enemy's smoke-house.   In kindling his camp-fire,
he would obey the general order to take only the top
rail of the neighboring fences, but would keep on taking
the top rail till there were none of the fences left.   The
trophies of his foraging expeditions which appeared
in the review consisted of pack-mules loaded with tur-
keys, geese, chickens, and bacon, and here and there a
chicken-coop strapped on to the saddle, with a cackling
brood peering out through the slats.   Then came cows,
goats, sheep, donkeys, crowing roosters, and in one instance a chattering monkey.   Mixed with these was a
procession of fugitive blacks—old men, stalwart women,
and grinning piccaninnies of all sizes, and ranging in
color from a raven's wing to a new saddle.   This portion
of the column called forth shouts of laughter and continuous rounds of applause.

Flowers were showered upon the troops in the same
profusion as the day before, and there was no abatement
in the uncontrollable enthusiasm of the vast assemblage
of citizens who witnessed the march.

Comparisons were naturally instituted between the Eastern and Western armies. The difference was much less than has been represented. The Army of the Potomac presented a somewhat neater appearance in dress, and was a little more precise in its movements. Sherman's army showed, perhaps, more of a rough-and-ready aspect and a devil-may-care spirit. Both were in the highest degree soldierly, and typical representatives of the terrible realism of relentless war.

At half-past three o'clock the matchless pageant had ceased. For two whole days a nation's heroes had been passing in review. Greeted with bands playing, drums beating, bells ringing, banners flying, kerchiefs waving, and voices cheering, they had made their last march. Even after every veteran had vanished from sight the crowds kept their places for a time, as if still under a spell and unwilling to believe that the marvelous spectacle had actually passed from view. It was not a Roman triumph, designed to gratify the vanity of the victors, exhibit their trophies, and parade their enchained captives before the multitude: it was a celebration of the dawn of peace, a declaration of the reëstablishment of the Union.

General Grant now stood in the front rank of the world's greatest captains. He had conquered the most formidable rebellion in the annals of history. The armies under his immediate direction in Virginia had captured 75,000 prisoners and 689 cannon; the armies under his general command had captured in April and May 147,000 prisoners and 997 cannon; making a total of 222,000 prisoners and 1680 cannon as the achievement of the forces he controlled.[1]

Most of the conspicuous soldiers in history have risen

---

[1] These figures relate to the final campaign alone. The whole year's capture were of course much larger. —EDITOR.

to prominence by gradual steps, but the Union commander came before the people with a sudden bound. Almost the first sight they caught of him was at Donelson. From that event to the closing triumph of Appomattox he was the leader whose name was the harbinger of victory. He was unquestionably the most aggressive fighter in the entire list of the world's famous soldiers. He never once yielded up a stronghold he had wrested from his foe. He kept his pledge religiously to " take no backward steps." For four years of bloody and relentless war he went steadily forward, replacing the banner of his country upon the territory where it had been hauled down. He possessed in a striking degree every characteristic of the successful soldier. His methods were all stamped with tenacity of purpose, originality, and ingenuity. He depended for his success more upon the powers of invention than of adaptation, and the fact that he has been compared at different times to nearly every great commander in history is perhaps the best proof that he was like none of them. He realized that in a sparsely settled country, with formidable natural obstacles and poor roads, and in view of the improvement in range and rapidity of fire in cannon and small arms, the European methods of warfare and the rules laid down in many of the books must be abandoned, and new means devised to meet the change in circumstances. He therefore adopted a more open order of battle, made an extensive use of skirmish-lines, employed cavalry largely as mounted infantry, and sought to cultivate the individuality of the soldier instead of making him merely an unthinking part of a compact machine. He originated the cutting loose from a base of supplies with large armies and living off the invaded country. He insisted constantly upon thorough coöperation between the different com-

mands, and always aimed to prevent operations of corps
or armies which were not part of a joint movement in
obedience to a comprehensive plan.   His marvelous
combinations, covering half a continent, soon wrought
the destruction of the Confederacy; and when he struck
Lee the final blow, the coöperating armies were so
placed that there was no escape for the opposing forces,
and within forty-seven days thereafter every Confederate army surrendered to a Union army.   He had no
hobby as to the use of any particular arm of the service.
He naturally placed his main reliance in his infantry,
but made a more vigorous use of cavalry than any of
the generals of his day, and was judicious in regulating
the amount of his artillery by the character of the
country in which he was operating.

His magnanimity to Lee, his consideration for his
feelings, and the generous terms granted him, served as
a precedent for subsequent surrenders, and had much
to do with bringing about a prompt and absolute cessation of hostilities, thus saving the country from a prolonged guerrilla warfare.

He was possessed of a moral and physical courage
which was equal to every emergency in which he was
placed.   He was calm amid excitement, patient under
trials, sure in judgment, clear in foresight, never depressed by reverses or unduly elated by success.   He
was fruitful in expedients, and had a facility of resource
and a faculty of adapting the means at hand to the ac-
complishment of an end which never failed him.   He
possessed an intuitive knowledge of topography, which
prevented him from ever becoming confused as to locality or direction in conducting even the most complicated movements in the field.   His singular self-reliance
enabled him at critical junctures to decide instantly
questions of vital moment without dangerous delay in

seeking advice from others, and to assume the gravest
responsibilities without asking any one to share them.

His habits of life were simple, and he enjoyed a physical constitution which enabled him to endure every
form of fatigue and privation incident to military service in the field.   His soldiers always knew that he was
ready to rough it with them and share their hardships
on the march.   He wore no better clothes than they,
and often ate no better food.   There was nothing in his
manner to suggest that there was any gulf between him
and the men who were winning his victories.   He never
tired of giving unstinted praise to his subordinates.   He
was at all times loyal to them.   His fidelity produced a
reciprocal effect, and is one of the chief reasons why
they became so loyally attached to him.   He was never
betrayed by success into boasting of his triumphs.   He
never underrated himself in a battle; he never overrated
himself in a report.

General Sheridan, in his "Memoirs," says of his chief,
in speaking of the later campaigns: "The effect of his
discomfitures was to make him all the more determined
to discharge successfully the stupendous trust committed to his care, and to bring into play the manifold
resources of his well-ordered mind.   He guided every
subordinate then, and in the last days of the rebellion,
with a fund of common sense and a superiority of intellect which have left an impress so distinct as to
exhibit his great personality.   When his military history
is analyzed after the lapse of years, it will show even
more clearly than now that during these, as well as his
previous campaigns, he was the steadfast center about
and on which everything else turned."

General Longstreet, one of his most persistent foes
on the field of battle, says in his reminiscences: "General Grant had come to be known as an all-round fighter

seldom, if ever, surpassed; but the biggest part of him was his heart." And again: "As the world continues to look at and study the grand combinations and strategy of General Grant, the higher will be his reward as a soldier."

While his achievements in actual battle eclipse by their brilliancy the strategy and grand tactics employed in his campaigns, yet the extraordinary combinations effected, and the skill and boldness exhibited in moving large armies into position, should entitle him to as much credit as the qualities he displayed in the immediate presence of the enemy. With him the formidable game of war was in the hands of a master.

INDEX

Aiken's Landing, Va., visitors from Washington to, 305

Alabama, proposed movement by Thomas and Wilson into, 386

"Alabama," the, fight with the *Kearsarge*, 254, 255

"Alabama" claims, the, 409

Alabama River, proposed military operations on the, 287

Alexandria, Va., Schofield moves to, 387

Alsop house, Va., Grant's headquarters near, 92

Ambulance, as a ladies' pleasure-carriage, 413, 414

Amelia Court-house, Va., Lee at, 454; Lee retreats from, 456

American volunteers, not mercenaries, 322

Ames, Maj.-gen. Adelbert, in Fort Fisher expeditions, 362, 370

Anderson, Lieut.-gen. Richard H., succeeds to Longstreet's command, 81; narrow escape from capturing Grant, 81; marches to Spottsylvania Court-house, 86; engagement with Warren and Sedgwick, 87; sent to Cold Harbor, 162

Anderson's Mill, Va., military movements near, 136

Anecdotes, the geometric excellence of, 220. For various anecdotes see the names of the narrators or their subjects.

Annapolis, Md., Burnside ordered to Virginia from, 36; plans for Schofield to rendezvous at, 387

Antietam, Md., the President's dream before the battle of, 497

Appomattox Court-house, Va., the surrender at, compared with that at Yorktown, 461; Grant moves to, 467, 468; the surrender at, 469 et seq., 484, 488, 489, 491, 503, 513; the "famous apple-tree," 470; McLean's house, 471 et seq.; McLean's removal from Bull Run to, 488

Appomattox River, the, military movements on, 78, 99, 189, 194, 201, 205, 206, 211, 234, 447, 457, 458, 462

Appomattox Station, Va., capture of Lee's trains at, 482

Armstrong's Mill, Va., military operations at, 311

Army, the, its officers as boatmen, 413; effects of wet weather on, 427, 428

Army of Georgia, the, in grand review at Washington, 510, 511

Army of Northern Virginia, the, confronting the Army of the Potomac, 36, 37; Grant's efforts to destroy its

Army of Northern Virginia—*continued*
supplies, 36; its component corps, 39; estimated strength, 39; surrender of, 458 et seq.; turns its back on the army of the Union, 488; Lee bids farewell to, 491

Army of the Cumberland, the, Gen. Thomas commanding, 1; under Grant's control, 2; Grant takes personal charge of, 3; successes of, 10; *H. P.'s* service in, 11–13; its love for Gen. Thomas, 12

Army of the James, the (Butler; Ord), capture of Fort Harrison, 299–302; movements against the South Side and Danville railroads, 230; visitors from Washington to, 304, 305; Butler relieved from command, 373, 374; plans for the spring campaign (1865), 387; Grant's telegram to, March 25, 1865, 404; reviewed by the President, 412–414; confronting Richmond, 426; final assault at Petersburg, 444–446, 448

Army of the Potomac, the, (Meade), Grant visits headquarters at Brandy Station, 22; Sheridan ordered to command the cavalry of, 23, 24, 39; Grant on, 25; *H. P.'s* service with, 29; Grant establishes his headquarters with, 31; Burnside ordered to support, 36; confronting the Army of Northern Virginia, 36, 37; Lee's army its objective, 37; its component corps, 39; crosses the Rapidan, 41 et seq.; moves along the Germanna road, 47; movement by the left flank, 76; Meade's anomalous position in, 114–116; embarrassed by its artillery, 129; Burnside's command joined to, 144, 145; Butler ordered to join, 147; reinforcements from Butler for, 160; familiarity of its officers with the battle-grounds of Virginia, 171; to cross the James, 187, 188; prepares to move, 190; losses from the Rapidan to the James, 192; lack of vigor before Petersburg, 210, 211; sickness in, 211; railroad facilities for, 212; the Sixth Corps returned to, 224; disposition of the corps before Petersburg, 224; its exposed position, 225; Grant at headquarters of, 225; Grant anticipates combined attacks on, 244; Meade attempts to resign his command, 246, 247; scheme of movement by the left flank, Oct. 27, 1864, 312; Grant's plans for further movements, 312; plans for the spring campaign (1865), 387; review of, 393; Sheridan to rejoin, 397, 401, 402; Parke commanding, 403; Sheridan's command separated from, 422; final

517